McDONALD INSTITUTE MONOGRAPHS

# Phylogenetic methods and the prehistory of languages

Edited by Peter Forster & Colin Renfrew

*Published by:*

McDonald Institute for Archaeological Research
University of Cambridge
Downing Street
Cambridge, UK
CB2 3ER
(0)(1223) 339336
(0)(1223) 333538 (General Office)
(0)(1223) 333536 (FAX)
dak12@cam.ac.uk
www.mcdonald.cam.ac.uk

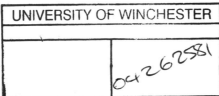

Distributed by Oxbow Books
*United Kingdom:* Oxbow Books, Park End Place, Oxford, OX1 1HN, UK.
Tel: (0)(1865) 241249; Fax: (0)(1865) 794449; www.oxbowbooks.com
*USA:* The David Brown Book Company, P.O. Box 511, Oakville, CT 06779, USA.
Tel: 860-945-9329; Fax: 860-945-9468

ISBN-10: 1-902937-33-3
ISBN-13: 978-1-902937-33-5
ISSN: 1363-1349 (McDonald Institute)



Edited for the Institute by Chris Scarre (*Series Editor*) and Dora A. Kemp (*Production Editor*).

Cover illustration: *The 10th-century Skarthi stone from Schleswig displaying Danish runes (Chapter 11) against a reconstructed tree of Indo-European languages (Chapter 14). (Skarthi stone courtesy of the Viking Museum Haithabu in Schleswig.)*

Printed and bound by Short Run Press, Bittern Rd, Sowton Industrial Estate, Exeter, EX2 7LW, UK.

This volume is dedicated to

Isidore Dyen

a pioneer in the
systematic multilateral analysis
of language relationships

# Contents

Contributors vii
Figures ix
Tables x

*Introduction* 1
Colin Renfrew & Peter Forster

**Part I** ***Classification***

*Chapter 1* Malagasy Language as a Guide to Understanding Malagasy History 11
Robert E. Dewar

*Chapter 2* Rapid Radiation, Borrowing and Dialect Continua in the Bantu Languages 19
Clare J. Holden & Russell D. Gray

*Chapter 3* Multilateral Comparison and Significance Testing of the Indo-Uralic Question 33
Brett Kessler & Annukka Lehtonen

*Chapter 4* Bantu Classification, Bantu Trees and Phylogenetic Methods 43
Lutz Marten

*Chapter 5* Quasi-cognates and Lexical Type Shifts: Rigorous Distance Measures for Long-range Comparison 57
Johanna Nichols

*Chapter 6* Phylogenetic Analysis of Written Traditions 67
Matthew Spencer, Heather F. Windram, Adrian C. Barbrook, Elizabeth A. Davidson & Christopher J. Howe

*Chapter 7* A Stochastic Model of Language Evolution that Incorporates Homoplasy and Borrowing 75
Tandy Warnow, Steven N. Evans, Donald Ringe & Luay Nakhleh

**Part II** ***Chronology***

*Chapter 8* How Old is the Indo-European Language Family? Illumination or More Moths to the Flame? 91
Quentin D. Atkinson & Russell D. Gray

*Chapter 9* Radiation and Network Breaking in Polynesian Linguistics 111
David Bryant

*Chapter 10* Inference of Divergence Times as a Statistical Inverse Problem 119
Steven N. Evans, Donald Ringe & Tandy Warnow

*Chapter 11* Evolution of English Basic Vocabulary within the Network of Germanic Languages 131
Peter Forster, Tobias Polzin & Arne Röhl

*Chapter 12* Convergence in the Formation of Indo-European Subgroups: Phylogeny and Chronology 139
Andrew Garrett

*Chapter 13* Why Linguists Don't Do Dates: Evidence from Indo-European and Australian Languages 153
April McMahon & Robert McMahon

*Chapter 14* Quantifying Uncertainty in a Stochastic Model of Vocabulary Evolution 161
Geoff K. Nicholls & Russell D. Gray

*Chapter 15* Estimating Rates of Lexical Replacement on Phylogenetic Trees of Languages 173
Mark Pagel & Andrew Meade

*Chapter 16* Interdisciplinary Indiscipline? Can Phylogenetic Methods Meaningfully be Applied to Language Data — and to Dating Language? 183
Paul Heggarty

*Glossary* 195

# Contributors

Quentin D. Atkinson
Department of Psychology, University of Auckland, Private Bag 92019, Auckland 1020, New Zealand.
*Email:* q.atkinson@auckland.ac.nz

Adrian C. Barbrook
Department of Biochemistry, Downing Site, Tennis Court Road, Cambridge, CB2 1QW, UK.
*Email:* acb18@mole.bio.cam.ac.uk

David Bryant
McGill Centre for Bioinformatics, 3775 University, Montréal, Québec H3A 2B4, Canada.
*Email:* bryant@mcb.mcgill.ca

Elizabeth A. Davidson
Department of Biochemistry, Downing Site, Tennis Court Road, Cambridge, CB2 1QW, UK.
*Email:* ead25@mole.bio.cam.ac.uk

Robert E. Dewar
McDonald Institute for Archaeological Research, Downing Street, Cambridge, CB2 3ER, UK.
*Email:* red30@hermes.cam.ac.uk

Steven N. Evans
Department of Statistics #3860, University of California at Berkeley, 367 Evans Hall, Berkeley, CA 94720-3860, USA.
*Email:* evans@stat.Berkeley.edu

Peter Forster
McDonald Institute for Archaeological Research, Downing Street, Cambridge, CB2 3ER, UK.
*Email:* pf223@cam.ac.uk

Andrew Garrett
Department of Linguistics, 1203 Dwinelle Hall, University of California, Berkeley, CA 94720-2650, USA.
*Email:* garrett@berkeley.edu

Russell D. Gray
Department of Psychology, University of Auckland, Private Bag 92019, Auckland, New Zealand.
*Email:* rd.gray@auckland.ac.nz

Paul Heggarty
8 Hobgate, Acomb, York, YO24 4HF, UK.
*Email:* paulheggarty@yahoo.fr

Clare J. Holden
Department of Anthropology, University College London, Gower Street, London, WC1E 6BT, UK.
*Email:* c.holden@ucl.ac.uk

Christopher J. Howe
Department of Biochemistry, Downing Site, Tennis Court Road, Cambridge, CB2 1QW, UK.
*Email:* ch26@mole.bio.cam.ac.uk

Brett Kessler
Psychology Department, Washington University in St Louis, Campus Box 1125, St Louis, MO 6313-48990, USA.
*Email:* bkessler@wustl.edu

Annukka Lehtonen
Department of Psychiatry, University of Oxford, Warneford Hospital, Oxford, OX3 7JX, UK.
*Email:* annukka.lehtonen@psych.ox.ac.uk

Lutz Marten
School of Oriental and African Studies, University of London, Thornhaugh Street, Russell Square, London, WC1H 0XG, UK.
*Email:* lm5@soas.ac.uk

April McMahon
English Language School of Philosophy, Psychology and Language Sciences, University of Edinburgh, 14 Buccleuch Place, Edinburgh, EH8 9LN, Scotland.
*Email:* amcmaho1@staffmail.ed.ac.uk

Robert McMahon
South East Scotland Genetic Services, Molecular Medicine Centre, Western General Hospital, Crewe Road South, Edinburgh, EH4 2XU, Scotland.
*Email:* rmcmahon@staffmail.ed.ac.uk

Andrew Meade
School of Animal and Microbial Sciences, University of Reading, Whiteknights, PO Box 228, Reading, RG6 6AJ, UK.
*Email:* a.meade@reading.ac.uk

Luay Nakhleh
Department of Computer Science, Rice University, 6100 Main St, MS 132, Houston TX, 77005-1892, USA.
*Email:* nakhleh@cs.rice.edu

Geoff Nicholls
Department of Statistics, University of Oxford, 1 South Parks Road, Oxford, OX1 3TG, UK.
*Email:* nicholls@stats.ox.ac.uk

Johanna Nichols
Department of Slavic Languages and Literatures, mailcode 2979, University of California, Berkeley, CA 94720, USA.
*Email:* johanna@berkeley.edu

Mark Pagel
School of Biological Sciences, University of Reading, Reading, RG6 6AJ, UK.
*Email:* m.pagel@reading.ac.uk

Tobias Polzin
HaCon Ing.ges.mbh, Lister Str. 15, 30163 Hannover, Germany.
*Email:* polzin@gmx.de

Colin Renfrew
McDonald Institute for Archaeological Research, Downing Street, Cambridge, CB2 3ER, UK.
*Email:* des25@cam.ac.uk

Donald Ringe
Department of Linguistics, 619 Williams Hall, University of Pennsylvania, Philadelphia, PA 19104-6305, USA.
*Email:* dringe@unagi.cis.upenn.edu

Arne Röhl
Genetic Ancestor Ltd, PO Box 503, Cambridge, CB1 0AN, UK.
*Email:* aroehl@geneticancestor.com

Matthew Spencer
Department of Mathematics and Statistics, Dalhousie University, Halifax, Nova Scotia, B3H 3J5, Canada.
*Email:* matts@mathstat.dal.ca

Tandy Warnow
Department of Computer Sciences, University of Texas at Austin, Austin, TX 78712, USA.
*Email:* tandy@cs.utexas.edu

Heather F. Windram
Department of Biochemistry, Downing Site, Tennis Court Road, Cambridge, CB2 1QW, UK.
*Email:* H.F.Windram@btinternet.com

## Figures


**I.1.** *Phylogeny: Charles Darwin's diagram from* The Origin of Species *illustrating 'the descent of the species ...'* 1
**I.2.** *Schleicher's family tree model for the Indo-European languages.* 2
**I.3.** *The intersecting fields of research into the origins of human diversity.* 2
**I.4.** *The wave theory for the distribution of innovations within a language family.* 4
**I.5.** *Word-coding methods used in this volume.* 5
**I.6.** *Classification of phylogenetic methods.* 6
**1.1.** *Madagascar and the Indian Ocean.* 12
**2.1.** *Geographical locations of the 95 Bantu and Bantoid languages used in the analysis.* 20
**2.2.** *Majority rule tree summarizing a Bayesian sample of 200 trees for 95 Bantu languages.* 21
**2.3.** *Consensus network summarizing the Bayesian sample of 200 trees for 95 Bantu languages.* 22
**2.4.** *Alternative possible topologies for the Bantu tree.* 23
**2.5.** *Illustrative splits graph.* 25
**2.6.** *Network of 95 Bantu and Bantoid languages, calculated using the Neighbor-Net method.* 26
**2.7.** *Networks of 48 East Bantu languages and 29 West Bantu languages, plus Tiv and Ejagham.* 27
**2.8.** *Network of 95 Bantu and Bantoid languages, calculated using the Neighbor-Net method.* 28
**4.1.** *The Bantu languages: geographic distribution.* 43
**4.2.** *Classification of 75 Bantu languages.* 48
**6.1.** *Elements of text evolution in an artificial text tradition containing 21 manuscripts and 856 locations.* 70
**6.2.** *Analysis of exemplar changes in the Prologue to The Wife of Bath's Tale.* 71
**6.3.** *Section of the Hg manuscript in the region of possible exemplar change.* 72
**8.1.** *Selection of languages and Swadesh list terms.* 94
**8.2.** *Cognate sets from Figure 8.1 expressed in a binary matrix showing cognate presence (1) or absence (0).* 94
**8.3.** *Character states for cognate sets 5 and 6 from Figure 8.1 are shown mapped onto a hypothetical tree.* 94
**8.4.** *Simple likelihood rate matrix adapted for modelling lexical replacement in language evolution.* 95
**8.5.** *The gamma distribution, used to model rate variation between sites.* 96
**8.6.** *Consensus network from the Bayesian MCMC sample of trees.* 97
**8.7.** *The Romance languages probably began to diverge prior to the fall of the Roman Empire.* 98
**8.8.** *Majority-rule consensus tree from the initial Bayesian MCMC sample of 1000 trees.* 99
**8.9.** *Frequency distribution of basal age estimates from filtered Bayesian MCMC sample of trees.* 100
**8.10.** *Frequency distribution of age estimates for the North and West Germanic subgroups.* 100
**8.11.** *Frequency distribution of basal age estimates from filtered Bayesian MCMC sample of trees.* 100
**8.12.** *Frequency distribution of basal age estimates from filtered Bayesian MCMC sample of trees.* 101
**8.13.** *Frequency distribution of basal age estimates from filtered Bayesian MCMC sample of trees.* 101
**8.14.** *Frequency distribution of basal age estimates from filtered Bayesian MCMC sample of trees.* 101
**8.15.** *Parsimony character trace for reflexes of Latin focus on the Romance consensus tree.* 104
**8.16.** *Frequency distribution of basal age estimates from filtered Bayesian MCMC sample of trees.* 105
**8.17.** *Majority-rule consensus tree for Swadesh 100-word list items only.* 106
**9.1.** *Two representations of the distances between Polynesian languages.* 113
**9.2.** *Timeline of Polynesian settlement, giving the date estimates and phases of settlement used in this paper.* 113
**11.1.** *Geographic locations of Germanic language samples.* 131
**11.2.** *Possible geographic and linguistic locations of Angles, Saxons and Jutes.* 132
**11.3.** *Unrooted network of 19 Germanic language samples.* 134
**13.1.** *Indo-European data, analyzed using SplitsTree.* 154
**13.2.** *Australian data from Nash (2002) analyzed using SplitsTree4.0.* 155
**13.3.** *Australian data from Nash (2002) analyzed using Neighbor-Net.* 155
**13.4a.** *Network for simulated hihi list (25 items), from full list with 10 per cent borrowing.* 156
**13.4b.** *Network for simulated lolo list (25 items), from full list with 10 per cent borrowing.* 156
**13.5.** *Germanic as drawn by Network3.0.* 157
**14.1.** *Distribution of the number of cognates per language and the number of languages to which cognates belong.* 163
**14.2.** *An example of the modelled cognate birth word death process.* 164
**14.3.** *One Indo-European language tree sampled from the posterior distribution of the data.* 168
**14.4.** *The distribution of the number of languages* $M_c$ *which possess a given synthetic data-cognate.* 169

**14.5.** *One language tree sampled from the posterior distribution of a subsample of 31 languages.* 170
**15.1.** *Indo-European and Bantu trees.* 176
**15.2.** *Rates of meaning evolution.* 177
**15.3.** *Frequency histogram of lexical half-lives derived from the data in Figure 15.2.* 178
**15.4.** *Instantaneous rate of evolution, q, versus the number of distinct cognate sets for a meaning.* 179
**15.5.** *Instantaneous rate of evolution, q, for the IE meanings versus the q obtained for the same Bantu meaning.* 179
**15.6.** *Branch lengths as estimated from binary-transformed data.* 180
**16.1.** *Rooted* FITCH *tree for Romance varieties using the results for phonetic similarity for the numerals one to ten.* 193

## Tables

**5.1.** *'Wheel' in Slavic languages.* 58
**5.2.** *Static, telic and transitive verbs for 'stand' in several Indo-European branches.* 59
**5.3.** *Static, telic, and transitive verbs for 'stand' in several Romance languages.* 60
**5.4.** *Ossetic 'stand'.* 61
**5.5.** *Stance verbs in languages from different families.* 63
**9.1.** *The accessibility matrix* **A**. 112
**9.2.** *The proportion of semantic slots for which the languages possess words that are not cognate).* 113
**9.3.** *Parameters and constants in the basic model.* 114
**11.1.** *Swadesh lists for 21 Germanic language samples.* between pp. 134 & 135
**12.1.** *Five numerals in PNIE and three NIE branches.* 144
**14.1.** *The per capita death rate, estimated from each of the age constrained clades in turn.* 169
**14.2.** *Effect of borrowing on reliability of root-time estimates using synthetic data simulated on a tree.* 169

# Introduction

## Colin Renfrew & Peter Forster

### The context of research

Colin Renfrew

The rapid development of computer-based methods for ordering great quantities of data has transformed the procedures of molecular genetics in recent years, just as such methods had earlier transformed classificatory biology. Phylogenetic methods now promise to have a significant impact upon the field of historical linguistics, and in particular to offer new interpretive procedures for considering the linguistic histories of very remote periods. The present volume is based upon the symposium 'Phylogenetic Methods and the Prehistory of Languages' held at the McDonald Institute for Archaeological Research in Cambridge in July 2004. It follows a number of earlier symposia directed towards the prehistory of languages, and follows in the wake of *Time Depth in Historical Linguistics* (Renfrew *et al.* 2000), deliberately seeking to use the expertise of those employing such methods in molecular genetics and related fields.

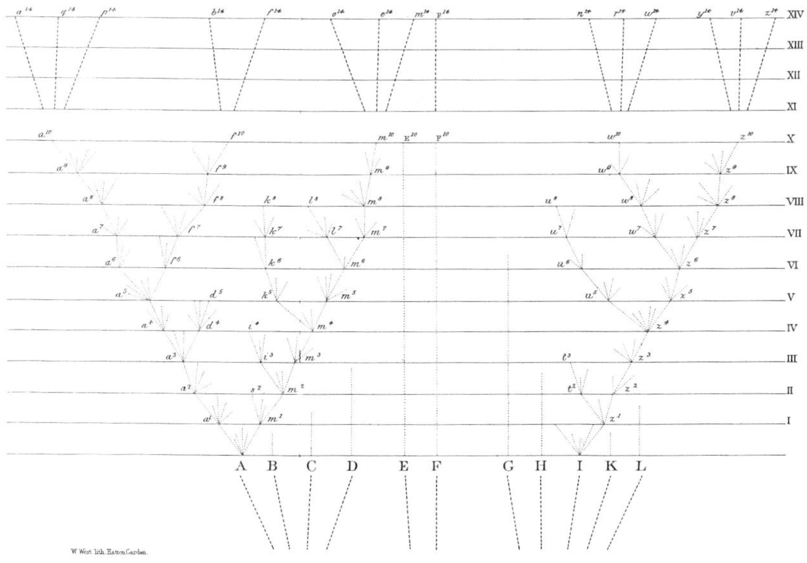


**Figure I.1.** *Phylogeny: Charles Darwin's diagram from* The Origin of Species *illustrating 'the descent of the species (A to L) of a genus large in its own country ... The intervals between the horizontal lines in the diagram, may represent each a thousand generations'.*

To study the prehistory of languages may seem at first sight, almost by definition, an impossible task. For languages come down to us from ancient times, if at all, in written form. The term 'prehistory' applied in any region refers to the stretch of time prior to the use of written records. Clearly to make statements about the nature of a language for a time prior to its first attestation by direct evidence requires some caution. But for more than two centuries historical linguists have developed sophisticated methods for doing just that, by observing relationships between languages, relationships which do carry implications about earlier states. For instance, when a language family is recognized by linguists and gains general acceptance, the proposal is frequently made that the observed family resemblances are best explained by common descent. The apparently related languages in the 'family' would thus have 'sprung from some common source' in the words of Sir William Jones (1786), namely from the hypothetical proto-language for the family in question. Jones was anticipated in this respect more than a century earlier by the Dutch scholar Marcus Zuerius van Boxhorn (van Driem 1997, 1039). The proto-language would have been spoken centuries, perhaps millennia earlier than the first surviving documents in the daughter languages. And of course there are cases where the ancestral proto-language for the surviving daughter languages actually is documented: Latin, as the parent of the Romance languages, being an obvious example.

Such statements about a proto-language are generally based upon large numbers of observations made upon the lexicon, morphology and phonology of the languages under review. But it is only relatively recently that analytical methods have become available for handling the great quantities of data that are potentially available. The methods of numerical taxonomy have, of course,

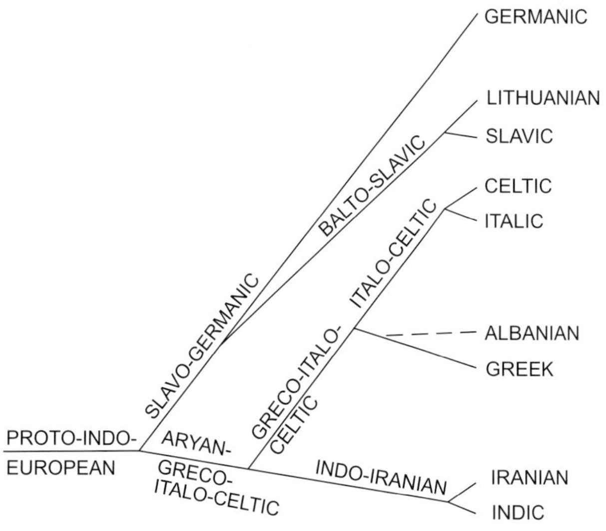


**Figure I.2.** *Schleicher's family tree model for the Indo-European languages (after Schleicher; Lehmann).*

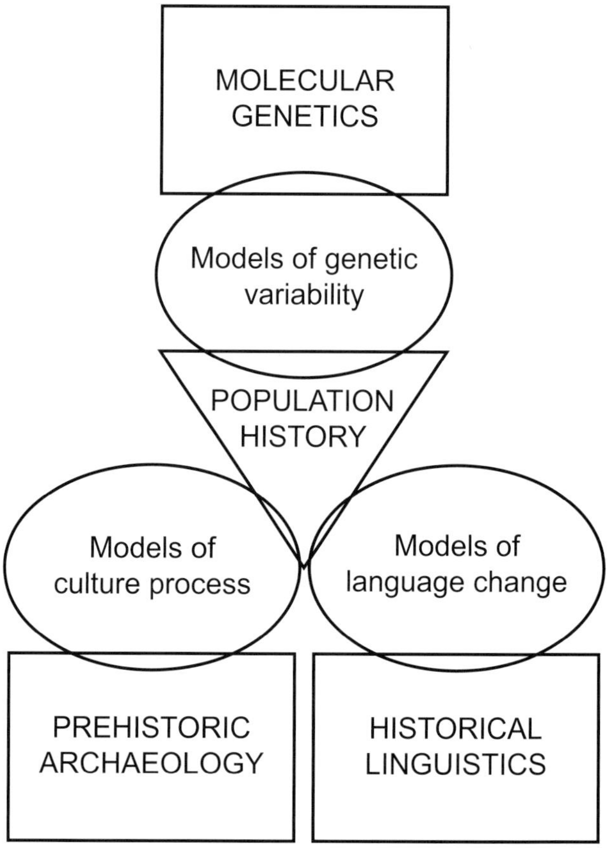


**Figure I.3.** *The intersecting fields of research into the origins of human diversity which are currently contributing to what may become a new synthesis between them (from Renfrew 1992; 2002).*

been available for some decades (e.g. Sokal & Sneath 1973), but it is with the advent of molecular genetics that more effective quantitative methods have become available, methods that have been developed in some cases to cope with the vast quantities of molecular data deriving from the Human Genome Project. They are frequently termed 'phylogenetic' methods because they operate by seeking to use the data to produce phylogenies, that is to say pathways or lines indicating the descent of groups. Often these phylogenies are described using a tree model (although network models are also in use). It was in this manner that Charles Darwin in 1859 envisaged the origin of species (Fig. I.1).

Darwin was considering the phylogeny of species and the descent of members of species as governed by natural selection, but the power of his phylogenetic model was soon applied in other fields including historical linguistics and archaeology (Pitt-Rivers 1875). In the field of historical linguistics Augustus Schleicher published already in 1863 his *Die Darwinsche Theorie und die Sprachwissenschaft*. His tree model for linguistic descent, applied to the languages of the Indo-European language family, was perhaps implicit in earlier work and in the very concept of the language family itself. In its dendritic form the notion of phylogeny today is generally based upon the Darwinian model (Fig. I.2), although it was anticipated by nearly 30 years in the 'stemmatic analysis' of the students of manuscripts such as Carl Gottlieb Zumpt (Timpanaro 1971, 44; see also Chapter 6 this volume).

Lines of descent need not, however, be illustrated exclusively in the form of a dendrogram, even when a unilineal succession is assumed, and as discussed below a network approach is the most common alternative.

The background to our symposium was of course a general interest in the application of such methods, which in a general sense are familiar to those acquainted with recent work in molecular genetics and archaeogenetics (e.g. Jobling *et al.* 2004; Renfrew & Boyle 2000), as well as to those participating in earlier meetings in the McDonald Institute's 'Prehistory of Languages' series (e.g. Renfrew *et al.* 2000; Bellwood & Renfrew 2002). In particular the work of Tandy Warnow and Don Ringe (e.g. Warnow 1997) in applying such approaches to the Indo-European family seemed of considerable interest, as did the work of Sergei Starostin and others in applying the methods of lexicostatistics to problems of time depth (Starostin 2000). The experience of Peter Forster in applying network methods, developed first with reference to molecular genetic data (Bandelt *et al.* 1995), then to linguistic problems (Forster *et al.* 1998) was also relevant. The great catalyst for our symposium was, however, the challenging paper by Russell Gray

& Quentin Atkinson (2003), in which phylogenetic methods were applied to the Indo-European language family, yielding dates for the first branchings within the Indo-European family much earlier than most historical linguists would have proposed. The application of a phylogenetic approach to produce not simply a structure for the language family in question, but also a chronology for the formation of that structure, seemed particularly promising. This and the pace of other related work on the application of such methods made the case for a fresh review involving most of the known specialists in this area particularly attractive.

The broader context for the discussions goes a little beyond the field of historical linguistics alone, and involves the interests of prehistoric archaeology as well as of molecular genetics (see Fig. I.3).

The relationships between archaeology and language have long been debated and have often proved contentious, and the literature is now vast (e.g. Blench & Spriggs 1997–99). Those between classical genetics and historical linguistics were reviewed in a magisterial volume by Luca Cavalli-Sforza and his colleagues (Cavalli-Sforza *et al.* 1994), although their earlier suggestions received short shrift from some linguists (Bateman *et al.* 1990). Those between archaeology and molecular genetics have been consolidated over the past decade within what may now be seen as the new discipline of archaeogenetics (Renfrew & Boyle 2000). Indeed there is the aspiration in some quarters that a 'new synthesis' between the disciplines (Renfrew 1991, 3) may now be emerging.

Certainly the renewed interest in these areas is reflected in papers in the present volume which are not specifically directed at the quantitative computations entailed in the application of phylogenetic methods. Robert Dewar, who in earlier work has argued the merits of reticulate rather than dendritic approaches to linguistic prehistory (Dewar 1995), reviews the relationships between linguistic and population history in Madagascar. His study reminds us that there are assumptions in the application of phylogenetic methods, such as the acceptance of single lines of descent, which should not be obscured by the undoubted efficacity of the numerical treatment implicit in such methods. This work is part of a larger body of research on Madagascar carried out at the McDonald Institute (Hurles *et al.* 2005; Vizuete-Forster *et al.* forthcoming).

The paper by Andrew Garrett likewise calls into question the assumption which underlies both tree and network approaches to phylogeny, namely that increasing divergence between taxonomic entities, accompanied by branching episodes, are the dominant processes. Johannes Schmidt (1872) was one of the first, with his 'wave theory' for linguistic innovation (Fig. I.4), to offer an alternative to the divergence and branching inherent in the model of Darwin and Schleicher.

The notion that processes of convergence rather than divergence might actually underlie the formation of a language family such as Indo-European was formulated by Trubetzkoy (1939). In general it has not found favour among linguists (see Aharon Dolgopolsky, quoted in Renfrew 1991, 9). But it has recently been utilized by Dixon (1997) in suggesting that some family-like resemblances, for instance in the Australian Pama-Nyungan family, may be explained in this way. In fact, so far as I am aware, no experienced historical linguist since Trubetzkoy has gone so far as to suggest that any specific language family has come about simply through the convergence of languages which were previously unrelated genetically. On the other hand it is clear that convergence as well as divergence processes can be at work between the languages *within* a given language family. This is the process which I have suggested (Renfrew 2000, 418; 2001, 42) might be termed *advergence*. On the long chronology for the development of the Indo-European languages which is proposed by Gray & Atkinson (2003) there are likely to be episodes of dispersal, of which the main one is perhaps to be associated with the dispersal of a farming economy from Anatolia. But there will be long periods also when advergence effects between those languages of the Indo-European family which are adjacently located result in further shared resemblances. These would not, however, be genetic effects, due to common descent from the shared proto-language (on the Schleicher model) but rather shared innovations (on the Schmidt model). They would be the effects which are generally felt to underlie the emergence of a *Sprachbund*, although in this case they are *Sprachbund* effects among languages which were already genetically related.

It is important therefore to take advergence effects into account. For, as Garrett indicates, episodes of advergence or convergence in this way may play an important role in language history. It remains to be seen how far these processes may complicate or impede the direct application of phylogenetic methods.

**Methods in phylogenetic linguistics**
Peter Forster

One aim of the conference was to bring together the available diversity of approaches in the emerging field of phylogenetic linguistics. For the same reason, we implemented a refereeing procedure for this volume which was designed to give each of the contributors maximal latitude and hence responsibility for her or

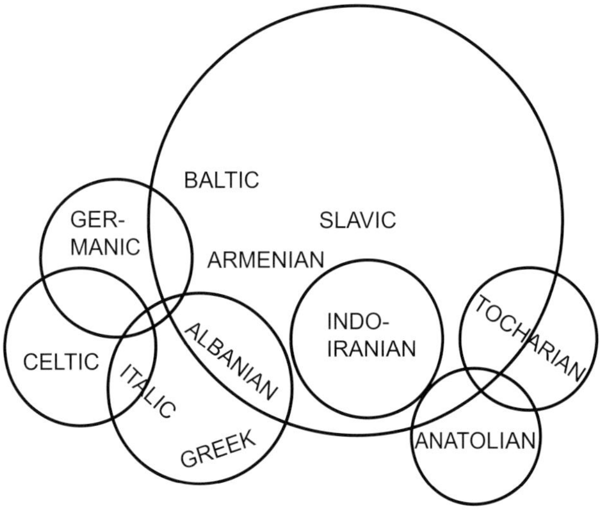


**Figure I.4.** *The wave theory for the distribution of innovations within a language family, as illustrated by Johannes Schmidt for the Indo-European languages (after Schmidt, and Lehmann).*

his chapter. Given this freedom, it is now interesting to scan these chapters for agreements and differences in approach between the various researchers.

The participants were in general agreement, both implicitly during the conference and as more explicitly documented in these pages, in their preference for network methods over tree methods to represent language evolution. This also holds true for the only chapter in the closely related field of manuscript evolution (Chapter 6 this volume), where it is uncontroversial that a new manuscript can arise as a combination of several existing manuscripts rather than pure descent from only one, yielding an evolutionary network of manuscripts rather than a tree.

A remarkable and quite unexpected area of agreement among many contributors concerns the choice of lexical data as the object of investigation, as opposed to phonological or morphological data. Specifically, the Swadesh 100- and 200-word lists (Swadesh 1955) are popular with several contributors. Although many readers will perceive this focus on the Swadesh basic lexicon as too narrow to encapsulate language evolution in all its aspects, the agreement on the Swadesh lists as a baseline does allow us to concentrate on the methodological differences concerning the choices of the phylogenetic method and the coding of the language data.

And it is in the coding of data where much of the debate arises. For example, the landmark paper by Gray & Atkinson published in 2003 drew the criticism of their Pennsylvanian colleagues both at the conference and in these pages (compare the debate between the chapters by Gray and colleagues versus Warnow and colleagues). The details of this controversy are expressed in rather technical terms, but in a nutshell, the New Zealand researchers chose to adapt the Indo-European data of Isidore Dyen (Dyen & Aberle 1974) into a binary coding scheme. What does this mean in a real example? Taking the first figure in Atkinson & Gray (Fig. 8.1 this volume) their six example languages have the words *water, Wasser, eau, acqua, nero* and *watar* for 'water'. In binary coding, these authors ask of each language the questions: Does a cognate of *Wasser* exist in English, yes or no? Does a cognate of *acqua* exist in English, yes or no? Does a cognate of *nero* exist in German? And so on, for all languages and words, with 'yes' and 'no' corresponding to zero and 1, respectively. The resulting binary-coded data are unobjectionable until one enters them into a phylogenetic method with the intention to reconstruct the ancestral prehistoric language; having inserted zeros into the data, it can then happen that the phylogeny reconstructs a hypothetical ancestral language which would not have a word for water. On the other hand, Gray and colleagues do not purport to employ their data for the reconstruction of ancestral languages, and their motivation for coding their data in this manner is a powerful one, namely to include into their analysis synonyms within one language, such as the German pair '*See*/*Meer*' for 'sea'.

Our own paper on the fragmentary corpus of ancient Gaulish published in 2003 is also taken to task, implicitly and explicitly, for example in Heggarty's and McMahon's chapters, because we expressly ignored etymological information prior to coding our items. Our response to similarly thoughtful criticisms is given elsewhere, but this is a good opportunity to compare the diverse lexical coding approaches employed in the chapters of this volume. To simplify this comparison, I have placed the chapters into an evolutionary tree in Figure I.5, with which the various coding procedures can be explained as follows.

Starting at the top of Figure I.5, the first question is how the words should be coded. Should they be coded by resemblance, in which case Spanish '*mucho*' and English 'much' would receive the same coding label, or should some prior knowledge of language history or etymology be included in the coding (which would then identify 'much' and '*mucho*' as being independently derived coincidental resemblances)? Johanna Nichols, and Brett Kessler & Annukka Lehtonen provide two chapters in which they opt for the resemblance approach. Using this approach, Kessler & Lehtonen produce evidence for the existence of a Uralic language family and an Indo-European language family, as a by-product of their paper. Their study is mainly concerned, however, with critically quantifying the power of the multilateral comparison technique advocated by Joseph Greenberg (1987, appendix).

Apart from the Nichols and Kessler chapters, the other authors in Figure I.5 follow the well-trodden Swadesh procedure of incorporating etymological scholarship into identifying cognates and labelling them with codes expressing their genetic relationship. This is the approach advocated by Paul Heggarty, which means that in Figure I.5 his chapter is placed on the branch to the right (or on the right branch, as many comparative linguists would argue). The Heggarty branch can now be further subdivided: when true cognates are present, they may be known to be loan words (e.g. English 'mountain' and French '*montagne*'), and it is then necessary to decide whether loan words should be included or excluded. The chapters by Bryant, Forster, Holden, McMahon and Pagel explicitly include loan words, while the remaining chapters by Atkinson, Nicholls and Warnow endeavour to purge their data of loans by coding loans with distinct labels. These two groups of chapters are therefore placed on separate branches in Figure I.5.

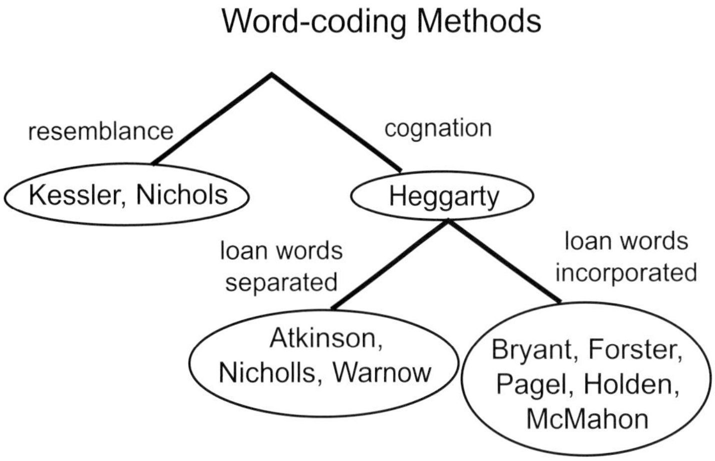


**Figure I.5.** *Word-coding methods used in this volume. Each chapter is a node labelled by the first author; note that Heggarty represents an internal node or branching point, while the others group into terminal nodes (often called tips or leaves). The derived character states (e.g. 'resemblance', 'loan words incorporated') are written alongside the lower ends of each link (often called 'edge').*

It is clear that no single one of the coding approaches summarized in Figure I.5 can in itself be considered 'better' or 'worse' than the others. Instead, the choice of coding must be tailored to the question that the researcher has set herself or himself. As a trivial example, a researcher wishing to analyze language contact may not be well served by data which have been coded to exclude all evidence of such contact (quoted from April McMahon, speaking on 27 November 2004 at the Ancient India and Iran Trust, Cambridge).

A brief note on phylogenetic methods is required within this general introduction. It is by no means possible to explain or even enumerate here all existing phylogenetic methods and their available computer programs, which number around 200. The interested reader may refer to the near-exhaustive compilation of available programs on the excellent website maintained by Joseph Felsenstein at the University of Washington. The weblink is http://evolution.genetics.washington.edu/phylip/software.html. It may, however, be helpful to touch upon those algorithms that are frequently referred to in these chapters. As depicted in Figure I.6, phylogenetic algorithms can be either tree algorithms or network algorithms. Tree algorithms have been around for several decades, whereas network algorithms are a more recent development, hence at present the former greatly outnumber the latter.

Tree algorithms attempt to recover evolutionary trees from the data, and will generally work well where languages have split from each other and subsequently have developed along their own paths. If the data are by nature not treelike (e.g. because languages have exchanged traits), then a tree applied to the raw data is not appropriate and either a judicious data coding is required (see above) or a network algorithm is indicated (see below). A second confounding factor for tree algorithms may be parallel independent evolution of traits, which may lead a tree algorithm to produce astronomically large numbers of equally plausible trees from one and the same data set. This second factor has been a major problem in genetics and motivated the development of network algorithms in the 1990s. As the name suggests, network algorithms generate graphs which contain reticulations (also known as cycles) depicting conflicting information in the data. Triangles, prisms, and high-dimensional cubes all constitute reticulations, and the simplest reticulation is the square. A step-by-step example for a toy network is provided in Forster *et al.* (1998).

Whether networks or trees, both approaches can be further subdivided into character methods and distance methods (Fig. I.6). What are characters and what are distances? In an example using 'bone' and 'leaf', English differs from German by the words for leaf (*Blatt*) and for bone (*Knochen*). Character methods would directly use the 'states' (i.e. translations) of

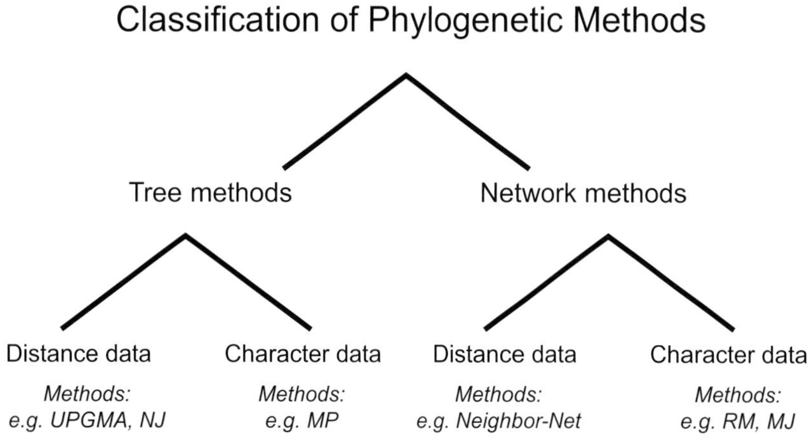


**Figure I.6.** *Classification of phylogenetic methods: NJ = Neighbour-Joining; MP = Maximum Parsimony; RM = Reduced Median; MJ = Median-Joining; UPGMA = Unweighted Pair Group Method with Arithmetic mean.*

these words to construct the tree or network. The linguist can then inspect the trees to see which words are postulated to have changed along which branches, and furthermore, which new words they have changed into. In distance methods, the trees would record only that German and English differ by a distance of two words, without specifying which words have changed along which branches. This potential disadvantage of distance methods may well be offset by other technical advantages in practice, and it is often difficult to predict *a priori* whether one method will be more suited to the task at hand than another.

Both tree and network algorithms may be seen as practical realizations of models, each with their own set of explicit or implicit assumptions. In fact, popular phylogenetic algorithms are sometimes accused of not making their assumptions explicit (Steele & Penny 2000). Several chapters in this book address the issue by developing models with explicit assumptions based to a greater or lesser degree on known or assumed mechanisms for language change. These statistical models are based either on a likelihood approach within a frequentist framework, or on a Bayesian approach. One particular challenge for all such models applied to lexical evolution is that we do not know all the possible cognate states for a word, unlike models for DNA where only the four nucleotides A, G, C, and T are available (Chapters 6 & 10 this volume). In general, there is a fine line to tread between invoking too stringent assumptions, some of which may not be as certain as assumed, and invoking too few assumptions for the model to capture the reality of language change (Chapter 8 this volume).

So far we have spoken only of unrooted trees and networks. Rooting procedures are mentioned only in passing rather than as a focus of any chapter, but it is important for the general reader to appreciate that in genetics it is common practice to produce unrooted graphs, before adding the root in the last step, for example by attaching an 'outgroup' (see Glossary). Alternatively one may include rooting information in the data by specifying the direction of change at the data level; this is possible for example for phoneme mergers which are thought to be effectively irreversible. Unrooted or insecurely rooted trees are of diminished value, especially when it the aim is to date deep branch points, as pointed out by Evans and colleagues (Chapter 10 this volume.

As for tangible results in this volume, some intriguing nuggets are on offer from this emerging field. Of particular interest to deep-time researchers are the chapters by Kessler & Lehtonen and Pagel & Meade which both penetrate deep into linguistic prehistory, but by using completely different methods. Although Kessler & Lehtonen demonstrate that a formal multilateral approach is insufficient to reconstruct a common ancestry between Uralic and Indo-European, they incidentally provide convincing statistical evidence for a Uralic family based solely on lexical resemblance without even resorting to phylogenetic methods. In the future, it would be interesting indeed to see how many more details can be gleaned when entering such data into phylogenetic methods. Pagel & Meade in their chapter identify lexemes whose half-life is on the order of thousands of years, providing new perspectives for linguistic chronologies. In this context, Bryant's chapter on Polynesian language evolution is also of interest, suggesting a rate of lexical evolution which is compatible with but possibly slower than that originally suggested by Swadesh. Among the new suggestions on classification we find the chapter by Forster and colleagues on Germanic lexical evolution (the proposed phylogeny will no doubt undergo evolution itself as the lexical data are expanded), and the chapter by Holden and colleagues on Bantu lexical evolution, which is extensively commented on from a linguist's perspective in the accompanying chapter by Lutz Marten.

Finally, it was a special pleasure to welcome to the Symposium Isidore Dyen, whose pioneering work particularly on the Indo-European languages, initiated more than 50 years ago, remains an important resource today, and we dedicate this Symposium volume to him.

## Acknowledgements

The editors wish first to thank the Management Committee of the McDonald Institute for Archaeological Research and the Institute's former Deputy Director Dr Chris Scarre both for their financial provision for the Symposium and for their consistent support over several years for the Prehistory of Languages Project. The research by Peter Forster and colleagues was partly funded by the Junge Akademie in Berlin for which we are grateful. The project as a whole, and the volumes in the Papers in the Prehistory of Languages series which have resulted, were initiated by the Alfred P. Sloan Foundation to whose vision the enterprise remains indebted.

For the organization of the Symposium 'Phylogenetic Methods in Historical Linguistics' which took place from 9–12 July 2004, they wish to acknowledge the assistance of: James Clackson, Katie Boyle, Manuel Arroyo-Kalin, Karin Haack and Mrs Deborah Parr.

In addition to the contributors to the present volume, the following participated in the Symposium: James Clackson, Sue Content, Sheila Embleton, Franz Manni, John Penney, Ian Roberts, Win Scutt, Stephen Shennan, Nicholas Sims-Williams, Natalia Slaska, Giselle Weiss (*Neue Zürcher Zeitung*) as well as the invited discussants, Bill Poser and Peter Schrijver, to whom we are very grateful. Isidore Dyen's paper to the Symposium, which was beyond the scope of this volume, is available at www.mcdonald.cam.ac.uk. Bound copies of the paper (Dyen 2004) have been deposited in the library of the McDonald Institute and in the University Library, Cambridge.

The editors acknowledge the Viking Museum Haithabu in Schleswig for providing the picture of the Skarthi stone for the cover.

The editors are pleased that this volume could be included in the Monograph series of the McDonald Institute. They wish to record their thanks to Shuichi Matsumura, Matthew Spencer, Vincent Macaulay and further anonymous specialists for acting as referees, to the anonymous reader of the entire volume, and to Dr Katie Boyle for kindly undertaking the copy editing, and their special gratitude to the Institute's Production Editor Miss Dora Kemp.

## References

Bandelt, H.-J., P. Forster, B.C. Sykes & M.B. Richards, 1995. Mitochondrial portraits of human populations using median networks. *Genetics* 141, 743–53.

Bateman, R., I. Goddard, R. O'Grady, V.A. Funk, R. Mooi, W.J. Kress & P. Cannell, 1990, Speaking with forked tongues: the feasibility of reconciling human phylogeny and the history of language. *Current Anthropology* 31, 1–24.

Bellwood, P. & C. Renfrew (eds.), 2002. *Examining the Farming/Language Dispersal Hypothesis*. (McDonald Institute Monographs.) Cambridge: McDonald Institute for Archaeological Research.

Blench, R. & M. Spriggs (eds.), 1997–99. *Archaeology and Language*, vols. I to IV. London: Routledge.

Cavalli-Sforza, L.L., P. Menozzi & A. Piazza, 1994. *The History and Geography of Human Genes*. Princeton (NJ): Princeton University Press.

Darwin, C., 1859. *The Origin of Species by Means of Natural Selection*. London: John Murray.

Dewar, R.E., 1995. Of nets and trees: untangling the reticulate and the dendritic in Madagascar's prehistory. *World Archaeology* 26, 301–18.

Dixon, R.M.W., 1997. *The Rise and Fall of Languages*. Cambridge: Cambridge University Press.

Dyen, I., 2004. The Basis of Linguistic Phylogenetics. Manuscript, McDonald Institute, University of Cambridge.

Dyen, I. & D.F. Aberle, 1974. *Lexical Reconstruction: the Case of the Proto-Athapaskan Kinship System*. Cambridge: Cambridge University Press.

Forster, P., A. Toth & H.-J. Bandelt, 1998. Evolutionary networks of word lists: visualising the relationships between Alpine Romance languages. *Journal of Quantitative Linguistics* 5(3), 174–87.

Gray, R. D. & Q.D. Atkinson, 2003. Language-tree divergence times support the Anatolian theory of Indo-European origin. *Nature* 426, 435–9.

Greenberg, J.H., 1987. *Language in the Americas*. Stanford (CA): Stanford University Press.

Hurles, M.A, B.C. Sykes, M.A. Jobling & P. Forster, 2005. The dual origin of the Malagasy in Island Southeast Asia and East Africa: evidence from maternal and paternal lineages. *American Journal of Human Genetics* 76, 894–901.

Jobling, M.A., M.E. Hurles & C. Tyler-Smith, 2004. *Human Evolutionary Genetics: Origins, Peoples and Disease*. New York (NY): Garland Science.

Jones, Sir W., 1786. Third anniversary discourse 'On the Hindus', reprinted in *The Collected Works of Sir William Jones*, 1807. London: John Stockdale, 23–46.

Pitt-Rivers, A.H.L.F., 1875. On the evolution of culture. *Proceedings of the Royal Institution of Great Britain* 7, 496–520 (under the author's signature A. Lane-Fox).

Renfrew, C., 1991. Before Babel, speculations on the origins of linguistic diversity. *Cambridge Archaeological Journal* 1(1), 3–23.

Renfrew, C., 1992. Archaeology, genetics and linguistic diversity. *Man* 27, 445–78.

Renfrew, C., 2000. 10,000 or 5,000 years ago? – Questions of time depth, in *Time Depth in Historical Linguistics*, eds. C. Renfrew, A. McMahon & L. Trask. (Papers in the Prehistory of Languages.) Cambridge: McDonald Institute for Archaeological Research, 413–39.

Renfrew, C., 2001. The Anatolian origins of Proto-Indo-European and the autochtony of the Hittites, in *Greater Anatolia and the Indo-Hittite Language Family*, ed. R. Drews. (*Journal of Indo-European Studies* Monograph 38.) Washington (DC): Institute for the Study of Man, 36–63.

Renfrew, C., 2002. Genetics and language in contemporary archaeology, in *Archaeology, the Widening Debate*, eds. B. Cunliffe, W. Davies & C. Renfrew. London: British Academy/Oxford: Oxford University Press, 43–76.

Renfrew, C. & K. Boyle (eds.), 2000. *Archaeogenetics: DNA and the Population Prehistory of Europe*. (McDonald Institute Monographs.) Cambridge: McDonald Institute for

Archaeological Research.
Renfrew, C., A. McMahon & L. Trask (eds.), 2000. *Time Depth in Historical Linguistics*. (Papers in the Prehistory of Languages.) Cambridge: McDonald Institute for Archaeological Research.
Schleicher, A., 1863. *Die Darwinsche Theorie und die Sprachwissenschaft*. Weimar.
Schmidt, J., 1872. *Die Verwandtschaftsverhältnisse der indogermanischen Sprachen*. Weimar: Böhlau.
Sokal, R.R. & P.H.A. Sneath, 1973. *Numerical Taxonomy*. London: Freeman.
Starostin, S., 2000. Comparative-historical linguistics and lexicostatistics, in *Time Depth in Historical Linguistics*, eds. C. Renfrew, A. McMahon & L. Trask. (Papers in the Prehistory of Languages.) Cambridge: McDonald Institute for Archaeological Research, 223–66.
Steele, M. & D. Penny, 2000. Parsimony, likelihood, and the role of models in molecular phylogenetics. *Molecular Biology and Evolution* 17, 839–50.
Swadesh, M., 1955. Towards greater accuracy in lexicostatistic dating. *International Journal of American Linguistics* 21, 121–37.
Timpanaro, S., 1971. *Die Entstehung der Lachmannschen Methode*. Hamburg: Helmut Buske Verlag.
Trubetzkoy, N.S., 1939. Gedanken über das Indogermanenproblem. *Acta Linguistica* 1, 81–9.
van Driem, G., 1997. *Languages of the Himalayas*. (2 vols.) Leiden: Brill.
Vizuete-Forster, M., S. Matsumura, P. Blumbach, R. Dewar & P. Forster, forthcoming. The genetic prehistory of female Asian lineages in Madagascar, in *Simulations, Genetics and Human Prehistory*, eds. S. Matsumura, C. Renfrew & P. Forster. (McDonald Institute Monographs.) Cambridge: McDonald Institute for Archaeological Research.
Warnow, T., 1997. Mathematical approaches to comparative linguistics. *Proceedings of the National Academy of Sciences of the USA* 94, 685–90.

# *Part I*

## *Classification*

# *Chapter 1*

# Malagasy Language as a Guide to Understanding Malagasy History

Robert E. Dewar

> On the entire coast between Mazalagem and Sadia, which has a length of about 130 leagues, they speak, on the coast itself, a language analogue to that of the *Cafres*, that is to say like that in Mozambique and Malindi [in reality, an idiom of a mixture of Swahili and Malagasy], and the natives resemble, in color and culture, the negros of Africa of whom, it seems, they are descendents. But a short distance from this coastline, as in all of the interior of the island and on all of the rest of the coastline, they only speak the *bouque* language [Malagasy], found only among these natives, and totally different from the *Cafre* language, but which is very like Malay, which proves in a manner almost certain that the first inhabitants came from Malacca. (Grandidier & Grandidier 1903–20, II, 21–2 [comments in brackets are Grandidiers']).[1]

This quotation is from the manuscript description of a voyage to Madagascar in 1613–14 written by the Portuguese priest Luis Mariano, and translated and published by the French scholars Alfred and Guillaume Grandidier. Although European sailors encountered Madagascar in 1500, Mariano has been credited with being the first to present 'serious notions' about Madagascar and its inhabitants (Deschamps 1965, 64). It is remarkable then that in the first serious discussion of the Malagasy people, phylogenetic notions of language, and their use in the inference of ancient population movements appear. It is also of interest that the Grandidiers chose to insert a clarification identifying the 'Cafre' language of the west coast as a mixture of Swahili and Malagasy, though they give no reason for doing so, nor is there any evidence of such a mixture. Indeed, this passage introduces well the central theme of this paper: the ways, both phylogenetic and otherwise, that the evidence of language can be used in the elucidation of Malagasy origins (cf. Dewar 1995). Before considering the linguistic evidence, it will be helpful to briefly review the other sources of our understanding of Malagasy origins.

Apart from the evidence offered by language, and to a limited extent by genetics, there are two other sources of data that have been used to establish the origins of the Malagasy. The first of these is comparative ethnology and technology, and the second are oral histories collected from the seventeenth century onwards. For the former, there are convincing demonstrations that traditional Malagasy agriculture, including herding, and technologies are a mix of items of both African and Southeast Asian origins. Such 'proofs' of disparate ultimate origins offer little evidence of the settlement process or indeed of chronology. The oral histories, which are of great importance in establishing local histories, are by their nature difficult to contextualize in an overview as broad as this one, and will only be briefly referred to.

### Background

Madagascar was one of the last substantial land masses of the tropical/subtropical world to be settled by people. Just why this is so can only be answered by speculation, but it is remarkable that an island of more than 600,000 km$^2$ located only about 400 km from the East African coast should have remained so long uninhabited. At present, there are several grounds for believing that settlement did not begin before about the beginning of the Common Era (Dewar & Wright 1993). Despite decades of archaeological research, no one has found any convincing traces of stone-age occupation. It appears nearly certain that the first settlers employed iron tools; iron did not fully replace stone tools anywhere in tropical Africa or Asia before about 200 BC. This provides a limit on the antiquity of settlement.

The earliest radiocarbon datings associated with human activity are possibly unreliable dates on butchered pygmy hippo (now extinct) bones from a coastal swamp in the southwest (MacPhee & Burney 1994). When calibrated, these dates have been taken as evi-

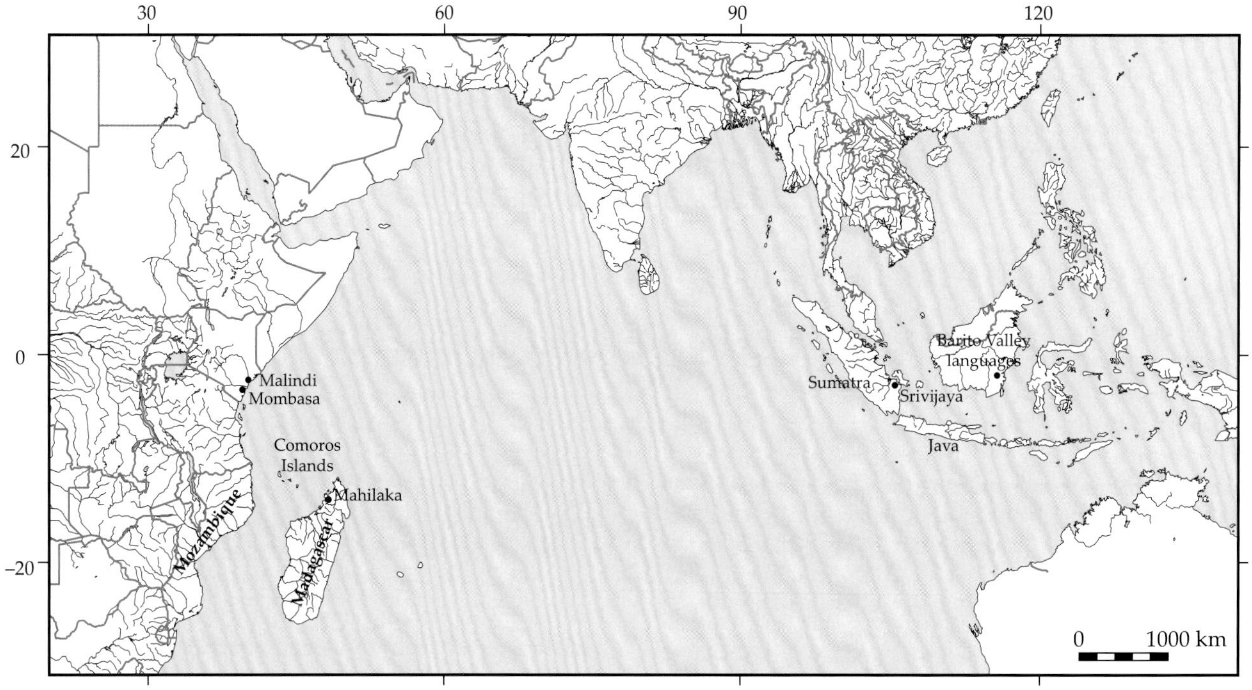


**Figure 1.1.** *Madagascar and the Indian Ocean.*

dence for hippo butchery on this coast in the first three centuries AD, but the bones are not associated with any equally ancient artefacts, nor any indication of human occupation. The earliest radiocarbon date from a sealed layer with evidence of occupation comes from a small rockshelter near the extreme northern coast and calibrates to about the fifth century AD (Dewar 1996). Although recovered with some artefacts and apparent culinary debris, this date is still something of an orphan, and none of the sparse collection of ceramic sherds with which it was found can be used to trace culture-historic relationships.

The earliest sites with substantial evidence for occupation are from the northeast coast and are reasonably well-dated to the late eighth to ninth century AD (Dewar & Wright 1993). These are roughly equivalent in age to the earliest settlements in the Comoros Islands, with which they share some ceramic traits (Allibert & Vérin 1996). They are also roughly contemporary with the origins of the 'mercantile and urban' Swahili tradition of East Africa (Horton & Middleton 2000). By the twelfth to thirteenth centuries AD, there are settlements known from the length of the island's coasts — from the extreme north to the extreme south, and along both the east and west coasts. These range in size from hamlets to the eleventh- to fifteenth-century urban entrepôt of Mahilaka on the northwest coast (Radimilahy 1998).

In sum, the archaeological record suggests that occupation in Madagascar was underway by no later than the late eighth century AD, with limited evidence to suggest that the island had been visited in earlier centuries. Who were these first settlers?

All the well-known sites from the eighth through the thirteenth centuries AD yield direct evidence of participation in the Indian Ocean trade network. Most commonly, these are ceramic sherds produced in the Near East, or China, but glass, carnelian, gold and silver beads are sometimes found as well (Dewar & Wright 1993; Radimilahy 1998; Wright & Fanony 1992). In the earliest villages of the northeast coast, there was the production of chlorite schist vessels, which later appear on East African sites, suggesting the production of exportable goods. It seems likely that the first settlers of Madagascar came there on board ships participating in the Indian Ocean trade. Once settled, they established herds and fields to feed themselves. Undoubtedly, they also sought exportable commodities along Madagascar's coast and in its forests and interior. In Mahilaka, there is evidence for the export of chlorite schist, gold, iron and crystal quartz, and it is likely that gums and resins, wood, and sea turtle scutes, were exported as well. Maritime trade continued, as, in the first years of the sixteenth century AD the Portuguese encountered ports along the northwest coast where there was regular trade with Malindi and Mombasa (Grandidier & Grandidier 1903–20, I, 21).

Given that trading may have formed the basis for at least some of the settlements on the island, it is likely that the settlement processes in Madagascar were heterogeneous. Some settlers may have spread to Madagascar as migrants seeking new lands for farming and herding. An obvious source would have been the nearby Comoros Islands. The earthenware ceramics of early Madagascar are clearly related to the ceramics of the Comoros, and to those of the Swahili coastline to the west. But other settlers obviously had roots on the opposite side of the Indian Ocean, and these may have arrived as the result of shipwrecks, or as temporary work parties of sailors and traders seeking to identify exportable goods, and to assemble them for returning trading vessels. The sixteenth-century Portuguese accounts describe several relatively small implantations of Islamic traders along the northwest coast, apparently recent migrants serving to gather and prepare commodities for trading partners (Grandidier & Grandidier 1903–20, I, 28, 41, 43, 117, 139 & 155–9). In the seventeenth century, the French established similar trading posts along the east coast, in part to supply their attempted colony in the southeast of Madagascar (cf. account of François Martin, in Grandidier & Grandidier 1903–20, IX). Earlier traders, based in Southeast Asia, may likewise have established trading settlements, although there is as yet no archaeological evidence of these. These may well have been principally communities of men, at least at the beginning, as the French trading posts were. Such settlers may have had little intention of residing permanently on Madagascar, although they may have been joined by other settlers, including women, if the commercial opportunities were attractive enough.

### Population genetics

The population of Madagascar is phenotypically heterogeneous, and this heterogeneity is as evident today as it was to Portuguese observers in the sixteenth century, who remarked upon the variations in skin-colour and hair texture. Some early observers attributed this to a mixture of African and Southeast Asian populations. Later, others attributed the darker-skinned populations to migrations from Melanesia. Still other scholars, responding to oral histories, attributed some of the lighter-skinned local populations to immigrations from the Persian Gulf. Finally, some attempted to explain the varying degrees of 'Asian' ancestry of local populations to two immigrations from Southeast Asia: one ancient, resulting in a population of largely mixed ancestry, and another much more recent, leaving largely 'Asian' descendents in the central highlands (for reviews of a large literature see Ferrand 1908; Vérin 1986).

There have, as yet, been only a limited number of published studies seeking to sort out these issues (recently reviewed, with additional data in Cox 2003). One clear conclusion is that the modern population of Madagascar has important genetic ancestry both in East Africa and Southeast Asia. A significant contribution from Melanesia seems unlikely. A second is that while there are differences in the proportion of Asian and African ancestry in different parts of the island, there is also marked heterogeneity in all regions, and a blended ancestry everywhere. Recently, Trefor Jenkins and Himla Soodyall of the University of Witwatersrand, with the assistance of Gwynn Campbell (now of McGill University) conducted a wide ranging genetic sampling of Madagascar. They have yet to publish definitive results.

### Language: dendritic approaches

In contrast to population genetics, where important results have been slow to appear, the analysis of Malagasy, the native language of almost all modern residents of Madagascar, is comparatively advanced and offers much insight into the settlement process of the island. At present Malagasy is the primary language of the vast majority of the Malagasy people. There is widespread use of French as a second language, and there are a limited number of villages where Swahili is a second language, and even a few villages where the descendents of nineteenth-century Makoa migrants from Mozambique have retained elements of their native language. The overwhelming dominance of Malagasy, however, is one of the great unifiers of the Malagasy people. Malagasy language is not, however, uniform from region to region. There are significant regional differences in spoken Malagasy, reflected principally in phonology and vocabulary, and these are often characterized as regional dialects; about two dozen dialects are recognized, although boundaries between dialects are often very fuzzy.

Malagasy is the westernmost member of the Austronesian language family. Austronesian has the greatest geographical distribution of any recognized language family, stretching from Eastern Polynesia to the aboriginal languages of Taiwan, and finally to Madagascar. It is also, perhaps because of this, a language family that has attracted much attention from historical linguists (see review in Pawley 2002). Austronesian linguists have also been among the most active in seeking to exploit their understanding of the language family's history in tracing out historical movements of ancient peoples, as anyone familiar with the debates surrounding the settlement of Oceania will know. Since Malagasy's resemblance to Malay was recognized before the crystallization of the methods of comparative linguistics, it has long been a famous, and curious case.

Historical linguists employ the comparative method to establish tree-like, or dendritic, models of linguistic relationships within a family. Languages, and then groups of related languages, are linked together on the basis of sharing innovative changes — usually phonological. These innovations are detected in regular correspondences between the phonological patterns in cognates — words whose similarity in meaning and sound pattern seem to be the product of descent from a common ancestral language. When cognates in adjacent branches of the tree show the appropriate sound correspondences, they can be 'reconstructed' as a part of the hypothetical parent language of the two branches. It is important to note that relationships between languages ought to established only upon what linguists call 'genetic' features: similarities by descent from a common ancestral language. Similarities due to chance resemblances, or to loan words cannot properly be used in the establishment of 'genetic' relationships.

In 1951, Otto Chr. Dahl demonstrated a close relationship between Malagasy and Maanjan, a language spoken today on Borneo (Dahl 1951). More recently, he has proposed that it is more proper to regard the ancestral relationship of Malagasy as linking to the Barito Valley languages of which Maanyan is a member (Dahl 1977). All of these languages are spoken in a relatively limited area of southeastern Kalimantan. Dahl's work has been regarded as of utmost importance, and a fact to be reckoned with in any reconstructed history of the settlement of Madagascar. It established, beyond any doubt, insular Southeast Asia as one of the homelands of Malagasy language and culture.

Dahl also offered an approximate date for the initial migration to Madagascar of about AD 400. This inference was based upon the limited number of Sanskrit loanwords found in Malagasy. These words all showed the phonological changes that distinguished Malagasy from Maanyan, and thus were assumed to have been loans established in the ancestor of Malagasy before the move across the Indian Ocean. Given that the number of Sanskrit loans were few in comparison to other Southeast Asian languages like Malay, Dahl argued that the migration must have occurred shortly after the beginning of Sanskrit influence in the region. He employed the epigraphic evidence of the introduction of Sanskrit into the region to establish his estimate of the chronology of migration. He has recently (1991) revised his estimate of initial migration to about the seventh century AD (see below).

The link between Malagasy and the Barito Valley languages does present certain difficulties for prehistorians. The most important is that none of the Barito Valley languages are spoken along coastal Kalimantan: these are all inland groups, without, so far as is known, any history of maritime activity. It is difficult to imagine any direct voyage from the Barito Valley to Madagascar. One solution is to posit an original homeland for the Barito Valley languages that included coastal regions, and may have included maritime activities, but there is little available evidence to support this. Dahl (1991) has suggested that two short South Sumatran inscriptions of the seventh century AD offer evidence of Maanyan occupation of that region, but the evidence is scant, and the argument highly speculative (Adelaar 1995).

## Linguistics: reticulate approaches

Complementary to the study of 'genetic' relations between languages is the study of the effects of processes associated with language contact — situations where adjacent languages or widespread bilingualism have detectable impacts on the development of a language. The most important recent study of language contact phenomena is that of Thomason & Kaufman (1988). This is a complex and somewhat controversial area, but it offers different insights from that available from the comparative method alone. First, it is an attempt to examine directly social conditions in the past that have resulted in language change. Second, it exploits evidence, for example of borrowings, that is by definition unused in the study of language phylogeny. It must be noted, however, that the most useful inferences are only evident after the phylogenetic relationships have already been well-established.

Two basic language contact processes are relevant to prehistorians of Madagascar: borrowing of words and interference (Thomason & Kaufman 1988). These are the result of different processes, although a single language, as Malagasy, may show signs of both. Each of these processes can have a range of effects on a language, from minor impacts, to major changes. It is also clear that languages differ in the extent to which they are susceptible to language contact change, so that it is not possible to clearly read past social conditions from language history. Nonetheless, careful examination of such language contact phenomena can yield important insights for prehistorians.

Borrowing from an adjacent language may reflect minor to major influences. At the minor end of the spectrum, where there is little bilingualism, and casual contacts between speakers of the two languages, the primary effect is the borrowing of words. Often, such borrowed words are labels for new and unknown items, and thus not replacements for words in the borrowing language's original vocabulary; English, a language with a propensity for borrowing, has accepted bagel (from Yiddish), toboggan (from Algonquian), and chutney (from Hindi) , among many others. Under more intensive interaction, involving extensive bilingualism over a long period, many more lexical items may be borrowed, and there may be structural and phonological changes in the borrowing language as well. Continuing with English as an example, there was extraordinary borrowing from Norman French into English as the result of William's conquest. As we shall see below, the various epochs of borrowing into Malagasy conform to the less intensive end of the spectrum.

Linguistic interference results from imperfect learning of a new language. The basic process is of a language community learning a second language, but failing to learn it perfectly and completely; in the process of learning, features of their native language become incorporated into their performance of the acquired language. Most of the time and particularly where the learning community is small relative to the population whose language they are acquiring, successive generations come to more and more perfectly acquire the new language. However, in other circumstances, particularly when both language communities, the native speakers and the learning speakers, are on more equal footing, aspects of the imperfect learning can later spread across the entire language community, i.e. the 'errors' of the learners can become standard. In contrast to borrowing, the errors associated with interference are more likely to occur in the realms of phonology and syntax rather than in lexical items (Thomason & Kaufman 1988). In the past, interference has often been labelled 'substratum', 'superstratum' or 'adstratum' influences, but Thomason & Kaufman prefer to lump these ill-defined categories into 'interference'.

Our understanding of language contact effects on Malagasy owe much to Dahl's research, and to that of Alexander Adelaar. Although Dahl died in 1992, at the age of 95, he was able to respond to the critiques of Adelaar, and to change his opinions in response. Differences remain between their two views of the development of Malagasy, but there are great areas of consensus. Their research offers much of interest to the prehistorian interested in Madagascar.

*In Insular Southeast Asia*

Adelaar (cf. 1995) has made a striking contribution in identifying loan words borrowed into Malagasy from other languages in Southeast Asia, presumably before the speakers of ancestral Malagasy moved across the Indian Ocean. First, he demonstrated, and Dahl (1991) agreed, that all of the approximately thirty words borrowed from Sanskrit into Malagasy showed phonological changes that could best be accounted for if they were first borrowed from Sanskrit into Malay or Javanese, and then subsequently acquired by the speakers of ancestral Malagasy. The Sanskrit loans are from various realms of meaning, but about a third are labels for months and/or seasons of the year.

In addition to loans ultimately from Sanskrit, Adelaar (1995 for a review) discovered a further array of words that were borrowed into ancestral Malagasy from other languages of western Indonesia, and many of these were accepted by Dahl (1991). By far the longest list of loan words is from Malay. There are others from Javanese, but it should be noted that there are many attested borrowings between Malay and Javanese. These words come from a variety of semantic fields, but interestingly, Adelaar (1996) has shown that the Malagasy system of cardinal directions was an adaptation of the Malay system. Sumatra and Java were centres of maritime activity and trading from early in the Common Era, and by the seventh century AD the Sumatran kingdom of Srivijaya was the dominant maritime and mercantile power of the region. It is not surprising that the Malay and Javanese should have been sources of borrowings into ancestral Malagasy since the route from Kalimantan to Madagascar must have passed this way, nor that it might include a set of terms so important for maritime life. Given the importance of the influence from Malay, both Dahl and Adelaar propose a 'pause' in the journey westward in the vicinity of Sumatra.

Adelaar (1995) also detects borrowings from the languages of South Sulawesi into Malagasy as well, in some cases, as borrowings into other Southeast Barito languages. As some of the peoples of South Sulawesi have been active mariners and merchants in recent centuries, it is not surprising that their languages may have been the source of loanwords. It is likely that these borrowings may have preceded the start of the move west from Kalimantan, yet there are some South Sulawesi loans that are not as yet known from other Southeast Barito languages, and may reflect later influences.

Still other Indonesian languages have been proposed as the sources of limited numbers of loanwords, but in all cases these seem to have had limited effects, and thus offer little of importance to the prehistorian.

How should we interpret these borrowings from Malay, Javanese, and South Sulawesi languages? First, Dahl and Adelaar have converged on the opinion that the limited impact of Sanskrit loans and the important impact of Malay on Malagasy suggests that the migration to the western Indian Ocean dated to (Dahl 1991) or at least commenced (Adelaar 1995) in the seventh century AD when Srivijaya established its preeminence. Adelaar (1991; 1995) has further proposed that the voyagers to the western Indian Ocean may not have been linguistically unified, and that the speakers of the Southeast Barito language may have been subordinates amongst the travellers. It is not unreasonable that a small party left behind to explore and exploit Madagascar's resources would have been largely drawn from subordinates, and that subsequent migrants would have adopted the local language. This suggestion is speculative, if reasonable, but as mentioned above the archaeological record is at present mute on this issue.

*In the Western Indian Ocean*

The Malagasy language, although unquestionably of Indonesian origin, has long been known to show features that reflect contact with languages of the western Indian Ocean, and especially with Bantu languages including Swahili. This was first made clear by the identification of loan words from East African languages. A good example is the standard word for cattle: *omby* in the Merina dialect. This is a loan word from a Bantu language; it has largely replaced the Indonesian term for cattle, *lambo*; *lambo* remains in the vocabulary, but its referent has shifted to another large mammal, the bush pig. Some Bantu loan words are common to all Malagasy dialects, but a number are only found in dialects of the western coast, where contact with Swahili was attested in the sixteenth century AD, and continues to the present. Dahl (1988) counted about 50 words in Malagasy that were, in one fashion or another, loans from Bantu.

Dahl (1954; 1988) has proposed, following earlier scholars, that loan words from East Africa reached Malagasy speech communities in two fashions: an early wave dating to near the arrival of Malagasy on the island, and then loans in subsequent centuries, particularly common in dialects along the western coast. He referred to the early wave of loans as resulting from a 'Bantu substratum' in Malagasy. Many linguists have been wary of postulated substratums in the development of languages, and most particularly where the substratum language is unknown. Dahl, however, showed that the substratum language was a Bantu language, and probably related to the Swahili subgroup languages of the Comoros. His substratum influence extended beyond loan words, for he noted phonological, morphological and syntactic innovations in Malagasy that seemed to be the result of the speech habits of Bantu language speakers being carried over into Malagasy. The most commonly cited change is in word endings. Southeast Barito words can end with consonants or vowels, but almost all Malagasy words end with a vowel, in conformance with Bantu languages.

Thomason & Kaufman (1988, 50) contrasted the effects of borrowing and of language shifting and showed each had different effects. As noted above, situations where the language contact effects are the result of long periods of bilingualism typically result in large numbers of borrowings of words, and eventually alterations in phonology and syntax. Language contact effects that are the result of imperfect learning among people shifting languages more commonly result in alterations of phonology and syntax, and do not necessarily involve the borrowing of words. They note, however, that some languages show both kinds of effects.

While the Bantu loanwords in Malagasy are prominent, they are not very large in number: Dahl counted about 50, and this compares to the 30 or so Malay loans noted by Adelaar. The phonological, morphological and syntactic changes attributed to the Bantu substratum seem relatively more important. This suggests that these are traces of language shift interference. Thomason & Kaufman argue that language-shift interference is more common when the shifting population is relatively large compared to the population of the community speaking the learned language. While the motivation for Bantu speakers to shift to Malagasy is unknown, the archaeological and historical evidence is concordant with such a shift.

Dahl (1988) notes that Bantu loan words often seem to fall into two domains: many are the names of domestic animals and plants, and others are words associated with tasks usually performed by women. He infers that women who were native speakers of Bantu languages may have played an important role in the development of the substratum, perhaps as wives to Malagasy-speaking men who arrived in Madagascar without wives.

Some regional populations of Madagascar, particularly along the southeast coast, trace their ancestry to migrations from the Persian Gulf, and there is strong linguistic evidence for Arab influence. There are many Arabic loan words, notably for names of the days of the week, that are common throughout the island. More importantly, the people of the southeast coast adopted Arabic script, and preserve a tradition of writing and reading these Arabic script documents. The language of these *sorabe* documents is Malagasy, or a blend of Malagasy and Arabic words (Versteegh 2001). Dahl (1991) and Adelaar (1995) differ on the likely path of this writing system to Madagascar; for Dahl it is likely a transmission from the northwest Indian Ocean, and for Adelaar possibly transmitted at a relatively late date from Indonesia. The oral histories of migrations from Arabia or the Persian Gulf ought not be easily dismissed, though they are difficult to interpret, particularly because similar traditions are common in Swahili groups along the East African coast.

## Conclusion

> Whatever view one may hold on how early Malagasy were influenced by other Indonesians, it seems necessary that we at least develop a more cosmopolitan view on the Indonesian origins of the Malagasy. A Southeast Barito origin is beyond dispute, but this is of course only one aspect of what Malagasy dialects and culture reflect today. Later influences were manifold, and some of these influences — African as well as Indonesian — were so strong that they have moulded the Malagasy language and culture in all its variety into something new, something for which a Southeast Barito origin has become a factor of little explanatory value (Adelaar 1995, 352–3).

Thus ends Adelaar's article 'Asian roots of the Malagasy: a linguistic perspective' (1995). The clear evidence of both African and Asian roots, in linguistic, cultural and biological realms, was evident to the seventeenth-century European observers. The evolving understanding of the development of the Malagasy language provides us with an even richer story of the origins of Malagasy language and culture. As additional archaeological evidence is acquired, and as more sophisticated evidence from population genetic studies is gathered and published, we will face the challenge of identifying the multiplicity of events and processes that were important in the historical development of the Malagasy people.

## Note

1. The translation from the Grandidiers' French translation of the Portuguese original is my own.

## References

Adelaar, A., 1991. New ideas on the early history of Malagasy, in *Papers in Austronesian Linguistics*, no. 1, ed. H. Steinhauer. Canberra: Department of Linguistics, Research School of Pacific and Asian Studies, Australian National University, 23–37.

Adelaar, A., 1995. Asian roots of the Malagasy: a linguistic perspective. *Bijdragen tot de Taal-Land en Volkenkunde* 151, 325–56.

Adelaar, K.A., 1996. Malagasy culture-history: some linguistic evidence, in *The Indian Ocean in Prehistory*, ed. J. Reade. London: Kegan Paul, 487–500.

Allibert, C. & P. Vérin, 1996. The early pre-Islamic history of the Comores Islands: links with Madagascar and Africa, in *The Indian Ocean in Prehistory*, ed. J. Reade. London: Kegan Paul, 461–70.

Cox, M.P., 2003. Genetic Patterning at Austronesian Contact Zones. Unpublished PhD Thesis, University of Otago, New Zealand.

Dahl, O.C., 1951. *Malgache et Maanjan*. Oslo: Egede-Instituttet.

Dahl, O.C., 1954. Le substrat bantou en Malgache. *Nørsk Tidsskrift for Sprogvidenskap* 17, 325–62.

Dahl, O.C., 1977. La subdivision de la famille Barito et la place du Malgache. *Acta Orientalia*, 38, 77–134.

Dahl, O.C., 1988. Bantu substratum in Malagasy. *Etudes Océan Indien* 9, 91–132.

Dahl, O.C., 1991. *Migration from Kalimantan to Madagascar*. Oslo: Norwegian University Press.

Deschamps, H., 1965. *Histoire de Madagascar*. 3rd edition. Paris: Berger-Levrault.

Dewar, R.E., 1995. Of nets and trees: untangling the reticulate and dendritic in Madagascar's prehistory. *World Archaeology* 26, 301–18.

Dewar, R.E., 1996. The archaeology of the early settlement of Madagascar, in *The Indian Ocean in Prehistory*, ed. J. Reade. London: Kegan Paul, 471–86.

Dewar, R.E. & H.T. Wright, 1993. The culture-history of Madagascar. *Journal of World Prehistory* 7, 417–66.

Ferrand, G., 1908. L'origine africaine des Malgaches. *Journal Asiatique* (Serie X) 10, 353–500.

Grandidier, A. & G. Grandidier, 1903–20. *Collections des Ouvrages Anciens Concernant Madagascar*, 9 vol. Paris: Comité de Madagascar.

Horton, M. & J. Middleton, 2000. *The Swahili: the Social Landscape of a Mercantile Society*. Oxford: Blackwell.

MacPhee, R.D.E. & D.A. Burney, 1994. Dating of modified femora of extinct dwarf *Hippopotamus* from southern Madagascar: implications for constraining human colonization and vertebrate extinction events. *Journal of Archaeological Science* 18, 695–706.

Pawley, A., 2002. The Austronesian dispersal: languages, technologies, and people, in *Examining the Farming/Language Dispersal Hypothesis*, eds. P. Bellwood & C. Renfrew. (McDonald Institute Monographs.) Cambridge: McDonald Institute for Archaeological Research, 251–73.

Radimilahy, C., 1998. *Mahilaka: an Archaeological Investigation of an Early Town in Northwestern Madagascar*. (Studies in African Archaeology 15.) Uppsala: Department of Archaeology and Ancient History.

Thomason, S.G. & T. Kaufman, 1988. *Langage Contact, Creolization and Genetic Linguistics*. Berkeley (CA): University of California Press.

Vérin, P., 1986. *The History of Civilization in North Madagasca*. Rotterdam: A.A. Balkema.

Versteegh, K., 2001. Arabic in Madagascar. *Bulletin of the School of Oriental and African Studies of the University of London* 64 (Part II), 177–87.

Wright, H.T. & F. Fanony, 1992. L'évolution des systèmes d'occupation des sols dans la vallée de la rivière Mananara au nord-est de Madagascar. *Taloha* 11, 16–64.

# Chapter 2

# Rapid Radiation, Borrowing and Dialect Continua in the Bantu Languages

Clare J. Holden & Russell D. Gray

## 1. Introduction

Despite several decades of study, several fundamental questions about Bantu linguistic relationships remain unresolved, as well as numerous questions of detail (see Chapter 4 this volume). Phylogenetic analysis has shown that Bantu languages fit a branching-tree model of evolution surprisingly well, but a tree model does not explain all the variation in the Bantu linguistic data. Moreover, several different Bantu trees appear to fit the data almost equally well. Our difficulties in resolving the Bantu tree are often ascribed to a lack of data and research, and it is true that there are many more Bantu languages than linguists. However there are probably also more fundamental reasons why a single Bantu tree has proven elusive, arising from the historical processes under which these languages developed. In this chapter, we show how the network-building method Neighbor-Net (Bryant & Moulton 2003) can be used to distinguish between different historical reasons why some linguistic relationships are not well resolved. We test three hypotheses for why some Bantu languages might not fit a tree model well: rapid radiation, linguistic borrowing and dialect chains, all thought to have been widespread within the Bantu family.

Bantu is a large family of over 450 languages that are spoken across sub-Equatorial Africa (Fig. 2.1). We define 'Bantu' in the sense of Ruhlen's (1991) 'Narrow Bantu'. Bantoid is the larger language group to which Bantu belongs. Bantoid belongs to the Niger-Kordofanian phylum, whose deepest branches are found in West Africa (Williamson & Blench 2000). Bantu languages are identified by codes originally assigned by Guthrie (1967–71), who classified Bantu languages into 15 zones (later expanded to 16), labelled A to S, based on geographical and linguistic criteria. (Many of these zones are probably not valid genetic groups.) Guthrie also divided the whole of Bantu into two large subdivisions, West Bantu and East Bantu (see Chapter 4 this volume). In this chapter, we use a modified version of Guthrie's codes taken from Bastin *et al.* (1999) (for a correspondence between the codes of Bastin *et al.* and Guthrie see Maho 2002). Bantu is thought to have originated in Cameroon or Nigeria, where the non-Bantu Bantoid languages are spoken today. The spread of Bantu is associated with the spread of farming; East Bantu in particular is associated with the Early Iron Age 'Chifumbaze' tradition in East and southeast Africa (Ehret 1998; Holden 2002; Phillipson 1993, 184–205; Vansina 1990).

## Part 1: Tree approaches to Bantu language phylogeny

A number of Bantu trees have been published, constructed using different samples of languages and different tree-building methods. Distance-based lexicostatistical methods have been widely used as a heuristic device to infer Bantu relationships (Nurse 1996; see Chapter 4, this volume). Bastin *et al.* (1999) published the most comprehensive lexicostatistical Bantu trees, including 542 languages and dialects. Their linguistic data comprised coded information on cognates for 92 items of basic vocabulary, derived from the Swadesh 100-word list of basic vocabulary, with eight meanings (such as 'snow') that are not present in Bantu excluded (Bastin 1983).

Subsequently, subsets of the data of Bastin *et al.* (1999) have been reanalyzed using phylogenetic tree-building methods, which use only innovations to define subgroups. In this respect, phylogenetic methods are comparable to the linguistic comparative method. Unlike the comparative method, however, phylogenetic methods use an explicit optimality criterion, such as maximum parsimony or likelihood, to choose among possible trees. Two further advantages of phylogenetic methods are that they let us test the

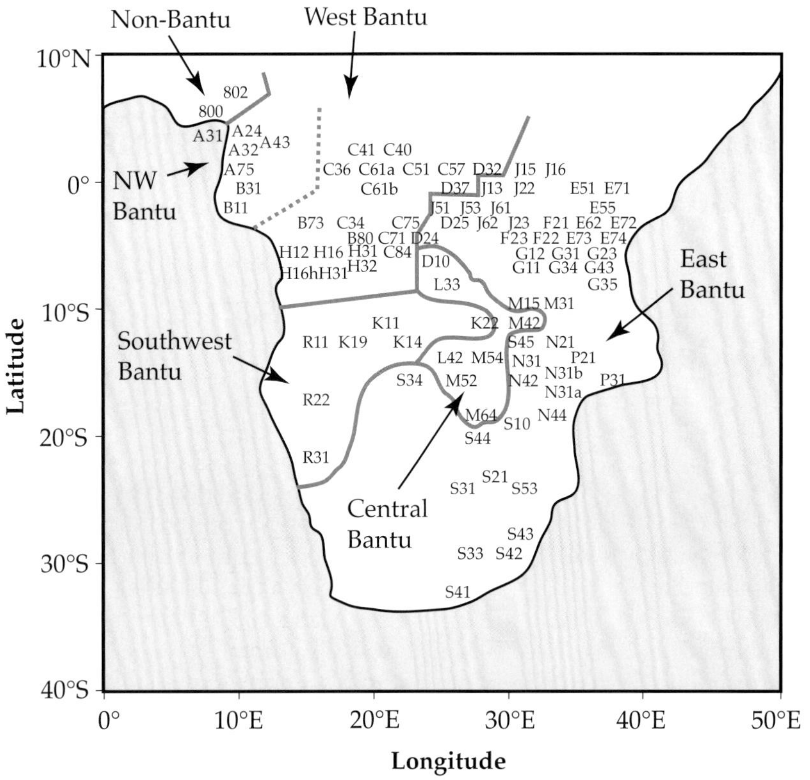


**Figure 2.1.** *Geographical locations of the 95 Bantu and Bantoid languages used in the analysis. Codes are a modified version of Guthrie's Bantu codes, taken from Bastin* et al. *(1999).*

fit of data on a tree using the consistency and retention indices, which measure the extent of homoplasy in the data set, and they allow us to evaluate the level of support in the data for each node, using tests such as bootstrap analysis, or, for Bayesian methods, by estimating the posterior probability of each node.

Holden (2002) reanalyzed 75 languages from Bastin *et al.*'s (1999) data set using maximum parsimony tree-building methods, implemented by the computer program PAUP*4.0 (Swofford 1998; see Fig. 4.2 this volume). More recently, we have used Bayesian MCMC (Markov chain Monte Carlo) methods to infer phylogeny for 95 Bantu languages from the same dataset, using using the computer programs MrBayes (Huelsenbeck & Ronquist 2001) and BayesPhylogenies (Pagel & Meade 2004) (Fig. 2.2; Holden *et al.* 2005). Instead of searching for the best tree(s) according to an optimality criterion, Bayesian methods sample trees in proportion to their likelihood, producing a sample of trees (usually several hundred) in which both more- and less-likely trees are included. One advantage of constructing a Bayesian tree sample is that it allows us to represent phylogenetic uncertainty in the sample, so that we do not have to treat the tree as if it were known without error, when, in fact, any tree remains simply a hypothesis about phylogeny. Our ability to reconstruct the true tree is inevitably limited by our data and our models of evolution; moreover, as we have noted, linguistic borrowing cannot be represented on a single tree.

Phylogenetic analysis suggests that Bantu basic vocabulary fits a tree model at least as well as typical biological data sets (Holden 2002; Sanderson & Donoghue 1989). For the 75-language Bantu tree constructed using equally weighted parsimony, Holden (2002) reported a consistency index (CI) of 0.65 and a retention index (RI) of 0.59; using weighted parsimony the CI was 0.72 and the RI was 0.68. These results indicate that Bantu linguistic evolution was substantially tree-like, at least for the basic vocabulary (other parts of the lexicon may be more prone to borrowing). This was at first a surprising result, since borrowing among Bantu languages is thought to be widespread, whereas gene flow and hybridization are thought to be rare among many biological taxa. However, a branching tree model does not explain all the variation among the Bantu languages; there remains considerable conflicting signal in the Bantu data, which could be due either to borrowing or parallel evolution. In comparative perspective, Indo-European is even more tree-like than Bantu (Bryant *et al.* 2005; Rexova *et al.* 2003), but Austronesian may be less so (Gray & Jordan 2000).

*Agreement and uncertainty among Bantu trees*

Comparing Bantu trees, it is apparent that several major questions about Bantu linguistic relationships remain unresolved. Conflicts among Bantu trees are illustrated in Figures 2.2–2.4. Figure 2.2 shows a majority rule tree summarizing a Bayesian sample of 200 Bantu trees, sampled from 2 million trees, constructed using a reversible model of evolution with the computer program MrBayes (Huelsenbeck & Ronquist 2001). The majority rule tree in Figure 2.2 shows all nodes present on at least half the trees in the sample, plus all other compatible groupings. Alternative tree topologies (not shown) were also present in the sample. Node labels indicate the proportion of trees in the sample in which each node

**Figure 2.2.** *Majority rule tree summarizing a Bayesian sample of 200 trees for 95 Bantu languages. Node labels indicate the proportion of trees in the sample containing that node; thus for example West Bantu languages formed a clade in 48 per cent of trees in the sample. This is equivalent to the posterior probability of each node.*

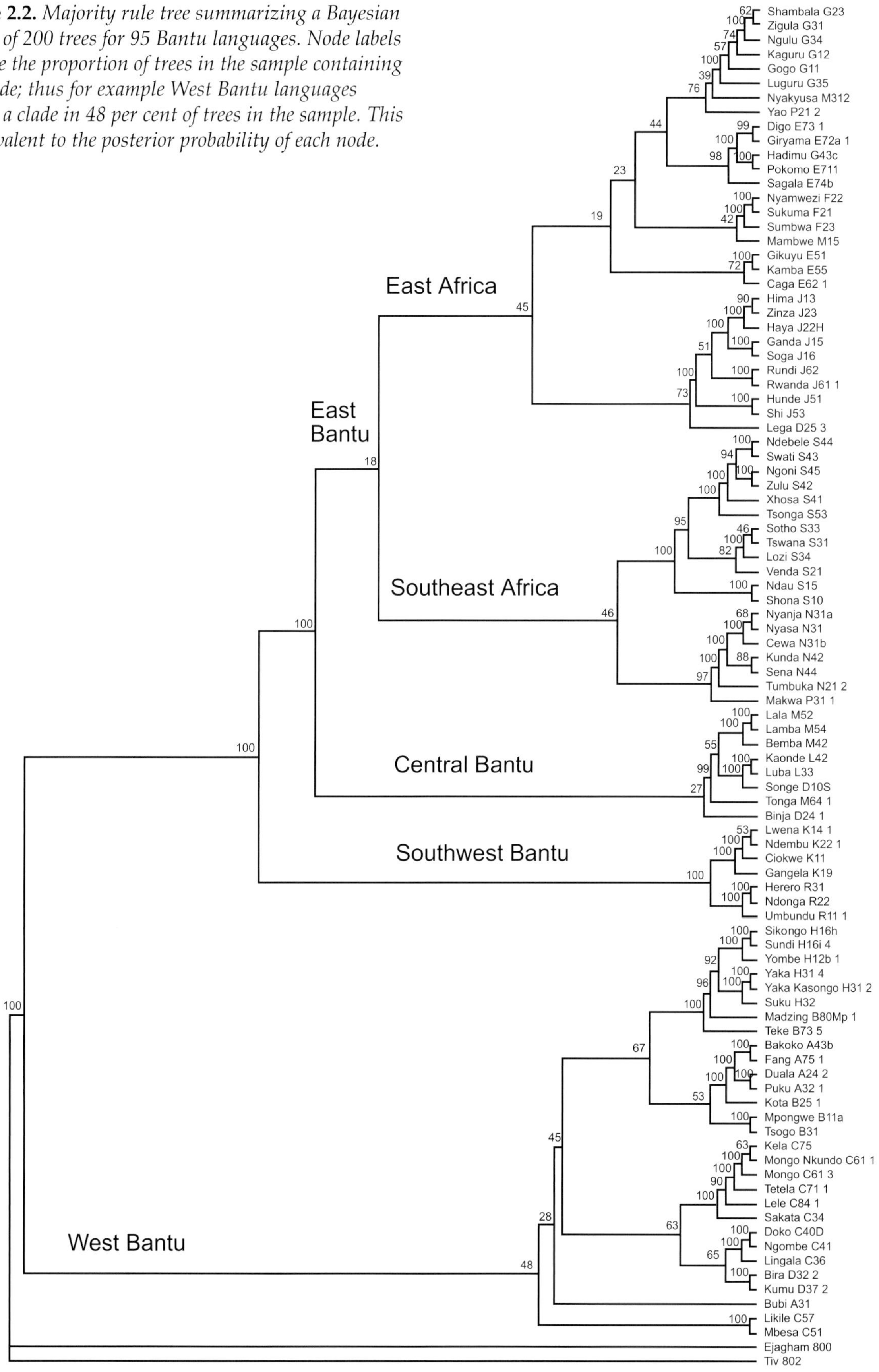

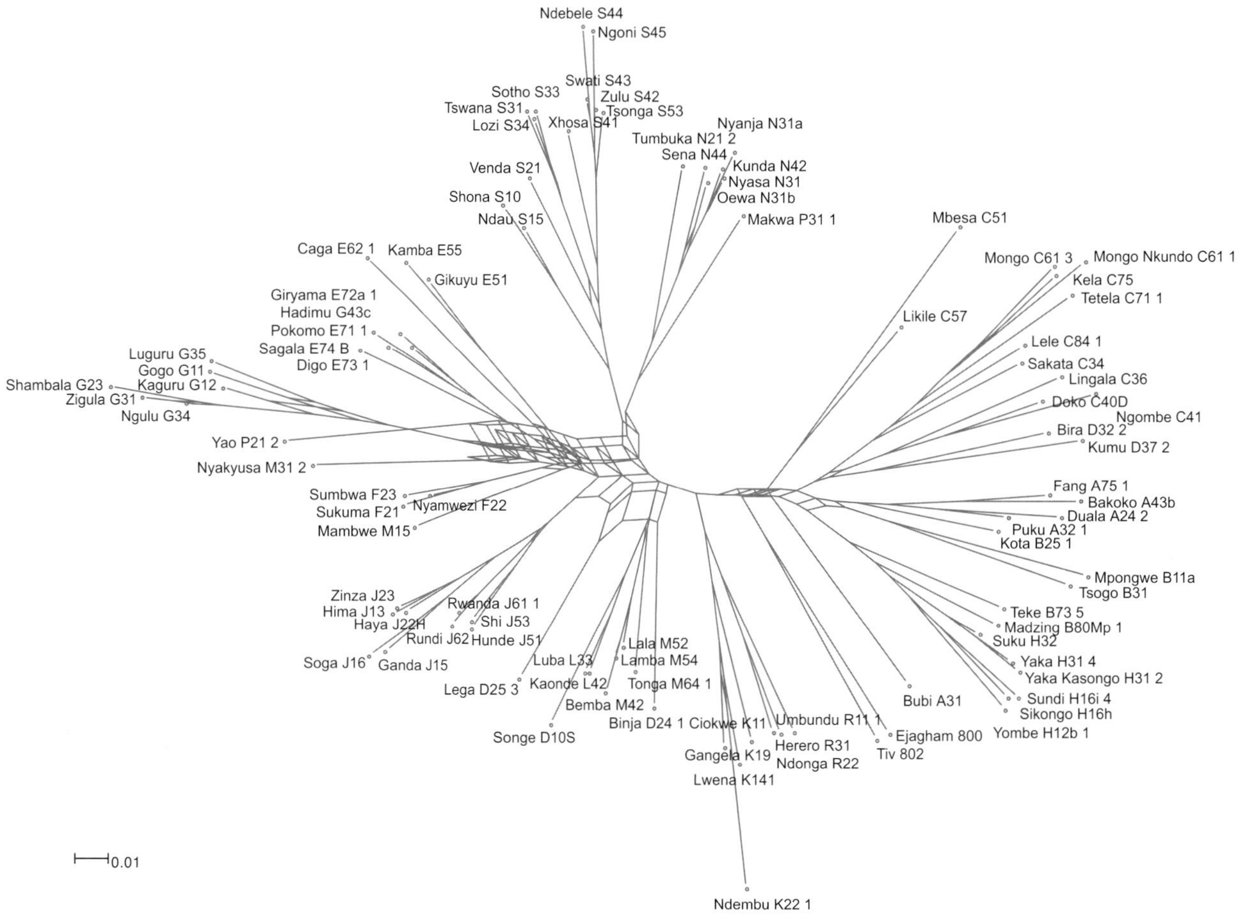


**Figure 2.3.** *Consensus network summarizing the Bayesian sample of 200 trees for 95 Bantu languages; threshold = 0.18. Most conflicts among trees involve the East Bantu languages in East Africa, with relatively little conflict among trees being associated with West Bantu languages.*

was found, which is equivalent to the posterior probability of that node. While many nodes were well supported in this analysis (being found in more than 95 per cent of trees in the sample) several nodes towards the root of the tree received much lower levels of support. An alternative summary of this tree sample, constructed using a consensus network (Holland & Moulton 2003), is shown in Figure 2.3. A consensus network allows us to represent the alternative tree topologies that were found in the sample. This consensus network (Fig. 2.3) shows trees present in more than 18 per cent of the sample. Examining the consensus network reveals that most alternative tree topologies involve the East Bantu languages spoken in East Africa, particularly Yao P21, which has conflicting affiliations with both East and Southeast Bantu languages (among the latter, especially with the N zone languages and Makwa P31). The 18 per cent threshold was chosen to illustrate the maximum amount of conflict among trees without becoming too visually complex; if we decrease this threshold, the main effect is to reveal even more complexity among the East African languages.

Figure 2.4 illustrates a range of plausible alternative Bantu trees. Figure 2.4a summarizes the Bayesian tree sample shown in more detail in Figure 2.2. Figure 2.4b shows a number of alternative Bantu tree topologies, found in other analyses that used a variety of methods including maximum parsimony (Holden 2002; see Fig. 4.2), Bayesian methods with a non-reversible model of evolution (Holden *et al.* 2005) and Neighbor-Joining (Saitou & Nei 1987; unpublished work by Holden). Figures 2.2–2.4 illustrate that there is significant uncertainty regarding the shape of Bantu history that we cannot currently resolve.

Summarizing across Bantu trees, we have divided Bantu into four major areas: West and East Bantu, and two groups of languages in Central and Southwest Africa that seem to be intermediate between West and East Bantu. These areas are shown on Figure 2.1. In phylogenetic analyses, languages in the intermediate zone usually cluster in two groups, labelled Central and Southwest Bantu on Figures 2.1 and 2.2 (Holden 2002; Holden *et al.* 2005). These categories broadly agree with much previous work in Bantu linguistics (Bastin *et al.* 1999; Heine 1973; Nurse 1996), although under Guthrie's traditional West and East Bantu division, our Southwest zone and parts of our Central zone would be grouped with West Bantu (see Chapter 4 this volume).

*West Bantu*

In our classification, West Bantu includes languages spoken in west-Central Africa, belonging to zones A, B, C, H and parts of D (Figs. 2.1–2.2). The most fundamental disputed question about the shape of Bantu history is whether or not West Bantu is monophyletic. In other words, do West Bantu languages share a unique common ancestor that is not also ancestral to East Bantu languages? Many published trees show the deepest splits on the Bantu tree to be *within* West Bantu, among the northwestern Bantu languages belonging to zones A and B (Bastin *et al.* 1999; Heine 1973; Holden 2002; Holden *et al.* 2005; Figs. 2.1 & 2.4b). The alternative hypothesis is that the deepest split on the tree is between East and West Bantu. The Bayesian tree sample summarized in Figure 2.2 supports this alternative hypothesis.

The status of West Bantu has profound consequences for reconstructing ancestral Bantu language and culture. If the earliest splits were within the northwestern Bantu languages of zones A and B, then those languages would become highly influential in reconstructing the earliest Bantu linguistic forms. Many historians, archaeologists and anthropologists also treat the Bantu language tree as a source of information about population history in this region (Ehret 1998; Holden & Mace 2003; Phillipson 1993; Schoenbrun 1998; Vansina 1984; 1990). Uncertainty in the tree has received little attention in such studies, although different researchers have used quite different trees. For example, in his classic study of political development in the Equatorial Bantu, Vansina (1990) assumed that there was a primary split between East and West Bantu; in contrast, Ehret (1998) subscribed to the alternative model that the deepest splits on the tree are within West Bantu languages. The topology of the tree chosen can have a significant effect on the conclusions of such studies; again, for example, in determining the influence of the northwestern Bantu-speaking societies for reconstructing of ancestral Bantu culture.

*East Bantu*

In our classification, East Bantu includes languages of zones E, F, G, J, N and S, plus some languages of

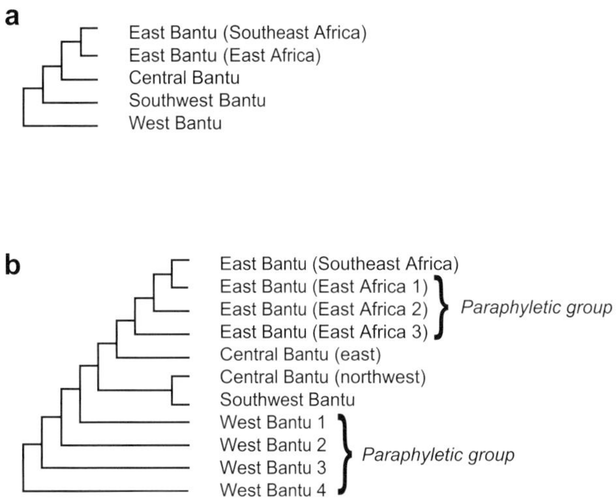


**Figure 2.4.** *Alternative possible topologies for the Bantu tree: a) summary of the Bayesian tree sample shown in Figure 2.2 — the five groups shown are monophyletic; b) summary of alternative Bantu trees, constructed using a variety of methods.*

zone M (Figs. 2.1–2.2). East Bantu is monophyletic on all published phylogenetic Bantu trees, but this clade is not well supported: it was not recovered in a bootstrap analysis (Holden 2002) and it has a very low posterior probability in Bayesian analyses (Holden *et al.* 2005; see also Fig. 2.2). Within East Bantu, the languages spoken in Southeast Africa, belonging to zones N and S, form a clade on previously-published phylogenetic trees. Languages in zone S often appear to be the most divergent within East Bantu when using ultrametric distance-based methods such as UPGMA; this is seen in some of the trees published by Bastin *et al.* (1999). However, maximum parsimony analysis (Holden 2002; see Fig. 4.2), which can display true branch lengths, suggests that this is because there was an increased rate of evolution among these languages. The languages spoken in East Africa sometimes form a clade within East Bantu, but not always (Fig. 2.4). In the present data set, the languages spoken in East Africa comprise zones E, F, G and J (Lakes Bantu), plus the individual languages Nyakyusa M31 and Yao P21 (Fig. 2.2).

Again, alternative relationships among East Bantu languages imply different historical scenarios for the spread of these languages and their speakers. Within East Bantu, was there a primary division between the languages spoken in East and Southeast Africa, as Ehret (1998) suggests? Or are the deepest splits within the East African languages, suggesting that the East Bantu originated there, perhaps in association with the Urewe archaeological tradition around Lake Victoria (Holden 2002; Phillipson 1993)?

*Southwest and Central Bantu*
Bantu languages that seem to be intermediate between West and East Bantu belong to zones K and R (Southwest Bantu), and to zones L and parts of M (Central Bantu). Central Bantu languages usually form a clade that is a sister-group to East Bantu (Figs. 2.2 & 2.4a). However, on some trees the Central languages split into an eastern and a western group, in which case the east-Central group usually forms a sister group to East Bantu, or occasionally to the southeastern (zones N-plus-S) clade within East Bantu, while the northwest-Central group clusters with Southwest Bantu (Fig. 2.4b). The position of the two languages Lega D25 and Binja D24 varies considerably across previously-published trees. They fall somewhere within, or as immediate outliers to, the East-plus-Central clade. The position of Southwest Bantu is also somewhat variable among the trees that have been proposed. On some maximum parsimony trees, Southwest Bantu clusters with West Bantu languages of zones C and H (Holden 2002; Fig. 4.2). However, on the widely cited tree published by Heine (1973), and in Bayesian analyses (Holden *et al.* 2005; Fig. 2.2) Southwest Bantu forms a sister group to Central-plus-East Bantu. But in the Bayesian tree sample summarized in Figure 2.2, there is very strong support (posterior probability = 1.0) for a clade which is a sister to Southwest Bantu and which comprises the languages of the Central Bantu and East Bantu regions of Figure 2.1 including Lega D25 and Binja D24 — regardless of how these languages are subgrouped among themselves.

*Why is a single Bantu tree elusive?*
It is unclear whether our difficulties in resolving the Bantu tree stem from a lack of data, or from a more fundamental mismatch between the actual process of Bantu evolution, often thought to be characterized by widespread borrowing and dialect continua, and a bifurcating tree model of language evolution. Regarding the lack of data, the linguistic data published by Bastin *et al.* (1999) comprised only 92 meanings. A 200-word vocabulary list would probably be preferable. All phylogenetic analyses by Holden have also used this data set, so potentially suffer from the same problem. Counteracting this limitation, we should note that most of these 92 items have numerous distinct word forms (see Chapter 15 this volume), comprising over 1600 cognates in the 95-language sample.

Regarding the tree model of linguistic evolution, trees are rather simplistic models of both biological and linguistic evolution. In biology, the importance of evolutionary processes such as hybridization, lateral gene transfer and recombination, especially in bacterial and viral evolution, is increasingly recognized (Boucher *et al.* 2003; Stone 2000; Woese 1998). Linguistic borrowing and the formation of creole languages are analogous to lateral gene transfer and hybridization (see Ringe *et al.* 2002, for a discussion of these phenomena). Parallel evolution can also give rise to ambiguous relationships among taxa. Such complex relationships cannot be represented on a single tree. When placed on a tree, admixed languages are usually positioned near the root of the branch of the parent language that contributed most to the mixed language (Bryant *et al.* 2005; Cavalli-Sforza *et al.* 1994). Unlike trees, which only permit branching and divergence among taxa, networks can also have reticulations among branches, making it possible to show more than one evolutionary pathway on a single graph. For this reason, networks may be preferable for describing linguistic relationships involving creoles, or among languages with extensive borrowing, as they allow us to represent more than one 'parent' per language.

**Part 2: Network approaches to Bantu language phylogeny**

In this analysis, we used a new network-building method, Neighbor-Net, to investigate the affiliations of those Bantu languages whose position varies across different trees. A primary question concerns the earliest Bantu history — can we resolve the question of whether there was a primary split between East and West Bantu, or whether the deepest splits on the tree are within West Bantu? The position of Southwest Bantu is also unclear from previous studies — is it a sister-group to East Bantu, or does it cluster with West Bantu languages? Is Central Bantu a valid group, or should it be split into two? Within East Bantu, are the Lakes (J) languages outliers to other languages, or do all East African languages form a clade?

Constructing a Bantu network also lets us distinguish between the different linguistic processes that might underlie the weak or conflicting signals for some parts of the Bantu tree. Such processes include rapid radiation and borrowing, the latter perhaps in the context of dialect continua. Rapid radiation may be inferred from a lack of phylogenetic signal, i.e. a rake- or star-shaped phylogeny, whereas reticulation would indicate possible borrowing. Reticulations can also pinpoint those languages which may have been involved in borrowing. Complex chains of conflicting relationships involving numerous languages may indicate that borrowing occurred in the context of dialect chains.

Under rapid radiation, a language diverges into several daughter languages very rapidly, so there is little time for linguistic innovations to accumulate in each branch before the subsequent further splitting of that branch. This leaves a weak phylogenetic signal that can be difficult to detect, so that the language tree appears to be star- or rake-shaped (Bellwood 1996). Borrowing is the transfer of linguistic elements from one language to another, often between neighbouring languages. Extensive borrowing can lead to conflicting affiliations (where a language shows similarities to more than one divergent language groups) that cannot be represented on a single tree.

Unlike tree-building methods, constructing a network does not force the data into a bifurcating tree. If the data are truly tree-like, then the Neighbor-Net method will return an unrooted tree, but if there are conflicts within the data then it will construct a splits graph, in which conflicting relationships are represented by reticulations or joining among branches. From the shape of the Neighbor-Net network, we can infer whether either rapid radiation or borrowing occurred in different parts of the Bantu language family. On a network, we would expect rapid radiation to result in a star-shaped phylogeny, with poorly marked hierarchical structure but no evidence for conflict among language groupings. We would expect borrowing to result in reticulation among branches, and we would expect dialect chains to be indicated by complex chains of reticulation involving numerous languages.

## Methods

*Data*

The sample included 93 Bantu languages and two non-Bantu Bantoid (hence simply 'Bantoid') languages, Tiv and Ejagham. The latter were used as outgroups to root the tree where appropriate (e.g. Fig. 2.2). Figure 2.1 shows the approximate geographical locations of the languages in the analysis.

The data set included all languages for which linguistic data were published in Bastin *et al.* (1999), and for which ethnographic data from the corresponding cultural group were published in the *Ethnographic Atlas* (Murdock 1967). This data set was designed to let us use our knowledge of Bantu language relationships to study other aspects of cultural evolution in these populations in the future; this is possible insofar as linguistic relationships reflect population history (Barbujani 1991; Cavalli-Sforza *et al.* 1988). The data set is similar to the 75-language data set used by Holden (2002; see Fig. 4.2), except that in the 75-language data set, languages with more than 5 per cent missing data were excluded, whereas they have been included here. For this analysis, the data were coded in a multistate form, i.e. with each column representing a meaning, and most meanings

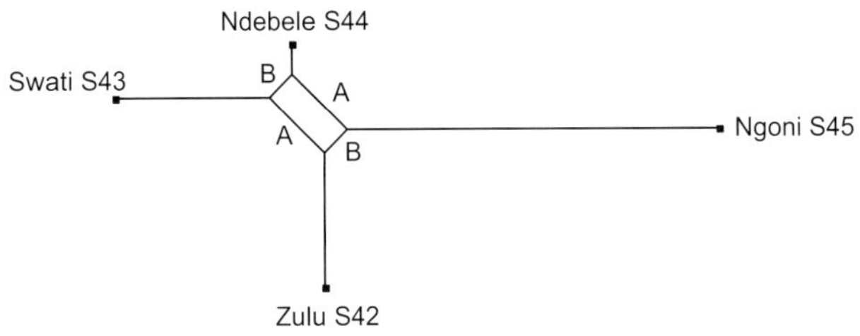


**Figure 2.5.** *Illustrative splits graph. Split A groups together Zulu and Ngoni versus Ndebele and Swati. Split B groups together Ndebele and Ngoni versus Swati and Zulu; there is more evidence for the first group than the second.*

having several different cognate forms. (We have also run this analysis with the data coded in binary form, i.e. each cognate having its own column; this made very little difference to the results.)

*Analysis*

Neighbor-Net (Bryant & Moulton 2003) is an agglomerative method for constructing networks that selects taxa on the basis of similarity and groups them together. The algorithms used in this method are analogous to the Neighbor-Joining method for building trees (Saitou & Nei 1987). In agglomerative tree-building methods, two taxa (or nodes) are chosen on the basis of similarity, then they are agglomerated (merged), the data matrix is reduced and we proceed to the next iteration. However, to construct a network, the Neighbor-Net method does not immediately agglomerate the selected taxa (or nodes). Instead, it waits until one of the chosen taxa (or nodes) has been grouped with a different node. Then the three nodes are reduced to two, and the process is repeated.

The Neighbor-Net method represents similarities within the data set as a splits graph, constructed from a distance matrix. Splits are bipartitions of the data. An example of a splits graph for four languages, Ndebele S44, Swati S43, Ngoni S45 and Zulu S42, is shown in Figure 2.5. Sets of parallel lines indicate a single bipartition (split) in the data. The box shape at the centre of the graph is characteristic of conflicting data. Split A groups together Zulu and Ngoni on the one hand, and Ndebele and Swati on the other. Split B groups together Ndebele and Ngoni on the one hand, and Swati and Zulu on the other. Branch lengths (or edge weights) are proportional to the support for a split in the data: thus there is more evidence for split A than for split B.

Distances between language pairs in the 95-language data set were calculated using PAUP v.4a (Swofford 1998), using mean character differences. Weighted splits were calculated and then represented as a splits graph using the computer program SplitsTree v4beta.06

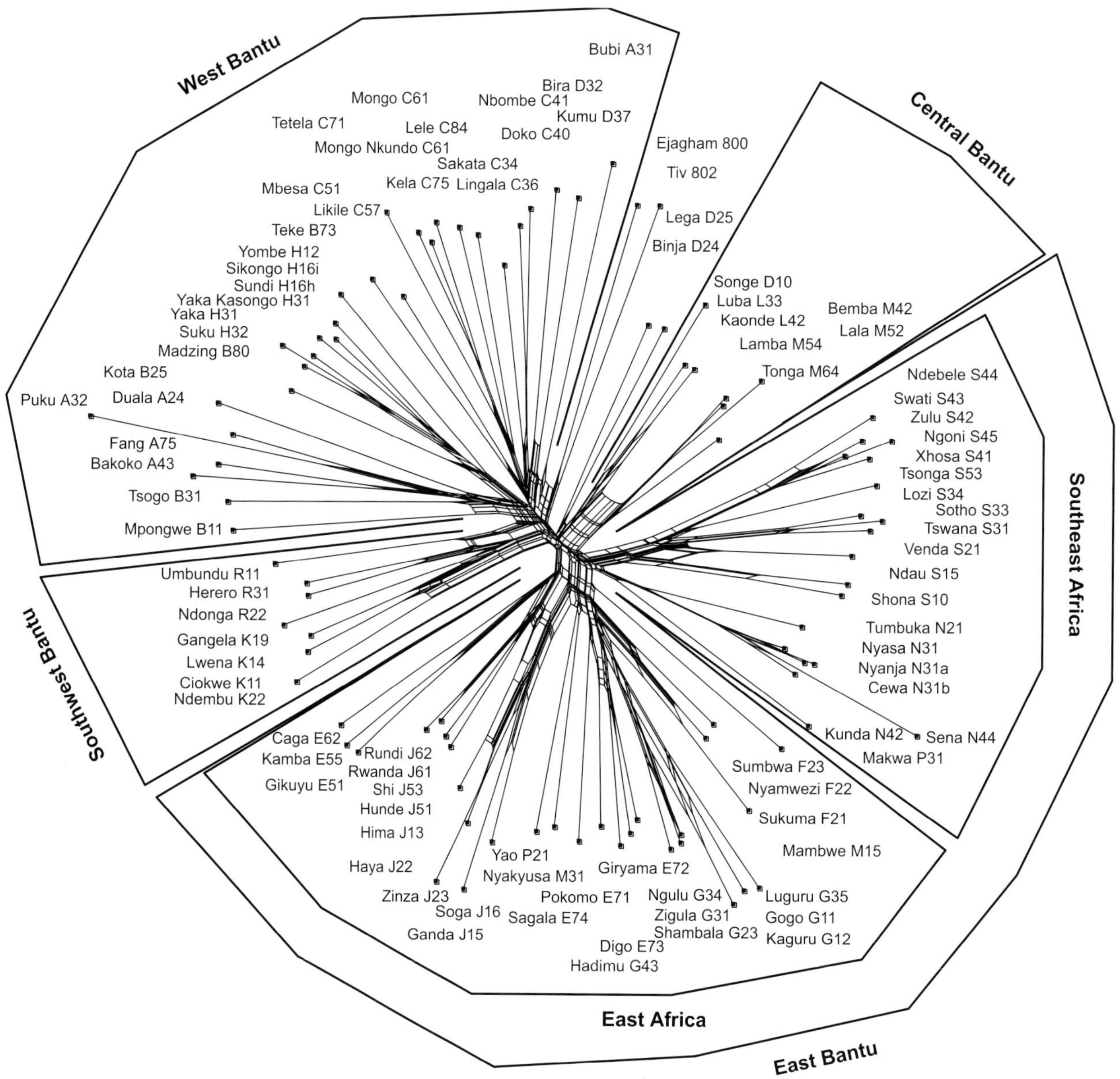


**Figure 2.6.** *Network of 95 Bantu and Bantoid languages, calculated using the Neighbor-Net method (Bryant & Moulton 2003). The major groups, West, East, Southwest and Central Bantu are indicated, with a division between languages spoken in East and Southeast Africa also shown for East Bantu.*

(Huson 1998; Huson & Bryant 2006). The complete Bantu network resulting from this analysis is shown in Figure 2.6. Separate splits graphs for East and West Bantu are shown in Figures 2.7a and 2.7b.

There is some evidence that Neighbor-Net may overfit the data, meaning that it produces some false splits (Nakhleh *et al.* 2005). However, such false splits have very small edge weights. To guard against the possibility of including false splits in our Bantu network, we also constructed a network from which edges weighted less than 0.002 were excluded; this cut-off point was essentially arbitrary. Eighty-seven of 331 edges or 26 per cent had weights less than 0.002. The network of weights greater than 0.002 is shown in Figure 2.8; it may be interpreted as a simplified and conservative estimate of the Bantu network.

## Results

A splits graph of the complete sample of 95 Bantu and Bantoid languages is shown in Figure 2.6. The major groups including West, East, Southwest and Central

Bantu are indicated. Figures 2.7a and b show splits graphs for East and West Bantu, respectively, allowing us to focus on relationships within those groups in more detail. The simplified splits graph of edge weights greater than 0.002 is shown in Figure 2.8. Unless specified, the following discussion refers to splits that are present on both the complete network (Fig. 2.6) and on the reduced network (Fig. 2.8).

On Figure 2.6, West Bantu languages cluster together on the top left of the graph, while East Bantu languages cluster to the bottom right. Southwest and Central Bantu occupy a space intermediate between West and East Bantu, with Central Bantu being closer to East Bantu, and Southwest Bantu closer to West Bantu. This is in line with our expectations from Bantu trees (cf. Figs. 2.2 & 2.4). Although the absolute positions of the languages have been rotated on Figure 2.8, the relative positions of languages remain the same.

*Central Bantu*

Although Central Bantu is clearly defined by splits dividing this group from other Bantu languages, there are also conflicting splits dividing Central Bantu into (a) a northwestern group comprising Kaonde L42, Luba L33 and Songe D10S, and (b) an eastern group comprising M-zone languages. The northwestern group is more similar to West and Southwest Bantu, plus a number of East Bantu languages that border the West Bantu area (see Fig. 2.1), including subzones J5, J6, E5 and E6 plus Hima J13. The east-Central group is more similar to the other East Bantu languages. This suggests that there was an area of contact, leading to borrowing or convergence, among languages on at least one side of this divide. Linguistically, Kaonde L42 falls within the northwestern group, but is also linked by conflicting splits to the eastern group. Geographically, Kaonde is closer to the eastern group (Fig. 2.1), so it seems likely that it originated as a northwest-Central language whose speakers later migrated south, and that there was subsequently borrowing between Kaonde and the east-Central languages.

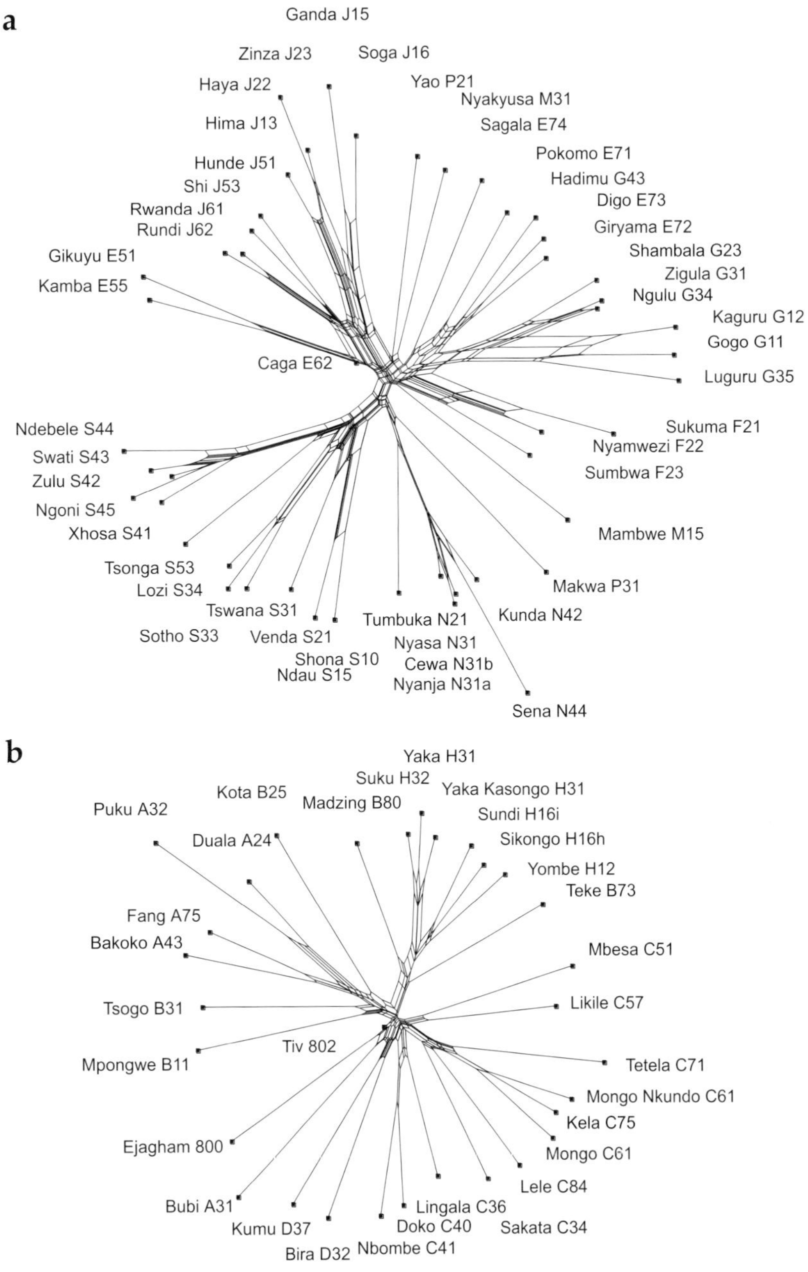


**Figure 2.7.** *a) Network of 48 East Bantu languages; relationships among East Bantu languages spoken in east Africa are particularly complex and conflicting. b) Network of 29 West Bantu languages, plus Tiv and Ejagham (Bantoid languages).*

*Southwest Bantu*

Southwest Bantu is very clearly separated from other languages, reflecting the robustness of this group in phylogenetic analysis (Fig. 2.2; Holden 2002). Figures 2.6 and 2.8 show a conflicting split linking Umbundu R11 to West Bantu (or alternatively, linking all the other Southwest Bantu languages to East-plus-Central Bantu). This split aside, the splits graphs (Figs. 2.6

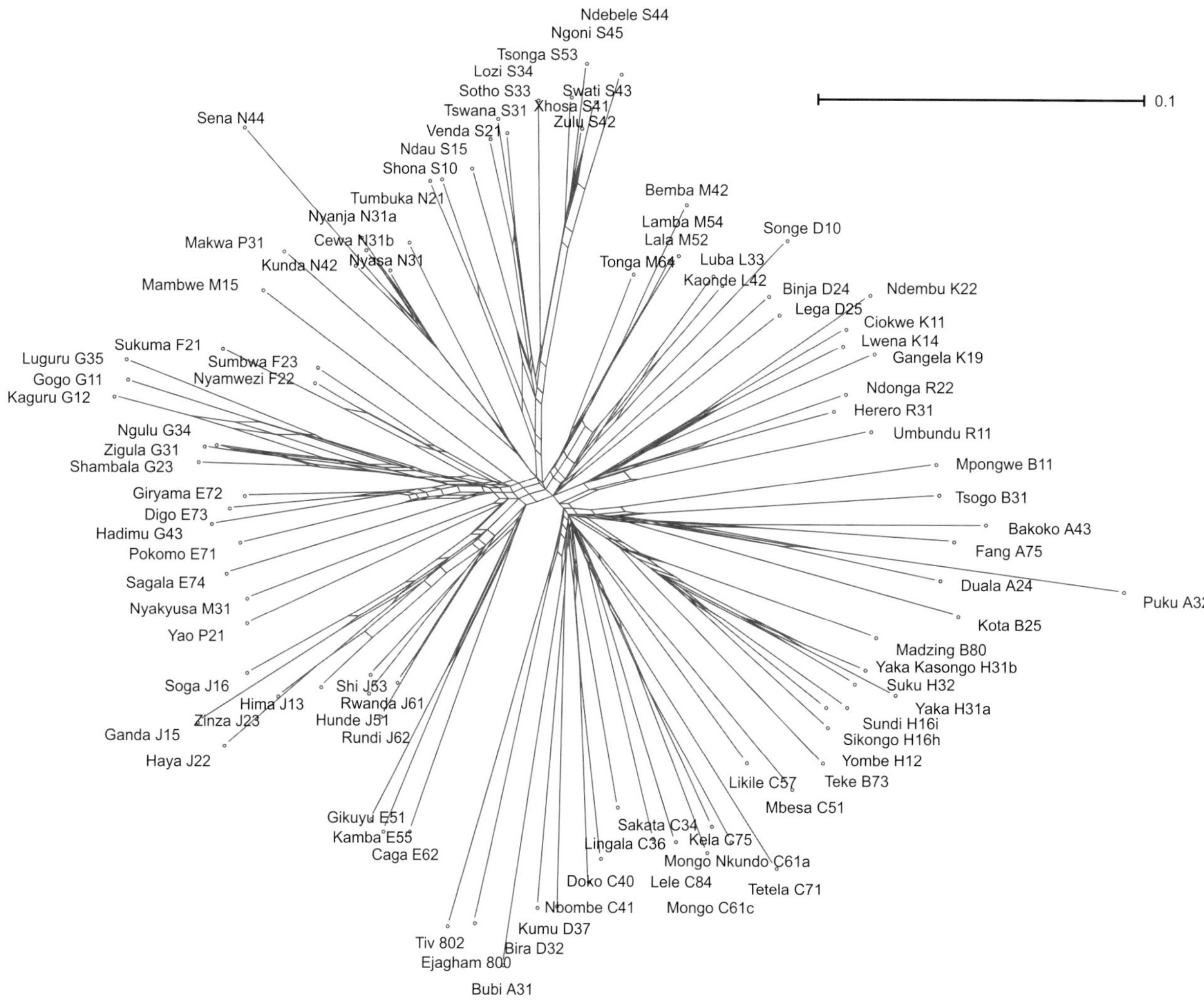


**Figure 2.8.** *Network of 95 Bantu and Bantoid languages, calculated using the Neighbor-Net method, showing only edge weights greater than 0.002.*

& 2.8) are consistent with a tree in which Southwest Bantu is an outlier to East-plus-Central Bantu, rather than clustering within West Bantu.

*East Bantu*

The following groups are supported by splits of varying lengths:

a) zone S;
b) zone N;
c) zone J (also known as Lakes Bantu);
d) zone F (including Sukuma F21, Nyamwezi F22 and Sumbwa F23).

Some of the most complex relationships in East Bantu appear among the East African languages of zones E (excluding E5 and E6), F and G. At the centre of the graph, there are no conflict-free major groupings among these languages, suggesting that these languages developed in a condition of dialect continua with borrowing across dialects (see Ringe *et al.* 2002 for discussion of an analogous situation among early Indo-European *'Satem'* languages). The early evolution of these languages appears to be the least tree-like of all the Bantu languages in this analysis. Later, some clearer groups emerge such as Kaguru G12 + Gogo G11 + Luguru G35, and zone F, but these languages also continue to be involved in extensive conflicting relationships (Figs. 2.6, 2.7a & 2.8).

Within the S-zone languages, Venda shows conflicting relationships, being grouped on the one hand with Ndau S15 plus Shona S10, and on the other hand with the S30, S40 and S50 languages (Figs. 2.6, 2.7a & 2.8). Venda is geographically adjacent to the groups it shares similarities with, suggesting that borrowing across neighbouring groups has occurred. However, it should be noted that adjacency alone does not *always* lead to linguistic convergence: historically specific factors must also have played a role.

*West Bantu*

In previous phylogenetic analyses, it has proven difficult to resolve the relationships among West Bantu languages. The deepest splits involving West Bantu languages receive very low support on trees (Fig. 2.2; Holden 2002; Holden *et al.* 2005).

Examining the splits graphs (Figs. 2.6, 2.7b & 2.8) suggests that there was a more or less simultaneous divergence of six groups of West Bantu languages. These include:

a) the H languages plus Madzing B80 and Teke B73;
b) Duala A24, Puku A32, Bakoko A43, Fang A75, Kota B25 and Tsogo A43;
c) Sakata C34, Mongo C61, Nkundo Mongo C61, Kela C75, Tetela C71 and Lele C84;
d) Lingala C36, Doko C40 and Ngombe C41;
e) Kumu D37 and Bira D32;
f) Likile C57 and Mbesa C51.

There is little evidence for conflict (borrowing) among West Bantu languages. The shape of the network suggests that our difficulties in resolving relationships among West Bantu languages may result from rapid early radiation of these languages, leaving little phylogenetic signal or deep hierarchical structure in the data.

We also wished to address the question of whether some northwestern Bantu languages are the most divergent relative to other Bantu languages. In the tree sample shown in Figure 2.2 the most divergent West Bantu languages are Bubi A31 and a pair consisting of Likele C57 and Mbesa C51. On the 75-language maximum parsimony tree shown in Figure 4.2, Mpongwe B11 is also highly divergent. Investigating the affiliations of these languages on the complete splits graph (Fig. 2.6) yielded the following results. Bubi, a long isolated language spoken on Bioko Island, is linked by one split to the outgroups Tiv 802 and Ejagham 800. Presumably these similarities are primitive (i.e. they result from ancestral similarities, which other Bantu languages have lost). Another split links Tiv, Ejagham, Bubi, Kumu D37 and Bira D32. These similarities (among far-flung languages) are probably also primitive. Another split links Bubi to Bira, Kumu, Doko C40 and Ngombe C41; these are all geographically peripheral West Bantu languages (Fig. 2.1). One split links together all the West Bantu languages apart from Mpongwe B11. These links are consistent with the view that Bubi A31, and possibly Mpongwe B11, diverged or became isolated early among the West Bantu languages, and lack some innovations that most other West Bantu languages share. No splits linking Likile C57 and Mbesa C51 to any particular West Bantu (or other) languages were detected.

With the exception of Bubi A31, there was no evidence that languages of zones A and B are particularly divergent, either among themselves, or in relation to other Bantu languages. Zones A and B (apart from Bubi) appear to cluster with zone H (Figs. 2.2–2.3, 2.6, 2.7b & 2.8).

**Discussion**

The results of this analysis suggest why persistent ambiguities in the Bantu tree remain, despite several decades of study. From the shape of the network it appears that different historical processes caused the ambiguities in the East and West Bantu parts of the tree. West Bantu languages underwent a rapid early radiation — near simultaneous divergence of several major West Bantu branches — resulting in a star-shaped phylogeny with little internal structure. With the exception of the isolated language Bubi A31 (and possibly Mpongwe B11) we found no evidence that the greatest divergence within Bantu involved languages of zones A and B. There is little evidence for borrowing among West Bantu languages, possibly indicating that these speech communities were more isolated from one another than were early East Bantu-speaking populations.

In contrast, both borrowing and dialect continua seem to have been important among East Bantu languages, especially in East Africa. There is extensive conflict at the centre of the graph, involving all East Bantu languages and also the eastern-Central Bantu languages. The fact that so many languages are involved suggests that the borrowing among these languages occurred early in their history, when their proto-languages were geographically closer together, possibly in the context of dialect continua. There also seems to have been ongoing borrowing among the Bantu languages of zones E (excluding E5 and E6), F and G in East Africa. However, there is a fairly tree-like structure among the Southeast African languages of zones N and S, indicating that subsequent divergence among these languages was substantially tree-like.

There is some evidence for more recent, localized borrowing, indicated by conflict involving fewer languages, for example that associated with Venda. Another case is the borrowing between Kaonde (a northwest-Central language) and the east-Central languages (Bemba, Lala and Lamba). Ethnographic evidence suggests that some of the languages that have experienced linguistic borrowing may have borrowed other cultural attributes along with vocabulary. For example, Kaonde-speakers are predominantly matrilineal, like the Bemba, Lala and Lamba, but unlike modern speakers of the other northwest-Central languages, Songe and Luba. A parsimonious interpretation is that after Kaonde speakers migrated south, they borrowed both linguistic elements and matrilineal descent from their new neighbours.

This analysis shows how, by constructing a network, we can move beyond the question of whether, or how well, Bantu languages fit a tree model. Although previous phylogenetic analysis of Bantu languages showed that relationships among these languages are more tree-like than we might have expected, a tree model does not explain all the variation among them (Holden 2002). Moreover, several alternative trees appear to fit the Bantu linguistic data almost equally well, so that we cannot, at present, define a single best tree. A network model lets us test alternative hypotheses for why some Bantu relationships may not be tree-like, including rapid radiation, borrowing and past dialect continua, providing new insights into why parts of the Bantu language family have remained intractable to phylogenetic analysis.

## Conclusion

Our results suggest that there was rapid early radiation among West Bantu languages; in contrast, there was extensive borrowing, partly within dialect continua, among East Bantu languages in East Africa. We propose that these are the underlying reasons why some parts of the Bantu language family have until now proven intractable to phylogenetic analysis.

## Acknowledgements

C.J.H. was supported by a Research Fellowship from the AHRB Centre for the Evolutionary Analysis of Cultural Behaviour at University College London (UCL). This research received additional funding from the Marsden Fund, Royal Society of New Zealand and the UCL Graduate School Research Projects Fund.

## References

Barbujani, G., 1991. What do languages tell us about human microevolution? *Trends in Ecology and Evolution* 6, 151–6.

Bastin, Y., 1983. Classification lexicostatistique des langues bantoues (214 releves). *Bull. Seanc. Acad. R. Sci Outre-Mer* 27, 173–99.

Bastin, Y., A. Coupez & M. Mann, 1999. Continuity and divergence in the Bantu languages: perspectives from a lexicostatic study. *Annales, Sciences humaines* 162, 1–226.

Bellwood, P., 1996. The origins and spread of agriculture in the Indo-Pacific region: gradualism and diffusion or revolution and colonization?, in *The Origins and Spread of Agriculture and Pastoralism in Eurasia*, ed. D.R. Harris. London: UCL Press, 465–98.

Boucher, Y., C.J. Douady, R.T. Papke, D.A. Walsh, M.E.R. Boudreau, C.L. Nesbo, R.J. Case & W.F. Doolittle, 2003. Lateral gene transfer and the origins of prokaryotic groups. *Annual Review of Genetics* 37, 283–328.

Bryant, D. & V. Moulton, 2003. Neighbor-Net: an agglomerative method for the construction fo phylogenetic networks. *Molecular Biology and Evolution* 21, 255–65.

Bryant, D., F. Filimon & R.D. Gray, 2005. Untangling our past: languages, trees, splits and networks, in *The Evolution of Cultural Diversity: a Phylogenetic Approach*, eds. R. Mace, C. Holden & S. Shennan. London: UCL Press, 69–85.

Cavalli-Sforza, L.L., E. Minch & J. Mountain, 1988. Reconstruction of human evolution: bringing together the genetic, archaeological and linguistic data. *Proceedings of the National Academy of Sciences of the USA* 85, 6002–6.

Cavalli-Sforza, L.L., P. Menozzi & A. Piazza, 1994. *The History and Geography of Human Genes*. Princeton (NJ): Princeton University Press.

Ehret, C., 1998. *An African Classical Age: Eastern and Southern Africa in World History, 1000 BC to AD 400*. Charlottesville (VA): University Press of Virginia.

Gray, R. & F. Jordan, 2000. Language trees support the express-train sequence of Austronesian expansion. *Nature* 405, 1052–5.

Guthrie, M., 1967–71. *Comparative Bantu: an Introduction to the Comparative Linguistics and Prehistory of the Bantu Languages*. Farnborough: Gregg International.

Heine, B., 1973. Zur genetischen Gliederung der Bantu-Sprachen. *African Language Studies* 14, 82–104.

Holden, C.J., 2002. Bantu language trees reflect the spread of farming across sub-Saharan Africa: a maximum-parsimony analysis. *Proceedings of the Royal Society of London* Series B 269, 793–9.

Holden, C.J. & R. Mace, 2003. Spread of cattle pastoralism led to the loss of matriliny in Africa: a co-evolutionary analysis. *Proceeding of the Royal Society of London* Series B 270, 2425–33.

Holden, C.J., A. Meade & M. Pagel, 2005. Comparison of maximum parsimony and Bayesian Bantu language trees, in *The Evolution of Cultural Diversity: a Phylogenetic Approach*, eds. R. Mace, C.J. Holden & S. Shennan. London: UCL Press, 53–65.

Holland, B. & V. Moulton, 2003. Consensus networks: a method for visualising incompatibilities in collections of trees, in *Algorithms in Bioinformatics*, eds. G. Benson & R. Page. Berlin: Springer-Verlag, 165–76.

Huelsenbeck, J.P. & F. Ronquist, 2001. MRBAYES: Bayesian inference of phylogeny. *Bioinformatics* 17, 754–5.

Huson, D.H., 1998 SplitsTree: a program for analyzing and visualizing evolutionary data. *Bioinformatics* 14, 68–73.

Huson, D.H. & D. Bryant, 2006. Application of phylogenetic methods in evolutionary studies. *Molecular Biology and Evolution* 32, 254–67.

Maho, J.F., 2002. Bantu Line-up: Comparative Overview of

Three Bantu Classifications, pp. 1–59. Unpublished manuscript. Goteborg, Sweden: Goteborg University. Available for download at www.african.gu.se/maho/jfmpubpapers.html.

Murdock, G.P., 1967. *Ethnographic Atlas*. Pittsburgh (PA): University of Pittsburgh Press.

Nakhleh, L., T. Warnow, C.R. Linder & K. St John, 2005. Reconstructing reticulate evolution in species — theory and practice. *Journal of Computational Biology* 12, 796–811.

Nurse, D., 1996. Historical classifications of the Bantu languages, in *The Growth of Farming Communities in Africa from the Equator Southwards*, vol. XXIX–XXX, ed. J.E.G. Sutton, Nairobi: British Institute in Eastern Africa, 65–75.

Pagel, M. & A. Meade, 2004. A phylogenetic mixture model for detecting pattern-heterogeneity in gene sequence or character-state data. *Systematic Biology* 53, 571–81.

Phillipson, D.W., 1993. *African Archaeology*. (Cambridge World Archaeology.) Cambridge: Cambridge University Press.

Rexova, K., D. Frynta & J. Zrzavy, 2003. Cladistic analysis of languages: Indo-European classification based on lexicostatistical data. *Cladistics* 19, 120–27.

Ringe, D., T. Warnow & A. Taylor, 2002. Indo-European and computational cladistics. *Transactions of the Philological Society* 100, 59–129.

Ruhlen, M., 1991. *A Guide to the World's Languages*, vol. 1: *Classification*. London: Edward Arnold.

Saitou, N. & M. Nei, 1987. The Neighbor-Joining method: a new method for reconstruction of phylogenetic trees. *Molecular Biology and Evolution* 4, 406–25.

Sanderson, M.J. & M.J. Donoghue, 1989. Patterns of variation in levels of homoplasy. *Evolution* 43, 1781–95.

Schoenbrun, D.L., 1998. *A Green Place, a Good Place: Agrarian Change, Gender and Social Identity in the Great Lakes Region to the 15th Century*. (Social History of Africa series.) Portsmouth: Heinemann.

Stone, G., 2000. Phylogeography, hypbridization and speciation. *Trends in Ecology and Evolution* 15, 354–5.

Swofford, D.L., 1998. PAUP*. Phylogenetic Analysis Using Parsimony (*and Other Methods). Sunderland (MA): Sinauer Associates.

Vansina, J., 1984. West Bantu expansion. *Journal of African history* 25, 129–45.

Vansina, J., 1990. *Paths in the Rainforests: Toward a History of the Political Tradition in Equatorial Africa*. London: James Currey.

Williamson, K. & R.M. Blench, 2000. Niger-Congo, in *African Languages: an Introduction*, eds. B. Heine & D. Nurse. Cambridge: Cambridge University Press, 11–42.

Woese, C., 1998. The universal ancestor. *Proceedings of the National Academy of Sciences of the USA* 95, 6854–9.

# *Chapter 3*

# Multilateral Comparison and Significance Testing of the Indo-Uralic Question

Brett Kessler & Annukka Lehtonen

Among Joseph Greenberg's many contributions to linguistics (Croft 2001; 2002), the one he may be best remembered for is his advocacy and prolific use of a methodology he called *multilateral comparison*. Using that technique, he claimed to demonstrate genetic relationship between many languages: four families in Africa (Greenberg 1963), previously unclassified languages of Papua and vicinity (the Indo-Pacific hypothesis: 1971), most of the native languages of the Americas (the Amerind hypothesis: 1987), and, most recently, a huge number of languages ranging across Eurasia and into North America (the Eurasiatic hypothesis: 2000; 2002). Indeed, Greenberg clearly believed that the technique was capable of demonstrating relationships among all languages. His last book presented preliminary evidence to support the notion that the Eurasiatic group was related to the Amerind languages (2002, 2–3), and he and his colleagues have often spoken of etyma purported to descend from a hypothesized Proto-World, the original human language (Bengtson & Ruhlen 1994; Ruhlen 1994, 101–24).

The prospect of making such great progress in uncovering the phylogeny of human language has excited many people and inspired them to apply multilateral comparison techniques to demonstrate the existence of very large genetic groups. At the same time, the reactions of the overwhelming majority of academic historical linguists have ranged from dismissive to hostile. Especially pursuant to the publication of the Amerind book (1987), several prominent linguists published detailed rebuttals of Greenberg's findings and of his methodology in general (e.g. Campbell 1988; Matisoff 1990; Ringe 1996; Salmons 1992).

In contrast, adherents of multilateral comparison have not presented a very rigorous explanation of their methodology. What has been offered does not proceed much beyond the most cursory geometrical sketch. One makes a tableau of words, where the columns represent many different languages, and the rows represent many different concepts; the data cells contain words expressing those concepts in the given languages. One then looks for columns that are more similar in corresponding rows than are other columns. Those similar columns are considered to be languages that are related, or more closely related to each other than to the other languages in the tableau (e.g. Greenberg 1993). Such a description immediately raises concerns because it seems essentially identical to a prescientific methodology known to have performed badly in the past (Poser & Campbell 1992). Occasional attempts to elaborate the methodology mathematically have only hurt its case. For instance, Greenberg & Ruhlen (1992) once claimed to show that a huge number of the world's language families are related because it is possible to find in each family some member language that has a word that has some connection to the concept 'swallow' (e.g. 'suck', 'neck', 'breast') and that has the consonants /m/, /l/, /k/, or most of them, or consonants that are similar. They argued that the probability of such a constellation of facts is vanishingly small; therefore the languages must be related. The computation was wrong on many levels (Hock 1993), but the most damning was the (admittedly widespread) assumption that a single low-probability event suffices to prove a hypothesis. Greenberg repeatedly expressed the idea that multilateral comparison is meant to be effective specifically because the huge data tableaux afford many opportunities to find interesting low-probability patterns. At the same time, he believed that the large amount of data afforded statistical protection against errors. But as many reviewers have pointed out, a strong case can be made for exactly the opposite assertion: that the more data one looks at, the more likely it is that one will find a sizeable number of interesting patterns that are simply coincidental, chance occurrences.

In light of such problems, it is perhaps understandable that there has been a backlash against multilateral comparison, with theorists sometimes insisting on procedures that are in all points its exact opposite. Instead of comparing lexemes, the traditional comparative method is meant to require comparing grammatical morphemes and the patterns of their use; instead of looking for similarities, one must specifically look for recurring sound correspondences; instead of being satisfied with matches in a small part of words, one must insist on matches involving at least a CVC sequence; instead of comparing many languages simultaneously, one must look at two at a time (e.g. Nichols 1996; Poser & Campbell 1992).

We concur that such recommendations are likely to result in a much smaller and more manageable set of interesting data that are much less likely to lead researchers into finding spurious connections between languages. However, we question whether such restrictions are either completely necessary or completely sufficient to solve the problem. Not sufficient, in that even the most rigorous classically trained linguists often remain unsure as to whether the number of recurrent sound correspondences they or a colleague have uncovered is enough to prove that languages are related. Not absolutely necessary, in that perhaps a convincing linguistic study can be performed without radically rejecting all of the principles of multilateral comparison.

In this paper we attempt to elaborate multilateral comparison into something that produces valid, convincing, and perhaps even useful results, while retaining as many of the properties of the methodology as possible. The tack we take is to graft on principles of statistical hypothesis testing so that one can evaluate whether the amount of similarities detected is significantly more than one would expect to see by chance. We take multilateral comparison as point of departure in part because it is an interesting case from a science-theoretic point of view: being diametrically opposed to mainstream techniques, it would not seem at first blush to be a promising candidate for rehabilitation. But in fact, we will show that certain aspects of the methodology make it especially useful for hypothesis testing.

**Significance testing in historical linguistics**

By now, several studies have addressed the general question of significance testing in historical linguistics; see, for example, the overview in Kessler (2001). Beginning with Ross (1950), all such methodologies exploit the idea that the connection between sound and meaning is arbitrary in a natural language. If one is given the words for 'black' and 'white' in a language but not told which one is which, there should be no way of solving the puzzle without knowledge of the language or perhaps of a related language. Due to this *arbitraire du signe* (Saussure 1916), if one can show that words for the same concept across two languages share some phonetic property significantly more than do words for different concepts, then that amounts to showing that the words and therefore the languages as a whole are historically connected. Further, if one can exclude the possibility of loans, then one is demonstrating genetic relationship. Of course, not all words are completely unmotivated; 'mother' tends to be similar across languages, and if one knows the words for 'black' and 'white' it is much easier to identify the words for 'blackness' and 'whiteness'. But it is generally believed that such cases can be identified with a little hard work.

Crucial to all significance testing is the proviso that all data be collected in a way unbiased with respect to the research hypothesis. All work after Ross (1950) addresses this by stipulating the use of a specific, predefined list of concepts. On encountering the concept 'black', the researcher is expected to objectively determine the single most usual word for 'black' in the two languages and enter them into the data set, totally without considering whether they constitute good evidence for the language relationship.

Significance-testing methodologies then require something to measure: What property of words should one look at in order to see if it is more abundant between words for the same concept than between words for different concepts? There have been two main threads of research here. One thread (e.g. Guy 1980; Kessler 1999; 2001; Ringe 1992; 1993; 1995; Ross 1950; Villemin 1983), following the traditional comparative method's emphasis on recurrent sound correspondences, has counted the number of times the same pairs of phonemes were found in words expressing the same concept. For example, in Ringe (1992), part of the evidence connecting English and Latin was the fact that an unusually high number of concepts (six) is expressed in Latin by words starting in /k/ and in English by words starting in /h/ (e.g. *cor, heart*; *cornu, horn*); any phonetic similarity between the two segments was deemed completely irrelevant. Another thread of research (e.g. Baxter & Manaster Ramer 2000; Oswalt 1970; 1998) has computed the phonetic similarity of the words. For example, Baxter & Manaster Ramer counted how many words begin with segments that are similar to each other. Latin /k/ couldn't match /h/ in their scheme, no matter how many words have that correspondence. But even a single pairing of phonetically similar sounds would be counted, such as /k/~/tʃ/.

The final step in significance testing is to determine whether the measure so computed is significantly greater than expected by chance. Various methods have been proposed, some simpler than others, all differing more or less in accuracy and general validity. Given the wide availability of fast computers, we now believe that the best solution in terms of reliability, accuracy, and applicability across a wide variety of methodologies is the Monte Carlo test of significance; see, for example, Kessler (1999; 2001) for its application to recurrence measures, and Baxter & Manaster Ramer (2000) for its use with phonetic similarity measures, all of which sources explain the theory. In a nutshell, the idea is that if we want to see what the relationship between words of the same meaning would look like across languages if only chance were involved, all we need to do is randomly rearrange the associations between the words and their meanings. Of course, any particular rearrangement is only one possible chance outcome; what we really want to do is to try all possible rearrangements and see what percentage of them has a measure better than or equal to the measure we actually found before rearranging. If five per cent of the rearrangements has such a high measure, we say that there is a five per cent probability that the relationship between the words is due to chance; or, more technically, we say that the results are significant at $p = .05$. Of course, even with high-speed computers it is impossible to do every rearrangement (a full permutation test) when large amounts of data are involved, but for all practical purposes, sampling a large number of random rearrangements (a Monte Carlo test) is just as good (Good 1994).

The significance-testing techniques we have briefly described here may raise two broad classes of objections. First, they ignore interesting classes of data, such as morphology. This is undeniably true, but no one has suggested that historical linguists abandon other methodologies when adding significance testing to their arsenal. It is simply the case that this particular tool requires unbiased, consistent collection of data for which mutual independence of form can be reasonably assumed, and in our present state of knowledge lexical lists afford the most reliable means to that end. Second, word lists have scary associations with glottochronology, which gained some disrepute due in part to inflated expectations for its precision (Embleton 2000). More damningly, virtually every amateur attempt to show connections between languages takes the form of pointing out phonetic similarities between words in a word list. However, problems with such approaches lie not in word lists themselves but in almost every other aspect of the methodology, such as collecting unbiased samples, matching up words by strictly defined criteria of semantic equality, and showing that the similarity is really greater than expected by chance. If such problems are corrected, Saussure's arbitrariness hypothesis actually makes word lists a very good choice for statistical analysis.

**Multilateral significance testing**

With this general background in mind, let us examine how such techniques may be applied to multilateral comparison. Some properties that characterize that methodology are:

- construction of flexible lexical word lists forming tableaux of words for the same concept across languages;
- use of similarity criteria rather than recurrent sound correspondences;
- simultaneous comparison across many languages.

To what extent can we apply these characteristics to hypothesis testing?

*Lexical lists*

As we have seen, the first property — working with lists of words that express the same concept in different languages — is already a staple in significance-testing research, and so we adopt it without hesitation. While Greenberg certainly studied grammatical elements, his work showed that lexical comparison proper can be treated as a separable methodology; for example, in his Eurasiatic work he presented lexical analysis in a separate monograph (2002). We propose therefore to restrict our purview here to lexical morphemes.

In one respect, however, we have chosen to depart somewhat from Greenbergian practice. We eschew the great length of the word lists reported in Greenberg's studies, which can number several hundred words. In general, it is true that increasing the amount of data increases the accuracy and significance of tests. Yet empirical studies show that increasing the size of word lists does not always help very much (Kessler 2001; Ringe 1992) and may in fact hurt the analysis. Some words are simply more probative than others because they are less subject to replacement. There is a point past which adding more words just waters down the data and makes it harder to uncover true relationships between languages. It is not clear just how small the lists can be. Although it is intriguing that Baxter & Manaster Ramer (2000) reported success using just 33 words from the Yakhontov list, the bulk of research has used one of the two Swadesh lists — 200 or 100 words (Swadesh 1952; 1955, respectively) — and in this study we stay within that conservative range.

In addition to being long, another property of Greenberg's word concept list is that it differed from study to study. These differences must be due in part to the convention against reporting negative data — words for which no cognates are found in a particular study are simply not mentioned — but in part to some real flexibility. We have undertaken to model such flexibility while bowing to the exigencies of controlled hypothesis testing: in particular, we must always guard against selecting words on the basis of what favours the research hypothesis.

We started with the Swadesh 200 list (1952) but omitted the concepts that are typically not fully lexical: 'and', 'at', 'because', 'few', 'he', 'here', 'how', 'I', 'if', 'in', 'not', 'some', 'there', 'they', 'this', 'we', 'what', 'when', 'where', 'who', 'with', 'ye'. We then introduced a process whereby the list would be reduced for specific comparisons, based on how suitable the remaining concepts were for the languages being tested. First, concepts were discarded outright if a language had no attested word for it (e.g. 'swim' in Gothic), or if all relevant words were sound symbolic (e.g. 'mother' in many languages), or loanwords (e.g. Latin *petra* 'stone', from Greek), or repeat a root that is used more typically elsewhere in the word list (e.g. 'dig' in Latin, *fodere*, is also used for 'stab').

Next, we assigned the remaining words a suitability factor, essentially an estimate of how likely it is that the word was truly old. This was a two-step process. First, for each individual language, we assigned each word a derivation factor, an estimate of how likely it was to have been derived from a different meaning. For example, the root of Latin *intestina* 'guts' clearly means 'in', and so it is given a high derivation factor. The other step of this process was to mark each concept by an estimate of its long-term retention rate. The score averages values reported in Swadesh (1955), Oswalt (1971), and values from three studies reported in Kruskal *et al.* (1973). The values given in the last are actually replacement rates, and were converted to retention scores using Oswalt's inverse power function transformation (1975). All values were given equal weight. A sixth term in the average indicated whether the semantic concept was used or advocated by a variety of language researchers: Swadesh (1955, where a refined, 100-item list was introduced), O'Grady, Black, and Hale (Alpher & Nash 1999), Yakhontov (Baxter & Manaster Ramer 2000), and Dolgopolsky (1986). For a given concept in a particular language, the suitability factor was its retention rate, proportionally reduced by the best (lowest) derivation rate of any of the words for that concept.

Finally, in any given comparison between languages, we ranked the concepts by the product of their suitability factor in each language, then used the top-ranking 100 words in the analysis. This process combines the best of two traditions: the Swadeshian tradition of using the universally most stable concepts for comparison — though enhanced by using a good deal of research unavailable to Swadesh himself — and the Greenbergian tradition of adapting the word lists to the study at hand. At the same time, nothing in the process biases the selection either in favour of or against the research hypothesis. The only disadvantage is that it requires a bit more thoughtful linguistic analysis than blindly following a word list, and it can be disappointing that one ends up discarding about half of one's painstakingly collected data. But in the end one does not wish a demonstration of linguistic relationship to fail because one has relied heavily on young words like *intestina* or on concepts subject to constant lexical replacement, like 'dirty', which has a retention rate of 3 on a scale of 0 to 100.

There is another way in which Greenberg's use of word lists was unusually flexible. In significance testing as well as almost all other uses of word lists, such as glottochronology, standard procedure has always insisted on selecting exactly one word to represent a concept in each language. Greenberg, however, never shied from using multiple words. In his Eurasiatic comparison (2002), for example, under the concept 'fire' he selected the Old Japanese word *pi* to compare with words like Greek *pyr*, but *atu-* 'hot' to compare with words like Old Irish *áith* (which he glossed as 'furnace'). Although it is hard to defend the imprecision of many of Greenberg's semantic matches, we must concede that often words have synonyms that are hard to choose between. Is there a way to incorporate into a significance test multiple words for individual concepts?

Multiple words would be difficult to handle in many standard statistical frameworks, but they turn out to be very tractable in Monte Carlo tests, because significance testing is done in exactly the same way as the initial measurements — except for having to rearrange and repeat thousands of times. We propose that when measuring the similarity or difference between two languages for a given concept that may be expressed by multiple words, one simply does all pairwise comparisons between the words, and takes their average. For example, if for the concept 'back' Old English offers both *hrycg* and *bæc* and Latin offers both *tergum* and *dorsum*, we would take four measurements: those for *hrycg* vs *tergum*, *hrycg* vs *dorsum*, *bæc* vs *tergum*, and *bæc* vs *dorsum*, then use the average of those four measurements. As long as exactly the same technique is performed during the rearrangements, the significance testing will be correct and unbiased.

*Phonetic similarity*

We have also seen that the second principle — the use of phonetic similarity measures — also has a precedent in significance testing. Its linguistic motivation is unassailable: words that have the same origin are, on average, more likely to sound alike than two randomly selected words that are not cognate; sounds do not always change, and when they do, they are more likely to change by small amounts than to become completely different. The only real problem is that one must define similarity precisely if one wishes to use it in a significance test.

As far as we can determine, Greenberg never published an explicit algorithm for quantifying the similarity of two words. Our proposal is to report the distance between the places of articulation of the first consonants of the word. More precisely, we suggest that one compute the phonetic difference between a pair of words by first isolating the first consonants of their roots; for all-vowel roots, the first vowel is used. Each of those two segments is scored according to its relative distance from the front of the mouth, in broad terms (labial, 0; dental to prepalatal, 4; palatal, 6; velar, 9; postvelar, 10); sounds with two places of articulation, like /w/, are given two scores (0, 9). The difference between two segments — and therefore between the two roots — is defined as the smallest absolute difference between all crosswise pairings of those scores. For example, /j/ would get a score of 6; when compared to /w/, |6–9| is smaller than |6–0|, so the distance between /j/ and /w/ is 3. In addition, half a point is added if the segments are not identical to each other.

This choice of similarity function is based on the observation that the place of articulation is the phonetic property most likely to remain constant over great amounts of time. It may appear objectionable that such a function throws away a lot of important data. However, as was the case with long word lists, it turns out that it actually does harm to include additional data that is weaker than the strongest datum, because counterevidence counts against the hypothesis just as surely as positive evidence counts for it. If place of articulation is more durable on average than voice, then requiring one to incorporate voice in a distance metric simply waters down the stronger evidence that place of articulation provides. In the end, counting any evidence beyond the most probative ends up weakening the case, leading one to falsely conclude that related languages are not related (see Kessler 2001 for some empirical tests).

*Multilateral comparison*

As far as we know, all previous work involving significance testing has been inherently bilateral, comparing two languages at a time. For example, even though Kessler (2001) performed many tests on eight different languages, all of the comparisons were bilateral; his discussion of multilateral comparison was small and disappointing. When looking for connections between the Indo-European languages and the Uralic languages, Oswalt (1998) did many bilateral comparisons, and Ringe (1998) used protolanguage reconstructions for the two families, thereby reducing a potentially very multilateral analysis to a bilateral analysis again. But Greenberg and his colleagues have repeatedly stressed that multilateralism is the essential nonnegotiable feature of their methodology (e.g. Greenberg 1993; 2000).

There are many interesting things one can do with multi-way interactions between multiple factors, many of which have an elegant mathematical description but pose a challenge for real-world interpretation. For example, there is a straightforward extrapolation of the Monte Carlo test for bilateral comparisons, where, instead of scrambling the connections between two columns (languages), one scrambles more columns. In the end, such a test may tell whether there is some connection between the languages that were entered. But what is the point of that? If one entered English, Basque, and Sumerian into a three-column table and found out only that there was some connection there somewhere, certainly the very next thing one would do would be to run bilateral tests to find out whether the relationship was restricted to a specific pair of those languages. So why not just do the bilateral comparisons in the first place?

It seems to us that the most immediately fruitful way to deploy multilaterality is not vertically but horizontally. If one knows that a set of languages is related, it is imaginable that that set of languages may prove a more useful comparandum against an unknown candidate language than would any of those languages singly. Even if it may not be immediately clear how that would work exactly, the intuition is probably clear. A language such as Albanian might be very difficult to identify with certainty as an Indo-European language if one could only compare it with a single other Indo-European language, and indeed it was accepted comparatively late into the fold (Bopp 1854). Only in the larger context, when one compares it with the pattern that emerges from considering the more easily grouped Indo-European languages, does the membership of Albanian become more evident.

We propose to emulate that multilateral capability in precisely the same way we have proposed treating multiple words for a concept in the same language. For example, if we know that Latin, Greek, and Gothic belong to the same group (call it Indo-European), we could build a data file where each concept lists words from all those languages. When we got to the concept 'five', we would have the set {*quinque*, *pente*, *fimf*}, precisely as if they were synonymous terms in one language. Then if we wanted to see whether Albanian belonged to this group, we would proceed exactly as if comparing Albanian to any single language. When we got to 'five', we would end up comparing the phonetic similarity of Albanian *pesë* to the set {*quinque*, *pente*, *fimf*}. By our proposed procedure, we would in effect measure the difference between *pesë* and each of those three words, and take the average. In general, as long as the selection of languages is unbiased, the larger the set, the more likely we will include a similar cognate which will bring up the average score for the comparison.

So, if languages are known to be related, they can be grouped together and treated as an entity in our multilateral comparisons. What if more than two groups remain after we have grouped known siblings? We propose a methodology analogous to a nearest-neighbour hierarchical clustering: perform comparisons between all pairs of groups and see which of the pairs is the most strongly connected, then group them together. Then repeat. More precisely, for each of the language comparisons that is significant at the .05 level, we compute the magnitude of the effect by first computing the total dissimilarity across all matching concepts (call that $m$), then computing what that would be by chance ($c$), then reporting the proportional improvement, $(c–m)/c$. The chance dissimilarity $c$ can be computed while doing the Monte Carlo significance test: it is simply the average of the total dissimilarity measures across all the rearrangements of the data.

This clustering technique gradually builds up a group that has at its core the most certainly related items. As it grows, it becomes easier to bring in outlying languages whose relationship is harder to establish. Crucially, though, while we believe that the power of the test grows, its bias does not. Just because a cluster might become more attractive as a partner to other Indo-European languages does not imply that it will be more likely to be chosen to partner with an unrelated language.

### Test case: Indo-Uralic

*Data and procedure*

The Indo-European and Uralic families are useful test cases of a methodology because each of them comprises many languages whose relationship with each other is now considered completely secure, but which vary widely in how obvious the connection is on the surface. While each family contains language groups whose interrelatedness must always have been obvious (e.g. the Germanic languages, the Balto-Finnic languages), the bulk of the connections weren't discovered until the late eighteenth century, and several others weren't acknowledged as members of the family until later (e.g. Albanian into Indo-European, Samoyedic languages into the Uralic group). A methodology's performance when confronted with these language families would give a good idea of its power.

The possibility of a genetic relationship between Indo-European and Uralic provides a test of a different kind. Such a relationship, nicknamed Indo-Uralic, has long been expected and often been claimed. It is a linchpin of most variants of the Nostratic hypothesis, and is an important element in Greenberg's Eurasiatic hypothesis. If a link between the two families can be demonstrated, it is happy news for almost everybody. If, on the other hand, a statistically rigorous version of multilateral comparison fails to uncover the connection between Indo-European and the family that most people consider to be its most likely neighbour, then the results of prior multilateral comparisons may be called into question.

Detailed information about the test can be found at our web site, http://BrettKessler.com/multilat. Here follows a synopsis.

Eleven Indo-European languages were chosen. Abundantly attested older languages (Old Church Slavic, Old English, Gothic, Classical Greek, Old High German, Old Irish, Classical Latin, Old Norse, and Sanskrit) were favoured because they should be closer to any putative Proto-Indo-Uralic ancestor and therefore make the connection easier to find. Albanian and Lithuanian, which are only attested relatively recently, were added to flesh out the range of languages considered. In the set of 11 languages, Old English, Gothic, Old High German, and Old Norse form a relatively recently diverging group whose interconnectedness is patent: the Germanic group. Lithuanian and Old Church Slavic form a branch, Balto-Slavic, that is less obvious but nowadays accepted by the vast majority of linguists. For Uralic, four mutually divergent languages were chosen: Finnish, Hungarian, Mari, and the Samoyedic language Nenets. XML files (W3C 2004) were built to store information about the words expressing each of the Swadesh 200 concepts for each of the languages. The words were gathered from a variety of sources without regard to the possibility of genetic cognacy with words from other languages in the study (Balg 1889; Buck 1949; Collinder 1955; 1957; Drizari 1957; Glare 1982; Kessler 2001; Köbler 2003a,b; Kulonen 2000; Lehtisalo 1956; Liddell & Scott 1889; Miklosich 1963; Moisio *et al.*

1995; Monier-Williams 1899; Országh 1959; Pewtress & Gerikas n.d.; Quin 1990; Ringe 1992; Sadeniemi 1966). An attempt was made to exclude all loanwords, motivated (sound symbolic) words, and words that share the same root with another word in the same language. For the Uralic languages, words that appear to be loans from Germanic or Balto-Slavic were excluded (principally words restricted to the Balto-Finnic languages), but not those that are merely suspected of being early Indo-European loans into Uralic as a whole (e.g. words for 'name' and 'water'; in Finnish, *nimi* and *vesi*), since these could also be interpreted as evidence for common descent from a shared ancestor. Suitability assignments were made for each concept, as described earlier.

Clustering multilateral analysis of the 15 languages was performed from the bottom up, as if pretending that we did not know of any existing relationships between any of the languages. We started with all pairwise comparisons among the 15 languages, took the pair that had the greatest significant magnitude at $p = .05$ or lower, combined them into a new group, then repeated with another round of pairwise comparisons, thenceforth treating that combined group exactly like a language. In each of the significance tests, the data was rearranged 100,000 times. This iterative process stopped when no language (or group) was found to be significantly related to any other language or group.

*Results*

In the initial iteration of the method, when all comparisons were bilateral comparisons between individual languages, the test found statistically significant evidence that 79 per cent of the pairings of intrafamily languages (an Indo-European language vs an Indo-European language, or a Uralic one vs a Uralic one) were related to each other. The most difficult Indo-European case was Albanian. While a connection was found between it and each of the Balto-Slavic languages, Old Irish, Greek and Sanskrit, the program reported insufficient evidence for linking it with Latin or any of the four Germanic languages. Some of the Germanic languages had trouble in other pairings: Norse was not connected with Church Slavic or Irish, and Gothic was not connected with Church Slavic or Greek. Greek did not get connected to the Balto-Slavic languages either. Within the Uralic family, the most trouble was caused by Nenets: while the program connected it with Mari, it did not report a connection between Nenets and either Hungarian or Finnish. None of the pairwise matches between Indo-European and Uralic languages were reported as significant.

High German and Gothic were found to be related at a significance level of $p = .00000$ with a magnitude of 78 per cent: the phonetic dissimilarity measure $m$ was only 84, much less than the chance measure $c$ of 382. Therefore that pair was pulled out and treated in the next iteration as a single language. The clusters formed by this process in successive clustering cycles were as follows:

| Magnitude | Grouping |
|---|---|
| 78% | High German with Gothic |
| 75% | English with the High German–Gothic group |
| 65% | Norse with English–High German–Gothic |
| 43% | Church Slavic with Lithuanian |
| 34% | Latin with Norse–English–High German–Gothic |
| 31% | Hungarian with Finnish |
| 24% | Albanian with Church Slavic–Lithuanian |
| 23% | Mari with Hungarian–Finnish |
| 21% | Sanskrit with Latin–Norse–English–High German–Gothic |
| 20% | Irish with Albanian–Church Slavic–Lithuanian |
| 14% | Greek with Sanskrit–Latin–Norse–English–High German–Gothic |
| 12% | Irish–Albanian–Church Slavic–Lithuanian with Greek–Sanskrit–Latin–Norse–English–High German–Gothic |
| 9% | Nenets with Mari–Hungarian–Finnish |

After this last iteration, the remaining two groups, representing the Indo-European and the Uralic languages respectively, were not found to be connected; the significance level was $p = .45$.

## Discussion and conclusions

A traditional bilateral approach to significance testing would have been essentially our first clustering cycle, which by itself yielded some paradoxical results that cannot easily be interpreted. The finding, for example, that Albanian is related to Greek, and Greek is related to Latin, but Albanian is not related to Latin has no real-world interpretation, at least not in terms of traditional Stammbaum phylogenetics. The result may be due to some experimental error — perhaps we were overly quick to reject suspected loans from Latin into Albanian but not perceptive enough to catch enough real loans from Greek — but most likely the result reflects uncertainty. A negative result can mean that two languages, although related, changed their vocabulary so fast that they simply do not any longer look much like each other. A positive result could occur simply because, if we are willing to accept matches at a five per cent significance level, then by definition we should expect five per cent of our tests to return a false positive. In view of these uncertainties, it is not clear how conflicting results could be meaningfully resolved at a bilateral level.

The multilateral approach successfully addressed this problem. By iteratively building up increasingly large groups starting with islands of certainty such as the Germanic languages and the Balto-Slavic languages, it eventually built up clusters that had sufficient useful comparanda to enable all the Indo-European languages to be identified and all the Uralic languages as well. It should be emphasized that this achievement is not inconsiderable. Both families contain languages that were only accepted as members after many decades of research on the respective families (Albanian in Indo-European, Nenets in Uralic) and which are not readily tractable even by other modern statistical methods. Ringe (1993) reported that his method had only marginal success dealing with Albanian in bilateral comparisons, and Marcantonio (2002, 136–53) failed to uncover sufficient statistical evidence for establishing a Uralic family.

The success in grouping these languages may be taken as a vindication of multilateral comparison. It supports what Greenberg always declared to be the central tenet of his methodology: comparing many languages synoptically can uncover evidence of relatedness that is not discernible bilaterally.

In two respects, however, this experiment fails to wholly vindicate Greenberg. Our methodology is not an exact duplication of multilateral comparison as it has generally been practised. We have introduced several techniques of experimental design that multilateralists rarely if ever discuss or, by implication, practice. Foremost among these are unbiased selection of comparanda, use of strict criteria for determining phonetic similarity, and a method of significance testing to see whether the evidence that turns up is more than expected by chance. To be fair, the majority of historical work lacks these qualities as well, and linguists of all stripes might profitably avail themselves of significance-testing techniques such as those presented here, when the amount of evidence they proffer for historical connections fails to immediately convince colleagues.

The other piece of bad news for the multilateralist research program is that this more rigorous version of the methodology failed to turn up any connection between Indo-European and Uralic. None of the pairwise tests were significant, and the $p$ value of .45 that was obtained when doing the last, great multilateral comparison is weaker by far than any value that would ever be considered to even hint at possible significance. Now we will be the first to admit that the failure to find positive results in any single test set is by no means definitive, and it is imaginable that our results would have been more positive if any number of parameters had been changed. For example, it is possible that some of the additional concepts used by Greenberg are unusually stable and therefore would have been more useful for detecting very old connections between languages. It is also conceivable that adding more languages to the data set would have changed the outcome. But until new evidence emerges, it is difficult to avoid the conclusion that the Indo-Uralic hypothesis is not well supported by the sort of data afforded by multilateral lexical comparison. Given that multilateralists generally believe that Uralic is one of the closest neighbours of Indo-European and therefore lies at the foundational level of much of their work, the validity of long-range multilateral analyses in general is called into question.

## References

Alpher, B. & D. Nash, 1999. Lexical replacement and cognate equilibrium in Australia. *Australian Journal of Linguistics* 19, 5–56.

Balg, G.H., 1889. *A Comparative Dictionary of the Gothic Language*. New York (NY): Westermann.

Baxter, W.H. & A. Manaster Ramer, 2000. Beyond lumping and splitting: probabilistic issues in historical linguistics, in Renfrew *et al.* (eds.), 167–88.

Bengtson, J.D. & M. Ruhlen, 1994. Global etymologies, in *On the Origin of Languages*, ed. M. Ruhlen. Stanford (CA): Stanford University Press, 277–336.

Bopp, F., 1854. *Über das Albanesische in seinen verwandtschaftlichen Beziehungen*. Berlin.

Buck, C.D., 1949. *A Dictionary of Selected Synonyms in the Principal Indo-European Languages*. Chicago (IL): University of Chicago Press.

Campbell, L., 1988. Review of Greenberg (1987). *Language* 64, 591–615.

Collinder, B., 1955. *Fenno-Ugric Vocabulary*. Stockholm: Almqvist and Wiksell.

Collinder, B., 1957. *Survey of the Uralic Languages*. Stockholm: Almqvist and Wiksell.

Croft, W., 2001. Joseph Harold Greenberg [obituary]. *Language* 77, 815–30.

Croft, W., 2002. Correction to Greenberg obituary. *Language* 78, 560–64.

Dolgopolsky, A.B., 1986. A probabilistic hypothesis concerning the oldest relationships among the language families of northern Eurasia, in *Typology, Relationship, and Time: a Collection of Papers on Language Change and Relationship by Soviet Linguists*, eds. V.V. Shevoroshkin & T.L. Markey. Ann Arbor (MI): Karoma, 27–50.

Drizari, N., 1957. *Albanian–English and English–Albanian Dictionary*. New York (NY): Ungar.

Embleton, S., 2000. Lexicostatistics/Glottochronology: from Swadesh to Sankoff to Starostin to future horizons, in Renfrew *et al.* (eds.), 143–65.

Glare, P.G.W. (ed.), 1982. *Oxford Latin Dictionary*. Oxford: Clarendon Press.

Good, P., 1994. *Permutation Tests: a Practical Guide to Resampling Methods for Testing Hypotheses.* New York (NY): Springer.

Greenberg, J.H., 1963. The languages of Africa. *International Journal of American Linguistics, supplement* 29(1), pt 2.

Greenberg, J.H., 1971. The Indo-Pacific hypothesis, in *Linguistics in Oceania*, ed. T.A. Sebeok. (Current Trends in Linguistics 8, vol. 1). The Hague: Mouton, 807–71.

Greenberg, J.H., 1987. *Language in the Americas.* Stanford (CA): Stanford University Press.

Greenberg, J.H., 1993. Observations concerning Ringe's *Calculating the Factor of Chance in Language Comparison. Proceedings of the American Philosophical Society* 137, 79–89.

Greenberg, J.H., 2000. *Indo-European and its Closest Relatives: the Eurasiatic Language Family: Grammar.* Stanford (CA): Stanford University Press.

Greenberg, J.H., 2002. *Indo-European and its Closest Relatives: the Eurasiatic Language Family: Lexicon.* Stanford (CA): Stanford University Press.

Greenberg, J.H. & M. Ruhlen, 1992. Linguistic origins of Native Americans. *Scientific American* 267, 94–9.

Guy, J.B.M., 1980. *Glottochronology without Cognate Recognition.* Canberra: Australian National University, Department of Linguistics.

Hock, H.H., 1993. Swallow tales: chance and the 'world etymology' MALIQ'A 'swallow, throat', in *CLS 29: Papers from the 29th Regional Meeting of the Chicago Linguistic Society*, vol. 1: *The Main Session*, eds. K. Beals, G. Cooke, D. Kathman, S. Kita, K.-E. McCullough & D. Testen. Chicago (IL): Chicago Linguistic Society, 215–38.

Kessler, B., 1999. Estimating the Probability of Historical Connections between Languages. Unpublished PhD dissertation, Stanford University.

Kessler, B., 2001. *The Significance of Word Lists.* Stanford (CA): Center for the Study of Language and Information.

Köbler, G., 2003a. *Altnordisches Wörterbuch.* http://www.koeblergerhard.de/anwbhinw.html.

Köbler, G., 2003b. *Neuhochdeutsch–althochdeutsches Wörterbuch.* http://www.koeblergerhard.de/germanistischewoerterbuecher/althochdeutscheswoerterbuch/nhd-ahd.pdf.

Kruskal, J.B., I. Dyen & P. Black, 1973. Some results from the vocabulary method of reconstructing language trees, in *Lexicostatistics in Genetic Linguistics*, ed. I. Dyen. The Hague: Mouton, 30–55.

Kulonen, U.-M. (ed.), 2000. *Suomen sanojen alkuperä: etymologinen sanakirja.* Jyväskylä: Gummerus Kirjapaino.

Lehtisalo, T., 1956. *Juraksamojedisches Wörterbuch.* Helsinki: Suomalais-Ugrilainen Seura.

Liddell, H.G. & R. Scott, 1889. *An Intermediate Greek–English Lexicon.* Oxford: Clarendon Press.

Marcantonio, A., 2002. *The Uralic Language Family: Facts, Myths and Statistics.* Oxford: Blackwell.

Matisoff, J.A., 1990. On megalocomparison. *Language* 66, 106–20.

Miklosich, F. von, 1963. *Lexicon Palaeoslovenico-Graeco-Latinum.* Neudruck der Ausg. Wien 1862–65. Aalen: Scientia.

Moisio, A., I.S. Galkin & V.N. Vasil'ev, 1995. *Suomalais-marilainen sanakirja.* Turku: Turun yliopisto.

Monier-Williams, M., 1899. *A Sanskrit–English Dictionary.* Delhi: Banarsidass.

Nichols, J., 1996. The comparative method as heuristic, in *The Comparative Method Reviewed*, eds. M. Durie & M. Ross. New York (NY): Oxford University Press, 39–71.

Országh, L., 1959. *Magyar-angol kéziszótár.* Budapest: Akadémiai Kiadó.

Oswalt, R.L., 1970. The detection of remote linguistic relationships. *Computer Studies* 3, 117–29.

Oswalt, R.L., 1971. Towards the construction of a standard lexicostatistic list. *Anthropological Linguistics* 13, 421–34.

Oswalt, R.L., 1975. The relative stability of some syntactic and semantic categories. *Working Papers on Language Universals* 19, 1–19.

Oswalt, R.L., 1998. A probabilistic evaluation of North Eurasiatic Nostratic, in Salmons & Joseph (eds.), 199–216.

Pewtress, H.H. & T. Gerikas (eds.), n.d. *Marlborough's English–Lithuanian and Lithuanian–English Dictionary.* London: Marlborough.

Poser, W.J. & L. Campbell, 1992. Indo-European practice and historical methodology, in *Proceedings of the Eighteenth Annual Meeting of the Berkeley Linguistics Society*, eds. L.A. Buszard-Welcher, L. Wee & W. Weigel. Berkeley (CA): Berkeley Linguistics Society, 214–36.

Quin, E.G. (ed.), 1990. *Dictionary of the Irish Language, Based mainly on Old and Middle Irish Materials.* Dublin: Royal Irish Academy.

Renfrew, C., A. McMahon & L. Trask (eds.), 2000. *Time Depth in Historical Linguistics.* (Papers in the Prehistory of Languages.) Cambridge: McDonald Institute for Archaeological Research.

Ringe, D.A., Jr, 1992. *On Calculating the Factor of Chance in Language Comparison.* Philadelphia (PA): American Philosophical Society.

Ringe, D.A., Jr, 1993. A reply to Professor Greenberg. *Proceedings of the American Philosophical Society* 137, 91–109.

Ringe, D.A., Jr, 1995. The 'mana' languages and the three-language problem. *Oceanic Linguistics* 34, 99–122.

Ringe, D.A., Jr, 1996. The mathematics of 'Amerind'. *Diachronica* 13, 135–54.

Ringe, D.A., Jr, 1998. Probabilistic evidence for Indo-Uralic, in Salmons & Joseph (eds.), 153–97.

Ross, A.S.C., 1950. Philological probability problems. *Journal of the Royal Statistical Society, Series B (Methodological)* 12(1), 19–59.

Ruhlen, M., 1994. *The Origin of Language: Tracing the Evolution of the Mother Tongue.* New York (NY): Wiley.

Sadeniemi, M. (ed.), 1966. *Nykysuomen Sanakirja.* Porvoo: WSOY.

Salmons, J., 1992. A look at the data for a global etymology: **Tik* 'finger', in *Explanation in Historical Linguistics*, eds. G.W. Davis & G.K. Iverson. Amsterdam: Benjamins, 207–28.

Salmons, J.C. & B.D. Joseph (eds.), 1998. *Nostratic: Sifting the Evidence.* Amsterdam: Benjamins.

Saussure, F. de, 1916. *Cours de Linguistique Générale.* Paris: Payot.

Swadesh, M., 1952. Lexico-statistic dating of prehistoric ethnic contacts. *Proceedings of the American Philosophical Society* 96, 452–63.
Swadesh, M., 1955. Towards greater accuracy in lexicostatistic dating. *International Journal of American Linguistics* 21, 121–37.
Villemin, F., 1983. Un essai de détection des origines du japonais à partir de deux méthodes statistiques, in *Historical Linguistics,* ed. B. Brainerd. Bochum: N. Brockmeyer, 116–35.
W3C, 2004. *Extensible Markup Language (XML).* http://www.w3.org/XML.

# Chapter 4

# Bantu Classification, Bantu Trees and Phylogenetic Methods

Lutz Marten

## 1. Introduction

Bantu languages pose a challenge for approaches to linguistic classification, since despite the establishment of the unity of the language group overall, no sub-classification of the Bantu languages has yet successfully been established. Several models have been used to come to such a classification, leading in part to different results. Most recently, Holden (2002) and Holden & Gray (Chapter 2 this volume) have employed phylogenetic methods for Bantu classification, which partly confirm previous studies. These results conflict, however, with a number of other previous classifications, which I present here, some of which are similarly based on quantitative methods. This presents both a methodological challenge, and leaves room for further studies in Bantu classification.

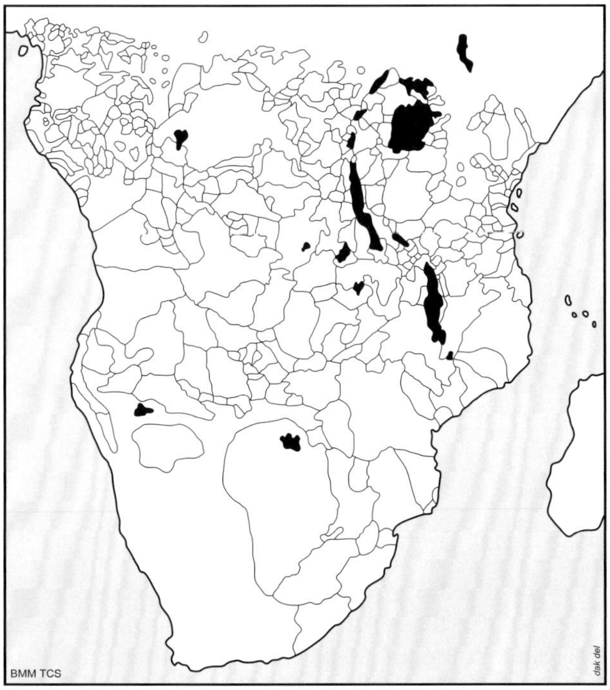


**Figure 4.1.** *The Bantu languages: geographic distribution.*

## 2. Bantu languages

Bantu languages are spoken in an area stretching from the Nigeria–Cameroon borderland in the northwest along just south of the Central African Republic up to southern Uganda and Central Kenya in the northeast, and southwards all the way to the Eastern Cape and to the Namib and Kalahari deserts in Namibia and Botswana.

Speakers of Bantu languages — somewhere in the range of 240 million people — thus occupy the larger part of sub-Saharan Africa (see Fig. 4.1, from Lowe & Schadeberg 1996). It is currently assumed that Bantu-speaking people originated in the northwest of the current Bantu area, that is, somewhere along the border between Nigeria and Cameroon, and that early Bantu speaking communities (and/or their languages) began to migrate east and southwards before about 3000 years ago, a movement which eventually, probably around 1000–2000 years ago, resulted in the present-day distribution (Ehret 1998; 2001; Vansina 1990).

There are estimated to be around 450–650 Bantu languages, including fairly well-known languages such as Swahili, Gikuyu, Bemba, or Zulu with substantive numbers of speakers and more or less long traditions of codification and literacy. However, the number of languages remains an estimate, for several reasons. One problem is, of course, the ultimately ill-defined notion of 'language', as opposed to 'dialect', a problem even more pressing for languages without a history of standardization and furthermore often bound up with socio-political-historical contingencies. For example, Nyanja in Zambia and Chewa in Malawi are mutually intelligible, but are often described as different languages for political reasons. Conversely, mutual intelligibility between different forms of Chaga in Tanzania is sometimes quite low, yet, these forms are usually referred to as dialects. For many Bantu languages, the relation between mutual intelligibility, structural similarity, and socio-historical closeness has yet to be described in detail.

A more specific problem with establishing the number of Bantu languages is that it is actually not quite clear what counts as a Bantu language and what does not. There is no question about this in the south and in the northeast of the Bantu area. In the south, the Bantu area is bordered by Germanic and Khoi-San languages and it is quite easy to see that, for example, Zulu and Herero are Bantu languages, while, for example, Afrikaans and Khoekhoegowab are not. Similarly, along the central and eastern parts of the northern Bantu borderland, Bantu languages border on Afro-Asiatic languages like Somali or Iraqw, or on Nilo-Saharan languages like Maasai or Luo. There are interesting contact phenomena in both the south and the northeast, but on the whole it is clear where the Bantu area ends. However, the neighbouring languages in the northwest are — like Bantu — Niger-Congo languages, and it is here, in eastern Nigeria, Cameroon, and in the north of the DRC where the decision as to which language counts as Bantu and which belongs to a different sub-branch of Niger-Congo becomes difficult, and where terms such as 'Semi-Bantu' (Johnston 1922) and 'Sub-Bantu' and 'Bantoid' (Guthrie 1948) have been coined.

Several scholars have proposed criteria for identifying Bantu languages, but often these have been useful for describing a 'prototypical' Bantu language — e.g. including noun classes, complex morphological systems, and CVC roots (cf. Guthrie 1948), but have proven to be not very helpful for making decisions in cases of doubt (Gerhardt 1981). Eventually, the only method for establishing Bantu as a genetically related language group, and thereby membership in it, is, of course, by providing a linguistic reconstruction and internal classification for all members. Alas, as yet, no such classification been established, despite the fact that the overall picture of the Bantu group has been sketched in outline over 100 years ago.

### 3. Bantu classification

That the languages of a large part of sub-Saharan Africa are related has been noted for a long time. As early as 1776, the Catholic missionary Abbé Proyart noted the relation between a number of western Bantu languages. Lichtenstein (1808) observed the relation between southern and eastern Bantu languages. In 1818, William Marsden commented on the relation between western and eastern Bantu languages that the

> instances of resemblance, in words expressing the simplest ideas, may be thought sufficient to warrant belief, that the nations by whom they are employed, must, at a remote period, have been more intimately connected (Tuckey 1818, 389)

a formulation which is — consciously or unconsciously — strikingly parallel to Sir William Jones's (1786 [1807]) famous observation that the Indo-European languages are related. Later, the first attempts at providing a comprehensive scientific study of the Bantu languages and their relationship were made, for example by Bleek (1862; 1869), who has been credited with coining the term 'Bantu' for the family, and Johnston (1919–22). However, it was Carl Meinhof (1899; 1910; 1932) who proposed the most influential model when he developed his Ur-Bantu, or Proto-Bantu (cf. also Dempwolff 1930–35 [1998]). Meinhof, professor for African languages in Hamburg, used a small number of test languages (Northern Sotho, Swahili, Herero, Duala, Nyakyusa and Sango in the first two editions; Northern Sotho, Swahili, Zulu, Nyakyusa and Kongo in the 1932 English edition), and applied the comparative method to reconstruct a hypothetical previous language, Proto-Bantu (PB), from which all Bantu languages were supposed to have developed. In using this method, he followed the Indo-European tradition, of which he was well aware, where the comparative method had been used to establish both the reconstructed Proto-Indo-European, and the sub-classification of it into different groups such as Romance, Germanic or Tocharian, which is often represented as a family tree. His procedure can be illustrated in a somewhat simplified manner with the examples from Swahili, Bemba, and Zulu below:

**Bantu cognates and reconstruction**

| | Swahili | Bemba | Zulu | PB | Gloss |
|---|---|---|---|---|---|
| (1) | *-lima* | *-lima* | *-lima* | **-lima* | 'cultivate' |
| (2) | *-tatu* | *-tatu* | *-thathu* | **-tatu* | 'three' |
| (3) | *n-goma* | *n-goma* | *isi-gubhu* | **-ɣoma* | 'drum' |
| (4) | *jiko* | *i-shiko* | *i-ziko* | **ɣîko* | 'fire-place' |
| (5) | *m-oto* | *umu-lilo* | *um-lilo* | **lilo*<br>**-lota* | 'fire'<br>'burn' |

The point of comparative reconstruction is that two words in different languages expressing the same idea have, following Saussure's (1916) insight about the arbitrariness of the linguistic sign, no reason at all to be of the same shape. If, however, two or more languages have consistently similar shapes for similar meanings, by way of explanation, they can be assumed to be related, and thus to share a common ancestor: that is, that the languages compared have developed from a single, older language. As a further step, one can try to reconstruct forms (e.g. words or sounds) for this older proto-language, which are conventionally prefixed with an asterisk, as the PB forms in (1–5) above. The examples in (1) above show that the word for 'cultivate' is *-lima* in all of our languages, and this is indeed the form which Meinhof reconstructs for PB. The examples in (2) show that Swahili and Bemba have *-tatu* for 'three', but that Zulu has *-thathu*, with two aspirated, rather than plain stops *t*. Meinhof here reconstructs **-tatu*, presumably partly on grounds of 'majority wins', and partly because there are more examples of aspiration of voiceless *t*s in Zulu, which is thus a good candidate for a systematic innovation in Zulu. The Zulu example here thus shows in addition to general relatedness how the comparative method leads to the establishment of sound correspondences (or 'laws'), such as, in this case, that PB /t/ becomes Zulu /$t^h$/. The examples in (3) and (4) illustrate more clearly the complexity of sound correspondences as they show different reflexes of the PB sound *ɣ, Meinhof's symbol for a reconstructed fricative, and how this fricative has different developments both across different languages, and in different phonological environments within individual languages. Thus, in the examples in (3), both in Swahili and Bemba (Zulu has a different word for 'drum', which requires a different explanation), *ɣ appears as velar stop /g/ when followed by a non-high vowel such as /o/ and preceded by a nasal (which is historically a class prefix). However, when followed by a 'tense' high vowel **î*, Meinhof's symbol for the highest front vowel in his PB seven-vowel system, *ɣ appears as affricate /dʒ/ in Swahili, as palatal fricative /ʃ/ in Bemba and as alveolar fricative /z/ in Zulu. To be useful for reconstruction, these correspondences have to be systematic rather than sporadic (which in fact they are), and then can be used to establish sound correspondences. The final examples illustrate a more problematic case. They show instances of the PB stem **lilo*, 'fire', in Bemba and Zulu, as well as the class prefix (for class 3), which is reconstructed as **umu-* and thus loses the second vowel in Zulu, and both vowels in Swahili. Again, this leads to the establishment of sound correspondences. The more interesting point to note here is the Swahili form *m-oto*. Since Swahili is a Bantu language, this exception needs to be explained by postulating internal or external innovation (such as borrowing). In this case, the word is likely to be a nominalization of a verbal root **-lota*, 'burn', that is, an internal innovation. Forms based on **lilo* and **-lota* are both found across wide parts of the Bantu area, without being in an obvious way related to specific possible sub-groups of Bantu. It is the scarcity of consistent, general sound correspondences across Bantu, as well as the inconsistent nature of lexical innovations and borrowings, such as illustrated by **lilo*/**-lota*, which have made it difficult to establish a sub-classification of Bantu so far.

However, by comparing his test languages, Meinhof was able to show that they were related, and, furthermore, that they corresponded more or less regularly to his reconstructed PB forms. In that sense, the genetic unity of Bantu was proven by the end of the nineteenth century, even though subsequent studies (notably Meeussen 1967; 1980) provided a more fine-grained picture of the hypothetical Proto-Bantu (see Schadeberg 2003 for more discussion).

From this point on, the relation of the Bantu languages to the wider Niger-Congo family was established following the 'mass comparison' approach by Greenberg (1963), but the internal genetic classification remains outstanding: Meinhof's (1932, 176) remark that 'an attempt to classify all Bantu languages must of necessity prove a failure' because we have not yet reached the stage in Bantu where we have 'accurate all-round knowledge of all the languages of the family' is echoed in 2001 by Nurse's (2001, 4) that a 'final linguistically-based historical classification of the Bantu languages has to be regarded as work in progress'. The most well-known Bantu classification to date is Guthrie's (1967–71) geographical referential classification, based on a large collection of data from about 200 Bantu languages which groups Bantu languages into 16 geographical zones grouped into two large groups — Western Bantu (zones A, B, C, D, H, L, K and R) and Eastern Bantu (zones D, E, F, G, M, N, P, S) — and assigns a letter and number to each language, a system which is widely used today (see Maho 2002 for discussion).

Despite being essentially a-historic, Guthrie's work has, however, had a great impact on studies of African history. Because the work provided a large-scale study of Bantu languages, it emphasized the question of how such a large area as the Bantu area could have come to be inhabited by speakers of very similar languages, and thus re-introduced an extended discussion about Bantu migration, or 'expansion'. Guthrie himself proposed that the Bantu languages originated in the Congo basin, but this idea has proven to be wrong — in a sometimes heated debate — and there is today wide-spread agreement, following arguments by Greenberg (1972) and later Vansina (1990), that the Bantu origin lies in southern Nigeria or the Nigerian-Cameroon borderland, whose Bantu languages show the highest degree of linguistic complexity (an idea in fact already proposed in Johnston 1919–22).

After the establishment of Bantu as a family at the turn of nineteenth century, progress has been made with regard to the overall position of Bantu within the African linguistic phyla, and much more comparative material has become available, in particular Guthrie's, which is still used in comparative studies of Bantu, and which triggered a new research tradition in Bantu history. However, no fully reconstructed family tree of the Bantu languages has become available yet.

**4. Internal classifications**

The somewhat surprising failure to establish a genetic sub-classification of Bantu has met with several reactions. At the centre of those has been the question of whether possibly the method of linguistic reconstruction as employed by Meinhof for his Proto-Bantu, and indeed in other language families, was unsuitable for the internal classification of Bantu. This discussion, of course, parallels discussions in the wider linguistic community, where it has been noted that linguistic change does not proceed as if it were rule-governed, but rather that novel pronunciations spread through the lexicon gradually (Wang 1969). Another, related, important aspect in the discussion is time depth, in that the comparative method might work better for longer time depths (Nichols 2003), and that possibly the spread of the Bantu languages is too recent to be classified by a family tree. More importantly, in the Bantu context, is the acknowledgement of contact phenomena, namely that communities do not by and large split and then never talk to speakers of other languages or dialects ever again (Thomason & Kaufman 1988). Rather, Bantu speakers are likely to have had contact with speakers of languages other than Bantu, but also with speakers of other Bantu languages, and multilingualism and diglossia are wide-spread across Africa. Transfer between dialects or closely related languages is difficult to detect retrospectively (Nurse 1997) and these 'convergence' effects make the establishment of family trees difficult, as traditional linguistic trees work on divergence effects. Finally, there is the further problem that the comparative method is very work-intensive, because it requires a thorough knowledge of all languages involved, that is, either native-speaker knowledge, or detailed descriptions of phonology, lexicon, and grammar, which often are not available for many Bantu languages.

In view of these problems, there have been three broad strategies towards Bantu sub-classification. The first one is to assume that comparative reconstruction will in fact eventually lead to a genetically valid tree for Bantu, and that the fact that it has not done so yet is due to the complexity of the task involved. In other words, that it is not surprising that, in view of the numbers of languages to be compared and the amount of detail required for a successful reconstruction, a genetic classification is still in progress. From this perspective, what needs to be done is to work on smaller subgroups, and once these smaller groupings are better understood, construct a larger tree upwards, until all Bantu languages are included. Nurse & Hinnebusch (1993), for example, provide a detailed study of the Sabaki languages of the northern East African coast, to which also Swahili belongs, and propose a genetic classification of them which takes into account phonological correspondences as well as lexical and grammatical features. This then leads to the establishment of a family tree, and the reconstruction of Proto-Northeast-Coast Bantu, which in turn can be incorporated into a larger tree. Similar reconstructions have been proposed for a number of groups within Bantu (see e.g. Doke 1954; Nurse 1999; 2001, Bastin *et al.* 2003; CBOLD 2004).

A second approach to the internal classification of Bantu is to abandon the comparative method altogether, and to develop methods which might be better suited to explain the distribution (and history) of the Bantu languages. This approach is followed, for example, in Möhlig (1981), who argues that a classic tree model of development is inapplicable to the Bantu case. Rather, Möhlig proposes a stratificational model, implying that there are several, layered proto-systems which underlie the current distribution of Bantu. The method employed in this model is, like in comparative reconstruction, based on phonological correspondences. However, the approach gives up on the idea that all Bantu languages can be reconstructed up to a single proto-from, as was implied by Meinhof. Thus, while this model recognizes the basic distinction between western Bantu (rainforest) and eastern Bantu (savanna) languages, it postulates a total of eleven proto-systems, or 'stratificational nuclei' (three forest nuclei and eight savanna nuclei), from which all Bantu languages can be derived by using regular sound correspondences, but which can not be derived from one another. A tentative historical explanation of this analysis would be to assume that Bantu speaking people (or their languages) migrated into sub-Saharan Africa not within one protracted migration, but rather through several, independent movements, each starting outside the Bantu area, and that periods of diverging movement were interspersed by periods of convergent language contact and transfer.

However, the probably most well-known approach to Bantu classification is the use of lexicostatistic methods, which is often seen as side-stepping the problem for the time being, and to work with smaller data samples, using 100- or 200-word lists for a usually large number of languages. In these, cognate forms are established, and the percentage of shared vocabulary is calculated. On the assumption that all languages undergo lexical change at a fairly similar rate, the degree of shared vocabulary is then an indication of the relatedness between the languages compared: the higher the percentage of shared vocabulary between two languages, the closer are the languages related. To ensure comparability, the words included in the method are usually taken from the so-called basic or non-cultural vocabulary which is said to be less subject to borrowing. The results of the calculation are easily represented in tree format, even though these trees are necessarily less well supported than trees resulting from the comparative method. Most researchers, at least in the Bantu context, view lexico-statistics consequently not as a replacement of comparative reconstruction, but rather as a shortcut to develop hypotheses about language relation which subsequently can be tested by the comparative method. Among the shortcomings of the method are that it works with a small set of examples for each language so that consequently stakes in the analysis of cognates are high; that it assumes an, ultimately unproven, even rate of change in the basic vocabulary; and that, of course, it has nothing to say about phonological, morphological or syntactic change. However, the advantage of the method is that it can be used for languages which are not yet fully described, and that is gives results fairly quickly. One of the most important results of a lexico-statistic study in Bantu is the classification proposed in Heine (1973) and in Heine *et al.* (1977), which confirms the division of Bantu into a western rainforest group, and a larger eastern and southern savanna group. This classification is one of the backbones of Vansina's (1990) account of Bantu migration, according to which western Bantu speakers slowly expanded into the tropical rainforests and the Congo basin, while eastern Bantu speakers migrated to the Great Lakes area and from there spread more rapidly across the savanna south of the rainforests (see also Nurse 1997; Ehret 2001).

More recent lexico-statistic studies are Bastin (1983) and Bastin *et al.* (1999). The most comprehensive of these, discussed further below, has results similar to Möhlig's studies, namely that the Bantu area is a convergence zone, characterized by language contact and borrowings, so that the appropriate analysis of the internal relationship of the Bantu languages is one based on geographic proximity with overlapping zones of linguistic closeness, and not on hierarchical branching as in classic tree methods.

## 5. Phylogenetic methods in Bantu classification

It is clear that lexico-statistic methods, despite possible shortcomings, have played and are playing an important role in current discussions about the classification of Bantu. Conversely, Bantu languages provide a good case study for the development of lexico-statistic methods. As pointed out above, there is no agreed genetic classification, but there are, in most cases at least, sufficient data available for running small-scale lexical comparisons of 100 or 200 words as are usually required for the establishment of lexico-statistic family trees. Furthermore, the Bantu area is an area where linguistic evidence is highly important for neighbouring disciplines such as archaeology, and for cross-disciplinary studies of the history of the region. Embleton (1986, 3) proposes that the development of the application of statistic methods in language comparison is a three-stage process, whereby as a first stage, a procedure is developed based on theoretical motivations or models, or past experience, which is applied, at the second stage, to data which are well-researched, such as Indo-European, and for which already a fairly established model of relationship exists, so as to test the new procedure's results compared to previously established ones and to improve it in light of this test. The third stage is to apply the, possibly refined, procedure to novel data, often from non-Indo-European languages, where no generally accepted classification exists. To the extent that the procedure results in reliable and testable results for Indo-European, it may lead to a better understanding of the non-Indo-European situation. The Bantu languages provide such an area where no established classification exists, and where the application of a new procedure which has proved useful in Indo-European might be profitable. One new procedure in statistics-based or quantitative language comparison is the application of computer-assisted tree-building algorithms for generating a range of trees compatible with the data, and for providing explicit parameters for choosing one tree over another (see McMahon & McMahon 2003). This procedure, developed in biology for the comparison of genetically differing species or groups and for the establishment of the best trees for representing biological genetic relationships, has been used with Indo-European data, including purely lexical as well as phonological and grammatical data (e.g. Ringe *et al.* 2002; Forster & Toth 2003; Gray & Atkinson 2003), but also, more pertinently to the present discussion, to Bantu languages by Bastin *et al.* (1999) and Holden (2002), Holden *et al.* (in press), Holden & Gray (Chapter 2 this volume).

Holden (2002) proposes a tree for Bantu based on 75 Bantu languages, which were selected not so

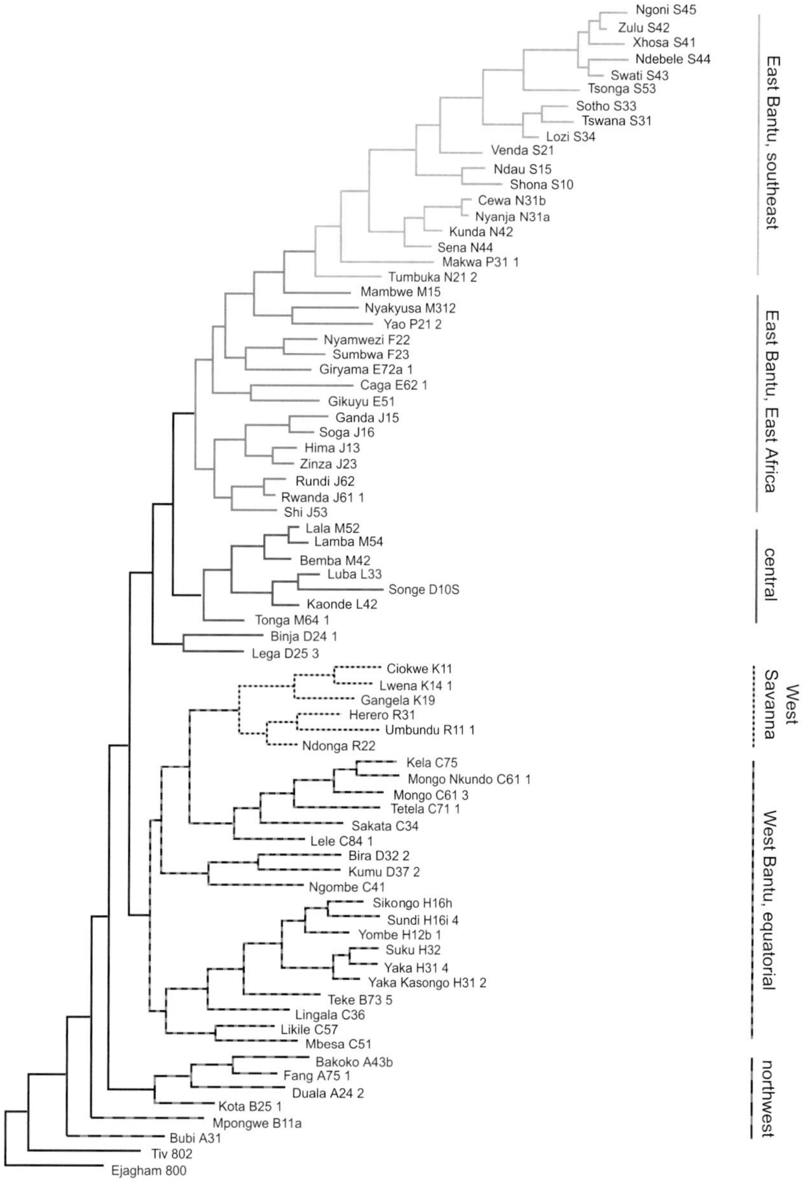


**Figure 4.2.** *Classification of 75 Bantu languages (from Holden 2002, 796).*

much according to linguistic criteria, but according to whether anthropological information about the speakers of the languages was available, as the research context for this project was to explore correlations between language relationship and anthropological characteristics. For the selected languages, data from Bastin *et al.* (1999) were used, namely 92 words of basic vocabulary for each language, coded for cognates. From these data a tree was constructed using a method called weighted maximum-parsimony, which selects the shortest tree for the data (see Fig. 4.2). The vertical lines on the right margin refer to her proposed historical analysis of the data, namely that the grouping of Bantu languages correlates with the archaeological hypothesis about the spread of farming across southern Africa.

In subsequent work, Holden *et al.* (in press) and Holden & Gray (Chapter 2, this volume) increased the number of languages included in the sample to 95, for which data from Bastin *et al.* (1999) were used. The difference between these studies is mainly in the phylogenetic methods used, which result in different representations of the relationships between the languages of the sample. Thus, while the tree reproduced here implies a hierarchical relationship between the languages included, later work includes networks as well as split graphs, which are better suited to express convergent relations. The advantage, in my mind, of using phylogenetic methods for Bantu languages is indeed that they result in several possible classifications for the same set of data, and thus provide hypotheses, to be tested further, rather than definitive results. However, before evaluating phylogenetic methods in Bantu studies more generally, some comments on the linguistic aspects of these particular studies deserve mentioning.

The first question concerns the languages chosen for these studies. As mentioned above, in Holden (2002), the criteria for including a language in the sample was the availability of corresponding anthropological data. However, from a linguistic perspective, selecting 100 or so sample languages out of the approximately 400–600 Bantu languages is an important factor for determining the results of the study (see Heine 1973). Out of the 75 languages in the sample in Holden (2002), two languages, Tiv and Ejaghem, are not Bantu languages narrowly defined, and are correctly found at the extreme branches in the tree, outside Bantu proper. The location of the remaining 73 languages is given below, according to their Guthrie zones.

**Test languages in Holden (2002) by Guthrie zone**

Zone A: Duala (A24), Bubi (A31), Bakoko (A43), Fang (A75)
Zone B: Mpongwe (B11), Kota (B25), Teke (B73)
Zone C: Sakata (C34), Lingala (C36), Ngombe

(C41), Mbesa (C51), Likile (C57), Nkundo (C61), Mongo (C61), Tetela (C71), Kela (C75)
Zone D: Songe (D10), Binja (D24), Lega (D25), Bira (D32), Kumu (D37)
Zone E: Gikuyu (E51), Caga (E62), Giryama (E72)
Zone F: Nyamwezi (F22), Sumbwa (F23)
Zone G: none
Zone H: Yombe (H12), Sundi (H16), Sikongo (H16), Kasongo (H31), Yaka (H31), Suku (H32)
Zone J: Hima (J13), Ganda (J15), Soga (J16), Zinza (J23), Shi (J53), Rwanda (J61), Rundi (J62)
Zone K: Ciokwe (K11), Lwena (K14), Gangela (K19)
Zone L: Luba (30), Kaonde (L41)
Zone M: Mambwe (M15), Nyakyusa (M31), Bemba (M42), Lala (M52), Lamba (M54), Tonga (M64)
Zone N: Tumbuka (N21), Cewa (N31), Nyanja (N31), Kunda (N42), Sena (N44)
Zone P: Yao (P21), Makwa (P31)
Zone R: Umbundu (R11), Ndonga (R22), Herero (R31)
Zone S: Shona (S10), Ndau (S15), Venda (S21), Tswana (S31), Sotho (S33), Lozi (S34), Xhosa (S41), Zulu (S42), Ngoni (S45), Swati (S43), Ndebele (S44), Tsonga (S53)

What is noteworthy in this distribution is the absence of any language from group G (which has 19 members in Guthrie, excluding the Swahili dialects), and the poor representation of groups P (14 members), with only Yao and Makwa, and group F (11 members), which has two languages from the same sub-group (Nyamwezi and Sumbwa). This means that the languages of Tanzania and Mozambique are rather under-represented, and that Northeast-Coast Bantu is represented with a strong leaning towards Kenyan languages. In Central Bantu, zone L has only two languages in the sample (Luba and Kaonde), out of 18 languages in zone L in Guthrie. In the northwest, zone A is represented by only four languages (Duala, Bubi, Bakoko and Fang) out of the 46 members (again, excluding dialects) of the group in Guthrie. In contrast, zone S, with 21 members (excluding dialects) is represented by 12 languages, that is, by more than half of the group. It is difficult to assess how the selection of languages specifically influences the result of the study, but it seems reasonable to expect that inclusion of more languages would result in a less tree-like result, as convergence effects would become more visible. In a way, this effect might be visible in the later Holden & Gray (Chapter 2 this volume) study, where an additional 20 languages are included, and where, partly due to different statistical techniques, but probably partly also due to the larger sample, convergence effects are more marked. The sample used by Holden & Gray (Chapter 2 this volume) includes a number of G languages, which were absent from the sample in Holden (2002), but retains the poor representation of zones F, L, and P, as opposed to the over-representation of zone S.

A second general point to note is the selection and analysis of vocabulary for the study. Holden's results are based on data published by Bastin *et al.* (1999). In this study, vocabulary questionnaires and written sources were used to construct a comparative data base of 92-word lists for 542 Bantu languages. One could criticize Bastin *et al.* (1999), and hence Holden's data set for this rather low number of lexical items. Embleton (1986, 92) recommends to the 'conscientious researcher' the use of 200-word lists as they are considerably more accurate than 100-word lists. It would thus be interesting to re-run Holden's procedure with a wider data base, based on a 200-word comparison. A related question is the (pre-)analysis of the data. In Bastin *et al.*'s (1999) study cognation judgements 'were informed by philological principles', taking into account the 'systematic sound-changes known to affect each language' (1999, 8). However, the actual judgements are not given. The problem here is that, on the one hand, cognation judgements are sometimes difficult to make, and, in this case, obviously depend on which systematic sound changes were known at the time of the judgement. On the other hand, borrowings, which have to be excluded from the set of cognate items, are difficult to detect within Bantu, especially in view of the overall structural similarity between Bantu languages, which are typologically fairly coherent — basic CVC roots, no consonant clusters except for nasal clusters, noun class morphology, complex verbal morphology, etc. So, in terms of data samples, both with respect to the quantity and quality of the data used, available phylogenetic studies of Bantu could be expanded to include more languages, more lexical items in the word lists compared, and ideally a more explicit account of cognation judgements. A particular interesting point in relation to data sample and results based on it is that Bastin *et al.* (1999) and Holden (2002) differ in their assessment of the role of borrowing in the Bantu area. While Bastin *et al.* (1999) conclude that a high level of borrowing has taken place in Bantu, Holden (2002), in contrast, claims that the level of borrowing is low, although both studies are based on the same data base. The important difference may well be that Holden (2002) only used a subset of 75 languages of the 542 languages used in Bastin *et al.* (1999).

### 6. Two quantitative studies of Bantu classification

Despite the methodological points made above, Holden's tree provides intriguing results, as it partly confirms previous studies, but is partly at odds with them as well. It would take much more space than available here to compare in detail Holden's results with all or even several previous approaches to Bantu classification. In what follows I am merely pointing out fits and misfits which I found striking. My main points of comparison here are the lexico-statistic study of Bastin *et al.* (1999), discussed in this section, and the geographical-referential classification of Guthrie (1967–71), as modified in Bastin *et al.* (1999), discussed in section 7.

As mentioned above, Bastin *et al.* (1999) propose a classification of 542 Bantu languages based on a quantitative statistic analysis of 92 words. After the initial cognation judgement, the relation between different languages is calculated according to the amount of shared vocabulary. Thus both Bastin *et al.* (1999) and Holden (2002) employ quantitative methods for Bantu classification. However, in terms of results, there is a marked difference between the two studies. While Holden (2002) implies that the tree derived by the phylogenetic methods she employed is a fairly true representation of the linguistic development of Bantu, Bastin *et al.* conclude rather the opposite namely that the results of their study, while being presentable in different trees and maps, point to the impossibility of finding any one format for presenting the complex linguistic relationship they discovered. Rather, the authors conclude that the lexico-statistic study of Bantu reveals a complex web of relationships, and that different results and classifications can be achieved by applying different parameters to the analytical mechanism. In particular, they present different trees (and maps) of the sample languages by varying the parameters of 'connectivity' (the degree of coherence within one postulated sub-group) and 'exclusivity' (the degree of how much vocabulary is shared with members outside of the postulated sub-group) and comment (1999, 223):

> ... groups that emerge from any attempt to impose a hierarchical structure on the Bantu languages largely fail to exhibit full connectivity or exclusivity. By varying the priority given to these two conflicting properties, it is possible to construct a series of trees which expose the ambiguities of relationship. It seems likely that such ambiguities reflect different 'periods of association' with other groups (which sometimes may reflect known history)'

Further trees are derived by using 'nearest neighbour' and 'furthest neighbour' computations, as well as intermediate trees ('variable neighbour') in which the thresholds of similarity are varied. These different trees provide a 'different perspective on linguistic relationships which are all part of the total picture' (1999, 109), so that no single tree can be taken to be the correct Bantu tree, and that Bantu languages display a 'continuity of converging intercommunication that cuts across possible diversity of origin' (1999, 223). In other words, the current distribution of Bantu languages is influenced by periods of contact and shared history, and by geographical proximity as much as by common origin, and therefore linguistic studies cannot provide evidence for 'simple' genetic trees, or be used without further interpretation for inference about history.

In terms of method, Bastin *et al.* conclude that, not surprisingly, tree models of linguistic relationship are poor tools (1999, 2):

> ... the substance of differentiation is innovation, and innovation is continually forging new communities. To the confusion of the tree model, shared innovation is independent of ancestry. The most we can say of two languages that display a number of innovations in common is that they have shared a period of linguistic community.

Furthermore, there is no clear correspondence between trees used in biology and in linguistics, as there is 'a sense of a radical difference between biological evolution and linguistic history: biological features are inherited, linguistic features are acquired' (1999, 3).

As pointed out above, I am not comparing Bastin *et al.*'s and Holden's approach in detail. However, it seems worth pointing out the contrasts between the results of the two studies on a general level. Bastin *et al.* deny the possibility of constructing any one family tree for Bantu in principle, while Holden (2002) proposes a version of a tree which is at least definite enough to be used to support historical hypotheses. The results reported in Holden & Gray (Chapter 2 this volume) seem to come closer to Bastin *et al.*'s results, in that several networks are presented. Yet Holden & Gray's conclusions with respect to the possibility of developing a sub-classification of Bantu with the aid of statistical methods are still more optimistic than those of Bastin *et al.* Wherever the truth in the matter lies, this difference, to me, indicates some caution about the use of quantitative methods in linguistics. McMahon & McMahon (2003) argue that one of the problems with the comparative method is that it rests 'on case law' (2003, 13), that is, there is no agreed procedure for testing it, and any two linguists may come up with very different analyses for the same problem, reflecting 'interference from individual linguists' opinion, either consciously or unconsciously' (2003, 14), as most historical linguists have already some idea about sub-groupings before starting to apply the comparative method. While I think that this is correct, in the case here, we have a similar scenario. Bastin *et al.*, presumably skeptical of genetic relationships, find that their analysis does not result in genetic sub-groupings. Holden, trying to find support for an archeological hypothesis with a family tree, finds a tree which does that. Both studies are based on presumably sound quantitative methods. It seems, thus, that quantitative methods are a highly useful and welcome addition for the study of linguistic relationship, and improve our methodological toolkit, but that the application of the method, and the interpretation of its results remains messy and subject to a certain degree of subjectivity.

## 7. Comparing Holden's results with Guthrie's classification

With all this in mind, let us go back to the classification proposed in Holden (2002), and see how it relates to the revised Guthrie classification, and discuss some more specific aspects of her analysis.

The updated Guthrie classification uses the coding system proposed by Guthrie (1967–71), so that, in order to assess similarities and differences between this classification, and the one proposed in Holden's tree, one thus can fairly easily check whether Holden's groupings correspond to languages with only one letter, and conversely, how languages with the same letter are distributed across the tree. Although this comparison does not, in some sense, compare like with like, as Guthrie's is a referential classification, while Holden's study is concerned with genetic relationship, comparing the two nevertheless is a good starting point for investigating how Holden's results relate to previous studies.

Starting from the root of the tree in Figure 4.1, the two 'wide Bantu' languages Tiv and Ejagham are separate branches and, as mentioned above, correctly analyzed as outside of Bantu proper (where 'correctly' here means, in agreement with the majority of previous studies, at least to my knowledge). The next two splits in the tree, Bubi (A31) spoken on Bioko island in the Bight of Biafra, and Mpongwe (B11), spoken in Gabon, versus the rest is different from the revised Guthrie classification, where the Bubi is grouped with the other three A languages in the sample, Duala, Bakoko and Fang, while Mpongwe is part of zone B, together with Kota (B25) and Teke (B73). On the other hand, Heine *et al.* (1977) have a separate Kande-Mpongwe branch. The splitting of the four B languages in Holden's sample into different sub-branches requires further investigation. In this respect, it is interesting to note that the Myene dialect cluster, to which Mpongwe belongs, is 'reported to have been partly submerged by the Fang' (Grimes 2004). For this group of languages, this leaves the curious position of Teke (B70) which is found in Holden's tree with several C and H languages. Disregarding details, the grouping of Bubi (A31) and Mpongwe (B11) as outliers of the tree, and of Kota (B25), Duala (A24), Fang (A75) and Bakoko (A43) as constituting a separate branch outside the rest of the sample languages seems to correspond with proposals to identify a northwestern forest group, made, with difference in detail, by several authors. In this respect, the tree supports the hypothesis that Northwest Bantu languages are differentiated at a higher node from the rest of Bantu than West and East Bantu. However, more recent work by Holden & Gray (Chapter 2 this volume) shows that different hypotheses about the relation between Northwest Bantu and the remaining Bantu languages can be supported by phylogenetic methods.

Moving along, the next big split in the tree divides a western branch (the part of the tree from Mbesa to Ciokwe) and a southeastern branch (from Lega to Ngoni) which are reminiscent of Guthrie's eastern vs western Bantu. Compared to Guthrie's division, the main difference is that in Holden's tree, Bira (D32) and Kumu (D37) are part of western Bantu, while they are eastern for Guthrie (although note that a number of D languages for Holden are eastern as well), and, conversely, that the two L languages in Holden's sample Luba (L30) and Kaonde (L41) come out as eastern, but as western in Guthrie. Within Holden's western group, the H languages (Kasongo to Sikongo) come out neatly as one branch, as do the R (Herero, Umbundu, Ndonga) and K (Ciokwe, Lwena, Gangela) languages, which also together form a distinct sub-branch. In contrast, the C languages in Holden's sample, while all in the western group, are scattered across several sub-branches. A further comment might be made with respect to the R, and to a lesser extent, K languages. Herero (R31) was found in Möhlig's (phonological based) study to be related to (N/P) languages spoken further east (cf. Möhlig 2000), but it seems that this was not picked up in Holden's study, and more generally that all of the Southwest Bantu languages are part of the eastern group in Heine *et al.*'s (1977) study. Bastin *et al.*, in their lexicostatistic study, generate several different trees where R languages are in different positions with respect to the rest of Bantu. In light of this, it is remarkable that here, these languages are grouped with a number of C languages, that is, closer to western Bantu. Holden

& Gray (Chapter 2 this volume) comment on possible conflicting evidence in the relation of Southwest Bantu to the rest of Bantu, but ultimately propose an analysis where Southwest Bantu is closer to East than to West Bantu.

Some smaller points in Holden's study are interesting in that they correlate with revisions proposed to Guthrie's classification as reported in Bastin *et al.* (1999), who re-classify Gangela as K19, as opposed to Guthrie's K12, corresponding to Holden's grouping together of Ciokwe (K11) and Lwena (K14) as opposed to Gangela. Similarly, Sikongo is unclassified in Guthrie, but both Sundi and Yombe are classified as H16. In contrast, Bastin *et al.* classify Sikongo and Sundi as H16, as opposed to Yombe, which becomes H12, which corresponds to the branching proposed in Holden's tree.

Before moving to the eastern branch, let us have a brief look at the D languages in Holden's tree. These are the only cases where languages of one Guthrie zone are found in both the western and the eastern branch: Bira (D32) and Kumu (D37) are in the western branch, while Songe (D10), Binja (D24) and Lega (D25) are in the eastern branch. Although Bira and Kumu on the one hand, and Binja and Lega on the other hand, belong to the same sub-groups within zone D (taking into account the reclassification of Kumu by Bastin *et al.* 1999), thus confirming these groupings in the tree, they are nevertheless, together with Songe, part of one zone, and at this level, the classification in Holden does not correspond well to Guthrie's. A result of this situation may be, as in similar cases discussed below, to highlight the need for further more detailed studies.

The internal grouping of the eastern group on the whole corresponds rather well to previous classifications. Again, there are instances of similarity in detail between Holden and the revised Guthrie classification, namely two examples in the S group. While Guthrie classified Ngoni and Swati as dialects (both S43), Bastin *et al.* re-classify Ngoni as S45, while Swati remains S43. Similarly, Lozi ('a nineteenth-century creole of an S.30 language' according to Ehret 1999, 49), K21 for Guthrie, is classified as S34 in Bastin *et al.* Both these re-classifications are reflected in Holden's tree. The internal classification of the S languages as a whole merits more discussion than space permits here, in view of the contact between different languages of the group on the one hand, and the dialect-chain like relation between some languages on the other (see e.g. Doke 1954; Hinnebusch 1999; Holden & Gray Chapter 2 this volume). In addition to the S group, Holden's classification presents distinct branches for the two sample languages of group F, as well as for the 'newly established' group J. This group is no part of the original Guthrie classification, but results from arguments against Guthrie's grouping in zones D and E, and the proposal to establish a new zone, zone J, comprising Guthrie's E10–E40 and D40–D50. This new group is reflected accurately as Holden's branch from Shi to Ganda. It is worth keeping in mind though, that there is as yet very little linguistic evidence for this group, other than lexical studies (cf. Nurse 1999, 9), and it is thus maybe not surprising that the group is reflected well here. There are also a number of discrepancies between Holden and Guthrie, especially in the Central Bantu area. For example, in the analysis of languages from group M, Bemba (M42), Lala (M52) and Lamba (M54) cluster together, but Tonga (M64), Mambwe (M15) and Nyakyusa (M31) are found in different branches of the tree. Similarly, the P language Makwa intervenes between the group of N languages in the sample, while the second P language Yao is found closer to the M language Nyakyusa. The two L languages Luba and Kasonde are grouped together with Songe (D10), which in turn is separated from other D languages as mentioned above. Partly because of this situation, Holden & Gray (Chapter 2 this volume) suggest that Central Bantu was an area of contact, resulting in partly conflicting tree representations.

With respect to the linguistic classification of the Bantu languages, then, Holden's tree provides a number of interesting points for discussion. Firstly, there are more detailed questions of discrepancy between her classification and those previously proposed, and a more detailed investigation of these might prove worthwhile. Of the points noted in the brief survey here, for example, in light of Holden's (2002) results, it is interesting to (re-)consider the internal coherence of groups C and D on the one hand, and L, M, N and P on the other hand, that is, those groups which are spread across different branches in Holden's tree. On a higher level of the tree, questions are raised as to the first splits in the tree — do the (or some) A and/or B languages form individual genetic branches? How good is the evidence for including the K and/or R languages in the western branch, rather than in the eastern branch? Some of these questions have indeed been addressed by Holden & Gray (Chapter 2 this volume). However, more generally, I think it would be useful to re-run the computation of the tree with different variables; on the one hand, with different computational variables, like those discussed by Bastin *et al.* (1999), and, on the other hand, with different data sets, as discussed in McMahon & McMahon (2003), by only taking into account, for example, the ten most widely shared items. Given computational space available, different subsets of vocabulary should be processed fairly easily, and differences and similarities between different trees should be illuminating, for example, for the establishment of contact (see McMahon & McMahon 2003, 50–52; Hinnebusch 1999). Of course, a further useful extension of the work would be to use a lager data set, both in terms of languages sampled, and in terms of vocabulary items included for each language.

## 8. Conclusion

In the previous sections, I have provided a brief outline of different approaches to Bantu classification. While there is comparatively widely shared agreement on the position, at least in outline, of Bantu within Niger-Congo, and on the unity of the Bantu languages, there is comparatively little agreement on the nature of this unity — to what extent it results from (historical) divergence or from (geographical and social) convergence. On the one end of the spectrum of positions adopted is Bastin *et al.*'s (1999) claim that the history of the Bantu-speaking people is characterized by mutual influence, contact, and convergence, so that tree models of language relationship are inapplicable to Bantu. In contrast, Holden (2002) found that the phylogenetic signal in the (admittedly smaller) sample of Bantu languages she used is strong enough to build meaningful trees for it. More recently, Holden & Gray's (Chapter 2 this volume) network approach seems to indicate that three different characteristics in the history of Bantu languages — rapid radiation, chain-like convergence, and tree-like divergence — can be observed from the data in their sample. It is interesting to note that all these approaches employed statistic-based methods, working with small (in fact the same) sets of cognate forms, and yet resulting in rather different over-all results. This is an indication of the fruitfulness of the use of statistical and phylogenetic methods in Bantu classification — different methods, even when, or maybe even especially when, applied to similar data yield different results which highlight the need for further study. Thus, for example, while the unity of zone S languages across different approaches indicates the fairly well-motivated establishment of this group, the ambiguous results with respect to, for example, Central Bantu languages show that an understanding of the complex relations involved in this group cannot fully be captured by the statistical methods employed. Rather, statistical methods help to create hypotheses which have to proved by more encompassing methods. These would include, presumably, more traditional methods of reconstruction, but also more refined phylogenetic methods, where this refinement is likely to result from: 1) samples which include more languages; 2) samples which include more lexical items; and 3) samples which include non-lexical features, such as phonological, morphological, and syntactic features. Although phylogenetic methods in linguistics are usually used with Swadesh-type lexical data-bases, there does not seem to be a methodological reason for restricting phylogenetic methods to lexical data as a point of principle. Restrictions in the size of the data sample are probably at least partly of a technical nature, related to available computational space, and as such likely to disappear with time. However, even within these constraints, a more densely populated data sample could include only a subset of Bantu groups, for example, only languages from Central Bantu. At least from a methodological point of view, it should be interesting to see how tree-like the results from such a sample would appear. Yet ultimately, of course, it is only through analysis of all Bantu languages that a successful classification of Bantu can be achieved.

## Acknowledgements

I am grateful to Clare Holden, Nancy Kula, Thilo Schadeberg and the audience at the Cambridge workshop for helpful comments. Parts of the results presented here have benefited from discussion within the network project Bantu Grammar: Description and Theory. Financial support for this project from the British Academy is hereby gratefully acknowledged.

## References

Bastin, Y., 1983. Essai de classification de quatre-vingt langues bantoues par la statistique grammaticale. *Africana Linguistica* 9, 11–108.

Bastin, Y., A. Coupez & M. Mann, 1999. *Continuity and Divergence in the Bantu Languages: Perspectives from a Lexicostatistic Study*. Tervuren: Musée royal d'Afrique Centrale.

Bastin, Y., A. Coupez, E. Mumba & T.C. Schadeberg, 2003. Reconstructions lexicales bantoues 3 – Bantu Lexical Reconstructions 3. Available on-line at http://linguistics.africamuseum.be/BLR3.html, accessed 03/04/04.

Bleek, W.H.I., 1862. *A Comparative Grammar of South African Languages*, part 1: *Phonology*. London: Trübner.

Bleek, W.H.I., 1869. *A Comparative Grammar of South African Languages*, part 2: *The Concord*. London: Trübner.

CBOLD: *Comparative Bantu Online Dictionary*, 2004. Available on-line at http://www.cbold.ddl.ish-lyon.cnrs.fr/, accessed 03/04/04.

Dempwolff, O., 1930–35 [1998]. *Induktiver Aufbau des Urbantu*, eds. L. Gerhardt & J. Roux, Cologne: Köppe.

Doke, C., 1954. *The Southern Bantu Languages*. London: Oxford University Press for the International African Institute.

Ehret, C., 1998. *An African Classical Age*. Oxford: James Curry.

Ehret, C., 1999. Subclassifying Bantu: the evidence of stem morpheme innovations, in *Bantu Historical Linguistics: Theoretical and Empirical Perspectives*, eds. J.-M. Hombert & L.M. Hyman. Stanford (CA): CSLI, 43–147.

Ehret, C., 2001. Bantu expansions: re-envisioning a central problem of early African history. *International Journal of African Historical Studies* 34, 5–41.

Embleton, S.M., 1986. *Statistics in Historical Linguistics*. Bochum: Brockmeyer.

Forster, P. & A. Toth, 2003. Toward a phylogenetic chronology of ancient Gaulidh, Celtic, and Indo-European. *Proceedings of the National Academy of Sciences of the USA* 100, 9079–84.

Gerhardt, L., 1981. Sprachvergleich und Rekonstruktion, in *Die Sprachen Afrikas*, eds. B. Heine, T.C. Schadeberg & E. Wolff. Hamburg: Buske, 375–405.

Gray, R. & Q. Atkinson, 2003. Language-tree divergence times support the Anatolian theory of Indo-European origin. *Nature* 426, 435–9.

Greenberg, J.H., 1963. *The Languages of Africa*. Bloomington (IN): Indiana University Press.

Greenberg, J.H., 1972. Linguistic evidence regarding Bantu origins. *Journal of African History* 13, 189–216. [Reprinted in *On Language: Selected Writings of Joseph H. Greenberg*, eds. K. Denning & S. Kemmer. Stanford (CA): Stanford University Press, 446–75.]

Grimes, M. (ed.), 2004. *Ethnologue: Languages of the World*. 14th edition. Available on-line at http://www.ethnologue.org, accessed 03/04/04.

Guthrie, M., 1948. *The Classification of the Bantu Languages*. London: Oxford University Press for the International African Institute.

Guthrie, M., 1967–71. *Comparative Bantu*. 4 vols. Farnborough: Gregg.

Heine, B., 1973. Zur genetischen Gliederung der Bantusprachen. *Afrika und Übersee* 56, 164–85.

Heine, B., H. Hoff & R. Vossen, 1977. Neuere Ergebnisse zur Territorialgeschichte des Bantu, in *Zur Sprachgeschichte und Ethnohistorie in Afrika*, eds. W.J.G. Möhlig, F. Rottland & B. Heine. Berlin: Reimer, 57–72.

Hinnebusch, T.J., 1999. Contact and lexicostatistics in Comparative Bantu studies, in *Bantu Historical Linguistics: Theoretical and Empirical Perspectives*, eds. J.-M. Hombert & L.M. Hyman. Stanford (CA): CSLI, 173–205.

Holden, C., 2002. Bantu language trees reflect the spread of farming across sub-Saharan Africa: a maximum parsimony analysis. *Proceedings of the Royal Society of London* Series B 269, 793–9.

Holden, C., A. Meade & M. Pagel, in press. Bantu language trees: a comparison of maximum parsimony and Bayesian methods, in *The Evolution of Cultural Diversity: a Phylogenetic Approach*, eds. R. Mace, C. Holden & S. Shennan. London: UCL Press.

Johnston, Sir H.H., 1919–22. *A Comparative Study of the Bantu and Semi-Bantu Languages*. 2 vols. Oxford: Clarendon.

Jones, Sir W., 1786 [1807]. *The Works of Sir William Jones, with the Life of the Author by Lord Teignmouth*, vol. III. London: John Stockdale and John Walker.

Lichtenstein, H.M.K., 1808. Bemerkungen über die Sprachen der südafrikanischen wilden Völkerstämme. *Allgemeines Archiv für Ethnographie und Linguistik* 1, 259–331.

Lowe, J.B. & T.C. Schadeberg, 1996. *Bantu MapMaker* v.3.1, computer programme. Available on-line at http://www.cbold.ddl.ish-lyon.cnrs.fr/Maps/BMM2.html, accessed 04/04/2004.

Maho, J., 2002. Bantu Line-Up. Unpublished manuscript, Göteborg University. Available on-line at http://www.african.gu.se/research/bantu.html, accessed 01/04/2004.

McMahon, A. & R. McMahon, 2003. Finding families: quantitative methods in language classification. *Transactions of the Philological Society* 101, 7–55.

Meeussen, A.E., 1967. Bantu grammatical reconstructions. *Africana Linguistica* 3, 79–121.

Meeussen, A.E., 1980. *Bantu Lexical Reconstructions*. Tervuren: Musée royal d'Afrique Centrale.

Meinhof, C., 1899. *Grundriss einer Lautlehre der Bantusprachen*. Leipzig: Brockhaus.

Meinhof, C., 1910. *Grundriss einer Lautlehre der Bantusprachen*. 2nd edition. Berlin: Reimer.

Meinhof, C., 1932. *Introduction to the Phonology of the Bantu Languages*, trans. N. van Warmelo. Berlin: Reimer.

Möhlig, W.J.G., 1981. Stratification in the history of the Bantu languages. *Sprache und Geschichte in Afrika* 3, 251–316.

Möhlig, W.J.G., 2000. The language history of Herero as a source of ethnohistorical interpretations, in *People, Cattle and Land*, eds. M. Bollig & J.-B. Gewald. Cologne: Köppe, 119–46.

Nichols, J., 2003. Diversity and stability in language, in *The Handbook of Historical Linguistics*, eds. B.D. Joseph & R.D. Janda. Oxford: Blackwell, 283–310.

Nurse, D., 1997. The contribution of linguistics to the study of history in Africa. *Journal of African History* 38, 359–91.

Nurse, D., 1999. Towards a historical classification of East African Bantu languages, in *Bantu Historical Linguistics: Theoretical and Empirical Perspectives*, eds. J.-M. Hombert & L.M. Hyman. Stanford (CA): CSLI, 1–41.

Nurse, D., 2001. *A Survey Report for the Bantu Languages*. Available at http://www.sil.org/silesr/2002/016/SILESR2002-016.htm, accessed 27/02/04.

Nurse, D. & T.J. Hinnebusch, 1993. *Swahili and Sabaki: a Linguistic History*. Berkeley (CA): University of California Press.

Proyart, L.B., 1776. *Histoire de Loango, Kakongo et autres Royaumes d'Afrique*. Paris. [Reprinted 1968. Farnborough: Gregg.]

Ringe, D., T. Warnow & A. Taylor, 2002. Indo-European and computational cladistics. *Transactions of the Philological Society* 100, 59–129.

Saussure, F. de, 1916. *Cours de linguistique générale*, eds. C. Bally & A. Sechehaye with collaboration of A. Reidlinger. Paris: Payot.

Schadeberg, T., 2003. Historical linguistics, in *The Bantu Languages*, eds. D. Nurse & G. Philippson. London: Routledge, 143–63.

Thomason, S.G. & T. Kaufman, 1988. *Language Contact,*

*Creolization and Genetic Linguistics*. Berkeley (CA): University of California Press.

Tuckey, J.K., 1818. *Narrative of an Expedition to Explore the River Zaire, Usually Called the Congo, in South Africa in 1816*. London: John Murray.

Vansina, J., 1990. *Paths in the Rainforests: Toward a History of Political Tradition in Equatorial Africa*. London: James Currey.

Wang, W., 1969. Competing changes as a cause of residue. *Language* 45, 9–25.

# *Chapter 5*

# Quasi-cognates and Lexical Type Shifts: Rigorous Distance Measures for Long-range Comparison

Johanna Nichols

## 1. Introduction

Systematic means of doing linguistic phylogenetics and estimating language family ages seem to have the same two requirements. First, character states are expected to be either identical due to inheritance (and therefore clade-defining) or non-identical due to changes in individual languages or branches; independent parallel development is an anomaly. More precisely, undetected parallel development is an anomaly, and most methods of linguistic phylogenetics endeavour to choose characters that are relatively unlikely to exhibit independent parallel development and/or remove instances of it from the data by hand. Second, it must be possible to distinguish strict cognates from non-cognates (the latter includes inter-branch borrowings), and this in turn requires that regular sound correspondences be identified. Unfortunately, these requirements preclude phylogenetics and estimating ages for some of the most interesting and important cases: language families for which the sound correspondences have not been worked out yet, language families for which regular sound correspondences cannot be established (a likely example is Afroasiatic, discussed below), and likely but not yet proven language families.

Here I present some lexical facts that may point to a way out of this dilemma. In stable lexical fields such as stance verbs ('sit', 'lie', 'stand'), lexical replacement is taken to be infrequent in general. However, a brief survey of Indo-European stance verbs suggests that lexical replacement is indeed infrequent in languages for which the basic stance verb is static or durative ('be standing', 'be in standing position'), but fairly frequent where the basic stance verb is telic or punctual ('stand up', 'assume standing position'). That is, the type of stance system determines the rate of replacement in stance verbs. Since type shifts in stance systems do occur occasionally, any very old language family is likely to exhibit at least a few of them, and if (like most families) it has rather few primary branches, the likelihood of ancient stance vocabulary surviving in several branches will be slim. Similarly, the likelihood that individual stance verbs will be good keys to ancient genealogical connections is slim. The ancient roots may survive, but not in the same senses.

Section 2 below argues that convergent development is common in languages, and that statistical means are needed for evaluating and weighting forms whose cognacy is probabilistic and non-unique by definition. Section 3 shows that recognizing past type shifts is not particularly difficult, so that it should be possible for searches for ancient cognates to be either directed or abandoned accordingly. Section 4 proposes and illustrates a method for casting about through an entire stance domain and a range of possible sound correspondences in search of possible ancient cognates. Section 5 considers the implications of lexical type shift for estimating language family ages from cognate retention rates. The concluding section summarizes the main properties of a phylogeny-drawing and age-estimating model that can work with probabilistic correspondences like those presented here.

This is a programmatic paper, intended to raise hypotheses based on observable behaviour of a pilot survey of a few languages.

## 2. Homoplasy in phylogenetic characters

Because language is transmitted rather than literally inherited, few of its component parts — words, syntactic constructions, morphological types, grammatical rules — are unique in particular languages. This means that the potential characters usable for phylogenetics are shot through with what is known as *homoplasy* or (in biology) *convergence* or (in linguistics) *independent parallel development.* In fact, probably all linguistic comparanda are homoplastic in at least

**Table 5.1.** *'Wheel' in Slavic languages.*

| | **Nominative** | **Genitive** |
|---|---|---|
| Old Church Slavic | kolo | kolese (same in Proto-Slavic) |
| Russian | koleso | kolesa |
| Ukrainian | kolo / koleso | kola / kolesa |
| Bulgarian | kolelo | pl. kolela |
| Serbian/Croatian | kolo | kola |
| Slovene | kolo | kolesa |
| Czech | kolo | kola |
| Slovak | koleso | kolesa |
| Polish, Kashubian | koło | koła |
| Upper Sorbian | koleso | kolesa |
| Lower Sorbian | kolaso | kolasa |

some degree. Therefore the only hope for phylogeny is to define characters that are known to be types rather than individuals and whose rigor rests on a probability of independent occurrence that is determinable and low enough for them to be useful.

Biological examples of homoplasy or convergence include independent development of functually comparable characters such as wings in birds and insects, seasonally changing white and dark coats or plumage in arctic animals, and omnivory in canids (which is independently both lost and developed several times in the canid lineage: see Harvey & Pagel 1991, 104). Linguistic analogues include such developments as independent parallel application of the same derivational process to the same root in different sister languages, mergers of cognate morphological categories, independent parallel semantic shifts, functionally similar grammaticalization of cognate morphemes, parallel typological developments, etc. An example of an independent parallel development in Slavic inflectional morphology is in Table 5.1.

In Proto-Slavic the word for 'wheel' was a neuter noun belonging to the minority consonant-stem declension with distinctive endings and mobile stress. The modern languages have lost the consonant-stem declension class and have shifted this word to the (productive) first declension (to which most neuter nouns now belong) and regularized the stem. Most languages have generalized the nominative stem, but Russian, Ukrainian (in part), Slovak, and Upper and Lower Sorbian have generalized the oblique stem. Bulgarian has a unique suffix (it preserves *kolá,* formerly plural 'wheels', in the meaning 'cart, car', testifying to generalization of the nominative stem). The shift to a productive declension class and generalization of the nominative stem are commonplace developments that are to be expected, and their appearance in several daughter languages is independent. Generalization of the oblique stem is much less common, but even so it is demonstrably independent in Russian, Slovak, and Sorbian: these languages have never been in contact, and the Russian generalization is secondary as the Proto-Slavic form was still attested in Old Russian a few centuries after the Proto-Slavic dispersal.

Homoplasy is at least a potential obstacle to accurate cladistics, as it replaces useful data points with material that is less informative to genealogy. It can even be a confounding factor, as homoplastic developments can be mistaken for clade-defining innovations. (For instance, in the early development of historical linguistics, the complex of head-final word order and suffixal morphology in several Eurasian language families was taken to be a family-defining feature; now we know it is a typologically harmonic complex. Ergativity in Basque and Georgian was also at first considered a possible genealogical trait, but it soon became clear that it is a moderately common alignment type.)

There is another problem with linguistic phylogenetics, in addition to homoplastic characters: it requires distinguishing cognates from non-cognate resemblants, and is by definition impossible for language families for which cognates and reconstructions are not available. A pressing example of this problem is Afroasiatic, a proven family but so old and diverse that regular correspondences cannot be reliably established for it. As a consequence the higher-level phylogeny of the family — the relationships between Semitic, Egyptian, Berber, Chadic, and the one or more branches that comprise Cushitic — cannot be determined. At present Afroasiatic is the only example of a family that can be demonstrated but not reconstructed, but almost certainly the search for deep genetic connections ongoing among comparative linguists will lead to some successes and they will be of the Afroasiatic type. It will be desirable to have a cladistic methodology capable of doing subgrouping on such families.

In addition, it would be useful to be able to determine a tentative (i.e. quasi-)phylogeny for sets of languages or families that are promising candidates for deeper relatedness but as yet unproven. Examples of such sets of possibly related families include the large groupings known as Penutian (in California and Oregon), northern Australian, the Trans-New Guinea grouping, Nostratic or Eurasiatic, Niger-Congo, and Nilo-Saharan. Testing other distributions, including archaeological evidence, against such a quasi-phylogeny could provide a measure of plausibility for the genealogical relatedness of the groupings.

Finally, a proper set of characters that accurately reflect phylogenetic distance will also be useful in dating, an important desideratum for historical linguists.

For all of these reasons, we need to be able to do reliable phylogeny on characters which are non-unique but admit of contextualization and statistical evaluation. Here I propose two kinds of potentially useful characters, both involving not single items (such as words or morphosyntactic types) but sets of items: lexical replacements in the context of lexical types and type shifts, and *quasi-cognates*, or resemblances in naturalistically defined ranges of form and meaning. Both will be illustrated here with material from the semantic field of stance predicates.

**Table 5.2.** *Static, telic and transitive verbs for 'stand' in several Indo-European branches.*

| **Branch** | **Language** | **Static** | **Telic** | **Transitive** |
|---|---|---|---|---|
| Germanic | English | stand | stand up | stand; put |
| Slavic | Proto-Slavic | *stojati | *stati | *staviti |
| Indo-Iranian | Sanskrit | stha:- | stha:- | stha:-p-aya |
| Celtic | Welsh | sefyll | sefyll | gosod / dodi 'put'[a] |
| Greek | | histe:mi | histe:mi[b] | histánai |
| Latin | | sto | consurgo, adsurgo, etc. 'rise (to one's feet)' | pono 'put' statuo 'put, stand' |

**Notes**
[a] Often with *i sefyll* 'standing', lit. 'to stand'
[b] Often prefixed.

## 3. Lexical type shifts: an example from stance verbs

The basic stance verbs, 'sit', 'stand', and 'lie', are among the more persistent lexical items, all three of these figuring in the Swadesh 100-word list and 'stand' in the Lohr high-retentive list (the latter given in McMahon & McMahon 2003). Stance predicates come in three common grammatical varieties: static ('stand, be standing', etc.); telic ('stand up; assume standing position');[1] and transitive ('put in standing position; stand (someone/something in a place)'). A language may treat any one of these three as basic and derive the others from it; or it may have suppletive roots in two or even all three.[2] A quasi-cognate approach, therefore, will search among all three senses for possibly cognate roots. Doing this for Indo-European sheds some light on rates of lexical change.

I will use the following terminology for three types of stance verb systems: base-static, base-telic, and base-transitive, depending on which of the grammatical varieties is elementary and which derived. (The terminology *base-static*, *base-telic*, etc. is intended to be analogous to *base-ten*, *base-twenty*, etc. as names for types of numeral systems. The terminology works best for the clear cases, but there will of course be some languages with mixed or inconsistent systems.) There are two indicators of which form is basic. The basic form may be the one from which one or more others are derived, e.g. English 'stand up' derived from 'stand', or Russian *sadit'sja* 'sit down' derived from *sadit'* 'put, seat, plant'. Or, in cases of lexical renewal, the basic form is the one which is first replaced by a renewing word, as when Latin *consurgo, adsurgo* 'rise (to one's feet)' replaced a telic derivative or inflectional form of *sto* 'stand', or East Iranian verbs meaning 'endure, last' replaced inherited 'stand' in the static sense. These histories illustrate lexical replacement by analogy as explicated by Kurylowicz (1947): a neologism replaces a word in its central sense, leaving the etymon intact only in its secondary or non-literal senses. (Both of these sets of examples are discussed again below.)

### *3.1. Lexical type shifts among stance verbs in Indo-European*

A quick survey of verbs meaning 'stand' shows that in most Indo-European branches (Table 5.2) the same root appears in both static and telic senses, often with a fairly fluid demarcation between the two senses. (In Sanskrit, for instance, the difference between static and telic is mostly a matter of present vs aorist tense.) Latin, however, is different, using a completely different and secondary verb in the telic sense (*consurgo, adsurgo*).

The modern Romance languages push the Latin trend even further, replacing telic and some static verbs with derivatives of the transitives. Romanian and Italian retain the original static verb, but the other languages replace even that (Table 5.3).

Indo-European languages generally tend to be at least weakly base-transitive in their overall lexical types, and the Slavic and Germanic branches strongly so (Nichols *et al.* 2004). Atypically for the base-transitive lexical type, modern Germanic and Slavic languages are base-static in their stance verbs. Latin has undergone a type shift to base-telic, replacing the inherited root for 'stand' with an unrelated one in the telic form. (The apparent root *surg-* is etymologically traced to *sub* 'up from under' and *reg-* 'direct, guide, lead', a verb which in its literal sense is transitive. Thus, consistent with the base-transitive tendencies of

**Table 5.3.** *Static, telic, and transitive verbs for 'stand' in several Romance languages.*

| Language | Static | Telic | Transitive[a] |
|---|---|---|---|
| Romanian | sta | se scula (în picioáre)<br>se ridicá (în picioáre) | scula (în picioáre)<br>ridica 'lift, raise'<br>pune (pe picioare) 'put' |
| Italian | stare in piedi | alzarsi (in piedi) | mettere in piedi<br>alzare 'lift, raise' |
| Catalan[b] | estar dret<br>estar dempeus | posar-se de peu / dret<br>aixecar-se | posar dret<br>aixecar 'lift, raise' |
| French | etre debout | se mettre debout<br>se lever | mettre debout<br>lever 'lift, raise' |
| Spanish | estar de pie | ponerse de pie<br>levantarse | poner de pie<br>levantar 'lift, raise' |
| Portuguese | estar de pé/em pé | pôr-se de pé/em pe<br>levantar-se | pôr de pe<br>levantar 'lift, raise' |

**Notes**

[a] The reflexive clitic *se* or *si* is a detransitivizer in all the languages. Not all relevant transitive forms are to be found in dictionaries.

[b] In Catalan, *llevar-se* means 'get out of bed, get up'. Its cognates in French, Spanish and Portuguese can have this meaning, but also mean simply 'stand up'.

Indo-European languages, this innovative telic verb is derived from a transitive.)

The daughter Romance languages remain faithful to the base-transitive and base-telic type and replace the telic forms with one or another neologism. In Table 5.3 the languages are listed in order of phylogenetic splitting: the first language to split off was Romanian, followed by Italian, followed by French and Catalan, and Spanish and Portuguese separated only in the late Middle Ages. The tree structure is reflected in some of the innovations: transitive LEVARE 'lift' becomes the base of the telic verb in all but Romanian and Italian; Spanish and Portuguese share the innovation of deriving the verb 'lift, raise' (*levantar-se*) from a participle. Romanian and Italian have different verbs for 'lift' (that of Italian is derived from the adjective ALTU 'high').

Evidently the telic verb 'stand up' is not at all stable in base-telic languages, as shown by its multiple independent replacements in Romance. Even the static verb has been replaced in most of the languages (often by a phrasal predicate that shares its prepositional phrase with the telic: French *debout* 'standing, upright', Spanish *de pie*, etc.). On the other hand, in the base-static majority of Indo-European languages the root for 'stand' is very stable. These different histories show that the stability of a lexeme can be relative to the lexical type of the language, so that using a Romance language in a lexicostatistical or glottochronological analysis might give incorrect results if the type shift were not recognized. A proper analysis of the wordlist distance of the Romance languages from the rest of Indo-European needs to be able to recognize the several lexical replacements as symptoms of a single shift of lexical type and measure distance accordingly. Such shifts are not frequent, and this means that the typological distance of the Latin/Romance branch from the rest is considerable and the shift could be useful for subgrouping. On the other hand, the shift is from the atypical base-static value to the typical base-telic value, given that Latin was base-transitive; thus the distance, though considerable, is not vast, and the shift is a natural one and not single-handedly diagnostic of subgrouping. The specific and unusual derivation of 'stand up; lift up' from a participle in Spanish and Portuguese is quirky enough to be a good diagnostic of subgrouping. Whether it will be a good diagnostic two millennia hence, when other evidence for the Spanish-Portuguese subgrouping will have been attenuated, depends on how stable a basic transitive verb like 'lift up' is in base-transitive, base-telic languages, and this we do not know yet.

Some of the East Iranian languages also replace static 'stand', but in doing so they exhibit the behaviour to be expected of a base-static language. Most Iranian languages, including the ancient East Iranian language Ossetic, preserve IE **steH-* in both static and telic senses, e.g. Avestan *sta:-, hišta-* 'stand'; *us-hišta-* 'stand up' (cited from Abaev 1979 s.v. *styn*). Several East Iranian daughter languages replace the static verb with **rap-* 'endure, last' (cf. Avestan *rap-* 'support, hold up') (Abaev 1973 s.v. *læwwyn*). Table 5.4 shows modern Ossetic data.

The Digor dialect is conservative, preserving **steH-* in both static and telic senses. Iron has the innovative word *læwwyn* in the static sense, and the transitive forms and one of the perfective telic forms are derived from this static verb. Its perfective *slæwwyn* seems to have occupied the central, literal part of the perfective range, 'stand up'; the examples cited by Abaev (1979) suggest that *styn* chiefly has the originally secondary senses of 'get up, rise, ascend'.

These East Iranian facts follow the trajectory of lexical replacement as described by Kurylowicz (1947), whereby innovations first appear in the central, literal part of a word's meaning. The static and telic verbs were originally the same (or at least had the same root, the telic probably with an originally directional prefix). The primary lexical meaning was the stance 'stand, be upright on one's feet', and this primary sense was renewed by a verb originally meaning 'endure, stay, be steadfast', meanings which are often implications or connotations of 'stand'. The descendant of **steH-* now remains in Iron Ossetic only in the telic sense, and the central part of its semantic range is being encroached on by the neologism in Digor. That is, the ancestral language was base-static and the original root now survives only in *non*-static senses.

**Table 5.4.** *Ossetic 'stand'.*

| | Static | Telic | Transitive |
|---|---|---|---|
| Imperfective[a] | I. læwwyn<br>'stand; stay'<br><br>D. læwwun, istun | styni<br><br><br>stun | læwwyn kænyn<br>'stop, detain;<br>help (s.o.) stand up' |
| Perfective[a,b] | I. slæwwyn,<br>alæwwyn,<br>fælæwwyn | slæwwyn, systyn | alæwwyn kænyn<br>'put (s.o.) on their feet; keep s.o. waiting, have s.o. stand' |

**Notes**
I. Iron dialect.
D. Digor dialect.
[a] The perfective/imperfective distinction is a regular derivational pairing in which the perfective (marked by prefixation) makes a static verb delimited or telic and makes a telic verb semelfactive (where the imperfective is iterative or habitual).
[b] Perfective and transitive examples from Digor happen not to be cited by Abaev or in other sources available to me.

*3.2. Mechanism of lexical type shifts*

If the East Iranian development just described is typical, lexical replacements will follow Kurylowicz's principle, with neologisms first taking root in the central, literal part of a word's meaning, displacing the inherited root to secondary senses (and then in due time ousting it in some of those as well). This means that lexical replacements can be a guide to lexical type. In base-static languages like the Iranian ones, lexical replacements will first appear in the literal sense of the static verb, while in base-telic languages like the Romance ones replacements appear first in the telic sense (and specifically in that part of its range having to do with the activity of rising up or getting up, rather than the part focusing on the achieved stance). The fact that replacement has occurred at all in East Iranian (which preserves the Indo-European base-static lexical type) can be explained as one of those replacements of a word by a more colourful near-synonym that happen from time to time in the history of languages. In a language family as old as Indo-European, we expect a few of these to have occurred over the millennia even in the very stable lexical domain 'stand'. That the original verb 'stand' has been replaced in Romance, however, is due to the fact that 'stand' is no longer a very salient lexical domain — or a very stable one for purposes of lexicostatistics.

Though much more work is needed on the diachrony of lexical type shifts, it can probably be modelled as taking place in three stages and following an S-shaped curve as such changes often do (Kroch 1989; Labov 1994; Weinreich *et al.* 1968). That is, there is a gradual build-up, a short period of rapid increase, and a gradual mop-up period in which a few holdout lexemes are replaced. The three stages, in more detail, are as follows.

(1) A word at a time, over a long period, a language makes occasional lexical replacements, in which for one reason or another derivational morphology or morphosyntactic behavior consistent with a new lexical type gradually comes to predominate. For instance, Pre-Latin replaces a number of inherited Indo-European lexemes with neologisms, one of which happens to be using a turn of phrase meaning 'direct oneself upwards' in lieu of 'rise' and 'stand up', initially a stylistic alternative to the inherited verb but eventually becoming the default way to say 'stand up'. When this happens the etymological connection of static 'stand' and telic 'stand up' is broken. Perhaps such innovations come to predominate because they fit well with some other aspect of the language's lexical typology (as basing telic 'stand' on a transitive verb may have fit well for Pre-Latin). Perhaps they reflect random drift. Perhaps they are calques on expressions in an influential neighboring or dominant language. Perhaps they are calques on a substratal language. Whatever the reason for their predominance, at some point they reach critical mass and new productive means of lexical formation and derivation arise.

(2) The point at which new means of lexical derivation arise can be thought of as the threshold or watershed marking the transition between types. In reality, of course, the transition is not instantaneous but is simply the rapid middle part of an S-curve.

(3) Once the new type is in place and determines lexical formation and derivation for the relevant sector of the vocabulary, a cascade of further lexical replacements takes place, implementing the new derivational patterns. That is, during the slow mop-up period at the end of one change there are numerous similar changes elsewhere in the system. For instance, suppose the shift to base-telic in Romance took place initially

among stance verbs and other verbs of physical action and location, and the cascade of subsequent innovations then produced suppletive pairings in non-stance verbs such as French *se rendre compte (de)* 'realize' (telic) beside *bien comprendre, concevoir nettement*, etc. 'realize' (static). (Contrast English, where the single verb *realize* can be either static or telic.) These additional replacements give the vocabulary a new cast and distance it lexically from cognate languages in a relatively short period of time.

What do we make, phylogenetically, of the fact that Latin and its descendants (or perhaps it is Proto-Italic and its descendants) manifest a different lexical type than their Indo-European sisters? Consider the scenario where Pre-Latin (or perhaps Proto-Italic), coming into close contact with Etruscan and other influential non-Indo-European languages of ancient Italy, calques their usage to the point that it undergoes a type shift. The daughters of Latin implement the new type so that their lexicons independently come to resemble that of Etruscan in structural type. (This is quite hypothetical; we actually know almost nothing of the lexical type of Etruscan.) This is then an acquired trait which has come to characterize the Latin/Romance branch, in part through separate parallel post-Latin developments.

I suggest that, where there is any reason to suspect contact, a known secondary development in daughter languages be regarded as a clade-defining trait even though we know it was only in rudimentary form in the protolanguage. The clade-defining event was interaction with a particular neighbour, and the seeds of the change were planted in the protolanguage. The daughter languages simply bring it to fruition, and their changes are not fully independent parallel developments (i.e. not true homoplasy or true convergence) but examples of what Sapir (1921, chap. 7) called *drift*: parallel, and often not simultaneous, developments in daughter languages due to invisible seeds planted in the protolanguage. Some cases of clade-forming secondary convergence like those discussed by Garrett (Chapter 12 this volume and 1999) may be due to this kind of gradual incarnation of invisible seeds, but presumably not all, as Garrett shows that this is not the case for Greek.

Will the Latin/Romance type shift be visible if we just use the glosses 'sit', 'stand', and 'lie' from the Swadesh list? It will not be very clearly visible, because the essence of the typology is derivation of stance-based verbs from each other, while the Swadesh list just uses one gloss from each stance-based set, the static one (which is the most stable member of the set in Latin and Romance, where the innovation-prone central part of the meaning range is the telic forms). Type shifts and differences of lexical type will be visible only if the linguist searches through (in the case of stance verbs) the full set of static, telic, and transitive glosses.

## 4. An application to long-range comparison

The different fates of verbs in the semantic field of 'stand' in Indo-European have implications for long-range comparison. Developments like those in Romance and Ossetic can remove even very stable words like 'stand' from standard vocabulary sets like the Swadesh 100-word list. Cognates so removed may survive elsewhere, as the descendant of **steH* 'stand' does in part of the telic range in Ossetic or as part of a phrasal verb in the static sense in Italian. Long-range comparison therefore needs to broaden the range of permitted senses so as to find such surviving cognates while retaining strict semantic controls that make possible statistical comparison. This section reports a pilot study in which quasi-cognates were sought in these extended semantic ranges in a comparison of material from different families.

I will refer to a set of verbs or verb glosses sharing the same stance component as a *stance domain*. Stance domains for the three basic stance predicates are SIT, STAND, and LIE. In the following, I focus on the first two. In the pilot study each stance domain was restricted to the same five kinds of glosses: static, telic, and three transitive ones: e.g. for SIT, 'seat (an adult), offer a seat', 'put (e.g. child) in sitting position', and 'set (inanimate object) down'. I sought the primary or basic verb in each of these senses in a convenience sample of seven languages from four families:

| | |
|---|---|
| Indo-European: | English |
| | Russian |
| | Spanish |
| Uralic: | Finnish |
| Kartvelian: | Georgian |
| East Caucasian: | Ingush |
| | Lak |

For long-range comparison we need to seek a phonologically resemblant word in any of the range of senses, and there should be evidence in the family (and ideally within each individual language) that any resemblant form detected is well-installed and potentially reconstructable in the semantic field: it should occur in more than one daughter language and in more than one of the senses. I call this latter consideration the *recurrence constraint*. It is met by the appearance of Romance descendants of **steH* in the

**Table 5.5.** *Stance verbs in languages from different families.*

| **STAND** | ***stand (up)*** | ***stand*** | ***have stand***[a] | ***stand***[a] | ***put (standing)***[a] | **C1**[b] | **C2**[b] |
|---|---|---|---|---|---|---|---|
| | **telic** | **static** | **causative** | **caus. anim.** | **caus. inan.** | | |
| English | stand (up) | stand | stand | stand | stand | T | T |
| Russian[c] | vstat' | stojat' | --/stavit'[g] | stavit' | stavit/('put') | T | T |
| Spanish[d] | levantarse;<br>*ponerse* de pie<br>pararse[e] | *estar* de pie<br><br>*estar* parado | *poner* de pie | levantar | poner derecho | N<br>?<br>P | P<br><br>N |
| Finnish | nousta | seisoa | 'put' | nostaa/('put') | nostaa/('put') | N | T |
| Georgian[c] | adgoma | dgoma | adgoma | aq'eneba | ('put') | | |
| Ingush[c] | ott | laatt | ottad.u | ottad.u | ottad.u; d.ott | Ø | T |
| Lak[c,d] | -.iz | -.a.c' | | | haz *d.an* | Ø | T |

| **SIT** | ***sit*** | ***sit*** | ***seat***[a] | ***set/put***[a] | ***put sitting***[a] | **C1** | **C2** |
|---|---|---|---|---|---|---|---|
| | **telic** | **static** | **causative** | **caus. anim.** | **caus. inan.** | | |
| English | sit (down) | sit | seat, sit | sit, set | ('put') | T | T |
| Russian[c] | {sed-} | sidet' | sadit' | sadit' | ('put') | T | T |
| Spanish[d] | asentarse | *estar* sentado | asentar | ('put') | ('put') | T | N |
| Finnish | istutaa[f] | istua | ('put') | ('put') | ('put') | T | -- |
| Georgian[c] | dadjdoma | djdoma/zi- | | dasvams | ('put') | T | T |
| Ingush[c] | waxou | d.aagha | waxoad.u | waxoad.u | d.ull/('put') | K | -- |
| Lak[c,d] | ssha99 *d.ik'wan* | sshaivk'un *ik'an* | | | | | |

**Notes**

[a] The notation ('put') means that the language uses one or more very general verbs 'put' which have no stance classification.
[b] C1, C2 = the first and second consonants in the root, stated as generic consonants: P = any labial; T = anterior obstruent; N = anterior resonant; K = posterior consonant; Ø = no initial consonant (for languages in which the first consonant of the root can be shown to pattern structurally or etymologically with the second consonant in related or analogous roots). Those listed are any that recur in the set for that language, in cognate glosses.
[c] Russian, Georgian, Ingush, and Lak are rendered in no-diacritics Latin (ch, sh, etc. as in English; 'dj' = voiced palatal affricate; 'w', for Ingush, = epiglottal pharyngeal; '9' for Lak = pharyngeal).
[d] Italics = auxiliary (inflection-bearing) verb in a phrasal verb.
[e] *pararse* and *parar* in American Spanish.
[f] The suffix *-tu-* is probably not synchronically segmentable in Finnish, but Rédei 1986ff., 629 shows that it is a suffix in Finnish (and Estonian).
[g] There is no standard lexicalized way to say this in Russian. Transitive *stavit'* can be used in a few expressions (e.g. teacher has child stand in corner).

static sense in both Romanian and Italian. Since Romanian is the most deeply divergent branch, occurrence of a cognate in Romanian and any other Romance language shows that the word is Proto-Romance. Nichols (2005) shows that the constraints implicit in such long-range works as Greenberg (1987) and Ruhlen (1998) are looser than these. Both have somewhat more lax constraints on resemblances in consonants; both permit free parsing rather than (as here) requiring a search of the first and second root consonants in that order; Ruhlen may have a similar semantic range, but Greenberg's semantic range is up to 14; neither has any recurrence constraint.

There is only one quasi-cognate evident among the two stance verbs in Table 5.5: STAND in Indo-European and Finnish has generic consonant T as both first and second consonant. (Strictly speaking, the word does not pass muster as a quasi-cognate unless it is confirmed elsewhere in Uralic, but as a preliminary example it suffices to illustrate the method.)

Obviously the chance of finding a match of generic consonants in a range of senses is greater than the chance of finding an identical or regularly correspondent consonant in a single sense. Therefore the number of matching words required for success in a quasi-cognate search is greater than the number required in strictly limited wordlist comparisons like those of Kessler (Chapter 3 this volume), Ringe (1992), Bender (1969), and others. By the criteria of Nichols 2005, the chance of finding, in a binary comparison, a generically resemblant two-consonant root in a search of five senses at 95 per cent confidence is 0.23 and 30 successes are needed on a 100-word list. This preliminary survey has found one such match between Indo-European and Uralic out of three stance verbs, a success rate which, if repeated over the entire 100-word list, would exceed the threshold of 30 and would strongly suggest genetic relatedness. In the pilot study there were no matches between Indo-European and East Caucasian. If this pattern of matches and non-matches were repeated over a larger survey, with Indo-European and Uralic showing a number of matches while East Caucasian had few or none with either of the others, the quasi-cognate search would be shown to be a good potential discriminant of probable vs. improbable relatedness.[3]

In addition, tabulating such data reveals typological differences between language families. All the languages except Spanish have base-static behaviour in one or the other of the verbs; only English and Russian have it for both verbs and in both transitive and intransitive verbs. Base-transitive lexicalization is evident for Spanish in the Appendix, and more generally evident for various Indo-European languages (Nichols *et al.* 2004). Finnish also has features of base-transitive lexicalization in stance verbs, with a separate word 'put' used in the transitive range instead of a derivative of the intransitive verb. (In the entries in the Appendix it resembles Spanish in overall pattern.) Since base-transitive lexicalization is not particularly common cross-linguistically, this resemblance is worth note.

To summarize, this preliminary application of a quasi-cognate search to the lexical domain of stance verbs seems to group Indo-European (excluding Romance) and Uralic together in terms of both consonant resemblances and lexical type. This tiny survey of three quasi-cognate ranges in seven languages is of course far from probative — as just stated, we would need over 30 such successes out of a 100-word list — but it does show that the method is feasible and has promise. Perhaps the most striking outcome is the fact that relaxing constraints on what counts as a match and including a range of senses did not cause matches to emerge in large numbers from all languages surveyed. This shows that quasi-cognate searches, properly constrained, can be rigorous enough to be of scientific interest.

## 5. Implications for the rate of lexical replacement

Above it has been argued that stability vs propensity for loss, as well as rate of loss, in wordlist comparisons must be relativized to the overall lexical typology of the language. Systematically surveying an entire limited semantic domain can reveal evidence of lexical type shifts in language families, and those shifts can explain sudden speedups in loss rate.

As I hope to have shown here, linguistic phylogenetics can be improved by some rethinking of what we use as characters. Be it noted that determining the lexical types of a set of languages and assessing their lexical retentions and replacements relative to the lexical types, or surveying whole quasi-cognate sets across a number of languages, is time-consuming and requires good linguistic resources and technical linguistic knowledge. There is no cheap and easy way to do any kind of wordlist survey, and a quasi-cognate search requires even more effort and expertise or resources than a closed wordlist survey.

Some historical linguists maintain that the fact that wordlist vocabulary loss is not metronomically regular across all languages and all lexical domains dooms all use of wordlists in dating language families. I have added to this picture evidence that even controlling for lexeme and family does not guarantee metronomicality: as in Romance we can have relatively rapid multiple loss and cascading lexical replacements due to shifts in lexical type. It is not enough to rank words for stability; we must also rank lexical types for different impacts on the stability of different kinds of lexemes. This further undermines the prospects of simple half-life models for accurate glottochronological dating.

On the other hand, the same results show that there is some chance of relativizing wordlist comparanda and their expected behaviour to overall lexical type. While a simple half-life model imposed uniformly on the entire lexicon does not give a very accurate estimate of age, a typologically sensitive one should be much more accurate — though it must be emphasized that even the best and most precise such procedure will never be more than an estimate.

## 6. Conclusions

What kind of model for determining phylogenies and estimating language family ages will be able to utilize facts like those discussed here? Its data will be not particular words with specific glosses and displaying particular sound correspondences, but probabilistic and approximate forms, meanings, and correspondences. Forms and meanings will both be expressed as a range based on common semantic and phonological changes — as in the quasi-cognate search shown in section 4 above, where resemblant or generic meanings ranged over, e.g. 'stand (static)', 'stand (telic)', and '(make/have) stand (transitive)' and resemblant or generic phonological segments ranged over all apical obstruents, all labials, etc. The model will utilize not only quasi-cognates but also typological information about the structure of lexical fields, derivational morphology, etc. in each language. Lexical data will come from various semantic fields and not just the stance verbs illustrated here. The model will compare quasi-cognates and also evaluate and weight factors that bear on the likelihood of cognacy and factors that increase or decrease the likely time depth.

Such a model will utilize data that is much more complex and much less determinate than current phylogenetic character data, and much more relativized to the grammatical and typological context. Identifying promising characters, typologies of their lexical and grammatical domains, common semantic shifts, and usable five-sense semantic ranges will be labour-intensive, as will working out chronological calibrations and weighted probable cognacy values. Though the job will be intricate, the kind of work to be done and how to go about doing it are straightforward matters for typology.

## Acknowledgements

Supported in part by the National Science Foundation (grants 96-16448 and 92-22294) and the Institute for Slavic, East European, and Eurasian Studies of the University of California, Berkeley. I thank my colleagues Shorena Kurtsikidze and Sirpa Tuomainen for Georgian and Finnish data respectively, Kathryn Klar for Welsh data, and Andrei Barashkov for advice on the Romance verbs. I thank the conference organizers, not least for their indulgence while I rewrote the paper drastically in order to expand on lexical type shifts in response to the conference discussion.

## Notes

1. In some languages some of these verbs may be ingressive (having an initial endpoint) rather than telic (having a final endpoint), but here I lump them together under the label 'telic'.
2. More accurately, there is a two-dimensional typological space defined by static vs telic and intransitive vs transitive as derivational bases, and languages are positioned at various points in this space. Here I discuss only the three points in this space where Indo-European languages tend to cluster.
3. To interpret this we would need to know something about lexical frequencies of different generic consonants in roots: perhaps these resemblances are no more than predictable results of preferences for having roots begin with anterior consonants. In Ingush, in contrast, posterior consonants are common verb-initially; see the discussion of closely related Chechen in Nichols 1997, 964–5.

## References

Abaev, V.I., 1958, 1973, 1979, 1989. *Istoriko-etimologicheskij slovar' osetinskogo jazyka*. (4 vols.) Moscow-Leningrad: AN.

Bender, M.L., 1969. Chance CVC correspondences in unrelated languages. *Language* 45, 519–36.

Garrett, A., 1999. A new model of Indo-European subgrouping and dispersal, in *Proceedings of the Twenty-fifth Annual Meeting of the Berkeley Linguistics Society*, eds. S.S. Chang, L. Liaw & J. Ruppenhofer. Berkeley (CA): BLS, 146–56.

Greenberg, J.H., 1987. *Language in the Americas*. Stanford (CA): Stanford University Press.

Harvey, P.H. & M.D. Pagel, 1991. *The Comparative Method in Evolutionary Biology*. Oxford: Oxford University Press.

Kroch, A.S., 1989. Reflexes of grammar in patterns of language change. *Language Variation and Change* 1, 199–244.

Kurylowicz, J., 1947. La nature des proces dits analogiques. *Acta Linguistica* 5.

Labov, W., 1994. *Principles of Linguistic Change*, vol. 1: *Internal Factors*. Oxford: Blackwell.

McMahon, A. & R. McMahon, 2003. Finding families: quantitative methods in language classification. *Transactions of the Philological Society* 101, 7–55.

Nichols, J., 1997. Chechen phonology, in *Phonologies of Asia and Africa*, eds. A.S. Kaye & P.T. Daniels. Winona Lake (IN): Eisenbrauns, 941–71.

Nichols, J., 2005. Of needles and haystacks: rules of thumb for wordlist comparisons. Under review.

Nichols, J., D.A. Peterson & J. Barnes, 2004. Transitivizing and detransitivizing languages. *Linguistic Typology* 8(2), 149–211.

Rédei, K., 1986ff. *Uralisches etymologisches Wörterbuch*. Budapest: Akadémiai Kiadó.

Ringe, D.A., Jr, 1992. *On Calculating the Factor of Chance in Language Comparison*. (Transactions of the American Philosophical Society 82(1).) Philadelphia (PA): American Philosophical Society.

Ruhlen, M., 1998. The origin of the Na-Dene. *Proceedings of the National Academy of Sciences of the USA* 95, 13,994–6.

Sapir, E., 1921. *Language*. New York (NY): Harcourt, Brace, & World.

Weinreich, U., W. Labov & M. Herzog, 1968. Empirical foundations for a theory of language change, in *Directions for Historical Linguistics*, eds. W.P. Lehmann & Y. Malkiel. Austin (TX): University of Texas Press, 95–188.

# Chapter 6

# Phylogenetic Analysis of Written Traditions

Matthew Spencer, Heather F. Windram, Adrian C. Barbrook, Elizabeth A. Davidson & Christopher J. Howe

Before the development of printing, texts were copied manually by scribes. In so doing, the scribes introduced changes. Some of these changes would have been accidental, whereas others would have been deliberate, perhaps in an attempt to restore what a scribe believed to be the correct version of the text. As copies of a text were in turn used as templates for further rounds of copying, the changes they contained would (usually) have been propagated, with additional changes introduced as well. Scholars have long studied the occurrence of variants in different versions ('witnesses') of a text, in the hope of shedding light on what the 'original' version of a text (if such an entity actually existed) might have been or of understanding what influences might have led to particular changes being made. The idea that systematic study of variants in a manuscript tradition might lead to a 'genealogy' of the manuscripts is generally termed 'stemmatic analysis'. It is often attributed to the nineteenth-century German philologist Karl Lachmann, although much of the detail of the approach relied on others (discussed by Salemans 2000, section 2.3). There are obvious parallels between the accumulation of changes in texts and the evolution of nucleic acid or protein sequences, and for many years scholars have applied the methods of phylogenetic analysis to the study of manuscript traditions (e.g. Platnick & Cameron 1977; Lee 1989; Robinson & O'Hara 1996; Robinson 1997; Barbrook *et al.* 1998; Salemans 2000; Lantin *et al.* 2004). Needless to say, the validity of some of these studies has been questioned by some (e.g. Hanna 2000; Cartlidge 2001). A particular point of concern has been the problem of 'contamination' where a scribe used more than one 'exemplar' (version) as a template when producing a copy (e.g. Hanna 2000, 165; Mink 2000; Deol 2001, 44), although the biological equivalent, lateral gene transfer, is increasingly recognized as an important phenomenon in sequence evolution (Howe *et al.* 2001; Boucher *et al.* 2003). In this paper we discuss a test of the applicability of phylogenetic methods to a manuscript tradition, and ways of improving the modelling of text evolution, including probabilistic models and methods for analyzing contamination.

### Evaluating text phylogenies

Why should we believe that phylogenetic methods work? In the analysis of written traditions, as with the analysis of language, the validity of phylogenetic methods has been queried by some. There are three categories of evidence for the applicability of these methods, arranged in descending order of power to convince a sceptic:

1. the methods perform well in tests where the true answer is known *a priori*;
2. the methods produce results that seem plausible to experts in the field, although we cannot be certain that the experts are right;
3. the methods have a compelling theoretical foundation, and we can show that the methods will perform well if we accept this foundation.

In biological systems, there have been a few successful tests of phylogenetic methods where the true phylogeny was under experimental control (e.g. Hillis *et al.* 1992). Molecular phylogenies have become the standard way of assessing relationships among organisms. Nevertheless, the results are not always clear-cut. For example, it is now widely accepted on the basis of molecular phylogenies that humans share more recent common ancestry with chimpanzees than with gorillas, despite the conflicting morphological and physiological evidence (Li 1997, 149–55). We have detailed probabilistic models of biological sequence evolution (e.g. Durbin *et al.* 1998, 41–4 & 193–7). The performance of phylogenetic methods in biology has been extensively studied by simulation (e.g. Nei 1991).

The situation is less satisfactory when phylogenetic methods are applied to text evolution. We review the evidence under each category in turn.

*1. True answer known* a priori*?*

There are circumstances in which the pathway of evolution of a written tradition may be known. For example, parts of the transmission history of an Icelandic narrative poetry sequence are known *a priori* because scribes explicitly identified the exemplar manuscript from which they copied. Maximum parsimony did a good but not perfect job of reconstructing this history (Robinson & O'Hara 1996).

In addition, it is also possible to mimic the evolution of a written tradition by contemporary copying of a text to generate an 'artificial' tradition whose evolution is known *a priori*. This information can then be used to test the reliability of different phylogenetic methods. We therefore produced an artificial text tradition in which 21 modern volunteer scribes copied from exemplar manuscripts, with a known pattern of transmission (Spencer *et al.* 2004a). The text was the first 834 words of an English translation of Wolfram von Eschenbach's medieval German poem *Parzival* (von Eschenbach 1980). The first scribe produced a handwritten copy of the printed text. We gave each subsequent scribe a photocopy of his or exemplar, instructing them only to copy accurately. The branching pattern of relationships between copies was chosen by us. We transcribed all copies into text files, aligned corresponding words, and produced a coded version for phylogenetic analysis in which words were replaced by arbitrary single-letter codes.

We supplied the aligned text and coded data to another member of the team, who received no information about the true phylogenetic relationships. He then attempted to reconstruct these relationships using a range of methods: maximum parsimony, neighbour-joining and split decomposition (we later added Neighbor-Net after the true phylogeny was known to the whole team). For maximum parsimony and neighbour-joining, we evaluated the accuracy of reconstructed trees using partition distance (Penny & Hendy 1985) and the triplet symmetric difference (implemented in COMPONENT 2, R.D.M. Page, http://taxonomy.zoology.gla.ac.uk/rod/cpw/index.html, downloaded 23/10/03) between the reconstructions and the true tree. No reconstruction was perfect, but all were fairly close to the true tree. Versions that were ancestral to others were consistently placed as terminal nodes on short edges rather than as internal nodes. This is not surprising as the methods were developed for the analysis of biological species in which ancestral forms are not generally present. Within such groups the branching order was sometimes incorrect, although with low statistical (bootstrap) support. For example, if a version A was the ancestor to versions B and C, the analysis in some cases would group A with one of B or C (with low support) rather than grouping B with C. For split decomposition and Neighbor-Net, we visually compared the reconstructions to the true phylogeny. Split decomposition correctly resolved a few groups of manuscripts, but left most relationships unresolved. Neighbor-Net showed strong support for most of the true relationships, along with weaker support for many relationships not found in the true phylogeny. Again, as might be expected, versions that should have been on internal nodes were shown on short terminal nodes. Although we cannot be sure that the behaviour of our modern volunteers is similar to that of medieval professional scribes, and our artificial tradition was not subject to contamination (see below), our study shows how accurate we might expect phylogenetic methods to be. Our results also highlight the need for methods that can place extant manuscripts on internal nodes.

*2. Answer agrees with expert opinion?*

There are many text traditions in which the results of a phylogenetic analysis have been compared with expert opinions (e.g. Lee 1989; Robinson 1997; Mooney *et al.* 2001; Lantin *et al.* 2004). For example, we compared the results of phylogenetic analysis of the thirty-five extant manuscript texts and three early printed copies of the *Kings of England* (a 105-line poem composed by John Lydgate in 1426) with the results of a conventional stemmatic analysis. We found good agreement between the conclusions of the two approaches (Mooney *et al.* 2001). In general, the verdict from similar studies with other traditions has been positive. Publication bias makes it difficult to decide whether this is a good representation of the success of phylogenetic methods. We might expect that someone who experiments with a phylogenetic method but does not obtain good results will not publish.

*3. A compelling theoretical foundation, and demonstrations that the methods perform well given this foundation?*

Many experts in textual criticism seem inclined to reject the use of phylogenetic methods, which they feel ignore too many important factors. For example, Hanna (2000) argues that phylogenetic methods are unlikely to perform well because they neglect the detailed philological knowledge available to human experts. It is interesting that similar concerns were raised when computational methods were first used for biological phylogenetics. For example, Crowson (1982) writes

> I cannot see how it could be possible to develop algorithms for these requirements [that ancestral species and sequences of adaptations should be

> biologically plausible], so I can see no prospect of computers replacing the functions of the controlled human imagination…

Jones (2001) suggests that rates of change vary substantially among branches in text traditions, and that this will reduce the accuracy of phylogenetic reconstruction. Cartlidge (2001) discusses the difficulties of coding text in the form of discrete characters, given the constraints of grammar and the possibility of variation operating on whole phrases rather than words.

## Modelling text evolution: probabilistic models

We feel that improving the mechanistic basis ('the model') for phylogenetic studies of text evolution will help make these studies more reliable and more acceptable to sceptics. Maximum likelihood (Felsenstein 1981) and Bayesian (Huelsenbeck *et al.* 2001) methods of phylogenetic inference are often viewed as the most reliable in biology, because they are based on explicit probabilistic models of sequence evolution. For DNA and protein data, the number of possible states at a site is fixed: there are four possible nucleotides or twenty different amino acids, respectively. We can thus model the evolution of DNA and protein sequences as a Markov chain with a finite number of states.

Text data are more complicated. In the following discussion, we assume that it is reasonable to split the text into locations (characters), each of which is independent. We know that this is not strictly true (Cartlidge 2001), even for biological sequences (Searls 2002; Robinson *et al.* 2003). Nevertheless, the level of linguistic information needed for more realistic treatments is difficult to acquire without a large amount of similar machine-readable text, which is unlikely to be available for most text traditions. For convenience, we refer to the text at a location as a word, although it may sometimes be more appropriate to use short phrases. We choose to work with words and short phrases because these are the kinds of variation traditionally studied by textual critics.

The number of possible words at a given location in the text is effectively infinite, and there may be words that are unobserved (either because they were in unsampled manuscripts or because by chance none of the scribes used them) whose probabilities of occurrence are not much lower than those of the observed words. Figure 6.1a shows how the number of words observed at a location increases as we resample more manuscripts from our artificial text tradition (Spencer *et al.* 2004a). For some locations, the same word occurred in all 21 manuscripts (a horizontal line at one state for all numbers of manuscripts sampled in Fig. 6.1a). For example, all manuscripts began with the word 'If'. Other locations had more observed states. For example, at a location where the original text had 'bite', the words 'bit', 'bet' and 'bile' sometimes occurred. The steepest line in the figure corresponds to 'Oh!', with 7 different forms, mostly punctuation variants. The more observed states over all 21 manuscripts, the stronger the tendency towards an upward trend even when almost all the manuscripts have been sampled (Fig. 6.1a). This suggests that for characters with many observed states, unobserved states are quite likely.

Because there is an effectively infinite number of possible states, we cannot immediately model text evolution using Markov chains with finite numbers of states. Furthermore, most possible transitions will not be observed because they are rare. Setting the probabilities of unobserved transitions to zero unduly restricts the behaviour of the model. Intuitively, texts containing the words 'cog' and 'dot' are more likely to be closely related if we allow the unobserved word 'dog' as a common ancestor than if we are restricted only to the observed words. We now discuss some ways of predicting the probabilities of unobserved transitions.

For our artificial text data, the probability that a word is changed during copying increases with the length of the word (Fig. 6.1b). This is consistent with the observation that word recognition is inversely proportional to the number of letters in the word (Pelli *et al.* 2003). Furthermore, the length of corresponding words changes relatively little during copying (Fig. 6.1c; see also Kukich 1992, section 2.1.2). We may therefore be able to capture many features of text evolution by sorting words into equivalence classes by length. Of course, word length is in principle infinite, but lumping all very long words into a single class is acceptable because very long words are rare.

Most miscopied words contain only a single error (Kukich 1992, section 2.1.1). This allows us to use word similarity as a match criterion for multiple alignment (Spencer & Howe 2004). We can measure word similarity using $n$-gram distance, where the $n$-grams of a word are the adjacent sets of $n$ letters. Here, we use $n = 3$, and add padding characters ('*') at the start and end of a word so that all letters are represented equally (Robertson & Willett 1998). For example, the word '**dwell**' has the 3-grams '**d', '*dw', 'dwe', 'wel', 'ell', 'll*', and 'l**'. The $n$-gram distance between two words is some function of the number of different $n$-grams found in one but not both words (Robertson & Willett 1998). The 3-gram distance between exemplar and copy words, where different, is not much affected by the length of the exemplar word (Fig. 6.1d), although there are constraints on the probability distri-

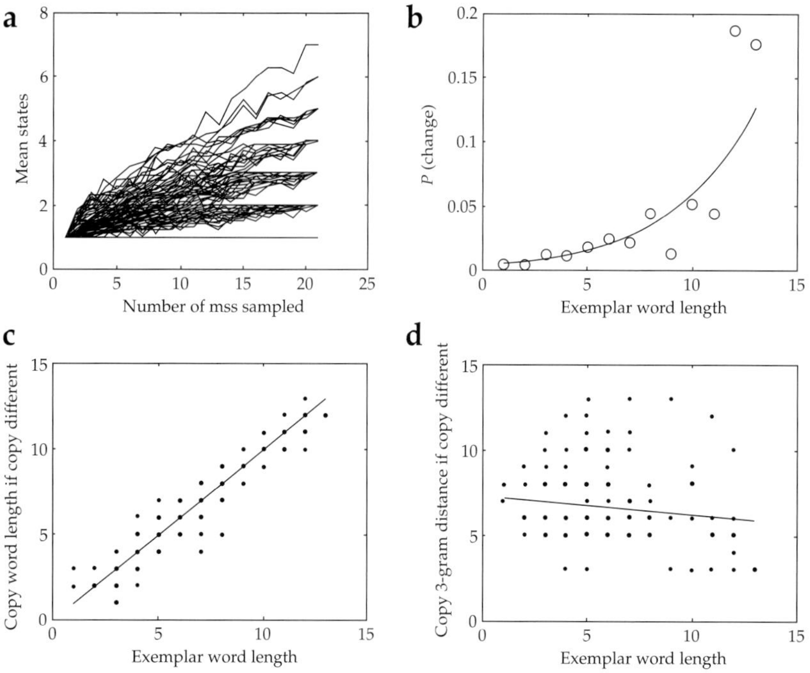


**Figure 6.1.** *Elements of text evolution in an artificial text tradition containing 21 manuscripts and 856 locations (characters), with 226 observations of different words in exemplar and copy at corresponding locations, out of a total of 16,332 exemplar-copy word pairs (Spencer* et al. *2004a). (a) The number of character states observed increases as more manuscripts are sampled. Each line connects the mean number of states for a single character over ten replicate resamplings of one to 21 manuscripts. (b) The probability* P *(change) that a word is changed during copying increases as word length increases. Each point is the probability of change estimated over all words of a given length in all manuscripts. The fitted line is a generalized linear model with quasibinomial errors, intercept –5.6 (standard error 0.23), slope 0.28 (standard error 0.04), parameters on log odds scale. The residual deviance is 25.85 on 11 degrees of freedom, scale parameter 2.15, deletion* F *test for slope* $F_{1,11} = 9.38$, $P = 0.011$. *(c) When exemplar and copy words are different, they remain about the same length. Each point is the length of a word in copy where the corresponding word in the exemplar was different. Small random numbers are added to both coordinates so the number of points is visible. The line is equal length in exemplar and copy. (d) When exemplar and copy words are different, the 3-gram distance between them is not much affected by exemplar word length. Each point is the 3-gram distance between an exemplar word and its copy, where the copy was different. We calculate 3-gram distance here as the number of 3-grams occurring in one but not both words, with two padding characters added at the start and end of each word to ensure equal representation of each letter. Small random numbers are added to both coordinates so the number of points is visible. The fitted line is a generalized linear model with Poisson errors, intercept 2.0 (standard error 0.06), slope –0.02 (standard error 0.01), parameters on log scale. The residual deviance is 124.99 on 224 degrees of freedom,* $\chi^2$ *for slope* = 3.33, P = 0.068.

bution (for example, the number of 3-grams different between a pair of different words cannot exceed the total number of 3-grams in both words).

Summarizing the empirical information, we can estimate the probability distribution of *n*-gram distance to an unobserved word, which is more or less independent of exemplar word length (Fig. 6.1d). We can estimate the distribution of length differences (among character states at a given location) and the probability of change from one character state to another (whether observed or unobserved), both of which are strongly dependent on exemplar word length (Figs. 6.1b & 6.1c). We could predict how often to choose an unobserved word using methods such as Good-Turing estimation (Orlitsky *et al.* 2003), which are widely used to predict the probabilities of unobserved events in language modelling (Manning & Schütze 1999, chap. 6). We still do not know what unobserved word to choose. We could sample from the *n*-gram and length difference distributions without specifying a particular unobserved word. Alternatively, we could use a corpus of relevant text to construct a large data base of possible but unobserved words with estimates of their frequencies. We have not yet experimented with these ideas.

Many textual critics prefer to work with regularized texts, in which apparently unimportant or misleading variants such as dialect and punctuation have been removed. This is equivalent to a binary division between a set of characters that are completely uninformative and a set of characters that are all equally informative. In contrast, the approach we are suggesting here, using models for the probability of change, will make much finer distinctions in quality of variants for stemmatic reconstruction. Many other factors such as position in the sentence, part of speech and rhyme may also be useful predictors of probability of change. We focused on word length because it is easy to measure and may have similar effects across languages and genres. Automatically identifying sentence boundaries, parts of speech and rhymes is much harder than measuring word length,

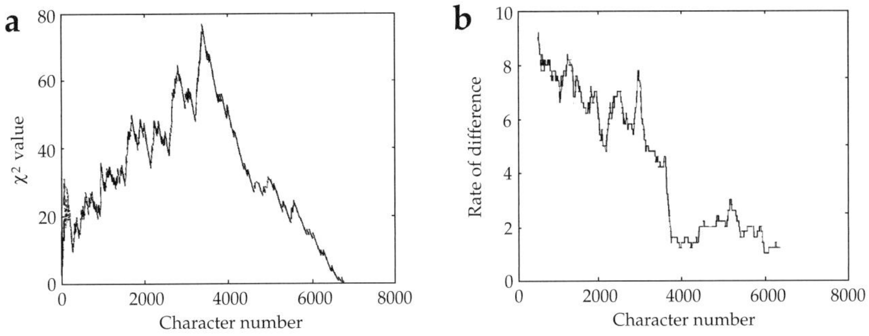


**Figure 6.2.** *Analysis of exemplar changes in the Prologue to The Wife of Bath's Tale. a) Plot of chi-squared values against the location in the text for the manuscripts El and Hg. The highest peak occurs at the location likely to be the site of manuscript recombination. b) Plot of the rate of differences between El and Hg (expressed as the percentage of differences in the region of coded text contained in a moving window of 501 characters) against the character number of the mid-point of the window.*

and the constraints on these features are likely to differ between works written in different languages, genres and metres. Nevertheless, the basic approach will be the same for any predictor.

In summary, we cannot model text evolution using the same kind of Markov chains as are used for DNA and protein sequences. The number of possible states is infinite for text data (where the states are words), but small and finite for DNA and protein sequences (where the states are nucleotides or amino acids). Instead, we could group words into length categories, because length is a good predictor of the probability of change. Where changes do occur, the word in the copy is usually of similar length to the word in the exemplar, and has similar *n*-grams. Predicting the probability of unobserved words is an unsolved problem.

### Modelling text evolution: reticulate evolution and contamination

Phylogenetic methods traditionally assumed that each entity is connected to each other by a single line of descent, thereby generating a treelike structure. In contrast, many biologists suspect that the transfer of genes between distantly-related organisms may have been important in the early evolution of life (e.g. Boucher *et al.* 2003). Detecting and representing this kind of reticulate evolution is difficult (Posada & Crandall 2001a,b; Posada 2002).

Similar problems occur in the study of text traditions. We have used methods such as split decomposition and reduced median networks to represent the relationships among manuscripts in contaminated text traditions (Barbrook *et al.* 1998; Spencer *et al.* 2004b). Another approach is to identify sections of text having tree-like transmission histories, and produce separate trees for each section. As described below (and Windram *et al.* 2005), we have attempted to devise a procedure by which scholars may be able easily to identify locations where it seemed likely that an exemplar change had occurred.

The Prologue to The Wife of Bath's Tale, part of *The Canterbury Tales* written by Chaucer in the late fourteenth century, was selected for this work. This tale consists of 830 lines of text and it is found in 58 manuscript copies. A CD-ROM of this tale containing full transcripts and facsimile copies of each of the manuscripts has already been published (Robinson 1996), facilitating access to information about any of the manuscripts used in the analysis. There is also a previous, non-quantitative study against which any results could be compared (Robinson 1997). The following procedure was developed for the detection of possible recombination sites.

Information on the text in each manuscript was coded as a NEXUS file, as in our previous studies, with one row per manuscript and one column (character) for each text location, corresponding to a word or short phrase. NEXUS is the standard format for phylogenetic analyses (Maddison *et al.* 1997). The NEXUS file was constructed by Peter Robinson (De Montfort University) from the transcripts in the CD-ROM using the COLLATE software package (Robinson 1994). The coded tale was split into quarters, and a neighbour-joining tree (Saitou & Nei 1987) was produced for each section using PAUP* (Swofford 2001). This enabled us to identify pairs of manuscripts that changed their relative affiliation throughout the text, e.g. Ellesmere (El) and Hengwrt (Hg). This pair of manuscripts is of considerable interest to scholars of *The Canterbury Tales*. They are both believed to have been written by the same scribe, and to be early copies of the *Tales*. It has been suggested that at least Hg was written soon after Chaucer's death in 1400 (Stubbs 2000).

A maximum chi-squared analysis was then performed for each pair of manuscripts. This was based on the maximum chi-squared method for detecting recombination in sequence data (Maynard Smith 1992). Originally, this was developed to detect the most likely site of DNA recombination, by comparing the observed number of differences between sequences with the expected number of differences if no recombination occurred. The calculation determines the chi-squared value for a break after each character in the

O lord the pyne I dide hem and the wo
Ful giltlees by goddes swete pyne
For as an hors I koude byte and whyne
I koude pleyne **and** I **was** in the gilt
Or ellis often tyme **I hadde** been spilt
Who so **that first to Mille comth** first grynt
I pleyned first so was oure werr stynt
They were ful glad to excusen hem **ful** blyue
Of thyng of which they neuere agilte hir lyue
Of wenches wolde I bern hem on honde
Whan that for syk **they myghte vnnethe** _ stonde
Yet tikled **I** his herte for that he
Wende that I hadde **had** of hym so greet chiertee
I swoor that _ my walkyng out by nyghte
Was for to espye wenches that he dighte
Vnder that colour hadde I many a myrthe
For al swich **wit is** yeuen vs in oure birthe
Deceite wepyng spynnyng god hath yeue
To wommen kyndely whil _ they may lyue
And thus of o thyng I auante me
At ende I hadde the **bet** in ech degree
By sleighte or force or by som maner thyng
As by continuel murmur or grucchyng
Namely abedde hadden they meschaunce
Ther wolde I chide and do hem no plesaunce
I wolde no lenger in the bed abyde
If that I felte his arm ouer my syde
Til he hadde maad his raunceon vn to me
Thanne wolde I suffre hym do his nycetee
And therfore euery man this tale I telle
Wynne who so may for al is for to selle
With empty hond men may none haukes lure
For wynnyng wolde I al his lust endure
And make me a feyned appetit
And yet in bacon hadde I neure delit
That made me that euere I wolde hem chyde
For thogh the Pope hadde seten hem bisyde
I wolde noght spare hem at hir owene bord
For by my trouthe I quytte hem word for word
As help me verray god omnipotent
Togh I right now sholde make my testament

**Figure 6.3.** *Section of the Hg manuscript in the region of possible exemplar change. Differences from El are marked. Places where an alternative word, or no word, is used in El are underlined and in bold. Where a word in El is not present in Hg, the underline has no text above it. Changes in word order are underlined with a broken line. Based on the transcription in Robinson (1996).*

sequence, with the highest value indicating the most likely site for recombination. A plot of chi-squared values against location in the text for the El/Hg pair (Fig. 6.2a) showed a clear maximum chi-squared value at character 3384, which corresponds with line 404 in the text. The probability of obtaining a maximum chi-squared value at least this large in the absence of a genuine break point is $1 \times 10^{-5}$.

We then plotted the rate of differences between the two manuscripts in a moving window (Fig. 6.2b). This indicates whether the two manuscripts become more or less similar to each other after the possible recombination point. For manuscripts El and Hg the plot showed that there was a decrease in the rate of differences (i.e. the manuscripts became more similar) in a region that corresponded with the location of the highest chi-squared value. The transcripts of the two manuscripts were then examined in the region of possible recombination (line 404) to see if the texts supported the results (Fig. 6.3). In the first half of the Prologue the two texts differ considerably, e.g. there are 16 differences between El and Hg in the 20 lines preceding line 404. However, there are no differences in the 20 lines immediately following line 404, and few changes thereafter.

Our results indicated that El becomes progressively more similar to Hg, with a sudden change of affiliation occurring at line 404, indicating a possible exemplar shift. These results were compared with Robinson's previous study (Robinson 1997), which states that 'After line 400, El changes character dramatically ... It is possible that for lines 420 onwards, El is actually based on the same exemplar as is Hg'. This indicates that the maximum chi-squared method gives plausible results (cf. criterion 2, evaluating text phylogenies).

Other methods have been suggested for detecting contamination in text traditions. For example, the shock waves approach (Wattel & van Mulken 1996) is based on visual inspection of plots of distances among all pairs of manuscripts. This is similar to the phylogenetic profiles method used for biological sequences (Weiller 1998). As originally implemented, neither method offers any statistical tests, although permutation tests are possible (Posada & Crandall 2001a; Posada 2002). To decide which approach is best, we need to evaluate the performance of these and other methods on real and simulated text traditions with shifts of exemplar at known locations.

## Conclusions

Phylogenetic methods are increasingly used to study the evolution of text traditions. We have shown that these methods perform well in simple cases where each text is descended from a single ancestor. Nevertheless, we do not currently have a realistic model of text evolution to underpin our analyses. Here, we suggested how it might be possible to develop such a model. A further complication is that many texts are descended from more than one ancestor. We have described one method for detecting points at which a text switches from one ancestor to another. In future, it will be interesting to compare the performance of different methods.

## Acknowledgements

We thank the Leverhulme Trust, the Daphne Jackson Trust, and the Arts and Humanities Research Board for support. Philippe Baret, Barbara Bordalejo, Anne-Catherine Lantin, Caroline Macé, Linne Mooney and Peter Robinson discussed this work with us.

## References

Barbrook, A.C., C.J. Howe, N. Blake & P. Robinson, 1998. The phylogeny of *The Canterbury Tales*. *Nature* 394, 839.

Boucher, Y., C.J. Douady, R.T. Papke, D.A. Walsh, M.E.R. Boudreau, C.L. Nesbø, R.J. Case & W.F. Doolittle, 2003. Lateral gene transfer and the origins of prokaryotic groups. *Annual Review of Genetics* 37, 283–328.

Cartlidge, N. ,2001. *The Canterbury Tales* and cladistics. *Neuphilologische Mitteilungen* 102, 135–50.

Crowson, R.A., 1982. Computers versus imagination in the reconstruction of phylogeny, in *Problems of Phylogenetic Reconstruction*, eds. K.A. Joysey & A.E. Friday. London: Academic Press, 245–55.

Deol, J.S., 2001. Text and lineage in early Sikh history: issues in the study of the Adi Granth. *Bulletin of the School of Oriental and African Studies* 64, 34–58.

Durbin, R., S. Eddy, A. Krogh & G. Mitchison, 1998. *Biological Sequence Analysis*. Cambridge: Cambridge University Press.

Felsenstein, J., 1981. Evolutionary trees from DNA sequences: a maximum likelihood approach. *Journal of Molecular Evolution* 17, 368–76.

Hanna, R., 2000. The application of thought to textual criticism in all modes — with apologies to A.E. Housman. *Studies in Bibliography* 53, 163–72.

Hillis, D.M., J.J. Bull, M.E. White, M.R. Badgett & I.J. Molineux, 1992. Experimental phylogenetics: generation of a known phylogeny. *Science* 255, 589–92.

Howe, C.J., A.C. Barbrook, M. Spencer, P. Robinson, B. Bordalejo & L.R. Mooney, 2001. Manuscript evolution. *Trends in Genetics* 17, 147–52.

Huelsenbeck, J.P., F. Ronquist, R. Nielsen & J.P. Bollback, 2001. Bayesian inference of phylogeny and its impact on evolutionary biology. *Science* 294, 2310–14.

Jones, A., 2001. The properties of a stemma: relating the manuscripts in two texts from *The Canterbury Tales*. *Parergon* 18, 35–53.

Kukich, K., 1992. Techniques for automatically correcting words in text. *ACM Computing Surveys* 24, 377–439.

Lantin, A.-C., P.V. Baret & C. Macé, 2004. Phylogenetic analysis of Gregory of Nazianzus' Homily 27. *Le poids des mots: Proceedings of the 7th International Conference on the Statistical Analysis of Textual Data*, Louvain-la-Neuve, 700–707.

Lee, A.R., 1989. Numerical taxonomy revisited: John Griffith, cladistic analysis and St. Augustine's *Quaestiones in Heptateuchem*. *Studia Patristica* 20, 24–32.

Li, W.-H., 1997. *Molecular Evolution*. Sunderland (MA): Sinauer Associates.

Maddison, D.R., D.L. Swofford & W.P. Maddison, 1997. NEXUS: an extensible file format for systematic information. *Systematic Biology* 46, 590–621.

Manning, C.D. & H. Schütze, 1999. *Foundations of Statistical Natural Language Processing*. Cambridge (MA): The MIT Press.

Maynard Smith, J., 1992. Analyzing the mosaic structure of genes. *Journal of Molecular Evolution* 34, 126–9.

Mink, G., 2000. Editing and genealogical studies: the New Testament. *Literary and Linguistic Computing* 15, 51–6.

Mooney, L.R., A.C. Barbrook, C.J. Howe & M. Spencer, 2001. Stemmatic analysis of Lydgate's 'Kings of England': a test case for the application of software developed for evolutionary biology to manuscript stemmatics. *Revue d'Histoire des Textes* 31, 275–97.

Nei, M., 1991. Relative efficiencies of different tree-making methods for molecular data, in *Phylogenetic Analysis of DNA Sequences*, eds. M.M. Miyamoto & J. Cracraft. New York (NY): Oxford University Press, 90–128.

Orlitsky, A., N.P. Santhanam & J. Zhang, 2003. Always Good Turing: asymptotically optimal probability estimation. *Science* 302, 427–31.

Pelli, D.G., B. Farell & D.C. Moore, 2003. The remarkable inefficiency of word recognition. *Nature* 423, 752–6.

Penny, D. & M.D. Hendy, 1985. The use of tree comparison metrics. *Systematic Zoology* 34, 75–82.

Platnick, N.I. & H.D. Cameron, 1977. Cladistic methods in textual, linguistic, and phylogenetic analysis. *Systematic Zoology* 26, 380–85.

Posada, D., 2002. Evaluation of methods for detecting recombination from DNA sequences: empirical data. *Molecular Biology and Evolution* 19, 708–17.

Posada, D. & K.A. Crandall, 2001a. Evaluation of methods for detecting recombination from DNA sequences: computer simulations. *Proceedings of the National Academy of Sciences of the USA* 98, 13,757–62.

Posada, D. & K.A. Crandall, 2001b. Intraspecific gene genealogies: trees grafting into networks. *Trends in Ecology and Evolution* 16, 37–45.

Robertson, A.M. & P. Willett, 1998. Applications of *n*-grams in textual information systems. *Journal of Documentation* 54, 48–69.

Robinson, D.M., D.T. Jones, H. Kishino, N. Goldman & J.L. Thorne, 2003. Protein evolution with dependence among codons due to tertiary structure. *Molecular Biology and Evolution* 20, 1692–704.

Robinson, P. (ed.), 1996. *Chaucer: the Wife of Bath's Prologue on CD-ROM*. Cambridge: Cambridge University Press.

Robinson, P.M.W., 1994. *Collate: Interactive Collation of Large Textual Traditions*. Oxford: Oxford University Centre for Humanities Computing.

Robinson, P., 1997. A stemmatic analysis of the fifteenth-century witnesses to The Wife of Bath's Prologue, in *The Canterbury Tales Project: Occasional Papers*, vol. II, eds. N. Blake & P. Robinson. London: Office for Humanities Communication Publications, 69–132.

Robinson, P.M.W. & R.J. O'Hara, 1996. Cladistic analysis of an Old Norse manuscript tradition, in *Research in Humanities Computing 4*, eds. S. Hockey & N. Ide. Oxford: Oxford University Press, 115–37.

Saitou, N. & M. Nei, 1987. The neighbor-joining method: a new method for reconstructing phylogenetic trees. *Molecular Biology and Evolution* 4, 406–25.

Salemans, B.J.P., 2000. *Building Stemmas with the Computer in a Cladistic, Neo-Lachmannian, Way*. Nijmegen: Katholieke Universiteit.

Searls, D.B., 2002. The language of genes. *Nature* 420, 211–17.

Spencer, M. & C.J. Howe, 2004. Collating texts using progressive multiple alignment. *Computers and the Humanities* 38, 253–70.

Spencer, M., E.A. Davidson, A.C. Barbrook & C.J. Howe, 2004a. Phylogenetics of artificial manuscripts. *Journal of Theoretical Biology* 227, 503–11.

Spencer, M., K. Wachtel & C.J. Howe, 2004b. Representing multiple pathways of textual flow in the Greek manuscripts of the Letter of James using reduced median networks. *Computers and the Humanities* 38, 1–14.

Stubbs, E. (ed.), 2000. *The Hengwrt Chaucer Digital Facsimile*. Leicester: Scholarly Digital Editions.

Swofford, D.L., 2001. *PAUP*. Phylogenetic Analysis Using Parsimony (*and other methods)*. Sunderland (MA): Sinauer Associates.

von Eschenbach, W., 1980. *Parzival*. London: Penguin Books.

Wattel, E. & M.J.P. van Mulken, 1996. Shock waves in text traditions: cardiograms of the mediaeval literature, in *Studies in Stemmatology*, eds. P. van Reenen & M. van Mulken. Amsterdam: John Benjamins Publishing Company, 105–21.

Weiller, G.F., 1998. Phylogenetic profiles: a graphical method for detecting genetic recombinations in homologous sequences. *Molecular Biology and Evolution* 15, 326–35.

Windram, H.F., M. Spencer & C.J. Howe, 2005. The identification of exemplar change in the Wife of Bath's prologue using the maximum chi-squared method. *Literary and Linguistic Computing* 20, 189–204.

# Chapter 7

# A Stochastic Model of Language Evolution that Incorporates Homoplasy and Borrowing

Tandy Warnow, Steven N. Evans, Donald Ringe & Luay Nakhleh

## 1. Introduction

The inference of evolutionary history, whether in biology or in linguistics, is aided by a carefully considered model of the evolutionary process and a reconstruction method which is expected to produce a reasonably accurate estimation of the true evolutionary history when the real data match the model assumptions and are of sufficient quantity. In molecular systematics (i.e. the inference of evolutionary histories from molecular data), much of the research effort has focused in two areas: first, the development of increasingly parameter-rich models of molecular sequence evolution, and second, the development of increasingly sophisticated software tools and algorithms for reconstructing phylogenies under these models. The plethora of software for reconstructing phylogenies from molecular data is staggering. By comparison, much less has been done in historical linguistics in terms of developing statistical models of character evolution or reconstruction methods, suggesting that there is perhaps much to be gained by doing so.

To date, although some models have been proposed for language evolution, all have failed in some significant ways. In particular, linguistic models either explicitly or implicitly have assumed that no homoplasy (i.e. parallel evolution and/or back-mutation) occurs (see for example Ringe *et al.* 2002; Taylor *et al.* 2000; Warnow 1997). Most, but not all, have not modelled borrowing between languages. In this paper, we go beyond earlier models by explicitly incorporating both homoplasy and borrowing into our model. We show that this model is not only quite rich, but reflects important properties of real linguistic characters. Our examination of phylogenetic inference under the model therefore has important ramifications for phylogenetic analyses of real data.

The paper is organized as follows. We present a model of language evolution that incorporates homoplasy in section 2. Computational issues involved with inferring phylogenetic trees under this model, including identifiability and calculating likelihood scores, are discussed in section 3; proofs of the mathematical results in this section are provided in an appendix. We then discuss how we can incorporate borrowing into our model for homoplasy, and discuss the issues for inferring evolution under both homoplasy and borrowing in section 4. We compare our model and its ramifications for phylogenetic analysis to biological models in section 5. We discuss the consequences for phylogenetic analysis in historical linguistics in section 6 and conclude in section 7 with a mention of a model similar to the homoplasy-free special case of ours that was proposed and investigated in (Mossel & Steel 2004) because of its rather simple theoretical properties.

## 2. A new model of language evolution on trees

Most of the models used in studies of language evolution explicitly or implicitly assume that evolution is treelike, and that linguistic characters evolve without homoplasy. We begin our discussion with a precise statement of what these assumptions mean.

### *2.1. The standard assumptions of language evolution*

The simplest models about language evolution are expressed in the following two statements:

- Evolution is treelike, i.e. the Stammbaum model applies.
- When a linguistic character changes its state, it changes to a new state not yet in the tree, i.e. there is no 'back-mutation' nor parallel evolution.

The first condition is understood in the linguistics community but the second condition is not quite as standard, and so it is worth discussing in greater detail.

The phenomenon of back-mutation and/or parallel evolution is called *homoplasy*. When there is no homoplasy in a character, then all changes of state for that character result in new states. When all the characters evolve without homoplasy down a tree, then the tree is called a *perfect phylogeny*, and each of the characters is said to be *compatible* on the tree.

When characters evolve without homoplasy, it is sometimes very easy to reconstruct the underlying unrooted tree, because each character yields definite information about the branching order within the tree. For example, if a character evolves so as to change only once in the tree, then that character defines a split of the leaves of the tree (i.e. the languages) into two parts, and that split is associated with the unique edge of the tree on which the character changes state. Characters that evolve in this way include practically unrepeatable phonological innovations, and are highly informative about evolutionary history.

The assumption that linguistic characters evolve without homoplasy is made implicitly in simulation studies (see McMahon & McMahon (2003) for one such paper), and was also made explicitly by Ringe & Warnow in their early work (Taylor *et al.* 2000) where they sought a tree on which all the characters were compatible. However, the pairing of these two assumptions, namely that evolution is treelike and that linguistic characters evolve without homoplasy (i.e. that perfect phylogenies exist) is too strong, as our analyses showed definitively that perfect phylogenies do not exist for our Indo-European (IE) data set.

One possible explanation for the inability to find perfect phylogenies is that the evolution isn't treelike, i.e. some contact between lineages must be inferred in order to explain the evolutionary process. In that case, the 'network model' makes sense, as described below. Non-treelike evolution is clearly realistic, since lexemes are transmitted between lineages. However, since sound changes can make the presence of such transmissions apparent, the character states that are assigned to lexemes that are borrowed are not identical (this is a direct consequence of the comparative method). Where reticulate evolution becomes problematic is when the borrowing is not detected, because then the comparative method will assign identical states to lexemes that are not actually cognate. Thus, although lexical characters are particularly vulnerable to borrowing, careful application of the comparative method can detect much — but not necessarily all — of the borrowing, and hence alleviate much of the problem involved in using lexical characters, at least with respect to this issue.

However, another possible explanation of the non-existence of perfect phylogenies is that characters may evolve with back-mutation or parallel evolution. Events of both types have been documented in linguistics; for instance, sound changes can occur repeatedly, resulting in phonological characters that exhibit parallel evolution (Ringe *et al.* 2002, 66–7), and a language can shift a semantic function from its morphology to its syntax, resulting in morphological characters that have back-mutations (see the discussion below).

Models that have incorporated borrowing into linguistic evolution while still assuming homoplasy-free evolution have been used in several simulation studies (McMahon & McMahon 2003) and in the inference of Indo-European evolution (Nakhleh *et al.* 2005). Such models thus explicitly assume that all incompatibilities of characters with the genetic tree must be explained by borrowing, since homoplasy is not permitted. Indeed, determining whether incompatibility is due to borrowing or homoplasy is one of the major challenges in historical linguistic reconstruction.

In order to make progress on this difficult question, we have begun by formulating a stochastic model of linguistic evolution that formally models homoplasy in ways that are consistent both with linguistic scholarship and with our own experience with Indo-European characters. We will show that inference of evolutionary trees is both theoretically possible and realistically feasible, even in the presence of homoplasy, provided that homoplasy can be identified and dealt with appropriately.

### 2.2. *Different types of linguistic characters*

There are three types of characters — lexical, morphological, and phonological. Here we assume that phonological characters are binary, and that all character state assignments are made on the basis of rigorous application of the Comparative Method (Hoenigswald 1960).

Homoplasy is an aspect of a character's evolution with respect to a particular set of languages, whereby a state for that character arises more than once in the evolutionary history of that set of languages. There are essentially two types of homoplasy: back-mutation (which means the reappearance of an ancestral state) and parallel evolution (whereby two languages have the same state, but no common ancestor of those languages has that state). Examples of both types of homoplasy exist in language evolution.

Homoplasy is possible for any type of linguistic character, although some characters are less likely to evolve with homoplasy than others. Our own study of linguistic characters in Indo-European suggests that true homoplasy (meaning either parallel evolution or back-mutation, not simple incompatibility due to borrowing) is very rare for morphological characters (although see the discussion later), but very likely for phonological characters and somewhat frequent for lexical characters. For example, phonological characters, which are frequently binary, can exhibit parallel evolution if the sound change is at all natural; loss of the consonant *h* is an example of such a sound change character that can evolve with parallel evolution. However, if phonological characters are based on phonemic mergers they do not exhibit back-mutation, since reversals of phonemic mergers do not occur.

Interestingly, linguistic scholarship makes it possible in many cases to identify the *homoplastic states* (that is, states which can arise more than once) based upon linguistic scholarship alone (i.e. before any phylogenetic analysis is done, and without reference to an estimated phylogeny), at least for morphological and phonological characters within the well-studied Indo-European family. For instance, the loss of /h/ in various Greek dialects and in late Latin is an obvious parallel development (Buck 1955; Sihler 1995); so is the merger of long /a:/ and long /o:/ in Germanic and in Slavic (but not in Baltic, which is more closely related to Slavic) (Brugmann 1897); among lexical characters, the use of 'nursery terms' originally meaning 'dad' as the usual words for 'father' in Gothic and Hittite must have occurred independently (Pokorny 1959), since those languages were never in contact at any time after their ancestors began to diverge. The ability to identify homoplastic states *in advance* of a phylogenetic reconstruction will allow us to infer the evolutionary history both accurately and efficiently, with ambiguity in the phylogenetic estimation only when there is not enough morphological and phonological character data to fully resolve the tree (or when we are unable to identify accurately the homoplastic states).

In addition, the number of homoplastic states is very small, at most one for either morphological or phonological characters, and lexical characters too seem to have a very small number of homoplastic states (most of the time only one, but in principle this number could be unbounded). For some morphological characters, homoplasy can be a back-mutation to the state of 'absence' or in parallel via mutations to a 'default' state. (We are grateful to Bill Poser for reminding us of the latter phenomenon.) An example of the former is the superlative in *-ism̥mo- (Brugmann 1906), which is clearly an innovation of Italo-Celtic that was subsequently lost in many Romance languages. Examples of the latter are scarce in archaic Indo-European languages but easier to find in their more modern descendants; for instance, the spread of the second-person singular ending /-st/ from the present indicative (where it originated) to the past and the subjunctive can be demonstrated to have occurred independently in English and German (Campbell 1962; Lühr 1984).

Phonological characters have homoplasy when the sound change occurs sufficiently naturally for it to arise more than once; in this case, the state indicating presence is the homoplastic state. In addition to the examples noted above, one can cite the merger of voiced and breathy-voiced stops in various clades of IE (Brugmann 1897), the merger of 'palatal' and 'velar' stops in a different but overlapping set of clades (including Hittite but *not* the Luvian subgroup of Anatolian) (Melchert 1987), and so on.

Thus, homoplastic states (ones that can arise more than once) within morphological and phonological characters can be easily identified, at least when the language family is well understood (even if its phylogeny is still unclear). On the other hand, the case of lexical characters is somewhat more difficult: even for the well-studied Indo-European family, accurate identification of homoplastic states without a given (and robust) phylogeny is not necessarily easy.

### 2.3. *Modelling character evolution*

We now state our parametric stochastic model of evolution.

In order to simplify the exposition, we will adopt the terminological convention that the term *homoplastic state* means a state that can appear homoplastically (i.e. one that can arise more than once in the tree). Thus the designation of a state as homoplastic is a feature of the model rather than the data: a homoplastic state may or may not appear in a homoplastic event in a particular random realization of the model (that is, in a particular data set).

We will assume that there is at most one homoplastic state per character (it is trivial to extend the analyses and proofs to the case where there is a fixed finite number of homoplastic states), that each homoplastic state can be identified before a phylogenetic analysis of the data, and that the probability of each substitution depends only upon the type of states that are involved (i.e. whether the states are homoplastic or not).

We now define a very general model of individual site evolution for linguistic characters. We will associate a stochastic substitution matrix to each combination of edge in the tree and each character, as follows. We denote the homoplastic state by $h^*$ for 'homoplastic', and the non-homoplastic states by $n$. The stochastic substitution matrix for the edge $e$ and character $c$ is defined by the following quintet:

- $p_{e,c}(n,h^*)$: the probability of a substitution of a non-homoplastic state with the homoplastic state.

- $p_{e,c}(n,n')$: the probability of a substitution of a non-homoplastic state with a new non-homoplastic state.
- $p_{e,c}(n,n)$: the probability of not changing, given that we start with a non-homoplastic state.
- $p_{e,c}(h^*,h^*)$: the probability of not changing, given that we start with the homoplastic state.
- $p_{e,c}(h^*,n)$: the probability of a substitution of the homoplastic state with a non-homoplastic state.

Thus $p_{e,c}(n,h^*) + p_{e,c}(n,n') + p_{e,c}(n,n) = 1$ and $p_{e,c}(h^*,h^*) + p_{e,c}(h^*,n) = 1$. Note that this is a very general model, since we do not assume that different characters have the same stochastic substitution matrices on any given edge, nor do we assume that these substitution matrices cannot change as we move across the tree. In this sense the model is highly unconstrained. Note also that we allow states to be 'sinks', so that once a language is in that state there is no possibility of changing state (that is, we allow $p_{e,c}(h^*,h^*) = 1$ or $p_{e,c}(n,n) = 1$).

*2.3.1. Modelling how different characters can evolve differently*

How we allow variation between characters in this model involves issues that are familiar in biological phylogenetics. Do we want to assume that the evolution along an edge results from the operation of a dynamic process that differs from character to character only by the rate with which substitutions occur? That is, do we want to impose the analogue of the rates-across-sites assumption from biology (see Evans & Warnow (2004) for a discussion of the rates-across-sites assumption and an extensive list of references)? Or do we want to only make the minimum assumption that all sites evolve down the same tree? As we will see, for the conditions we assume — namely, that we can identify the homoplastic states — we do not need to make any assumptions constraining how characters can vary in their evolutionary processes in order to be able to reconstruct the tree. This is a surprising result that distinguishes our model from other models which do not explicitly assume the existence of sufficient homoplasy-free states.

*2.3.2. How the model works for different character types*

There are two different types of characters we will consider: those which represent the presence or absence of a given feature (phonological characters are the main example of this type), and those for which there is an unbounded number of possible homoplasy-free states.

*Characters indicating presence/absence:* For the first type of character (which reflects our binary phonological characters), the two possible states represent presence or absence, and evolution proceeds from absence to presence. Sound changes can occur more than once, but once a sound change has occurred in the tree, all nodes below the edge on which the sound change occurs will be recognizable as having undergone the sound change (i.e. parallel evolution is possible, but back-mutation is impossible). Thus, $p_{e,c}(h^*,n) = 0$ and $p_{e,c}(h^*,h^*) = 1$. We will make one quite mild additional assumption, which is that for such characters, $0 < p_{e,c}(n,h^*) < 1$ for all edges $e$ in the tree.

*All other characters:* For other types of characters (i.e. morphological and lexical), each state represents a different form for the character (semantic slot for the lexical characters), and hence there is an unbounded number of states for these characters. Morphological characters and lexical characters can have both types of homoplasy (back-mutation and parallel evolution), but in both cases we assume that the homoplastic states can be identified. (We acknowledge that in the case of lexical characters this identification may not be as reliable as in the cases of morphological or phonological characters; our mathematical analysis that follows addresses the case where we are able to make this identification.) We again make a mild assumption, which is that $0 < p_{e,c}(n,n') < 1$ for all edges $e$ in the tree.

## 3. Inference of evolutionary history under our model

We will now discuss issues involved with inferring evolutionary history under our models, beginning with the theoretical issue of identifiability, and then addressing actual methods for inferring evolutionary histories.

### *3.1. Identifiability*

The first issue is whether the model is *identifiable*. In essence, this is a question that asks whether it is possible to uniquely determine the model, as well as its associated parameters, from the probability of each possible pattern at the leaves. We leave that general question open, but show a positive answer to the fundamental question of whether the evolutionary tree (albeit not the location of the root nor the parameters of the evolutionary process) is identifiable:

**Theorem 3.1.** *The model tree (modulo the placement of the root and the parameters of evolution) is identifiable, provided that we are able to identify correctly the homoplastic states.*

The proof of this theorem is given in the appendix.

### 3.2. *Algorithms for inferring evolution under our model*

Because the model tree is identifiable, this means that it is possible to reconstruct, with complete accuracy, the underlying (unrooted) evolutionary tree for a language family — provided that there are enough data, we use appropriate methods, and the family evolves under the model. Note that this statement does not imply the ability to estimate to any degree of accuracy other features about the evolutionary history — such as the location of the root, the parameters $p_{e,c}(\cdot,\cdot)$, dates at internal nodes if we assume a model in which there is a functional dependence between the $p_{e,c}(\cdot,\cdot)$ and such dates, etc.

Also, we need to qualify our statement about completely accurate reconstruction of the tree. Mathematically, having data on even an infinite number of characters may not be enough to reconstruct the tree perfectly if, as we consider more characters, the corresponding rates of linguistic evolution become slower or faster too precipitously. For example, suppose that we actually have an infinite number of lexical or morphological characters $c$, and for some edge $e$, we have $\sum_c (1 - p_{e,c}(h^*,h^*)) < \infty$ and $\sum_c (1 - p_{e,c}(n,n)) < \infty$. Then by a standard result from probability theory (the Borel-Cantelli lemma), with probability one only finitely many characters will exhibit a change of state on the edge $e$, and there is positive probability that no characters exhibit a change on $e$. In particular, if this state of affairs holds for every edge, then the data will 'freeze' after a certain point and all leaves will exhibit the same state for all but a finite number of characters — implying that we are unable to reconstruct the tree with certainty. Similarly, if $\sum_c p_{e,c}(h^*,h^*) < \infty$ and $\sum_c p_{e,c}(n,n) < \infty$ for an edge $e$, then (again by the Borel-Cantelli lemma) with probability one all but finitely many characters will exhibit a change on edge $e$ and there is positive probability that every character exhibits a change on $e$. If this state of affairs holds for every edge, then with probability one only finitely many characters will be informative and for the remaining characters the languages at the leaves of the tree will appear to be completely unrelated.

Note that this problem also occurs for models proposed for molecular evolution, and so this issue is not particular to the linguistic model we propose. However, if such pathologies are not present, then under our model algorithms for reconstructing phylogenetic trees can be designed which will yield reliable estimates of the true tree, as we now show.

#### *3.2.1. Algorithms for inferring evolution under morphological or lexical characters*

For morphological and lexical characters (i.e. those characters with an unbounded number of *possible* homoplasy-free states), there are two simple algorithms which will reconstruct the true tree. Each uses knowledge of the homoplasy-free states in order to infer explicit constraints on the topology of the underlying tree. The first method infers bipartitions on the leaf-set and is the simplest algorithmically, but also requires (probabilistically) more data in order to resolve the tree completely. The second method infers quartet trees and is algorithmically more complex, but can use the data more efficiently.

*Algorithm 1 (bipartition-based):* The first algorithm seeks bipartitions defined by two distinct homoplasy-free states. If a character exhibits two homoplasy-free states and no other states in the family, then (under the assumptions of the model) the bipartition it defines on the set of languages corresponds to an edge in the tree. We therefore just collect all such bipartitions, and use standard polynomial time methods for constructing the minimal tree consistent with all the bipartitions (see Gusfield 1990). Given enough characters of this type to infer each edge on which there is a change, we can reconstruct the true tree for the language family.

*Algorithm 2 (quartet-based):* Consider a character in which states 1 and 2 are known not to be homoplastic. Suppose languages $A$ and $B$ both have state 1 and languages $C$ and $D$ both have state 2. In this case, the only possible form for the tree on $A$, $B$, $C$, $D$ is $AB \mid CD$ (i.e. there must be at least one edge separating the languages $A$ and $B$ from $C$ and $D$). The algorithm proceeds as follows. First, we examine each character in turn, and for each pair of non-homoplastic states, we construct the trees on four-language sets using this rule. Then, after we have computed the set of all such quartet tree constraints, we seek a tree that is consistent with all the input constraints. Finding the tree that meets all the constraints is a computational problem that is in general NP-hard to solve (i.e. hard to solve efficiently) it is equivalent to perfect phylogeny which is NP-hard (Bodlaender *et al.* 1992; Steel 1992), but under some conditions is solvable in a time that is polynomial in the number of languages (i.e. 'computationally feasible'). In particular, if the correct subtree is given for all quartets of languages, then the problem is solvable in polynomial time.

#### *3.2.2. Algorithms for phonological characters*

There are two approaches for using binary phonological characters. The first is to use linguistic knowledge to screen the data set and remove all characters which have evolved with any homoplasy. This is the traditional approach, which tries to only use those phonological characters that represent very unusual sound changes, unlikely to evolve in parallel (Hoenigswald

1960). The use of complex phonological characters is an example of this type — any single simple phonological character might be likely to evolve in parallel, but the conjunction of independent ones together might represent a highly unusual such character. For instance, the sequence of sound changes (a) Grimm's Law (Streitberg 1896), (b) Verner's Law (Streitberg 1896), (c) shift of stress to initial syllables, and (d) merger of unstressed /e/ with /i/ unless /r/ follows immediately — occurring in that order — is a complex phonological character which is probably sufficient to validate the Germanic clade even without further evidence (Ringe 2005). (On the other hand, each of the sound changes of this complex character can be shown to have close parallels elsewhere: (a) in Armenian, (b) in late Middle English, (c) in Italic, Celtic, Latvian, etc., and (d) in Hittite and various other languages.)

Provided that such a screening can be done, phonological characters can then be quite useful for inferring evolution, since each then represents a binary split that must hold for the true tree.

Analyzing unscreened phonological characters can also be done, using the technique for estimating evolutionary distances we provide in the appendix, and applying methods such as neighbour joining (Saitou & Nei 1987) which are guaranteed to be correct on *tree-like* distances (also called *additive* distances). Such an approach is guaranteed to be correct, but the conditions under which the approach holds are not necessarily realistic. The conditions for correct reconstruction of the true tree include that there be a fair abundance of phonological characters, and that they all be drawn from the same distribution. That is, unlike the case of either morphological or lexical characters, we cannot use any individual phonological character to yield information about the evolutionary tree, and instead must use the aggregate information among all the phonological characters. Therefore, all the characters must actually be essentially identical in their evolutionary process — a condition we do not impose on morphological or lexical characters. They can have different *rates* of evolution, but the rates of evolution must be drawn from a distribution which we can estimate from the data. These are strong conditions, and will not necessarily hold in practice. (Such issues arise in most statistical models — and in particular, in most statistical models that are used in molecular systematics.)

## 4. Reticulate evolution in linguistics

In this section we explain how we model borrowing between languages, using phylogenetic *networks*. When there is no contact between languages after they have diverged, the Stammbaum model can be used to describe the evolution of the languages. In this case, a rooted tree is used to model how languages evolve from a common ancestor. However, when there is contact between two languages after they have diverged, a different type of model is needed. One such approach, which is appropriate when an underlying tree (the so-called *genetic* tree) can still be reasonably defined, is a *network* model. In this case, additional edges, representing contact between language communities that co-exist in time and are geographically proximate, are added to the rooted tree. These additional edges indicate the flow of linguistic characters between two groups, and hence are bi-directional (since the transmission of characters can go both ways, in general).

The contact edges are actually pairs of directed edges, one directed edge for each of the two orientations. Every node in the network (other than the root) has a unique parent node, but may also *borrow* a state (i.e. receive a state, and replace its current state with the new state) from a neighbour, to whom it is connected by contact edges. We make two mild assumptions: first, that no state changes occur on a contact edge, and second, that no node in the tree has more than one contact edge incident with it, and so has at most one neighbour.

An important issue in modelling linguistic evolution using networks is whether we will allow a language to inherit a state for a character, as well as borrow a state for that character from one of its neighbours, without replacing its inherited state by the borrowed state. In this paper we only allow replacement rather than allowing the two states to co-exist; thus, we do not allow polymorphism (two or more states for a character in a language) to occur as a result of borrowing. Thus, we assume that the evolutionary process operates first genetically, so that each node receives its state from its genetic parent, but that state will be replaced if the node borrows a state from a neighbour.

This assumption allows us to assert that each character evolves down a tree contained within the network, since we can define the tree by picking, for each node of the network, the node from which it obtains its state (either by inheritance or by borrowing). Thus, every character has a treelike evolution, even if the tree on which it evolves is not the genetic tree. (If the character evolves without any borrowing, then its tree will be the genetic tree, and otherwise its tree will include one or more contact edges, and hence differ from the genetic tree.)

The parameters associated with the evolutionary process involved in borrowing determine the relative probabilities of each character to be borrowed, as well as the degree of contact of each borrowing edge. Thus, we will have the parameter $\kappa_e$, where $e$ is a directed contact edge, indicating the probability of transmission via contact in that direction of the most easily transmitted character. We also have the parameter $\pi_c$ for a character $c$, which determines its probability of being borrowed. Therefore, the probability of character $c$ being transmitted on edge $e$ is $\pi_c \times \kappa_e$. These parameters allow us to determine for a given character $c$, the probability of the character evolving down each of the trees contained within the network.

Since every character evolves down a tree contained within the network, and we have described the process by which the tree on which the character evolves is chosen, it suffices to describe the evolutionary process on trees. More generally, it is straightforward to combine any given model of treelike evolution with this reticulate evolution model, since each character evolves in a treelike fashion on some tree contained within the network (in statistical parlance, our model is a *mixture* of treelike models).

However, inferring an accurate reticulate evolutionary scenario presents several difficulties; only some simple situations can be readily handled (in particular, we can infer a network with one contact edge under this model, since such networks are defined by their collections of bipartitions, but this is not generally true). In order to extend the inference to be able to handle more borrowing, it may be necessary to identify which characters evolve on the same evolutionary tree within the network. When this can be done, then if there are enough characters to determine each of the trees contained within the network, the network itself may be identified (under some conditions) from its constituent trees. However, determining the network from its constituent trees is not a trivial matter, though some cases can be handled efficiently (see Nakhleh 2004). On the other hand, the assumption that we can determine which characters evolve on the same tree is potentially unrealistic. Hence, inference under a model that allows both borrowing and homoplasy may be fairly challenging. Eliminating one of these two factors — borrowing or homoplasy — certainly makes inference much easier.

## 5. Comparison with models of molecular evolution

The model we present here is a fairly simple model which imposes one major assumption (the ability to detect homoplastic states) but is otherwise highly unconstrained. In particular, we allow characters to evolve without any common mechanism, assuming only that they evolve down the same tree. Under this model, we are able to show identifiability, linear time likelihood calculations, and most importantly, inference of the underlying (unrooted) evolutionary tree that is efficient with respect to data and with respect to running time.

By comparison, all models of molecular evolution that are in use make strong assumptions about the common mechanisms governing the different characters; without such strong assumptions, identifiability is lost, and it becomes impossible to reconstruct the true underlying tree from even infinite data.

Since some of the interest in phylogenetic reconstruction for historical linguistics has been for dating internal nodes, a few additional remarks are in order. Our discussion of what is achievable without imposing a common mechanism model shows that we can reconstruct the underlying unrooted tree, but not the parameters of the model. If dating of internal nodes is desired, much more information about the evolutionary processes is needed; in particular, the different characters in the data set must be assumed to evolve under a common model with either the same quintet of probabilities for all edges, or quintets that are related under a rates-across-sites model, with a known (or estimable) distribution of rates. These are very strong requirements, and may not hold in practice. Making these assertions with any degree of confidence is probably beyond what can be done at this date; inferring dates without having a basis for making these assertions is therefore potentially quite problematic. Indeed, it may be best to avoid making such inferences until the validity of assertions along these lines can be evaluated.

## 6. Consequences for phylogenetic analysis in linguistics

Inference of evolutionary history under our model rests upon being able to identify homoplastic states, since this allows us to reconstruct the true tree (given enough data) without having to remove any characters from the data set. In practice, several issues complicate this issue. The first is that even in the case where all the homoplastic states can be identified prior to the phylogenetic analysis, the presence of borrowing can make the inference of evolution difficult, except when the total amount of borrowing is quite low. Therefore, characters that are resistant to borrowing and for which homoplastic states are identifiable, will be much more useful in a phylogenetic analysis. This means that morphological characters are the most valuable, since they are most resistant to borrowing, have a very low incidence of homoplasy, and the homoplastic states (when they exist) are most easily identified, especially in archaic Indo-European languages (Meillet 1925). The second issue is that the identification of homoplastic states requires a very thoroughly trained and knowledgeable historical linguist, and that even the most skilled linguist may not be able to accurately identify all the homoplastic states. Finally, insufficient data present the problem of incomplete resolution within a phylogenetic analysis. Therefore, in practice, phylogenetic analyses within historical linguistics are likely to remain somewhat ambiguous, whether due to insufficient data or insufficient identification of homoplastic states.

Note that this discussion assumes that all characters are kept, and none are removed from the data set. What about the traditional approach in which the data are screened, and all characters suspected of homoplasy are deleted before the phylogenetic analysis (Hoenigswald 1960; Garde 1961)? This approach is controversial in part because of its potential to be biased (i.e. it may be that the characters are not really homoplastic so much as inconsistent with a presumed phylogeny), but in any event once a data set is modified through this process, the resultant *screened* data require somewhat different handling than our methods described in this paper. In particular, our approach for phonological data assumes that the characters evolve identically and independently. Once the character set is modified through this process, while the independence assumption will still hold, the identical distribution of character evolution will not necessarily still hold. Thus, the proposed technique for analyzing phonological characters cannot be applied in this case. Instead, since the characters will be presumed to now evolve without homoplasy (assuming all characters that are homoplastic have been successfully identified and deleted), the traditional approach of treating each binary phonological character as being homoplasy-free can be used. Thus, screening data for homoplasy, and deleting all such characters, can be applied successfully (although great care must be exercised not to delete characters that simply do not agree with one's assumptions), but phylogeny reconstruction on such modified data sets requires different techniques.

This commentary reflects the different issues involved in analyzing each type of data. Lexical characters, being the most easily borrowed, and having the most difficult-to-detect homoplastic states, are the most difficult to use (Porzig 1954). Phonological characters, on the other hand, are somewhat more interesting to discuss — they are frequently homoplastic, but homoplasy in phonological characters is relatively easily identified; while traditional methods may eliminate all phonological characters suspected of homoplasy, this paper shows how to properly analyze the full set of phonological characters without deleting suspicious characters from the data set. Morphological characters, being the most resistant to both borrowing and homoplasy, however, are likely to be the most valuable for phylogenetic analysis of languages.

In practice, we must also consider whether the model fits the data, and whether we will have enough data (meaning enough independent characters) in order to obtain a sufficiently accurate estimate of evolution. The assumptions of the model may, of course, not hold for the data set in question — the most difficult aspect to ensure is that we can identify the homoplastic character states for every character. This requires a great deal of linguistic competence, and also a great deal of knowledge of the particular family, and even then may not be guaranteed to be correct. Hence, from a practical standpoint, this is still a problem area. Finally, if a tree does not fit the data set, so that contact must be inferred, we can guarantee success but only in a somewhat limited way: if the evolutionary history does not include too much borrowing (specifically, too many contact edges), we should still be able to infer the evolutionary history. Quantifying the limits of how much borrowing can be allowed is part of our ongoing research.

## 7. Related work

The research most closely related to our work is (Mossel & Steel 2004), which studies a no-common-mechanism model of evolution in which there is no homoplasy. This model is mathematically equivalent to the special case of ours that obtains when homoplasy is not allowed. The authors present a reconstruction method using quartets similar to the one we described, but improve upon it by using the observation that not all quartets are necessary to determine the tree. They give a precise quantification of when it is possible to reconstruct the tree with high probability very efficiently (in terms of the amount of data required). Their analysis can be carried over to our somewhat more general situation to give the following result.

**Theorem 7.1.** *Suppose that the tree* T *is binary and has* n *leaves (that is, there are* n *languages). Assume further that there are constants* $0 < a < b < 1$ *such that* $a \leq p_{e,c}(n,n') \leq b$ *for all edges e and characters* c. *Then for any given* $0 < \varepsilon < 1$ *there are constants* $\gamma$ *and* $\delta$ *depending on* a, b, $\varepsilon$ *such that if the number of characters is at least* $\gamma + \delta \log n$, *then the tree can be correctly reconstructed from the data with probability at least* $1 - \varepsilon$. *Moreover, there is a polynomial-time (in* n*) algorithm for the reconstruction.*

## 8. Conclusions

In this paper we have presented a new model of linguistic character evolution that allows for homoplasy and borrowing between languages. We have shown that both morphological and lexical characters are sufficient to identify the true tree, even without a rates-across-sites assumption, provided that we can identify homoplastic states and the amount of borrowing is limited. We have also provided a new technique for analyzing phonological characters, which allows us to keep characters that evolve with homoplasy, and which will also identify the true tree provided that all phonological characters evolve identically and independently. Thus, our research extends the current models of linguistic character evolution and provides new techniques for analyzing linguistic data. We have also provided an initial attempt for the inference of reticulate (non-tree) evolution in historical linguistics.

It is worth noting that our research is an extension of linguistic methodology, rather than a radical departure; the techniques we propose are consistent with existing techniques, while allowing for better use of the available data. Furthermore, the research also provides a mathematical explanation for the belief within the historical linguistic research community that the choice of data is extremely important, and that morphological and phonological characters in general are better than lexical characters with respect to phylogeny reconstruction.

## 9. Appendix

### *9.1. The model*

We begin with a summary of the model of evolution. The graphical component of the model is a rooted phylogenetic network $N$, which is a rooted tree $T$ along with contact edges, where the presence of a contact edge represents the assumption that there is contact between two language communities at a given point in time. Thus, we always work with pairs of contact edges, one edge in each of the two orientations, between two nodes in $T$, and each of these individual directed edges $e = (v,w)$ is associated with a parameter $\kappa_e$ which is the probability of transmission of character states from $v$ to $w$. Note that $\kappa_{(w,v)}$ may not be equal to $\kappa_{(v,w)}$. Note also that because contact edges can only take place between nodes that are able to co-exist, not all networks defined as unions of rooted trees with contact edges are feasible — certain additional constraints must also exist. Thus, while it is not necessary otherwise to incorporate time into the model, we may also require that the nodes of the tree be associated with a date, so that these dates decrease as you move from the root towards the leaves, and so that contact edges exist only between nodes that have the same date.

The model also is equipped with a set of characters, and a probability distribution on the set. Thus, each site evolves under a random process, selected at random (under this distribution) from the set. Each character in the set is equipped with a probability distribution for the state type (i.e. homoplastic or non-homoplastic) at the root of the tree, and a collection of the transition probabilities (the $p_{e,c}(\cdot,\cdot)$ parameters) between the two types of states for each edge in the tree. Letting $h^*$ denote the unique homoplastic state for a given character and $n$ denote a non-homoplastic state, these transition probabilities are given by $p_{e,c}(n,n)$, $p_{e,c}(n,h^*)$, $p_{e,c}(n,n')$, $p_{e,c}(h^*,h^*)$ and $p_{e,c}(h^*,n)$. Each character $c$ is also equipped with a relative probability $\pi_c$ of being borrowed, so that the probability that character $c$ is transmitted across a borrowing edge $e$ is $\pi_c \kappa_e$.

*Notes:* In our discussion earlier we discussed how the parameters of the different types of characters might be constrained by their type; thus, for example, since binary phonological characters have only two states — one of which is non-homoplastic and the other potentially homoplastic — we would have $p_{e,c}(n,n') = 0$ for any phonological character on any edge $e$. The description given here is just the more general one. Note also that this model, as described, is a linguistic equivalent of the *no-common-mechanism* model of Tuffley & Steel (1997).

In order to fully specify this model, we need to delineate the actual collection of non-homoplastic states and then specify the precise mechanism for picking from the non-homoplastic states when a substitution is to result in such a state. The requirement that any change to a non-homoplastic state always results in a new state forces the set of such states to be uncountable. Since we are treating all non-homoplastic states as being on an equal footing, it suffices to label the set of non-homoplastic states by any nice uncountable set such as the unit interval and to pick a state according to the uniform probability distribution whenever a substitution is to result in a non-homoplastic state.

### *9.2. A dynamic form of the model*

In other stochastic models for character evolution in both linguistic and biological phylogenetics, the substitution probabilities for an edge are derived from the net effect of a continuous dynamic substitution process occurring along the edge — typically a Markov chain. We can also introduce such a structure into our framework as follows.

Now each edge $e$ for character $c$ will have a *length* $t_{e,c}$ and we imagine a rate one Poisson process of substitution events running for 'time' $t_{e,c}$, so that the expected number of substitution events on the edge is $t_{e,c}$.

What happens at each substitution event is determined by a quintuple of probabilities $q_{e,c}(h^*,h^*)$, $q_{e,c}(h^*,n)$, $q_{e,c}(n,h^*)$, $q_{e,c}(n,n)$, and $q_{e,c}(n,n')$, where $q_{e,c}(h^*,h^*) + q_{e,c}(h^*,n) = 1$ and $q_{e,c}(n,h^*) + q_{e,c}(n,n) + q_{e,c}(n,n') = 1$. The interpretation of, say, $q_{e,c}(n,h^*)$ is that it is the probability that a given substitution event will result in a change from a non-homplastic state $n$ to the unique homoplastic state $h^*$.

If $q_{e,c}(h^*,h^*) \neq 0$ or $q_{e,c}(n,n) \neq 0$, then we can have substitution events that are 'spurious' in the sense that they don't actually result in any change in the state of the character.

In order to derive the corresponding quintuple $p_{e,c}(\cdot,\cdot)$, we first observe that if we combine all of the non-homoplastic states into a single state, then the 'clumped' evolution is still Markovian and is just a two state Markov chain with rate matrix (that is, infinitesimal generator matrix)

$$\begin{pmatrix} -q_{e,c}(h^*,n) & q_{e,c}(h^*,n) \\ q_{e,c}(n,h^*) & -q_{e,c}(n,h^*) \end{pmatrix}$$

We can explicitly diagonalize this matrix and hence exponentiate it in closed form to get

$$p_{e,c}(h^*,h^*) = \frac{q_{e,c}(n,h^*) + \exp(-t_{e,c}(q_{e,c}(h^*,n) + q_{e,c}(n,h^*)))q_{e,c}(h^*,n)}{q_{e,c}(h^*,n) + q_{e,c}(n,h^*)}$$

$$p_{e,c}(h^*,n) = \frac{q_{e,c}(h^*,n) - \exp(-t_{e,c}(q_{e,c}(h^*,n) + q_{e,c}(n,h^*)))q_{e,c}(h^*,n)}{q_{e,c}(h^*,n) + q_{e,c}(n,h^*)}$$

$$p_{e,c}(n,h^*) = \frac{q_{e,c}(n,h^*) - \exp(-t_{e,c}(q_{e,c}(h^*,n) + q_{e,c}(n,h^*)))q_{e,c}(n,h^*)}{q_{e,c}(h^*,n) + q_{e,c}(n,h^*)}$$

$$p_{e,c}(n,n) + p_{e,c}(n,n') = \frac{q_{e,c}(h^*,n) + \exp(-t_{e,c}(q_{e,c}(h^*,n) + q_{e,c}(n,h^*)))q_{e,c}(n,h^*)}{q_{e,c}(h^*,n) + q_{e,c}(n,h^*)}$$

To complete the computation of the quintuple $p_{e,c}(\cdot,\cdot)$, we just need to find $p_{e,c}(n,n)$ and then get $p_{e,c}(n,n')$ by subtraction. Now $p_{e,c}(n,n)$ is the probability that any substitution on the edge is from $n$ to itself. The per-substitution-event rate at which that chain exits the state $n$ is $q_{e,c}(n,n') + q_{e,c}(n,h^*) = 1 - q_{e,c}(n,n)$, and thus

$$p_{e,c}(n,n) = \exp(-t_{e,c}(1 - q_{e,c}(n,n))).$$

This dynamic model could be further constrained to provide linguistic equivalents of standard molecular evolution models. For example, requiring that $t_{e,c}$ has the product form $\alpha_e \times \beta_c$ would result in the analogue of the rates-across-sites assumption.

### 9.3. *Identifiability*

The following two lemmas provide the fundamental techniques that we will use in proving identifiability of the underlying unrooted tree.

**Lemma 9.1.** *Let* T *be an unrooted binary tree, leaf-labelled by the set* L *of languages. Let* Q(T) *denote the set of all the subtrees of* T *induced by quartets of languages drawn from* L. *Then* T *is defined by the set* Q(T). *That is, if* T′ *is an unrooted binary tree with* Q(T′) = Q(T), *then* T = T′. *Let* C(T) *denote the set of bipartitions defined by the edges of the tree* T. *Then if* T *is an unrooted binary tree with* C(T′) = C(T), *then* T = T′. *Furthermore, given* C(T) *or* Q(T), *it is possible to recover* T *in polynomial time.*

The proof is well known in the computational biology literature (see, for example Kim & Warnow 1999), and is omitted.

**Lemma 9.2.** *Let* T *be an unrooted binary tree with positive edge weights* $w : E \to \mathbb{R}_+$, *where* E *is the set of edges of* T. *Let* $[D_{i,j}]$ *be a matrix defined by* $D_{i,j} = \sum_{e \in P_{i,j}} w(e)$, *where* i *and* j *are leaves of* T *and* $P_{i,j}$ *is the collection of edges on the path connecting* i *and* j. *Then* T, *and the associated edge weights, are uniquely determined by* $[D_{i,j}]$, *and can be constructed from the matrix in polynomial time.*

The first part (uniqueness of the tree and edge weights) of this theorem is given in Buneman (1971) and the polynomial time algorithm for obtaining $T$ and $w$ is given in Waterman *et al.* (1977).

#### 9.3.1. *Morphological and lexical characters*

Recall that in our model we make the assumptions that for morphological and lexical characters we can identify all homoplastic states, and that $0 < p_{e,c}(n,n') < 1$ for all edges $e$ in the tree. Suppose that the probability of a non-homoplastic state at the root is non-zero. Now let $c$ be a morphological or lexical character, and let $e$ be an arbitrary edge in $T$. Consider the probability that the state of $c$ at the root is non-homoplastic, and that $c$ changes exactly once — on the edge $e$ — to a new non-homoplastic state. By our assumptions the probability of this is strictly positive. Furthermore, given these events, the character $c$ defines a bipartition on the leaf set into two sets, defined by the edge $e$. Thus, given the states of the leaf set defined by the character $c$, we can infer the edge $e$. It is also easy to see that any bipartition of the leaf set defined by two non-homoplastic states has zero probability if that bipartition does not correspond to an edge in the tree. Therefore, given the probability distribution on bipartitions of the leaf-set defined by two non-homoplastic states, we can infer the tree $T$ (but not the root location). Therefore, the underlying unrooted tree $T$ is identifiable under this model. (A similar argument can be used to prove identifiability from the quartet trees defined on the basis of pairs of non-homoplastic states.)

*9.3.2. Binary phonological characters*

We consider binary phonological characters. We will prove identifiability of the full model (the underlying tree and the associated $p_{e,c}(\cdot,\cdot)$ parameters, but not the location of the root). Our proof relies only upon the assumption that the root state is known and is not homoplastic.

In binary phonological characters, the root state is 0 and indicates absence of the sound change, and all transitions are from absence to presence (indicated by 1). Thus, we allow $0 \rightarrow 1$ substitutions, but no $1 \rightarrow 0$ substitutions.

Let $\rho_{e,c}$ denote the probability of a $0 \rightarrow 1$ substitution on the edge $e$ (i.e. $\rho_{e,c} = p_{e,c}(n,h^*)$). Recall that we assume that for all edges $e$ we have $0 < \rho_{e,c} < 1$. Set $l_{e,c} = -\log(1 - \rho_{e,c})$ and call $l_{e,c}$ the length of the edge $e$. We define $l_c(P_{i,j})$, the length of a path $P_{i,j}$ between leaves $i$ and $j$, to be the sum of the lengths of the edges in the path. To ensure identifiability, we need only to show that we can compute $l_c(P_{i,j})$ for all pairs of leaves $i$ and $j$ in the tree, given the probabilities of the patterns at the leaves.

We know the probability that both $i$ and $j$ are in state 0, and we also know the probabilities that each is individually in state 0. The probability that i is in state 0 is just $\prod_{e\in P_{r,i}}(1-\rho_{e,c})$, where $r$ is the root, and we can compute the probability that $j$ is in state 0 similarly. The probability that both $i$ and $j$ are in state 0 is $\prod_{e\in P_{r,v}}(1-\rho_{e,c}) \times \prod_{e\in P_{v,i}}(1-\rho_{e,c}) \times \prod_{e\in P_{v,j}}(1-\rho_{e,c})$, where $v$ is the most recent common ancestor of $i$ and $j$. Therefore,

$$\prod_{e\in P_{i,j}}(1-\rho_{e,c}) = \frac{\Pr[i=0 \,\&\, j=0]^2}{\Pr[i=0]\Pr[j=0]}.$$

Equivalently, the length of the path $P_{i,j}$ is set by

$$l_c(P_{i,j}) = -2\log(\Pr[i=0 \,\&\, j=0]) + \log(\Pr[i=0]) + (\Pr[j=0]).$$

Since lengths of paths are identifiable, so (by Lemma 9.2) is the tree. Hence model trees are identifiable from binary phonological characters if we require $0 < \rho_{e,c} < 1$.

*9.3.3. Morphological and lexical characters revisited*

Although identifiability of the tree $T$ was established above for morphological and lexical characters, we would like to point out that a distance argument analogous to that used for binary phonological characters can also be used in this setting if the model doesn't allow homoplasy. This observation has the practical consequence that it enables distance-based reconstruction methods to be used for morphological and lexical characters when there is no homoplasy permitted.

We therefore assume for some character $c$ that the root state is non-homoplastic $p_{e,c}(n,h^*) = 0$ for all edges $e$. Then for two leaves $i$ and $j$ we have, in the notation above, that

$$-\log \Pr[i \text{ and } j \text{ in the same state}] = \sum_{e\in P_{i,j}}\{-\log(p_{e,c}(n,n))\}$$

and we can apply Lemma 9.2 to establish identifiability of the tree provided $0 < p_{e,c}(n,n) < 1$ for all $e$ and $c$ (which is equivalent to $0 < p_{e,c}(n,n') < 1$ for all $e$ and $c$ because of our assumption that $p_{e,c}(n,h^*) = 0$).

If we are in the setting of section 9.2, then the edge weight $-\log(p_{e,c}(n,n))$ is $t_{e,c}(1 - q_{e,c}(n,n))$. In particular, if we impose the rates-across-sites assumption that $t_{e,c} = \alpha_e \times \beta_c$, then the vectors of edge weights for different characters are just scalar multiples of each other.

### 9.4. Likelihood calculations

Because of the independence of the characters, it suffices to show how to compute likelihoods for single characters. Hence, let $c$ be a single character, and (as usual) let $c(x)$ denote the state of $x$ under the character $c$.

We begin by preprocessing the tree in order to assign states (when possible) to internal nodes. This is possible for every internal node that is on a path between two leaves with the same non-homoplastic state. The result of this labelling yields rooted subtrees, denoted by $t$, so that within each subtree $t$ every two leaves that have the same state have state $h^*$. The question is how to calculate the likelihood for this special case.

*9.4.1. Notation*

We begin with some notation. We distinguish between the case where a node is labelled with $h^*$, and where a node has a non-homoplastic state, denoted by $n$.

A *marking* of a rooted subtree $t$ is a set of edges of $t$ along with the kind of event (mutation to $h^*$, or homoplasy-free mutation) that occurs on each edge. A marking allows us to determine the equivalence relation on the nodes of the tree defined by the character. Thus, some such markings will have probability 0 since they will be incompatible with the pattern at the leaves, and others will have non-zero probability. Given a marking of a subtree $t$, the probability of the data given the marking will be either 0 (if the marking is incompatible) or 1 (if the marking is compatible). Hence we only need to compute the probabilities of the markings which are compatible with the pattern at the leaves.

We let the set of all markings of edges of the subtree $t$ be denoted by $M(t)$.

We let $M^{h^*}(t)$ denote all markings of the subtree $t$ which have the root labelled by $h^*$, and $M^n(t)$ denote all markings of the subtree in which the root is labelled by a non-homoplastic state (i.e. something other than $h^*$).

We let $DM^n(t)$ denote the markings of $t$ which have the root labelled by a non-homoplastic state, but labelled distinctly from all leaves below the root.

We let $SM^n(t)$ denote the markings of $t$ which have the root labelled by a non-homoplastic state, and identically labelled as some leaf below the root.

When we write $\Pr[M^n(t)]$, $\Pr[SM^n(t)]$, $\Pr[DM^n(t)]$, or $\Pr[M^{h^*}(t)]$, we mean the probability of the character states at the leaves of the tree $t$, over all markings of the tree $t$ with the properties defined by the referenced set.

Before we show how we compute the various probabilities, we need to define two more quantities. The subtrees we will work with are always rooted subtrees, but have two different forms. Let $v$ be a node in the tree $T$. We denote the subtree of $T$ rooted at $v$ by $T_v$. However, if $v$ is not a leaf and if $a$ is one of $v$'s children, then we denote $T(v,a)$ the tree rooted at $v$ with one child $a$, along with $T_a$. Thus, there will be two types of subtrees $t$ — those whose root has one child, and those whose root has two children.

We are now ready to show how we compute all the probabilities we need.

*9.4.2. The base case:* t *is a leaf*

If $t$ is a leaf then $c(t)$ is already defined, and in this case we can compute the various probabilities we need to compute.

Thus, $\Pr[M^{h^*}(t)] = 1$ if $c(t) = h^*$, and $\Pr[M^{h^*}(t)] = 0$ if $c(t) \neq h^*$. (We set $\Pr[M^n(t)]$ in the opposite way.) Similarly, $\Pr[SM^n(t)] = 1$ if $c(t) \neq h^*$, and $\Pr[SM^n(t)] = 0$ if $c(t) = h^*$. Finally, $\Pr[DM^n(t)] = 0$ for all leaves $t$.

*9.4.3. The inductive case:* t *is not a leaf*

We can then establish the following identities.

(1) $\Pr[M^n(t)] = \Pr[SM^n(t)] + \Pr[DM^n(t)]$ (definition)
(2) $\Pr[M(t)] = \Pr[M^{h^*}(t)] + \Pr[M^n(t)]$ (definition)
(3) $\Pr[M^{h^*}(T(v,a))] = p_{e,c}(h^*,h^*)\Pr[M^{h^*}(T_a)] + p_{e,c}(h^*,n)\Pr[M^n(T_a)]$
(4) $\Pr[M^{h^*}(T_v)] = \Pr[M^{h^*}(T(v,a))]\Pr[M^{h^*}(T(v,a'))]$, where $a$ and $a'$ are the two children of $v$
(5) $\Pr[SM^n(T(v,a))] = p_{e,c}(n,n)\Pr[SM^n(T_a)]$
(6) $\Pr[SM^n(T_v)] = \Pr[SM^n(T(v, a))]\Pr[DM^n(T(v,a'))] + \Pr[DM^n(T(v,a))]\Pr[SM^n(T(v,a'))]$, where $a$ and $a'$ are the two children of $v$. Note that this suffices because of our preprocessing step — which results in the case that in every subtree, two leaves which share the same state of a given character must both have the homoplastic state $h^*$.
(7) $\Pr[DM^n(T(v,a))] = p(n,h^*)\Pr[M^{h^*}(T_a)] + p_{e,c}(n,n')\Pr[M^n(T_a)] + p_{e,c}(n,n)\Pr[DM^n(T_a)]$
(8) $\Pr[DM^n(T_v)] = \Pr[DM^n(T(v,a))]\Pr[DM^n(T(v,a'))]$, where $a$ and $a'$ are the two children of $v$.

Hence, the probability of the states at the leaves can be computed in linear time, given the probabilities of substitution on the edges, for all characters.

## Acknowledgements

The authors would like to thank the McDonald Institute for inviting them to submit this paper.

## References

Bodlaender, H., M. Fellows & T. Warnow, 1992. Two strikes against perfect phylogeny. *Proceedings of the 19th International Colloquium on Automata, Languages, and Programming*. (Lecture Notes in Computer Science.) Vienna: Springer Verlag, 273–83.

Brugmann, K., 1897. *Grundriss der vergleichenden Grammatik der indogermanischen Sprachen*, vol. 1. 2nd edition. Strassburg: Trübner.

Brugmann, K., 1906. *Grundriss der vergleichenden Grammatik der indogermanischen Sprachen*, vol. 2. 2nd edition. Strassburg: Trübner.

Buck, C.D., 1955. *The Greek Dialects*. Chicago (IL): University of Chicago Press.

Buneman, P., 1971. The recovery of trees from measures of dissimilarity, in *Mathematics in the Archaeological and Historical Sciences: Proceedings of the Anglo-Romanian Conference, Mamaia, 1970*, eds. F.R. Hodson, D.G. Kendall & P. Tautu. Edinburgh: Edinburgh University Press, 387–95.

Campbell, A., 1962. *Old English Grammar*. Revised edition. Oxford: Clarendon Press.

Evans, S.N. & T. Warnow, 2004. Unidentifiable divergence times in rates-across-sites models. *IEEE/ACM Trans-*

*actions on Computational Biology and Bioinformatics* 1, 387–95.

Garde, P., 1961. Réflexions sur les differences phonétiques entre les langues slaves. *Word* 17, 34–62.

Gusfield, D., 1990. Efficient algorithms for inferring evolutionary trees. *Networks* 21, 19–28.

Hoenigswald, H.M., 1960. *Language Change and Linguistic Reconstruction.* Chicago (IL): University of Chicago Press.

Kim, J. & T. Warnow, 1999. *Tutorial on Phylogenetic Tree Estimation.* Presented at ISMB (Intelligent Systems for Molecular Biology) 1999, Heidelberg, Germany. Available electronically at http://kim.bio.upenn.edu/~jkim/media/ISMBtutorial.pdf.

Lühr, R., 1984. Reste der athematischen Konjugation in den germanischen Sprachen, in *Das Germanische und die Rekonstruktion der indogermanischen Grundsprache,* eds. J. Untermann & B. Brogyanyi. Amsterdam: Benjamins, 25–90.

McMahon, A. & R. McMahon, 2003. Finding families: quantitative methods in language classification. *Transactions of the Philological Society* 101, 7–55.

Meillet, A., 1925. *La Méthode Comparative en Linguistique Historique.* Oslo: Aschehoug.

Melchert, H.C., 1987. PIE velars in Luvian, in *Studies in Memory of Warren Cowgill,* ed. C. Watkins. Berlin: de Gruyter, 182–204.

Mossel, E. & M. Steel, 2004. A phase transition for a random cluster model on phylogenetic trees. *Mathematical Biosciences* 187(2), 189–203.

Nakhleh, L., 2004. Phylogenetic Networks in Biology and Historical Linguistics. Unpublished PhD thesis, University of Texas at Austin.

Nakhleh, L., D. Ringe & T. Warnow, 2005. Perfect phylogenetic networks: a new methodology for reconstructing the evolutionary history of natural languages. *Language, Journal of the Linguistic Society of America* 81(2), 382–420.

Pokorny, J., 1959. *Indogermanisches etymologisches Wörterbuch.* Bern: Francke.

Porzig, W., 1954. *Die Gliederung des indogermanischen Sprachgebiets.* Heidelberg: Winter.

Ringe, D., 2005. *A Linguistic History of English,* vol. 1: *From Proto-Indo-European to Proto-Germanic.* Accepted for publication by Oxford University Press.

Ringe, D., T. Warnow & A. Taylor, 2002. Indo-European and computational cladistics. *Transactions of the Philological Society* 100(1), 59–129.

Saitou, N. & M. Nei, 1987. The neighbor-joining method: a new method for reconstructing phylogenetic trees. *Molecular Biology and Evolution* 4, 406–25.

Sihler, A., 1995. *New Comparative Grammar of Greek and Latin.* Oxford: Oxford University Press.

Steel, M., 1992. The complexity of reconstructing trees from qualitative characters and subtrees. *Journal of Classification* 9, 91–116.

Streitberg, W., 1896. *Urgermanische Grammatik.* Heidelberg: Winter.

Taylor, A., T. Warnow & D. Ringe, 2000. Character-based reconstruction of a linguistic cladogram, in *Historical Linguistics 1995*, vol. 1: *General Issues and Non-Germanic languages*, eds. J.C. Smith & D. Bentley Amsterdam: Benjamins, 393–408.

Tuffley, C. & M. Steel, 1997. Links between maximum likelihood and maximum parsimony under a simple model of site substitution. *Bulletin of Mathematical Biology* 59(3), 581–607.

Warnow, T., 1997. Mathematical approaches to comparative linguistics. *Proceedings of the National Academy of Sciences of the USA* 94, 6585–90.

Waterman, M.S., T.F. Smith, M. Singh & W.A. Beyer, 1977. Additive evolutionary trees. *Journal of Theoretical Biology* 64, 199–213.

# *Part II*

## *Chronology*

# *Chapter 8*

# How Old is the Indo-European Language Family? Illumination or More Moths to the Flame?

Quentin D. Atkinson & Russell D. Gray

## 1. An electric light on a summer night

The origin of Indo-European has recently been described as 'one of the most intensively studied, yet still most recalcitrant problems of historical linguistics' (Diamond & Bellwood 2003, 601). Despite over 200 years of scrutiny, scholars have been unable to locate the origin of Indo-European definitively in time or place. Theories have been put forward advocating ages ranging from 4000 to 23,000 years BP (Otte 1997), with hypothesized homelands including Central Europe (Devoto 1962), the Balkans (Diakonov 1984), and even India (Kumar 1999). Mallory (1989) acknowledges 14 distinct homeland hypotheses since 1960 alone. He rather colourfully remarks that

> the quest for the origins of the Indo-Europeans has all the fascination of an electric light in the open air on a summer night: it tends to attract every species of scholar or would-be savant who can take pen to hand (Mallory 1989, 143).

Unfortunately, archaeological, genetic and linguistic research on Indo-European origins has so far proved inconclusive. Whilst numerous theories of Indo-European origin have been proposed, they have proven difficult to test. In this chapter, we outline how techniques derived from evolutionary biology can be adapted to test between competing hypotheses about the age of the Indo-European language family. We argue that these techniques are a useful *supplement* to traditional methods in historical linguistics. This chapter is a development and extension of previous work on the application of phylogenetic methods to the study of language evolution (Gray & Atkinson 2003; Atkinson & Gray 2006; Atkinson *et al.* 2005).

## 2. Two theories

There are currently two main theories about the origin of Indo-European. The first theory, put forward by Marija Gimbutas (1973a,b) on the basis of linguistic and archaeological evidence, links Proto-Indo-European (the hypothesized ancestral Indo-European tongue) with the Kurgan culture of southern Russia and the Ukraine. The Kurgans were a group of semi-nomadic, pastoralist, warrior-horsemen who expanded from their homeland in the Russian steppes during the fifth and sixth millennia BP, conquering Danubian Europe, Central Asia and India, and later the Balkans and Anatolia. This expansion is thought to roughly match the accepted ancestral range of Indo-European (Trask 1996). As well as the apparent geographical congruence between Kurgan and Indo-European territories, there is linguistic evidence for an association between the two cultures. Words for supposed Kurgan technological innovations are notably consistent across widely divergent Indo-European sub-families. These include terms for 'wheel' (**rotho-*, **k$^w$(e)k$^w$l-o-*), 'axle' (**aks-lo-*), 'yoke' (**jug-o-*), 'horse' (**ekwo-*) and 'to go, transport in a vehicle' (**wegh-*: Mallory 1989; Campbell 2004). It is argued that these words and associated technologies must have been present in the Proto-Indo-European culture and that they were likely to have been Kurgan in origin. Hence, the argument goes, the Indo-European language family is no older than 5000–6000 BP. Mallory (1989) argues for a similar time and place of Indo-European origin — a region around the Black Sea about 5000–6000 BP (although he is more cautious and refrains from identifying Proto-Indo-European with a specific culture such as the Kurgans).

The second theory, proposed by archaeologist Colin Renfrew (1987), holds that Indo-European languages spread, not with marauding Russian horsemen, but with the expansion of agriculture from Anatolia between 8000 and 9500 years ago. Radiocarbon analysis of the earliest Neolithic sites across Europe provides a fairly detailed chronology of agricultural dispersal. This archaeological evidence indicates that agriculture spread from Anatolia, arriving in Greece at some time during the ninth millennium BP and reaching as far as the British Isles by 5500 BP (Gkiasta *et al.* 2003). Renfrew maintains that the linguistic argument for the Kurgan theory is based on only limited evidence for a few enigmatic Proto-Indo-European word forms. He points out that parallel semantic shifts or widespread borrowing can produce similar word forms across different languages without requiring that an ancestral term was present in the proto-language. Renfrew also challenges the idea that Kurgan social structure and technology was sufficiently advanced to allow them to conquer whole continents in a time when even small cities did not exist. Far more credible, he argues, is that Proto-Indo-European spread with the spread of agriculture — a scenario that is also thought to have occurred across the Pacific (Bellwood 1991; 1994), Southeast Asia (Glover & Higham 1996) and sub-Saharan Africa (Holden 2002). On the basis of linguistic evidence, Diakonov (1984) also argues for an early Indo-European spread with agriculture but places the homeland in the Balkans — a position that may be reconcilable with Renfrew's theory.

The debate about Indo-European origins thus centres on archaeological evidence for two population expansions, both implying very different time-scales — the Kurgan theory with a date of 5000–6000 BP, and the Anatolian theory with a date of 8000–9500 BP. One way of potentially resolving the debate is to look outside the archaeological record for independent evidence that allows us to test between these two time depths. Genetic studies offer one potential source of evidence. Unfortunately, due to problems associated with admixture, slow rates of genetic change and the relatively recent time-scales involved, genetic analyses have been unable to resolve the debate (Cavalli-Sforza *et al.* 1994; Rosser *et al.* 2000). Another potential line of evidence is contained in the languages themselves, and it is the linguistic evidence we shall turn to now.

### 3. The demise of glottochronology and the rise of computational biology

Languages, like genes, chronicle their evolutionary history. Languages, however, change much faster than genes and so contain more information at shallower time depths. Conventional means of linguistic inquiry, like the comparative method, are able to infer ancestral relationships between languages but cannot provide an absolute estimate of time depth. An alternative approach is Morris Swadesh's (1952; 1955) lexicostatistics and its derivative 'glottochronology'. These methods use lexical data to determine language relationships and to estimate absolute divergence times. Lexicostatistical methods infer language trees on the basis of the percentage of shared cognates between languages — the more similar the languages, the more closely they are related. Words are judged to be cognate if they can be shown to be related via a pattern of systematic sound correspondences and have similar meanings (see Fig. 8.1 for some examples). This information can be used to construct evolutionary language trees. Glottochronology is an extension of this approach to estimate divergence times under the assumption of a 'glottoclock', or constant rate of language change. The following formulae can be used to relate language similarity to time along an exponential decay curve:

$$t = \frac{\log C}{2 \log r}$$

where $t$ is time depth in millennia, $C$ is the percentage of cognates shared and $r$ is the 'universal' constant or rate of retention (the expected proportion of cognates remaining after 1000 years of separation: Swadesh 1955). Usually, analyses are restricted to the Swadesh word list, a collection of 100–200 basic meanings that are thought to be relatively culturally universal, stable and resistant to borrowing. These include kinship terms (e.g. mother, father), terms for body parts (e.g. hand, mouth, hair), numerals and basic verbs (e.g. to drink, to sleep, to burn). For the Swadesh 200-word list, a value of 81 per cent is often used for $r$.

Linguists have identified a number of serious problems with the glottochronological approach:

1. Much of the information in the lexical data is lost when word information is reduced to percentage similarity scores between languages (Steel *et al.* 1988).
2. The methods used to construct evolutionary trees from language distance matrices have been shown to produce inaccurate results, particularly where rates of change vary (Blust 2000).
3. Languages do not always evolve at a constant rate. Bergsland & Vogt (1962) compared present-day languages with their archaic forms and found evidence for significant rate variation between languages. For example, Icelandic and Norwegian were compared to their common ancestor, Old Norse, spoken roughly 1000 years ago. Norwegian has retained 81 per cent of the vocabulary of Old Norse, correctly suggesting an age of approximately 1000 years. However, Icelandic has retained over 95 per cent of the Old Norse vocabulary, falsely suggesting that Icelandic split from Old Norse less than 200 years ago.
4. Languages do not always evolve in a tree-like manner (Bateman *et al.* 1990; Hjelmslev 1958). Borrowing between languages can produce erroneous (or, in extreme cases, meaningless) language trees. Also, widespread borrowing can bias divergence time estimates by making languages seem more similar (and hence younger) than they really are.

These problems have led many linguists to completely abandon any attempt to derive dates from lexical data. For example, Clackson (2000, 451) claims that the data and methods 'do not allow the question "When was Proto-Indo-European spoken?" to be answered in any really meaningful or helpful way'.

Fortunately, none of these problems are unique to linguistics. It is ironic that whilst computational methods in historical linguistics have fallen out of favour over the last half-century, computational biology has thrived. In much the same way as linguists use information about current and historically attested languages to infer their history, evolutionary biologists use DNA sequence, morphological and sometimes behavioural data to construct evolutionary trees of biological species. Questions of relatedness and divergence dates are of interest to biologists just as they are to linguists. As a result biologists must also deal with the problems outlined above: nucleotide sequence information is lost when data is analyzed as distance matrices (Steel *et al.* 1988); distance-based tree-building methods may not accurately reconstruct phylogeny (Kuhner & Felsenstein 1994); different genes (and nucleotides) evolve at different rates and these rates can vary through time (Excoffier & Yang 1999); and finally, evolution is not always tree-like due to phenomena such as hybridization and horizontal gene transfer (Faguy & Doolittle 2000).

Despite these obstacles, computational methods have revolutionized evolutionary biology. Rather than giving up and declaring that time-depth estimates are intractable, biologists have developed techniques to overcome each problem. Here, we describe how these biological methods can be adapted and applied to lexical data to answer the question 'How old is the Indo-European language family?'

## 4. From word lists to binary matrices

In order to estimate phylogenies accurately we need to overcome the problem of information loss encountered in lexicostatistics and glottochronology. This requires a large data set with individual character-state information for each language. Lexical data are ideal because there are a large number of well-studied characters available and these can be divided into meaningful evolutionary units known as *cognate sets* (as described above, words are judged to be cognate if they can be shown to be related via a pattern of systematic sound correspondences and have similar meaning). Cognate words from different languages can be grouped into cognate sets that reflect patterns of inheritance. Owing to the possibility of unintuitive or misleading similarities between words from different languages, expert knowledge of the sound changes involved is required in order to make cognacy judgements accurately. For example, knowledge of regular sound correspondences between the languages is required to ascertain that the English word *when* is cognate with Greek *pote* of the same meaning. Conversely, English *have* is not cognate with Latin *habere* despite similar word form and meaning.

To estimate tree topology and branch lengths accurately requires a large amount of data. Our data was taken from the Dyen *et al.* (1992) Indo-European lexical data base, which contains expert cognacy judgements for 200 Swadesh list terms in 95 languages. Dyen *et al.* (1997) identified eleven languages as less reliable and hence they were not included in the analysis presented here. Three extinct languages (Hittite, Tocharian A and Tocharian B) were added to the data base in an attempt to improve the resolution of basal relationships in the inferred phylogeny. Multiple references were used to corroborate cognacy judgements (Adams 1999; Gamkrelidze & Ivanov 1995; Guterbock & Hoffner 1986; Hoffner 1967; Tischler 1973; 1997). For each meaning in the data base, languages were grouped into cognate sets. Some examples are shown in Figure 8.1.

By restricting analyses to basic vocabulary such as the Swadesh word list the influence of borrowing can be minimized. For example, although English is a Germanic language, it has borrowed around 60 per cent of its total lexicon from French and Latin. However, only about 6 per cent of English entries in the Swadesh 200-word list are clear Romance language borrowings (Embleton 1986). Known borrowings were not coded as cognate in the Dyen *et al.* data base. For example, the English word *mountain* was not coded as cognate with French *montagne,* since it was obviously borrowed from French into English after the Norman invasion. Any remaining reticulation can be detected using biological methods such as split decomposition, which can identify conflicting signal. The issue of borrowing in lexical data is discussed in more detail by Holden & Gray (Chapter 2 this volume; see also Bryant *et al.* 2005).

We can represent the information in Figure 8.1 most simply as binary characters in a matrix, where the presence or absence of a particular cognate set in a particular language is denoted by a 1 or 0 respectively. Figure 8.2 shows a binary representation of the cognate information from Figure 8.1. Using this coding procedure we produced a matrix of 2449 cognacy judgements across 87 languages. Alternative coding methods are also possible, such as representing the data as 200 meaning categories each with multiple character states. It has been argued that semantic categories are the fundamental 'objects' of linguistic

| | | | | |
|---|---|---|---|---|
| English | here$^{1}$ | sea$^{5}$ | water$^{9}$ | when$^{12}$ |
| German | hier$^{1}$ | See$^{5}$, Meer$^{6}$ | Wasser$^{9}$ | wann$^{12}$ |
| French | ici$^{2}$ | mer$^{6}$ | eau$^{10}$ | quand$^{12}$ |
| Italian | qui$^{2}$, qua$^{2}$ | mare$^{6}$ | acqua$^{10}$ | quando$^{12}$ |
| Modern Greek | edo$^{3}$ | thalassa$^{7}$ | nero$^{11}$ | pote$^{12}$ |
| Hittite | ka$^{4}$ | aruna-$^{8}$ | watar$^{9}$ | kuwapi$^{12}$ |

**Figure 8.1.** *Selection of languages and Swadesh list terms. Cognacy is indicated by the numbers in superscript.*

| Meaning | here | | | | sea | | | | water | | | when |
|---|---|---|---|---|---|---|---|---|---|---|---|---|
| Cognate set | 1 | 2 | 3 | 4 | 5 | 6 | 7 | 8 | 9 | 10 | 11 | 12 |
| English | 1 | 0 | 0 | 0 | 1 | 0 | 0 | 0 | 1 | 0 | 0 | 1 |
| German | 1 | 0 | 0 | 0 | 1 | 1 | 0 | 0 | 1 | 0 | 0 | 1 |
| French | 0 | 1 | 0 | 0 | 0 | 1 | 0 | 0 | 0 | 1 | 0 | 1 |
| Italian | 0 | 1 | 0 | 0 | 0 | 1 | 0 | 0 | 0 | 1 | 0 | 1 |
| Greek | 0 | 0 | 1 | 0 | 0 | 0 | 1 | 0 | 0 | 0 | 1 | 1 |
| Hittite | 0 | 0 | 0 | 1 | 0 | 0 | 0 | 1 | 1 | 0 | 0 | 1 |

**Figure 8.2.** *Cognate sets from Figure 8.1 expressed in a binary matrix showing cognate presence (1) or absence (0).*

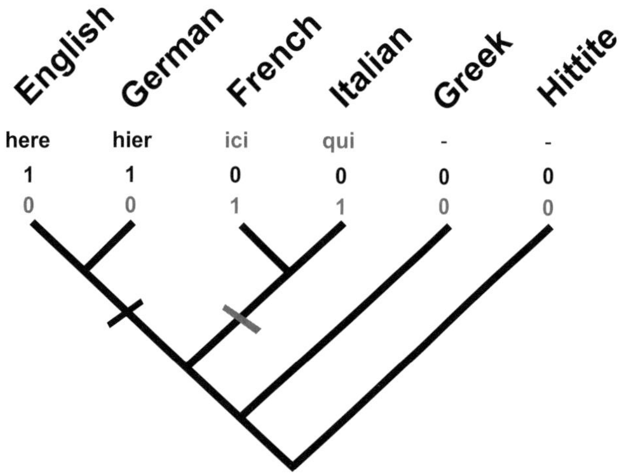


**Figure 8.3.** *Character states for cognate sets 5 (black) and 6 (grey) from Figure 8.1 are shown mapped onto a hypothetical tree. Implied character state changes can then be reconstructed on the tree. The black and grey bands show a likely point at which cognate sets 5 and 6 were gained. We can use this information to evaluate possible evolutionary scenarios.*

change (see Evans *et al.* Chapter 9 this volume) and that binary coding of the presence or absence of cognate sets is thus inappropriate. However, cognate sets constitute discrete, relatively unambiguous heritable evolutionary units with a birth and death (see Nicholls & Gray, Chapter 14 this volume) and there is no reason to suppose they are any more or less fundamental to language evolution than semantic categories. Further, coding the data as semantic categories makes it difficult to deal with polymorphisms (i.e. when a language has more than one word for a given meaning — e.g. for the meaning 'sea' German has both *See* and *Meer*). It also significantly increases the number of parameters required to model the process of evolution. Pagel (2000) points out that, if each word requires a different set of rate parameters, then for just 200 words in 40 languages there are 1278 parameters to estimate. We thus used a binary coding of cognate presence/absence information to represent linguistic change in our analysis.

As well as avoiding the problem of information loss, analyzing cognate presence/absence information allows us to explicitly model the evolutionary process. *Unlike lexicostatistics and glottochronology, we do not count the number of cognates shared between languages, nor do we calculate pair-wise distances between languages.* Instead, the distribution of cognates is mapped onto an evolutionary language tree (see Fig. 8.3), and likely character state changes are inferred across the whole tree.

### 5. Models are lies that lead us to the truth

When biologists model evolution, they lie: they lie about the independence of character state changes across sites; they lie about the homogeneity of substitution mechanisms; and they lie about the importance of selection pressure on substitution rates. But these are lies that lead us to the truth. Biological research is based on a strategy of model-building and statistical inference that has proved highly successful (Hillis

| | 0 | 1 |
|---|---|---|
| 0 | $-u\pi_1$ | $u\pi_1$ |
| 1 | $u\pi_0$ | $-u\pi_0$ |

**Figure 8.4.** *Simple likelihood rate matrix adapted for modelling lexical replacement in language evolution. This is a time-reversible model that allows for unequal equilibrium frequencies of 1s and 0s (cognate presence and absence). The model parameters are u (the mean substitution rate), and $\pi_0$ and $\pi_1$ (which represent the relative frequencies of 1s and 0s).*

1992; Hillis *et al.* 1996; Pagel 1999). The goal for biologists is not to construct a model so complex that it captures every nuance and vagary of the evolutionary process, but rather to find the simplest model available that can reliably estimate the parameters of interest.

Model choice is thus a balance between over- and under-fitting parameters (Burnham & Anderson 1998). Adding extra parameters can improve the apparent fit of a model to data, however, sampling error is also increased because there are more unknown parameters to estimate (Swofford *et al.* 1996). Depending on the question we are trying to answer, this added uncertainty can prevent us from estimating the model parameters from the data to within a useful margin of error. In many cases, adding just a few extra parameters can create a computationally intractable problem. Conversely, a model that is too simple can produce biased results if it fails to capture an important part of the process (Burnham & Anderson 1998). There is thus a compromise between biased estimates and variance inflation.

The strategy that has proved successful in biology is to start with a simple model that captures some of the fundamental processes involved and increase the complexity as necessary. For example, nucleotide substitution models range from a simple equal rates model (Jukes & Cantor 1969), to more complex models that allow for differences in transition/transversion rates, unequal character state frequencies, site specific rates, and auto-correlation between sites (Swofford *et al.* 1996). Although even the most complicated models are simplifications of the process of evolution, often the simplest substitution model captures enough of what is going on to allow biologists to extract a meaningful signal from the data. Levins (1966) gives three reasons why we should use a simple model. First, violations of the assumptions of the model are expected to cancel each other out. Second, small errors in the model should result in small errors in the conclusions. And third, by comparing multiple models with reality we can determine which aspects of the process are important.

Likelihood evolutionary modelling has become the method of choice in phylogenetics (Swofford *et al.* 1996). The likelihood approach to phylogenetic reconstruction allows us to explicitly model the process of language evolution. The method is based on the premise that we should favour the tree topology/topologies and branch-lengths that make our observed data most likely, given the assumptions of our model — i.e. we should favour the tree with the highest likelihood score. We can evaluate possible tree topologies for a given model and data by modelling the sequence of cognate gains and losses across the trees.

Likelihood models have a number of advantages over other approaches. First, we can work with explicit models of evolution and test between competing models. The assumptions of the method are thus overt and easily verifiable. Second, we can increase the complexity of the model as required. For example, as explained below, we were able to test for the influence of rate variation between cognate sets and, as a result, incorporate this into the analysis using a gamma distribution. And third, model parameters can be estimated from the data itself, thus avoiding restrictive *a priori* assumptions about the evolutionary processes involved (Pagel 1997).

Likelihood models of evolution are usually expressed as a rate matrix representing the relative rates of all possible character state changes. Here, we are interested in the processes of cognate gain and loss, respectively represented by 0 to 1 changes and 1 to 0 changes on the tree (see Fig. 8.3). We can model this process effectively with a relatively simple two-state time-reversible model of lexical evolution (shown in Fig. 8.4). We extended this simple model by adding a gamma shape parameter ($\alpha$) to allow rates of change to vary between cognate sets according to a gamma distribution. This was implemented after a likelihood ratio test (Goldman 1993) showed that adding the gamma-shape parameter significantly improved the ability of the model to explain the data ($\chi^2 = 108$, $df = 1$, $p < .001$). Essentially, the gamma distribution provides a number of different rate categories for the model to choose from when assigning rates to each cognate set. The gamma distribution for different values of $\alpha$ is shown in Figure 8.5. A suitable value for $\alpha$ can be estimated from the data.

Our model assumes that the appearance and disappearance of cognates is randomly distributed about some mean value. This rate can vary between cognate sets and (with the addition of rate smoothing — described below) rates of change can vary through time in a constrained way. Whilst historical, social, and cultural contingencies can undoubtedly influence

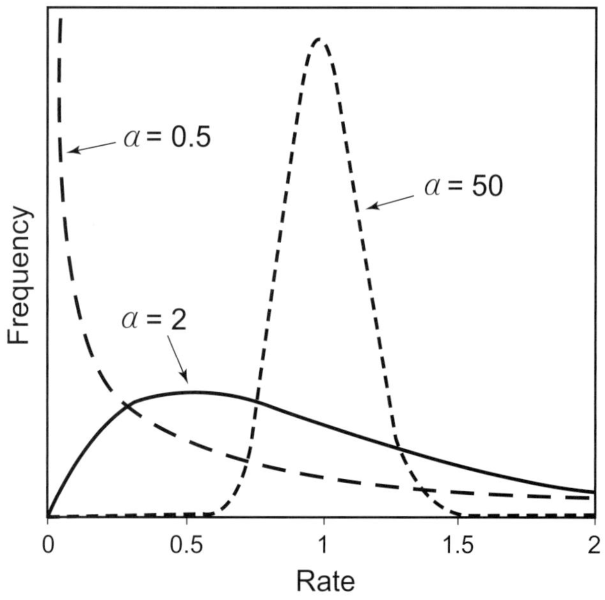


**Figure 8.5.** *The gamma distribution, used to model rate variation between sites. Three possible values for α are shown. For small values of α (e.g. α = 0.5), most cognate sets evolve slowly, but a few can evolve at higher rates. As α increases, the distribution becomes more peaked and symmetrical around a rate of 1 — i.e. rates become more equal (e.g. α = 50).*

the process of linguistic change, we explicitly reject Warnow *et al.*'s (Chapter 7 this volume) counsel of despair, that language evolution is so idiosyncratic and unconstrained that inferring divergence dates is impossible. Language evolution is subject to real-world constraints, such as human language acquisition, expressiveness, intelligibility, and generation time. We cannot help but quote Ringe *et al.* (2002, 61) on this point:

> Languages replicate themselves (and thus 'survive' from generation to generation) through a process of native-language acquisition by children. Importantly for historical linguistics, that process is tightly constrained.

These constraints create underlying commonalities in the evolutionary process that we can, and should, be trying to model.

Evans *et al.* (Chapter 10 this volume) argue that our model is 'patently inappropriate' because it assumes that all characters are independent. In biology, this is known as the I.I.D. (identically and independently distributed) assumption. Evans *et al.* correctly point out that the I.I.D. assumption is violated when individual meanings in the Swadesh word list are broken up into characters representing multiple cognate sets. Specifically, if a particular cognate set is present in a language, it will be less likely that other cognate sets for the same meaning will also be present. However, we do not think that this lack of independence biases our results. The issue of independence will be dealt with in detail in section 10.2.

### 6. Bayesian inference of phylogeny

It is not usually computationally feasible to evaluate the likelihood of all possible language trees — for 87 languages there are over $1 \times 10^{155}$ possible rooted trees. Further, the vast number of possibilities combined with finite data means that inferring a single tree will be misleading — there will always be uncertainty in the topology and branch-lengths. If we are to use our results to test hypotheses we need to use heuristic methods to search through 'tree-space' and quantify this phylogenetic uncertainty. Bayesian inference is an alternative approach to phylogenetic analysis that allows us to draw inferences from a large amount of data using powerful probabilistic models without searching for the 'optimal tree' (Huelsenbeck *et al.* 2001). In this approach trees are sampled according to their posterior probabilities. The posterior probability of a tree (the probability of the tree given the priors, data and the model) is related by Bayes's theorem to its likelihood score (the probability of the data given the tree) and its prior probability (a reflection of any prior knowledge about tree topology that is to be included in the analysis). Unfortunately, we cannot evaluate this function analytically. However, we can use a Markov Chain Monte Carlo (MCMC: Metropolis *et al.* 1953) algorithm to generate a sample of trees in which the frequency distribution of the sample is an approximation of the posterior probability distribution of the trees (Huelsenbeck *et al.* 2001). To do this, we used *MrBayes*, a Bayesian phylogenetic inference programme (Huelsenbeck & Ronquist 2001).

MrBayes uses MCMC algorithms to search through the realm of possible trees. From a random starting tree, changes are proposed to the tree topology, branch-lengths and model parameters according to a specified prior distribution of the parameters. The changes are either accepted or rejected based on the likelihood of the resulting evolutionary reconstruction — i.e. reconstructions that give higher likelihood scores tend to be favoured. In this way the chain quickly goes from sampling random trees to sampling those trees which best explain the data. After an initial 'burn-in' period, trees begin to be sampled in proportion to their likelihood given the data. This produces a distribution of trees. A useful way to summarize this distribution is with a consensus tree or consensus network (Holland & Moulton 2003)

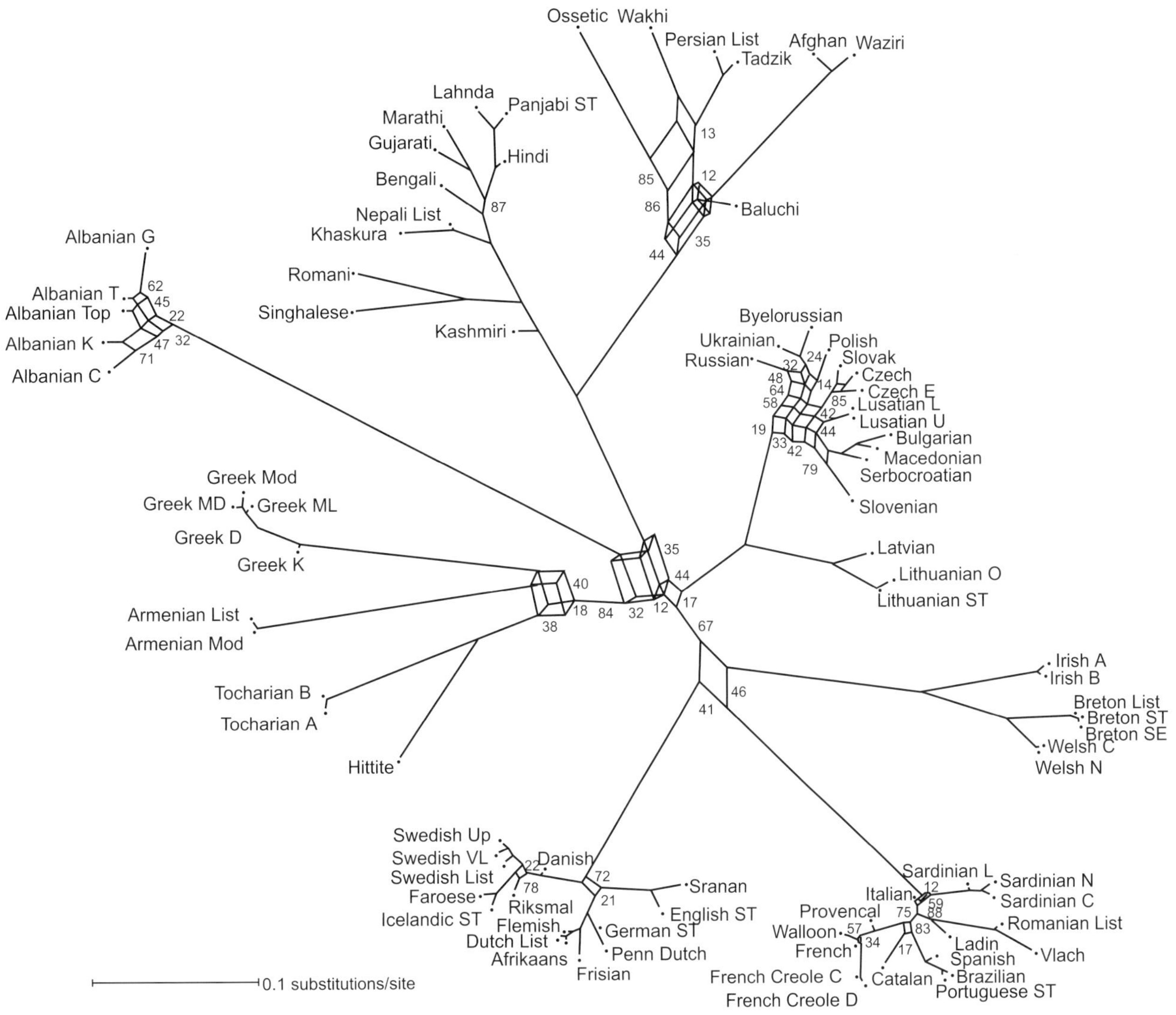


**Figure 8.6.** *Consensus network from the Bayesian MCMC sample of trees. Values express the posterior probability of each split (values above 90 per cent are not indicated). A threshold of 10 per cent was used to draw this splits graph — i.e. only those splits occuring in at least 10 per cent of the observed trees are shown in the graph. Branch lengths represent the median number of reconstructed substitutions per site across the sample distribution.*

depicting uncertainty in the reconstructed relationships. These graphs are, however, just useful pictorial summaries of the analysis. The fundamental output of the analysis is the distribution of trees.

The consensus network from a Bayesian sample distribution of 100 trees is shown in Figure 8.6. The values next to splits give an indication of the uncertainty associated with each split (the posterior probability, derived from the percentage of trees in the Bayesian distribution that contain the split). For example, the value 41 next to the parallel lines separating Italic and Celtic from the of the Indo-European sub-families indicates that that split was present in 41 per cent of the trees in the sample distribution. Similarly, the split grouping Italic and Germanic languages was present in 46 per cent of the sample distribution.

## 7. Rate variation and estimating dates

There are at least two types of rate variation in lexical evolution. First, rate variation can occur between cognates. For example, even in the Swadesh word list, the Indo-European word for *five* is highly conserved (1 cognate set) whilst the word for *dirty* is highly variable (27 cognate sets). This is akin to site-specific rate variation in biology. Biologists can account for

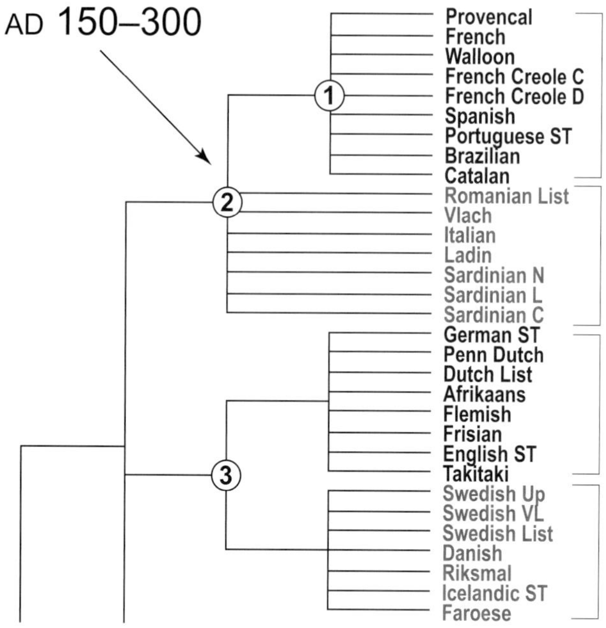


**Figure 8.7.** *The Romance languages (derived from Latin) probably began to diverge prior to the fall of the Roman Empire. We can thus constrain the age of the point on the tree which corresponds to this divergence event (2). Using this rationale 14 nodes were constrained, including an Iberian French node (1) and a Germanic node (3).*

this type of rate variation by allowing a distribution of rates. As mentioned above, we used a model of cognate evolution that allowed for gamma distributed rate variation between cognates.

Second, rates of lexical evolution can vary through time and between lineages. Clearly this will cause problems if we are trying to estimate absolute divergence times on the inferred phylogenies since inferred branch-lengths are not directly proportional to time. Again, biologists have developed a number of methods for dealing with this type of rate variation. We used the penalized-likelihood method of rate smoothing implemented in *r8s* (*version 1.7*; Sanderson 2002a), to allow for rate variation across each tree. Sanderson (2002b) has shown that, under conditions of rate variation, the penalized-likelihood rate-smoothing algorithm performs significantly better than methods that assume a constant rate of evolution.

In order to infer absolute divergence times, we first need to calibrate rates of evolution by constraining the age of known points on each tree in accordance with historically attested dates. For example, the Romance languages (derived from Latin) probably began to diverge prior to the fall of the Roman Empire. We can thus constrain the age of the node corresponding to the most recent common ancestor of the Romance languages to within the range implied by our historical knowledge (see Fig. 8.7). We constrained the age of 14 such nodes on the tree in accordance with historical evidence (see Atkinson & Gray 2006). These known node ages were then combined with branch-length information to estimate rates of evolution across each tree. The penalized-likelihood model allows rates to vary across the tree whilst incorporating a 'roughness penalty' that costs the model more if rates vary excessively from branch to branch. This procedure allows us to derive age estimates for each node on the tree. Figure 8.8 shows the consensus tree for the initial Bayesian sample distribution of 1000 trees,[1] with branch lengths drawn proportional to time. The posterior probability values above each internal branch give an indication of the uncertainty associated with each clade on the consensus tree (the percentage of trees in the Bayesian distribution that contain the clade). For example, the value 67 above the branch leading to the Italo-Celto-Germanic clade indicates that that clade was present in 67 per cent of the trees in the sample distribution. We can derive age estimates from this tree, including an age of 8700 BP at the base of the tree — within the range predicted by the Anatolian farming theory of Indo-European origin.

A single divergence time, with no estimate of the error associated with the calculation, is of limited value. To test between historical hypotheses we need some measure of the error associated with the date estimates. Specifically, uncertainty in the phylogeny gives rise to a corresponding uncertainty in age estimates. In order to account for phylogenetic uncertainty we estimated the age at the base of the trees in the post-burn-in Bayesian MCMC sample to produce a probability distribution for the age of Indo-European. One advantage of the Bayesian framework is that prior knowledge about language relationships can be incorporated into the analysis. In order to eliminate trees that conflict with known Indo-European language groupings, the original 1000 tree sample was filtered using a constraint tree representing these known language groupings [(Anatolian, Tocharian, (Greek, Armenian, Albanian, (Iranian, Indic), (Slavic, Baltic), ((North Germanic, West Germanic), Italic, Celtic)))]. This constraint tree was consistent with the majority-rule consensus tree generated from the entire Bayesian sample distribution. The filtered distribution of divergence time estimates was then used to create a confidence interval for the age of the Indo-European language family. This distribution could then be compared with the age ranges implied by the two main theories of Indo-European origin (see Fig. 8.9). The results are clearly consistent with the Anatolian hypothesis.

Not all historically attested language splits were used in our analysis. One means of validating our

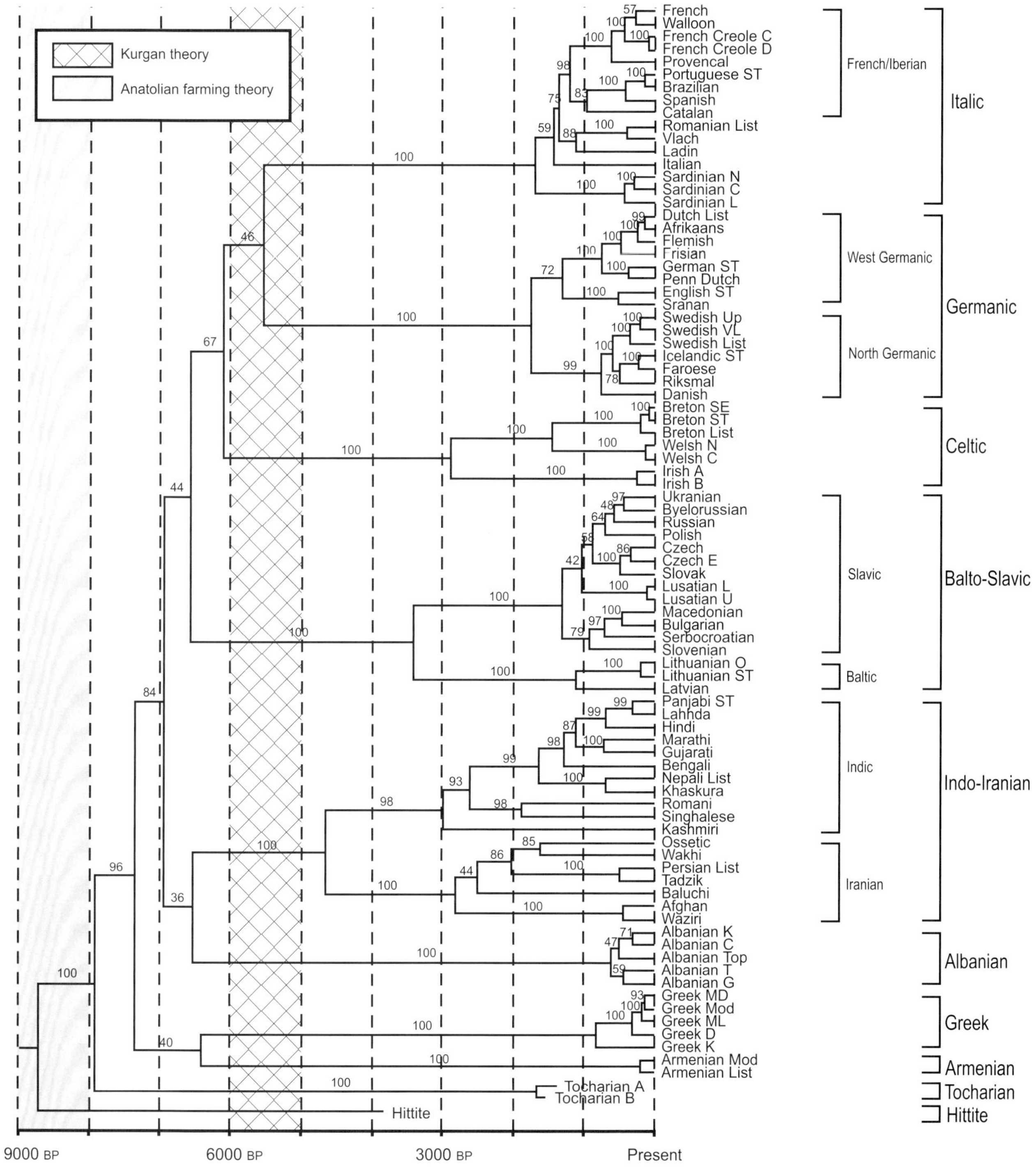


**Figure 8.8.** *Majority-rule consensus tree from the initial Bayesian MCMC sample of 1000 trees (Gray & Atkinson 2003). Values above each branch indicate uncertainty (posterior probability) in the tree as a percentage. Branch-lengths are proportional to time. Shaded bars represent the age range proposed by the two main theories — the Anatolian theory (grey bar) and the Kurgan theory (hatched bar). The basal age (8700 BP) supports the Anatolian theory.*

methodology is to produce divergence time distributions for nodes that were not constrained in the analysis and compare this to the historically attested time of divergence. For example, Figure 8.10 shows the inferred divergence time distributions for the North and West Germanic subgroups. The grey band in

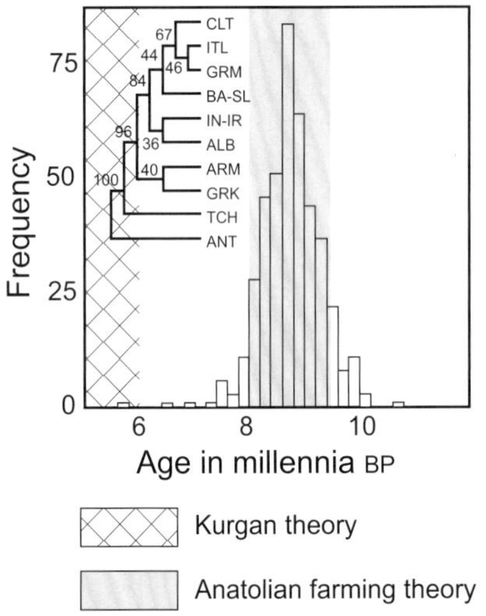


**Figure 8.9.** *Frequency distribution of basal age estimates from filtered Bayesian MCMC sample of trees for the initial assumption set* (n = 435)*. The majority-rule consensus tree for the entire (unfiltered) sample is shown in the upper left.*

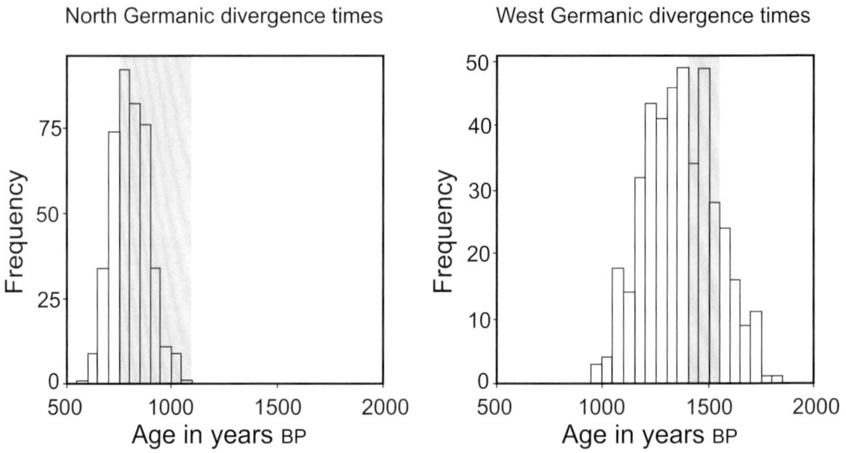


**Figure 8.10.** *Frequency distribution of age estimates for the North and West Germanic subgroups across filtered Bayesian MCMC sample of trees* (n = 433)*. The grey bands indicate the historically attested time of divergence.*

these figures indicates the likely age of each subgroup based on the historical record. The age estimates for the North Germanic clade correspond with written evidence for the break up of these languages between AD 900 and AD 1250. Similarly, estimated ages of the West Germanic clade are consistent with historical evidence dating the Anglo-Saxon migration to the British Isles about 1500 years ago.

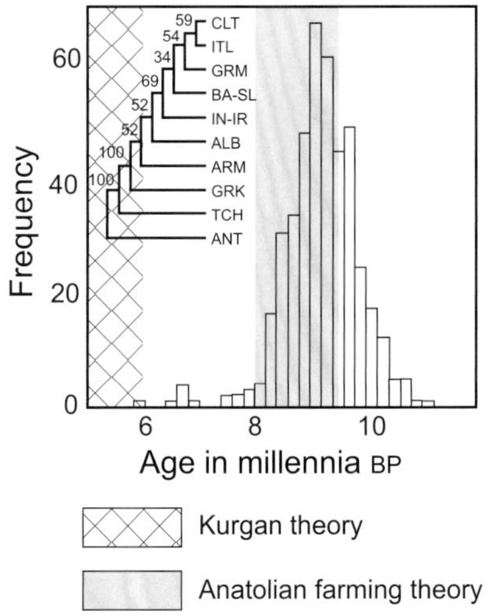


**Figure 8.11.** *Frequency distribution of basal age estimates from filtered Bayesian MCMC sample of trees for analysis with doubtful cognates excluded* (n = 433)*. The majority-rule consensus tree for the entire sample is shown in the upper left.*

## 8. Testing robustness

A key part of any Bayesian phylogenetic analysis is an assessment of the robustness of the inferences. To do this we tested the effect of altering a number of different parameters and assumptions of the method.

### *8.1. Bayesian 'priors'*

Initializing each Bayesian MCMC chain required the specification of a starting tree and prior parameters (*'priors'*) for the analysis. The sample Bayesian distribution was the product of ten separate runs from different random starting trees. Divergence time and topology results for each of the separate runs were consistent. Other test analyses were run using a range of priors for parameters controlling the rate matrix, branch-lengths, gamma distribution and character state frequencies. The inferred tree phylogeny and branch-lengths did not noticeably change when priors were altered.

### *8.2. Cognacy judgements*

The Dyen *et al.* (1992) data base contained information about the certainty of cognacy judgements. Words were coded as 'cognate' or 'doubtful cognates'. In the initial analysis we included all cognate information in an effort to maximize any phylogenetic signal. However, we wanted to test the robustness of our results to changes in the stringency of cognacy decisions. For this reason, the analysis was repeated with doubtful cognates excluded. This produced a similar age range to the initial analysis, indicating that our results were robust to errors in cognacy judgements (see Fig. 8.11).

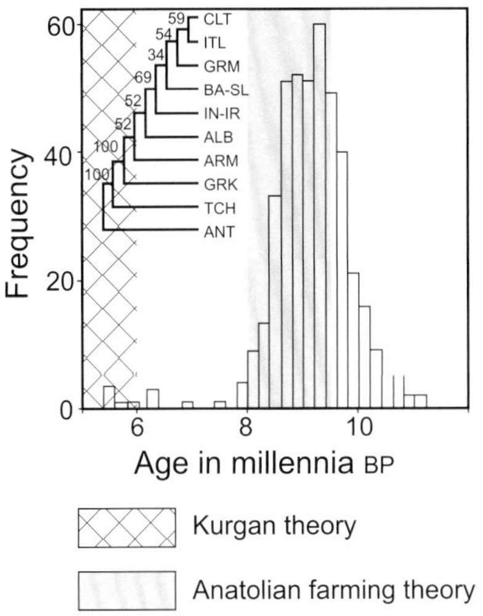


**Figure 8.12.** *Frequency distribution of basal age estimates from filtered Bayesian MCMC sample of trees using revised Celtic age constraint of between 1800 BP and 2200 BP. The majority-rule consensus tree for the entire sample is shown in the upper left.*

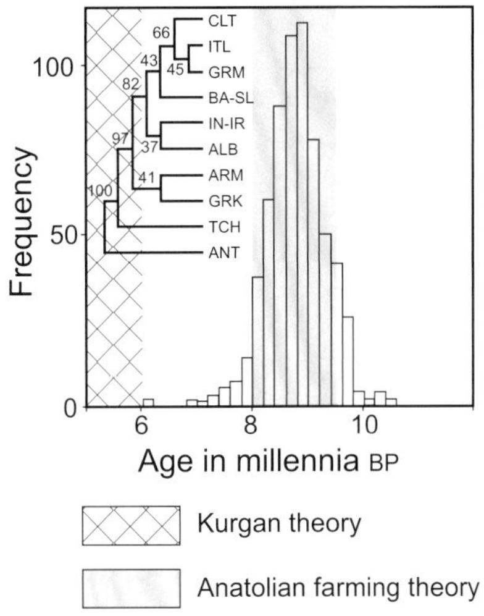


**Figure 8.13.** *Frequency distribution of basal age estimates from filtered Bayesian MCMC sample of trees using minimum set of topological constraints [(Anatolian, Tocharian, (Greek, Armenian, Albanian, (Iranian, Indic), (Slavic, Baltic), (North Germanic, West Germanic), Italic, Celtic))]* (n = 670)*. The majority-rule consensus tree for the entire sample is shown in the upper left.*

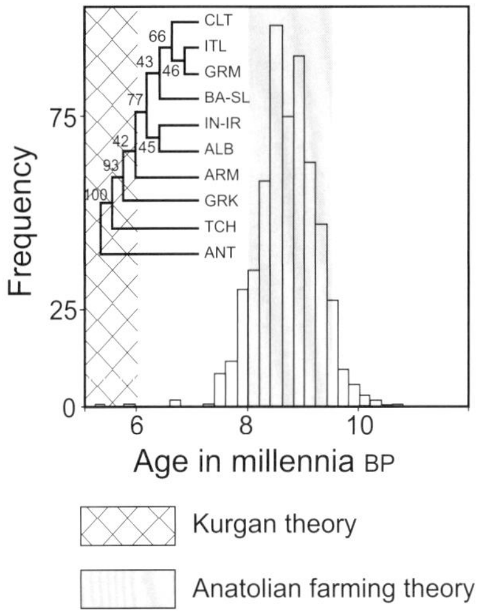


**Figure 8.14.** *Frequency distribution of basal age estimates from filtered Bayesian MCMC sample of trees with information about missing cognates included* (n = 620)*. The majority-rule consensus tree for the entire sample is shown in the upper left.*

*8.3. Calibrations and constraint trees*

At the conference on which this volume is based, a question was raised about the age constraint used for Insular Celtic. It was suggested that whilst we used a maximum age constraint of 2750 BP, an age constraint of between 2200 BP and 1800 BP would have been more suitable. We do not wish to engage in debates about the correct age of the Insular Celtic divergence, however, a re-analysis of the data using the suggested ages serves to demonstrate the robustness of our results to variations in age constraints. Figure 8.12 shows the distribution of divergence times using the much later Celtic age constraints. Clearly, our results are robust to alterations in this age constraint. In fact, the step-by-step removal of each of the 14 age constraints on the consensus tree revealed that divergence time estimates were robust to calibration errors across the tree. For 13 nodes, the reconstructed age was within 390 years of the original constraint range. Only the reconstructed age for Hittite showed an appreciable variation from the constraint range. This may be attributable to the effect of missing data associated with extinct languages. Reconstructed ages at the base of the tree ranged from 10,400 BP with the removal of the Hittite age constraint, to 8500 BP with the removal of the Iranian group age constraint. The results are highly robust calibration errors because of the large number of age constraints we used to calibrate rates of lexical evolution across the tree.

We also wanted to be sure that the constraint tree used to filter the Bayesian distribution of trees had not systematically biased our results. Figure 8.13 shows the divergence time distribution for the initial data set after filtering using a minimum set of topological constraints [(Anatolian, Tocharian, (Greek, Armenian, Albanian, (Iranian, Indic), (Slavic, Baltic), (North Germanic, West Germanic), Italic, Celtic))]. Again, the divergence time distribution was consistent with the Anatolian farming theory.

*8.4. Missing data*

Another possible bias was the effect of missing data. Some of the languages in the Dyen *et al.* (1992) data base may have contained fewer cognates because information about these languages was missing. For example, the three extinct languages (Hittite, Tocharian A & Tocharian B) are derived from a limited range of source texts and it is possible that some cognates were missed because the terms were not referred to in the source text. This may have biased divergence time estimates by falsely increasing basal branch-lengths. Nicholls & Gray (Chapter 14 this volume) point out that we should expect fewer cognates to be present in the languages at the base of the tree anyway — the fact that Hittite has 94 cognates whilst most languages have around 200, does not necessarily imply that data is missing. Nonetheless, we tested for the effect of missing data by including information about whether or not the word for a particular term was missing from the data base. If we could not rule out the possibility that a cognate was absent from a language because it had not been found or recorded, then that cognate was coded as missing (represented by a '?' in the matrix). Encoding missing cognate information in this way means that we can account for uncertainty in the data itself using the likelihood model — the unknown states become parameters to be estimated. Analyzing this recoded data also produced an age range consistent with the Anatolian theory (see Fig. 8.14).

*8.5. Root of Indo-European*

Finally, we tested the effect of the rooting point for the trees. In the previous analyses, trees were rooted with Hittite. Although this is consistent with independent linguistic analyses (Gamkrelidze & Ivanov 1995; Rexová *et al.* 2003), other potential root points are possible. It could be claimed that a Hittite root biases age estimates in favour of the Anatolian hypothesis. We thus reran the rate-smoothing analysis rooting the consensus tree in Figure 8.8 with Balto-Slavic, Greek, Tocharian and Indo-Iranian groups. In all four cases the estimated divergence time *increased* to between 9500 BP and 10,700 BP.

## 9. Discussion

The time-depth estimates reported here are consistent with the times predicted by a spread of language with the expansion of agriculture from Anatolia. The branching pattern and dates of internal nodes are broadly consistent with archaeological evidence indicating that between the tenth and sixth millennia BP a culture based on cereal cultivation and animal husbandry spread from Anatolia into Greece and the Balkans and then out across Europe and the Near East (Gkiasta *et al.* 2003; Renfrew 1987). Hittite appears to have diverged from the main Proto-Indo-European stock around 8700 years ago, perhaps reflecting the initial migration out of Anatolia. Indeed, this date exactly matches estimates for the age of Europe's first agricultural settlements in southern Greece (Renfrew 1987). Following the initial split, the language tree shows the formation of separate Tocharian, Greek, and then Armenian lineages, all before 6000 BP, with all of the remaining language families formed by 4000 BP. We note that the received linguistic orthodoxy (Indo-European is only 6000 years old) does approximately fit the divergence dates we obtained for most of the branches of the tree. Only the basal branches leading to Hittite, Tocharian, Greek and Armenian are well beyond this age. Interestingly, the date range hypothesized for the Kurgan expansion does correspond to a rapid period of divergence on the consensus tree. According to the divergence time estimates shown in Figure 8.8, many of the major Indo-European sub-families — Indo-Iranian, Balto-Slavic, Germanic, Italic and Celtic — diverged between six and seven thousand years ago — intriguingly close to the hypothesized time of the Kurgan expansion. Thus it seems possible that there were two distinct phases in the spread of Indo-European: an initial phase, involving the movement of Indo-European with agriculture, out of Anatolia into Greece and the Balkans some 8500 years ago; and a second phase (perhaps the Kurgan expansion) which saw the subsequent spread of Indo-European languages across the rest of Europe and east, into Persia and Central Asia.

## 10. Response to our critics

*10.1. The potential pitfalls of linguistic palaeontology*

A number of linguists have claimed that *linguistic palaeontology* offers a compelling reason why the arguments we have presented must be wrong: Proto-Indo-Europeans are claimed to have had a word for 'wheel' (**k$^w$(e)k$^w$l-o-*) but wheels did not exist in Europe 9000 years ago. The case is based on a widespread distribution of apparently related words for wheel in Indo-European languages. This is often presented as a knock-down argument against any age of Indo-European older than 5000 to 6000 years (when wheels first appear in the archaeological record). However, there are at least two alternative explanations for the distribution of terms associated with wheel and wheeled transport.

First, independent *semantic* innovations from a common root are a likely mechanism by which we can account for the supposed Proto-Indo-European reconstructions associated with wheeled transport (Trask 1996; Watkins 1969). Linguists can reconstruct word forms with much greater certainty than their meanings. For example, upon the development of wheeled transport, words derived from the Proto-Indo-European term **kwel-* (meaning 'to turn, rotate') may have been independently co-opted to describe the wheel. On the basis of the reconstructed ages shown in Figure 8.8, as few as three such semantic innovations around the sixth millennium BP could have accounted for the attested distribution of terms related to **k^w(e)k^wl-o-* 'wheel' (one shift just before the break up of the Italic-Celtic-Germanic-Balto-Slavic-Indo-Iranian lineage, one shift in the Greek-Armenian lineage, and one shift [or borrowing] in the Tocharian lineage).

The second possible explanation for the distribution of terms pertaining to wheeled vehicles is widespread borrowing. Good ideas spread. Terms associated with a new technology are often borrowed along with the technology. The spread of wheeled transport across Europe and the Near East 5000–6000 years ago seems a likely candidate for borrowing of this sort. Linguists are able to identify many borrowings (particularly more recent ones) on the basis of the presence or absence of certain systematic sound correspondences. However, our date estimates suggest that most of the major Indo-European groups were just beginning to diverge when the wheel was introduced. We would thus expect the currently attested forms of any borrowed terms to look as if they were inherited from Proto-Indo-European — they may thus be impossible to reliably identify.

Both of these arguments are discussed in more detail elsewhere (Watkins 1969; Renfrew 1987; Atkinson & Gray 2006). It suffices to say that both the power and the pitfalls of linguistic palaeontology are well known. We are disappointed that in their rush to dismiss our paper in the media, otherwise scholarly and responsible linguists have claimed much greater certainty for their semantic reconstructions than is justifiable. This does not mean that we think there is no issue here. Ideally, we should aim to synthesize all lines of evidence relating to the age of Indo-European. Ringe (unpublished manuscript) presents a careful summary of the terms related to wheeled vehicles in Indo-European. He argues that words for 'thill' (a pole that connects a yoke or harness to a vehicle) and 'yoke' can confidently be reconstructed for Proto-Indo-European. He notes that reflexes of **k^w(e)k^wl-o-* 'wheel' have not been found in Anatolian languages but exist in Tocharian A and B and other Indo-European languages, and hence can be reconstructed for the common ancestor of all non-Anatolian Indo-European languages. Ringe claims that the specific forms of these words make parallel semantic changes or borrowing extremely implausible. It would be extremely useful to attempt to quantify just how unlikely such alternative scenarios are. Until all the assumptions of these arguments are formalized, and the probability of alternative scenarios quantified, it will remain difficult to synthesize all the different lines of evidence on the age of Indo-European.

*10.2. Independence of characters*

As mentioned in section 5, Evans *et al.* (Chapter 10 this volume) claim our evolutionary model of binary character evolution is 'patently inappropriate' because it assumes independence between characters when our characters are clearly not independent. However, we do not believe that any violation of independence necessarily biases our time-depth estimates. We note that the assumption of independence does not hold for nucleotide or amino acid sequence data either. For example, compensating substitutions in ribosomal RNA sequences result in correlation between paired sites in stem regions (Felsenstein 2004). However, biologists still get reasonably accurate estimates of phylogeny despite violations of this assumption. In fact, *nothing in the Evans* et al. *paper demonstrates that coding the data as binary characters, rather than the multistate characters, will produce biased results.* Pagel & Meade (Chapter 15 this volume) demonstrated that, on the contrary, binary and multi-state coded data produce trees that differ in length by a constant of proportionality. In other words, the binary and multi-state trees are just scaled versions of one another. Since we estimate rates of evolution for each tree using the branch lengths of that tree, scaling the branch lengths does not affect our results. Pagel & Meade (Chapter 15 this volume) also approximated the effect of violations of the independence assumption on the MCMC analysis by 'heating' the likelihood scores. They inferred that violations of independence would produce higher posterior probability values but would have little effect on the consensus tree topology. This means that we may have underestimated the error due to phylogenetic uncertainty but our estimates will not be biased towards any particular date.

Finally, treating cognate sets as the fundamental unit of lexical evolution does not, as Evans *et al.* (Chapter 10 this volume) argue, constitute an 'extreme violation' of the independence assumption. Almost all of the languages in the Dyen *et al.* (1992) data base contain polymorphisms, meaning that for a given language there exist multiple words of the same meaning. The polymorphisms in our data are a reflection of the nature of lexical evolution. Specifically, they demonstrate a lack of strict dependence between cognate sets within meaning categories — i.e. a word with a given meaning can arise in a language that already has a word of that meaning. Models of lexical evolution that do not allow polymorphisms (e.g. Ringe *et al.* 2002) could also be labelled as 'patently inappropriate' because they assume that for a word to arise in a language any existing words with that meaning must be concomitantly lost from the language. This is not always the case. Ringe *et al.* (2002) note that although the words 'small' and 'little' have

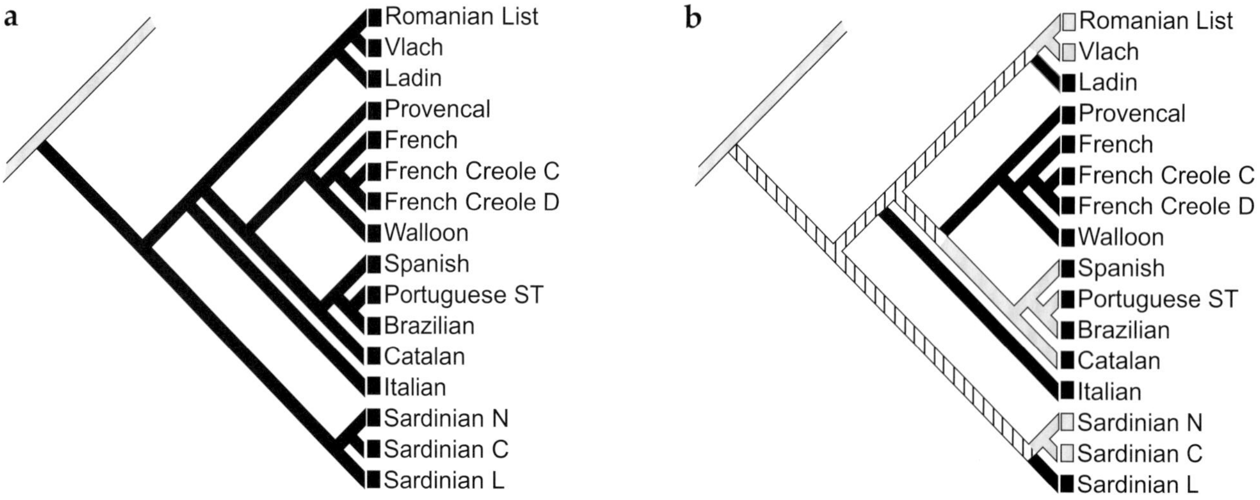


**Figure 8.15.** a) *Parsimony character trace for reflexes of Latin focus (originally 'hearth' but borrowed as 'fire') on the Romance consensus tree. Black indicates presence of the character, grey indicates absence and dashed indicates uncertainty. This shows borrowing across the whole Romance subgroup — evolutionary change is inferred at the base of the subgroup with no change within the subgroup, falsely inflating divergence time estimates.* b) *as with (a) but for reflexes of Latin testa (originally 'cup, jar, shell' but borrowed as 'head'). Here the borrowing is not across the whole Romance subgroup — evolutionary change is inferred within the subgroup.*

very similar meanings, they have persisted together in English for over a thousand years. Our binary coding procedure allows us to represent such polymorphisms with ease. The presence of polymorphisms means that dependencies between cognate sets are not as strong as Evans *et al.* claim. A further factor that weakens the dependencies between the cognate sets arises from the 'thinning' process that occurs in lexical evolution. The observed cognate sets do not represent the full compliment of actual cognates that arose in Indo-European (see Nicholls & Gray Chapter 14 this volume). Some cognates that existed in the past will not have persisted into present-day languages and any unique 'cognates' were not included in the analysis. This 'thinning' of the cognates also acts to reduce dependencies between characters in the analysis and thus further weakens any effect of violations of independence. Further research by Atkinson *et al.* (2005) using synthetic data has shown that violations of the independence assumption do not significantly affect date estimates.

*10.3. Confidence in lexical data*

From a phylogenetic viewpoint the lexicon is a tremendously attractive source of data because of the large number of possible characters it affords. However, we are aware that many historical linguists are sceptical of inferences based purely on lexical data. Garrett (Chapter 12 this volume) argues that borrowing of lexical terms, or *advergence,* within the major Indo-European subgroups could have distorted our results. He identifies a number of cases where an ancestral term has been replaced by a different term in all or some of the daughter languages, presumably via borrowing:

> Thus Latin *ignis* 'fire' has been replaced by reflexes of Latin *focus* 'hearth' throughout Romance, and archaic Sanskrit *hanti* 'kills' has been replaced by reflexes of a younger Sanskrit form *marayati* throughout Indo-Aryan.

Garret argues correctly that, where a word has been borrowed across a subgroup after the initial divergence of the group, our method will infer that the word evolved in the branch leading up to that subgroup (see Latin *focus* example: Fig. 8.15a). This will falsely inflate the branch lengths below the subgroups and deflate branch lengths within each group. Since we estimate rates of evolution on the basis of within-group branch lengths, it is argued that we will underestimate rates of change and hence overestimate divergence lower in the tree. However, this argument requires that two special assumptions hold. First, any borrowing must occur across a whole subgroup and only across a whole subgroup. When terms are not borrowed across the whole group there is no systematic bias to infer changes in the branch leading to the group. Depending on the distribution of borrowed terms, advergence can even produce the opposite effect, falsely inflating branch lengths within subgroups and hence causing us to underestimate divergence times. It seems unlikely that all or even most borrowed terms were borrowed across an entire subgroup. Garrett highlighted 16 instances of borrowing within Indo-European subgroups.[2] These were presumably selected because they were thought to reflect the sort of advergence pattern that would bias our results. Of these, at least 6 are unlikely to favour inferred language change at the base of a subgroup.[3] Figure 8.15b shows the example of the Romance term for 'head'.

Second, even if we accept the first assumption, we must assume that the proposed process of advergence is unique to contemporary languages. As Garrett (Chapter 12 this volume) puts it, this requires 'the unscientific assumption that linguistic change in the period for which we have no direct evidence was radically different from change we can study directly'. Rather than arguing that borrowing was rare at one stage and then suddenly became common across all of the major lineages at about the same time, it seems more plausible to suggest that borrowing has always occurred. If the same process of advergence in related languages has always occurred then the effect of shifting implied changes to more ancestral branches will be propagated down the tree such that there should be no net effect on divergence time calculation. For example, borrowing within Italic may shift inferred changes from the more modern branches to the branch leading to Italic, but borrowing between Proto-Italic and its contemporaries will also shift inferred changes from this branch to ancestral branches. This means that whilst we may incorrectly reconstruct some proto-Indo-European roots, our divergence time calculation will not be affected. We maintain that although advergence has undoubtedly occurred throughout the history of Indo-European, and that this may have affected our trees, this effect is likely to be random and there is no reason to think it will have significantly biased our results. Atkinson *et al.* (2005) analyzed synthetic data with simulated borrowing, and found that date estimates were highly robust to even high levels of borrowing.

Ringe *et al.* (2002) argue that non-lexical characters such as grammatical and phonological features are less likely to be borrowed (although they also note that parallel changes in phonological and morphological characters are possible). To avoid potential problems due to lexical borrowing they coded 15 phonological and 22 morphological characters as strict constraints in their analyses (they did not throw out the remaining 333 lexical characters). While we agree that phonological and morphological characters would be very useful, we believe there are good reasons to trust the inferences based on the lexical data in our case. The Dyen *et al.* (1992) data has had much of the known borrowing filtered from it. Further, the relationships we infer between Indo-European languages are remarkably similar to those inferred by linguists using the comparative method. Our results are not only consistent with accepted language relationships, but also reflect acknowledged uncertainties, such as the position of Albanian. Our time-depth estimates for internal nodes of the Indo-European tree are also congruent with known historical events (i.e. when constraints were removed step-by-step from each of the 13 internal constraint points, the reconstructed ages were within 390 years of the original constraint range: Gray & Atkinson 2003). Significantly, if we constrain our trees to fit the Ringe *et al.* (2002) typology we get very similar date estimates to our initial consensus tree topology. In short, there is nothing to indicate that either our tree typologies or date estimates have been seriously distorted by the use of just lexical data.

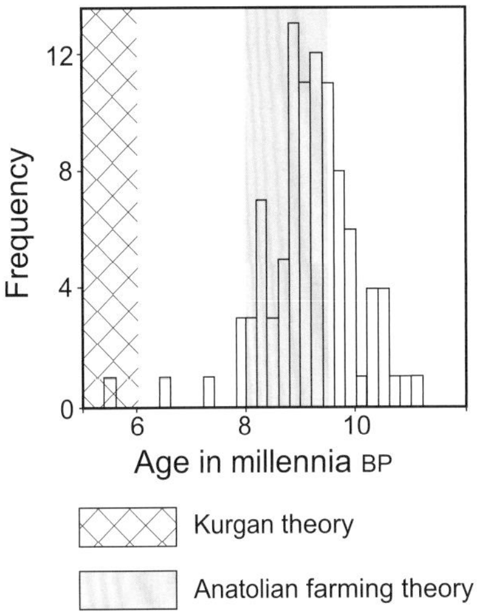


**Figure 8.16.** *Frequency distribution of basal age estimates from filtered Bayesian MCMC sample of trees using Swadesh 100-word list items only* (n = 97).

Determined critics might still claim that the remaining undetected lexical borrowing that undoubtedly exists in the Dyen *et al.* data (see Nicholls & Gray Chapter 14 this volume) has led us to make erroneous time-depth inferences at the root of the Indo-European tree. The Swadesh 100-word list is expected to be more resistant to change and less prone to borrowing than the 200-word list (Embleton 1991; McMahon & McMahon 2003). If undetected borrowing has biased our tree topology and divergence time estimates then the 100-word list might be expected to produce different estimates. To assess this possibility we repeated the analysis using only the Swadesh 100-word list items. Figure 8.16 shows the results of this analysis. Predictably, with a smaller data set variance in the age

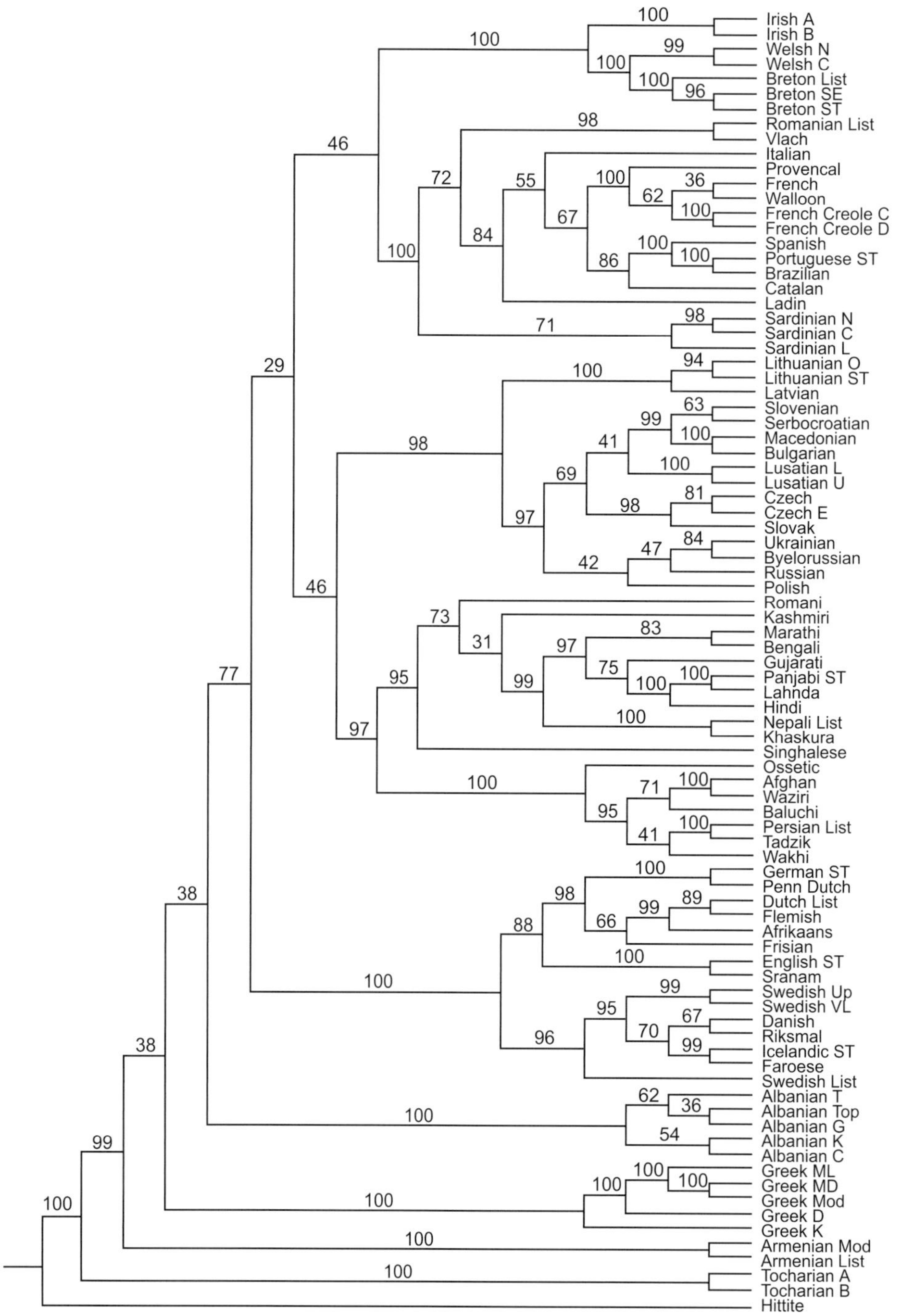


**Figure 8.17.** *Majority-rule consensus tree (unfiltered) for Swadesh 100-word list items only. Values above each branch express uncertainty (posterior probability) in the tree as a percentage.*

estimates increased. However, the resulting age range was still consistent with the Anatolian theory of Indo-European origin. Interestingly, the majority rule consensus tree (shown in Fig. 8.17) is *slightly* different to that obtained from the full data set. It contains a Balto-Slavic-Indo-Iranian group and an Italo-Celtic group. Ringe *et al.*'s (2002) compatibility analysis also found these clades. The low posterior probability values for these groups mean that we should not over-interpret the certainty of these deeper relationships, but clearly the possibility that undetected lexical borrowing is obscuring some of the deeper relationships would repay further attention. We emphasize that this possible borrowing does not appear, however, to affect our time-depth estimates for the root of the tree.

It is interesting to note that whilst our methodology produced consistent results using the Swadesh 100- and 200-word list, Tischler's (1973) glottochronological analysis was affected by the choice of word list. Tischler generated Indo-European divergence times using pair-wise distance comparisons between languages under the assumption of constant rates of lexical replacement. Using the Swadesh 200-word list, he calculated that the core Indo-European languages (Greek, Italic, Balto-Slavic, Germanic and Indo-Iranian) diverged around 5500 BP whilst Hittite diverged from the common stock around 8400 BP. This is in striking agreement with the timing depicted in Figure 8.8. However, the same calculation using the Swadesh 100-word list, produced a Hittite divergence time of almost 11,000 BP. Other inferred divergence times were also older. Tischler favoured the 200-word list results because they tended to be more consistent and were based on a larger sample size. However, the disparate 100 word list ages led Tischler to conclude that the divergence times for Hittite (and a number of other peripheral Indo-

European languages, including Albanian, Armenian and Old Irish) were in fact anomalous and he instead favoured an age for Indo-European of between 5000 and 6000 years, reflecting the break-up of the core languages. He explained the apparent earlier divergence of Hittite, Albanian, Old Irish and Armenian as an artefact of borrowing with non-Indo-European languages or increased rates of change.

## 11. Conclusion

The analyses we have presented here are far from the last word on the vexed issue of Indo-European origins. We expect that 'every species of scholar and would be savant who can take pen to hand' will still be drawn to the question of Indo-European origins. However, in contrast to some of the more pessimistic claims of our critics, we do not think that estimating the age of the Indo-European language family is an intractable problem. Some of these critics have argued that it is hard enough to get the tree typology correct, let alone branch lengths or divergence times. From this point of view all efforts to estimate dates should be abandoned until we can get the tree exactly right. We think that would be a big mistake. It would prematurely close off legitimate scientific inquiry. The probability of getting the one 'perfect phylogeny' from the $6.66 \times 10^{152}$ possible unrooted trees for 87 languages is rather small. Fortunately we do not need to get the tree exactly correct in order to make accurate date estimates. Using the Bayesian phylogenetic approach we can calculate divergence dates over a distribution of most probable trees, integrating out uncertainty in the phylogeny. We acknowledge that estimating language divergence dates is difficult, but maintain it is possible if the following conditions are satisfied:

a) a data set of sufficient size and quality can be assembled to enable the tree and its associated branch lengths to be estimated with sufficient accuracy;
b) most of the borrowing is removed from the data;
c) an appropriate statistical model of character evolution is used (it should contain sufficient parameters to give accurate estimates but not be over-parameterized);
d) multiple nodes on the tree are calibrated with reliable age ranges;
e) uncertainty in the estimation of tree topology and branch lengths are incorporated into the analysis;
f) variation in the rate of linguistic evolution is accommodated in the analysis.

The analyses of Indo-European divergence dates we have outlined above go a long way to meeting these requirements. The Dyen *et al.* (1997) data set we used in our analyses contains over two thousand carefully coded cognate sets (condition a). Dyen *et al.* excluded known borrowings from these sets (condition b). The two state, time-reversible model of cognate gains and losses with gamma distributed rate heterogeneity produced accurate trees (i.e. congruent with the results of the comparative method and known historical relationships)[4] (condition c). When the branch lengths were combined with the large number of well-calibrated nodes (condition d), the estimated divergence dates were also in line with known historical events. The Bayesian MCMC approach allowed us to incorporate phylogenetic uncertainty into our analyses (condition e), and to investigate the consequences of variations in the priors, tree rooting, and stringency in cognate judgements. Finally, rate smoothing allowed us to estimate divergence dates without the assumption of a strict glottoclock (condition f). *We challenge our critics to find any paper on molecular divergence dates that uses as many calibration points, investigates the impact of so many different assumptions, or goes to the same lengths to validate its results.*

In the words of W.S. Holt, history is 'a damn dim candle over a damn dark abyss'. Although we see reason for careful scholarship when attempting to estimate language divergence dates, we see no justification for pessimism here. Far from dancing around the question of Indo-European origins like moths around a flame, with the light of computational phylogenetic methods we can illuminate the past.

### Notes

1. Ten million post burn-in trees were generated using the MrBayes (Huelsenbeck & Ronquist 2001). To ensure that consecutive samples were independent, only every 10,000th tree was sampled from this distribution, producing a sample size of 1000.
2. The proposed borrowings were: in Romance — ear, fire, liver, count, eat, head and narrow; in Germanic — leaf, sharp and think; and in Indic — kill, night, play, suck, flower and liver. We note that this list was not intended by Garrett to be a comprehensive account of all possible borrowings.
3. Borrowings that are unlikely to favour inferred language change at the base of a subgroup or that would favour inferred language change within a subgroup are: in Romance — ear, head, narrow; in Germanic — leaf; and in Indic — flower and liver.
4. We do, however, agree that the question of model specification would repay further investigation (see Nicholls & Gray Chapter 14 this volume; Pagel Chapter 15 this volume; Atkinson *et al.* 2005).

### References

Adams, D.Q., 1999. *A Dictionary of Tocharian B.* (Leiden Studies in Indo-European 10.) Amsterdam: Rodopi. Available via online data base at S. Starostin & A. Lubotsky (eds.), *Database Query to A dictionary of Tocharian B.* http://iiasnt.leidenuniv.nl/ied/index2.html.

Atkinson, Q.D. & R.D. Gray, 2006. Are accurate dates an intractable problem for historical linguistics? in *Mapping our Ancestry: Phylogenetic Methods in Anthropology and Prehistory,* eds. C. Lipo, M. O'Brien, S. Shennan & M. Collard. Chicago (IL): Aldine, 269–96.

Atkinson, Q.D., G. Nicholls, D. Welch & R.D. Gray, 2005. From words to dates: water into wine, mathemagic or phylogenetic inference? *Transactions of the Philological Society* 103(2), 193–219.

Bateman, R., I. Goddard, R. O'Grady, V. Funk, R. Mooi, W. Kress & P. Cannell, 1990. Speaking of forked tongues: The feasibility of reconciling human phylogeny and the history of language. *Current Anthropology* 31, 1–24.

Bellwood, P., 1991. The Austronesian dispersal and the origin of languages. *Scientific American* 265, 88–93.

Bellwood, P., 1994. An archaeologist's view of language macrofamily relationships. *Oceanic Linguistics* 33, 391–406.

Bergsland, K. & H. Vogt, 1962. On the validity of glottochronology. *Current Anthropology* 3, 115–53.

Blust, R., 2000. Why lexicostatistics doesn't work: the 'Universal Constant' hypothesis and the Austronesian languages, in *Time Depth in Historical Linguistics,* eds. C. Renfrew, A. McMahon & L. Trask. (Papers in the Prehistory of Languages.) Cambridge: McDonald Institute for Archaeological Research, 311–32.

Bryant, D., F. Filimon & R.D. Gray, 2005. Untangling our past: Pacific settlement, phylogenetic trees and Austronesian languages, in *The Evolution of Cultural Diversity: Phylogenetic Approaches*, eds. R. Mace, C. Holden & S. Shennan. London: UCL Press, 69–85.

Burnham, K.P. & D.R. Anderson, 1998. *Model Selection and Inference: a Practical Information-Theoretic Approach.* New York (NY): Springer.

Campbell, L., 2004. *Historical Linguistics: an Introduction*. 2nd edition. Edinburgh: Edinburgh University Press.

Cavalli-Sforza, L.L., P. Menozzi & A. Piazza, 1994. *The History and Geography of Human Genes.* Princeton (NJ): Princeton University Press.

Clackson, J., 2000. Time depth in Indo-European, in *Time Depth in Historical Linguistics,* eds. C. Renfrew, A. McMahon & L. Trask. (Papers in the Prehistory of Languages.) Cambridge: McDonald Institute for Archaeological Research, 441–54.

Devoto, G., 1962. *Origini Indeuropeo.* Florence: Instituto Italiano di Preistoria Italiana.

Diakonov, I.M., 1984. On the original home of the speakers of Indo-European. *Soviet Anthropology and Archaeology* 23, 5–87.

Diamond, J. & P. Bellwood, 2003. Farmers and their languages: the first expansions. *Science* 300, 597.

Dyen, I., J.B. Kruskal & P. Black, 1992. *An Indoeuropean Classification: a Lexicostatistical Experiment.* (Transactions 82(5).) Philadelphia (PA): American Philosophical Society.

Dyen, I., J.B. Kruskal & P. Black, 1997. FILE IE-DATA1. Available at http://www.ntu.edu.au/education/langs/ielex/IE-DATA1.

Embleton, S., 1986. *Statistics in Historical Linguistics.* Bochum: Brockmeyer.

Embleton, S.M., 1991. Mathematical methods of genetic classification, in *Sprung from Some Common Source,* eds. S.L. Lamb & E.D. Mitchell. Stanford (CA): Stanford University Press, 365–88

Excoffier, L. & Z. Yang, 1999. Substitution rate variation among sites in mitochondrial hypervariable region I of humans and chimpanzees. *Molecular Biology and Evolution* 16, 1357–68.

Faguy, D.M. & W.F. Doolittle, 2000. Horizontal transfer of catalase-peroxidase genes between archaea and pathogenic bacteria. *Trends in Genetics* 16, 196–7.

Felsenstein, J., 2004. *Inferring Phylogenies.* Sunderland (MA): Sinauer.

Gamkrelidze, T.V. & V.V. Ivanov, 1995. *Indo-European and the Indo-Europeans: a Reconstruction and Historical Analysis of a Proto-Language and Proto-Culture.* Berlin: Mouton de Gruyter.

Gimbutas, M., 1973a. Old Europe *c.* 7000–3500 BC, the earliest European cultures before the infiltration of the Indo-European peoples. *Journal of Indo-European Studies* 1, 1–20.

Gimbutas, M., 1973b. The beginning of the Bronze Age in Europe and the Indo-Europeans 3500–2500 BC. *Journal of Indo-European Studies* 1, 163–214.

Gkiasta, M., T. Russell, S. Shennan & J. Steele, 2003. Neolithic transition in Europe: the radiocarbon record revisited. *Antiquity* 77, 45–62.

Glover, I. & C. Higham, 1996. New evidence for rice cultivation in S., S.E. and E. Asia, in *The Origins and Spread of Agriculture and Pastoralism in Eurasia,* ed. D. Harris. Cambridge: Blackwell, 413–42.

Goldman, N., 1993. Statistical tests of models of DNA substitution. *Journal of Molecular Evolution* 36, 182–98.

Gray, R.D. & Q.D. Atkinson, 2003. Language-tree divergence times support the Anatolian theory of Indo-European origin. *Nature* 426, 435–9.

Guterbock, H.G. & H.A. Hoffner, 1986. *The Hittite Dictionary of the Oriental Institute of the University of Chicago.* Chicago (IL): The Institute.

Hillis, D.M., 1992. Experimental phylogenetics generation of a known phylogeny. *Science* 255, 589–92.

Hillis, D.M., C. Moritz & B.K. Marble, 1996. *Molecular Systematics.* 2nd edition. Sunderland (MA): Sinauer.

Hjelmslev, L., 1958. *Essai d'une Critique de la Methode dite Glottochronologique. Proceedings of the Thirty-second International Congress of Americanists, Copenhagen, 1956.* Copenhagen: Munksgaard.

Hoffner, H.A., 1967. *An English–Hittite Dictionary*. New Haven (CT): American Oriental Society.

Holden, C.J., 2002. Bantu language trees reflect the spread of farming across Sub-Saharan Africa: a maximum-parsimony analysis. *Proceedings of the Royal Society of London* Series B 269, 793–9.

Holland, B. & V. Moulton, 2003. Consensus networks: a method for visualising incompatibilities in collections of trees, in *Algorithms in Bioinformatics, WABI 2003,* eds. G. Benson & R. Page. Berlin: Springer-Verlag, 165–76.

Huelsenbeck, J.P. & F. Ronquist, 2001. MRBAYES: Bayesian inference of phylogeny. *Bioinformatics* 17, 754–5.

Huelsenbeck, J.P., F. Ronquist, R. Nielsen & J.P. Bollback, 2001. Bayesian inference of phylogeny and its impact on evolutionary biology. *Science* 294, 2310–14.

Jukes, T.H. & C.R. Cantor, 1969. Evolution of protein molecules, in *Mammalian Protein Metabolism*, vol. 3, ed. M.N. Munro. New York (NY): Academic Press, 21–132.

Kuhner, M.K. & J. Felsenstein, 1994. A simulation comparison of phylogeny algorithms under equal and unequal evolutionary rates. *Molecular Biology and Evolution* 11, 459–68.

Kumar, V.K., 1999. *Discovery of Dravidian as the Common Source of Indo-European*. Retrieved Sept. 27th 2002 from http://www.datanumeric.com/dravidian/.

Levins, R., 1966. The strategy of model building in population biology, *American Scientist* 54, 421–31.

Mallory, J.P., 1989. *In Search of the Indo-Europeans: Languages, Archaeology and Myth.* London: Thames & Hudson.

McMahon, A. & R. McMahon, 2003. Finding families: quantitative methods in language classification. *Transactions of the Philological Society* 101, 7–55.

Metropolis, N., A.W. Rosenbluth, M.N. Rosenbluth, A.H. Teller & E. Teller, 1953. Equations of state calculations by fast computing machines. *Journal of Chemical Physics* 21, 1087–91.

Otte, M., 1997. The diffusion of modern languages in prehistoric Eurasia, in *Archaeology and Language*, eds. R. Blench & M. Spriggs. London: Routledge, 74–81.

Pagel, M., 1997. Inferring evolutionary processes from phylogenies. *Zoologica Scripta* 26, 331–48.

Pagel, M., 1999. Inferring the historical patterns of biological evolution. *Nature* 401, 877–84.

Pagel, M., 2000. Maximum-likelihood models for glottochronology and for reconstructing linguistic phylogenies, in *Time Depth in Historical Linguistics*, eds. C. Renfrew, A. McMahon & L. Trask. (Papers in the Prehistory of Languages.) Cambridge: The McDonald Institute for Archaeological Research, 413–39.

Renfrew, C., 1987. *Archaeology and Language: the Puzzle of Indo-European Origins.* London: Cape.

Rexová, K., D. Frynta & J. Zrzavy, 2003. Cladistic analysis of languages: Indo-European classification based on lexicostatistical data. *Cladistics* 19, 120–27.

Ringe, D., n.d. Proto-Indo-European Wheeled Vehicle Terminology. Unpublished manuscript.

Ringe, D., T. Warnow & A. Taylor, 2002. Indo-European and computational cladistics. *Transactions of the Philological Society* 100, 59–129.

Rosser, Z.H., T. Zerjal, M.E. Hurles *et al.*, 2000. Y-chromosomal diversity in Europe is clinal and influenced primarily by geography, rather than by language. *American Journal of Human Genetics* 67, 1526–43.

Sanderson, M., 2002a. *R8s, Analysis of Rates of Evolution*, version 1.50. http://ginger.ucdavis.edu/r8s/

Sanderson, M., 2002b. Estimating absolute rates of evolution and divergence times: a penalized likelihood approach. *Molecular Biology and Evolution* 19, 101–9.

Steel, M., M. Hendy & D. Penny, 1988. Loss of information in genetic distances. *Nature* 333, 494–5.

Swadesh, M., 1952. Lexico-statistic dating of prehistoric ethnic contacts. *Proceedings of the American Philosophical Society* 96, 453–63.

Swadesh, M., 1955. Towards greater accuracy in lexicostatistic dating. *International Journal of American Linguistics* 21, 121–37.

Swofford, D.L., G.J. Olsen, P.J. Waddell & D.M. Hillis, 1996. Phylogenetic Inference, in *Molecular Systematics*, eds. D.M. Hillis, C. Moritz & B.K. Marble. 2nd edition. Sunderland (MA): Sinauer, 407–514.

Tischler, J., 1973. *Glottochronologie und Lexicostatistik.* Innsbruck: Innsbrucker Verlag.

Tischler, J., 1997. *Hethitisch-Deutsches Worterverzeichnis.* Dresden: Probedruck.

Trask, R.L., 1996. *Historical Linguistics.* New York (NY): Arnold.

Watkins, C., 1969. *Indogermanische Grammatik III/1. Geschichte der Indogermanischen Verbalflexion.* Heidelberg: Carl Winter Verlag.

# Chapter 9

# Radiation and Network Breaking in Polynesian Linguistics

David Bryant

## 1. Introduction

The exploration and settlement of Polynesia was surely one of the greatest navigational feats in all human history. At a time when Europeans were tentatively edging out into the Mediterranean, Austronesians had colonized half the globe (King 2003). It was once thought that all of this exploration was carried out in primitive sailing vessels capable only of coastal navigation (Sharp 1956). Sharp claimed that the Polynesians had neither the technology nor the skills required for intentional voyages of longer than 200 miles from a coastline. Hawaii, Easter Island and New Zealand were discovered by accident, perhaps when the early sea-farers were blown off course in a storm.

For many, this process of accidental settlement followed by isolation made Polynesia a convenient laboratory for studying cultural, genetic, and linguistic evolution (Goodenough 1957). Polynesian societies were assumed to be more or less isolated from external influences and from each other. Consequently, Polynesia was one place where phyletic (tree-based) models of linguistic and cultural evolution could be applied without hesitation.

However the 'myth of primitive isolation' (Terrell *et al.* 1997) has been deconstructed. Sharp's theory of accidental discovery has given way to theories of systematic and intentional exploration. Polynesian sailing, navigational, and exploratory techniques were far more sophisticated than had been at first thought (Kirch & Green 2001). Hawaii, Easter Island, and New Zealand were discovered not by accident, but through planned and systematic exploration. Indeed the initial discoveries were followed by multiple return voyages. Eastern and western Polynesia were linked by extensive trading networks. The Polynesian islands were far from isolated.

Pawley & Green (1984) describe the different theories for Polynesian exploration using two *modes* of settlement:

*Radiation*, where islands are settled and then, for the most part, isolated. This corresponds to *allopatric* or *peripatric* speciation in evolutionary biology, as is well described by a tree-based model.

*Network breaking*, where groups of islands are settled and at first in close contact, but gradually divergences between different islands appear. The initial period of interaction creates a *dialect chain*. This corresponds to *sympatric* speciation in evolutionary biology.

Kirch & Green (2001) stress that analyses must incorporate *both* modes. The network-breaking model is more suited for closely clustered islands, while the radiation model is more appropriate for remote islands. Of course, it is difficult to quantify exactly what is close and what is remote, in this context.

The possibility of frequent and widespread linguistic exchanges between different societies poses a difficult challenge for phylogenetic linguistics. If we limit ourselves to tree-building methods, parsimony *or* model based, we run the risk of being severely misled. Recent exchanges may make some languages appear to have diverged far more recently than they actually did, and can lead to incorrectly derived histories (Terrell *et al.* 1997).

If the amount of borrowing between languages is minimal then network-based methods (e.g. Bryant & Moulton 2004) may be able to reconstruct the history of exchanges. However, if the interactions were continuous and widespread it may not actually be *possible*, for any method, to reconstruct the complete history of all past exchanges and interactions.

This situation is not unique to linguistics. In population genetics, there are generally not enough data to reconstruct the exact phylogenetic history of the genomes being studied, recombination or not (e.g. Stephens & Donnelly 2000). However, powerful statistical techniques can be employed to make estimates, or test hypotheses, by integrating over *all* possible

**Table 9.1.** *The accessibility matrix* **A**.

| | 1 | 2 | 3 | 4 | 5 | 6 | 7 | 8 | 9 | 10 | 11 |
|---|---|---|---|---|---|---|---|---|---|---|---|
| 1. Tonga | 0.0 | .020 | .014 | .0080 | .0098 | .0080 | .0049 | .011 | .0040 | .0013 | .010 |
| 2. Samoa | .020 | 0.0 | .012 | .010 | .0076 | .0067 | .0085 | .0076 | .0045 | .0022 | .011 |
| 3. S. Cooks | .014 | .012 | 0.0 | .010 | .024 | .013 | .0067 | .020 | .0062 | .0036 | .011 |
| 4. N. Cooks | .0080 | .010 | .010 | 0.0 | .010 | .0067 | .0049 | .0094 | .0049 | .0022 | .0045 |
| 5. Tahiti | .0098 | .0076 | .024 | .010 | 0.0 | .018 | .0089 | .044 | .0098 | .0040 | .0089 |
| 6. Marquesas | .0080 | .0067 | .013 | .0067 | .018 | 0.0 | .0058 | .024 | .0089 | .0045 | .0053 |
| 7. Hawaii | .0049 | .0085 | .0067 | .0049 | .0089 | .0058 | 0.0 | .0094 | .0036 | .0013 | .0040 |
| 8. Tuamotu | .011 | .0076 | .020 | .0094 | .044 | .024 | .0094 | 0.0 | .015 | .0049 | .011 |
| 9. Mangareva | .0040 | .0045 | .0062 | .0049 | .0098 | .0089 | .0036 | .015 | 0.0 | .0062 | .0036 |
| 10. Easter | .0013 | .0022 | .0036 | .0022 | .0040 | .0045 | .0013 | .0049 | .0062 | 0.0 | 0.0 |
| 11. NZ | .010 | .011 | .011 | .0045 | .0089 | .0053 | .0040 | .011 | .0036 | 0.0 | 0.0 |

histories. The fact that we cannot reconstruct the exact history does not prevent us from making inferences about parameters or features of the data.

In this chapter, we do not even try to reconstruct an explicit history for Polynesian languages. Instead we look at a more general question: do the patterns of language similarity support a *radiation* model or a *network-breaking* model? We develop a model for language evolution in Polynesia that incorporates accessibility of islands, language innovations, exchanges between islands, and differing island settlement dates. We derive exact and analytic formulae for the language differences expected under this model, and use these results to estimate the rate of language change and inter-island exchange that has occurred. Our analysis demonstrates (with many caveats) the existence of substantial and continual exchanges between islands.

## 2. The data

### 2.1. *The accessibility matrix*

The islands of Polynesia are not equidistant from each other. Some are separated by just a few days' sailing; others, like New Zealand, by several weeks. Distance is not the only factor affecting how easy it is to get from one island to another, though it is the most important. A large island with high mountains is easier to find (and return to) than a small atoll that is barely above sea level. Irwin (1992) incorporated these factors into an *accessibility matrix*. We modify Irwin's matrix by restricting the islands to the 11 for which we have linguistic data, and by normalizing the entries so that they sum to one. The accessibility matrix **A** that we use is presented in Table 9.1.

### 2.2. *Linguistic data*

Our Polynesian linguistic data, kindly supplied by Russell Gray, was extracted from the enormous POLLEX data base (Biggs 1998). The data was coded as multi-state *lexical characters*, following (Ringe *et al.* 2002; Bryant *et al.* 2005). Each character corresponds to a *semantic slot*, or word meaning. We used the 200 semantic slots from the Swadesh list of core vocabulary (Swadesh 1952). The character coding for a particular semantic slot is an assignment of states to each language, with two languages assigned the same state if and only if they possess words that are true cognates for that semantic slot. See (Ringe *et al.* 2002) and (Bryant *et al.* 2005) for examples and discussion of this coding.

For each pair of islands we computed the proportion of semantic slots for which the two islands had words that are not cognate. The resulting distance matrix is presented in Table 9.2. Multi-dimensional scaling (MDS) (using XGVIS: Buja & Swayne 2002) and Neighbor-Net (Bryant & Moulton 2004) reveal similar patterns (Fig. 9.1). In both analyses we see a clear east–west division, with Tonga and Samoa well separated from the remaining languages. There is little or no indication of further subdivisions within the eastern Polynesian islands in the MDS, however the Neighbor-Net supports the division into Tahitic (Tahiti, Tuamotu, NZ, S. Cooks) and Marquesic languages, with Hawaii and Northern Cooks somewhat ambiguous.

### 2.3. *Settlement dates*

Figure 9.2 shows a hypothetical time-line for settlement of the Polynesian islands. The dates were estimated (somewhat roughly) from a summary of archaeological evidence made by (Kirch & Green 2001). These dates correspond to the earliest archaeological evidence for human presence. The date for Tuamotu was extrapolated from the date for the Austral Islands.

**Table 9.2.** *The proportion of semantic slots for which the languages possess words that are not cognate).*

| | 1 | 2 | 3 | 4 | 5 | 6 | 7 | 8 | 9 | 10 | 11 |
|---|---|---|---|---|---|---|---|---|---|---|---|
| 1. Tonga | 0.0 | 0.2159 | 0.4395 | 0.4737 | 0.4648 | 0.4523 | 0.4434 | 0.4660 | 0.4208 | 0.4633 | 0.4544 |
| 2. Samoa | 0.2159 | 0.0 | 0.3966 | 0.3848 | 0.4023 | 0.3984 | 0.3954 | 0.4131 | 0.3793 | 0.3943 | 0.4312 |
| 3. S. Cooks | 0.4395 | 0.3966 | 0.0 | 0.2132 | 0.1727 | 0.2583 | 0.2298 | 0.1992 | 0.2263 | 0.3163 | 0.2212 |
| 4. N. Cooks | 0.4737 | 0.3848 | 0.2132 | 0.0 | 0.2042 | 0.2318 | 0.2533 | 0.2406 | 0.2017 | 0.2439 | 0.3438 |
| 5. Tahiti | 0.4648 | 0.4023 | 0.1727 | 0.2042 | 0.0 | 0.2381 | 0.2315 | 0.1588 | 0.2316 | 0.2660 | 0.2472 |
| 6. Marquesas | 0.4523 | 0.3984 | 0.2583 | 0.2318 | 0.2381 | 0.0 | 0.2209 | 0.2298 | 0.1814 | 0.2319 | 0.2843 |
| 7. Hawaii | 0.4434 | 0.3954 | 0.2298 | 0.2533 | 0.2315 | 0.2209 | 0.0 | 0.2368 | 0.2215 | 0.2657 | 0.2609 |
| 8. Tuamotu | 0.4660 | 0.4131 | 0.1992 | 0.2406 | 0.1588 | 0.2298 | 0.2368 | 0.0 | 0.2471 | 0.3017 | 0.2061 |
| 9. Mangareva | 0.4208 | 0.3793 | 0.2263 | 0.2017 | 0.2316 | 0.1814 | 0.2215 | 0.2471 | 0.0 | 0.2067 | 0.3234 |
| 10. Easter Island | 0.4633 | 0.3943 | 0.3163 | 0.2439 | 0.2660 | 0.2319 | 0.2657 | 0.3017 | 0.2067 | 0.0 | 0.3891 |
| 11. NZ | 0.4544 | 0.4312 | 0.2212 | 0.3438 | 0.2472 | 0.2843 | 0.2609 | 0.2061 | 0.3234 | 0.3891 | 0.0 |

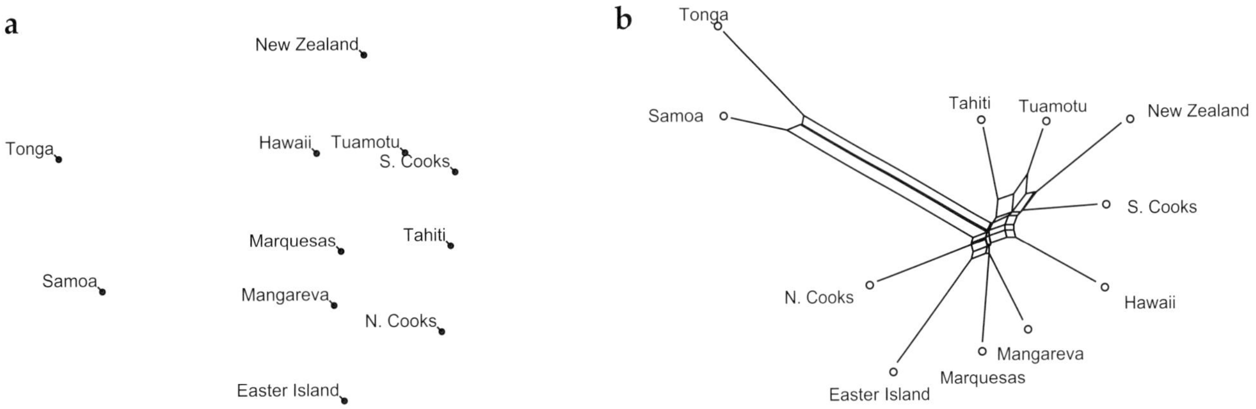


**Figure 9.1.** *Two representations of the distances between Polynesian languages: a) output from a two-dimensional multi-dimensional scaling analysis; b) Neighbor-Net.*

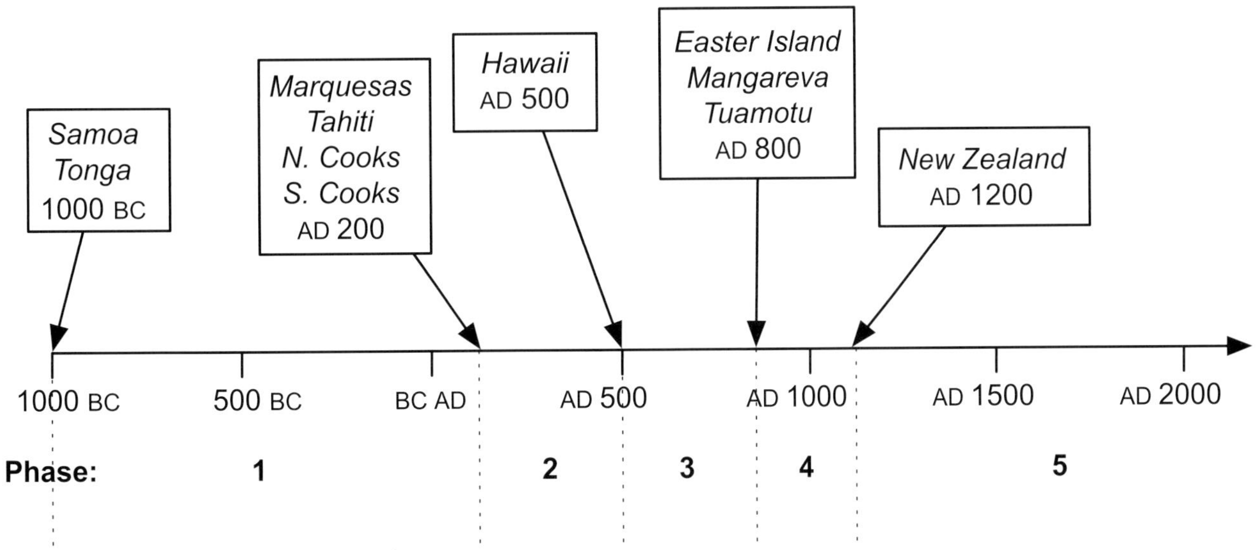


**Figure 9.2.** *Timeline of Polynesian settlement, giving the date estimates and phases of settlement used in this paper.*

## 3. Constructing a model of Polynesian language evolution

In this section we detail our probabilistic model of language evolution on these eleven Polynesian islands. We are only interested in the patterns of cognate and non-cognate words for the 200 semantic slots. For us, a language history is an assignment of states for every character (semantic slot) for every point of time, for every island settled by that time. At a given time, two islands have the same state for a given slot if and only if, at that time, they possessed words for that slot that were cognate. Time ranges from 0 (1000 BC) to 3004 (the present).

Our model is *Markovian*, in the sense that the probabilities of a specific language assignment at time $t+h$, given the assignment at time $t$, is independent of the assignments for all times before $t$. In other words, only the current state of the system affects what happens next.

We model the progressive settlement of different islands by defining five *settlement phases* (see Fig. 9.2). The phases are delimited by the settlement times, and are numbered one to five. The number of settled islands, and therefore the number of islands involved in potential exchanges, changes for every phase.

Our model assumes (implicitly) that settlement of the different islands was a discrete event, with the islands introduced in each phase being settled on the exact dates given in Figure 9.2. A more sophisticated model would incorporate variability and estimation error into these settlement times. However this change would make the analysis a lot more complicated, and it is not immediately apparent that we would get a significantly better fit of the model to the data.

Let $S^{(i)}$ denote the set of islands that have been settled by phase $i$, where $i$ ranges from 1 to 5. Thus $S^{(1)}$ contains Tonga and Samoa only, while $S^{(5)}$ contains all eleven islands.

### *3.1. Initialization*

At time $t = 0$ Samoa and Tonga are the only settled islands. For each semantic slot we assign the same state to both islands.

### *3.2. During a phase*

There are two kinds of events that can occur during a given phase $i$: exchanges and innovations. Each occurs according to a *Poisson process*, with a different rate for each different event. We have tried to keep both events as simple as possible. This is appropriate if we are to test null hypotheses regarding the processes of language mutation and borrowing. However in both cases we are clearly modelling highly complex processes with very simple ones. Future versions could apply more sophisticated models.

*Exchange events:* Exchange events from island $a$ to island $b$ in $S^{(i)}$ occur with rate $\tau\mathbf{A}_{ab}$ per semantic slot per unit time with values for $\mathbf{A}_{ab}$ taken from Table 9.1. When an exchange occurs, a word in a semantic slot for the language on island $a$ is copied into the corresponding slot for island $b$.

*Word-innovation events:* A word innovation occurs at a rate $\mu$ per semantic slot per populated island. The word resulting from an innovation is not cognate with any of the words used in any other language.

### *3.3. Between phases*

The borderlines between phases correspond to settlement events. Suppose we are between phase $i$ and phase $i + 1$. Each island in $S^{(i+1)}$ that is not in $S^{(i)}$ is settled from a randomly chosen island in $S^{(i)}$. The probability that $b \in S^{(i+1)}$ is settled from $a \in S^{(i)}$ is

$$\frac{\mathbf{A}_{ab}}{\sum_{x \in S^{(i)}} \mathbf{A}_{xb}}.$$

The language of a newly settled island is copied from the island that settles it.

### *3.4. Relation to the radiation and network-breaking models*

We have described a relatively simple stochastic model with two parameters, $\tau$ and $\mu$. During each phase, the amount of exchange (borrowing) between different islands is determined by $\tau$. The probabilities of exchange between two islands correlate with the ease of migrating from one island to another. There would be a lot of exchange between some islands, while remote islands will be relatively isolated. The rate of innovation is determined by $\mu$, and innovations are more likely to persist on remote islands where there is less chance they will be 'corrected'.

If we set $\tau = 0$ then we obtain the radiation model, with no exchange between islands after settlement.

**Table 9.3.** *Parameters and constants in the basic model.*

| **Parameters** | |
|---|---|
| $\tau$ | Rate of exchange (transfer of cognates) |
| $\mu$ | Rate of mutation/innovation |
| **Constants** | |
| $\mathbf{A}$ | Accessibility matrix |
| $N$ | Number of semantic slots |
| $r$ | Number of possible cognates per semantic slot |
| $S^{(i)}$ | Islands inhabited during phase $i$. |
| $\sigma(a,b)$ | Probability that island $b$ is settled from island $a$. |

Cognate patterns generated according to this model will be completely tree-like. If we want to distinguish between the radiation model and the network-breaking model we can study the effect of increasing the parameter $\tau$.

## 4. Derivation of the expected differences between languages

Having formalized our model, we now study the patterns of linguistic differences that it generates. In this section we derive expectations for the pair-wise differences between sites.

For the remainder of the section we consider a single, arbitrary, semantic slot. The expected number of differences between languages follows directly, irrespective of whether or not the different slots are independent.

Let $C_{ab}(t)$ denote the event that island $a$ and island $b$ have cognate words (that is, the same state) for the semantic slot at time $t$. Let $c_{ab}(t)$ denote the probability $P[C_{ab}(t)]$ that $C_{ab}(t)$ holds.

If $t$ occurs during the middle of phase $i$ then, by definition $c_{ab}(t) = 0$ whenever either $a$ or $b$ are not in $S^{(i)}$, that is, when $a$ and $b$ have not both been settled by phase $i$.

We will determine the probabilities $c_{ab}(t)$ by solving a system of ordinary differential equations (ODEs). Let $t$ be a point in time in the middle of one of the settlement phases. Let $h$ be a value that is small enough such that $t + h$ is in the same phase. We will consider the limit of

$$\frac{c_{ab}(t+h)-c_{ab}(t)}{h} \qquad (1)$$

as $h$ goes to zero. This equals the derivative $\frac{d}{dt}c_{ab}(t)$.

*4.1. Background: 'little oh'* o(h) *notation*

Before proceeding we briefly review the 'little oh' notation $o(h)$. Writing

$$P[\text{Event } X] = \lambda h + o(h)$$

for some real number $\lambda$ is identical in meaning to writing

$$\lim_{h\to 0}\frac{P[\text{Event } X]-\lambda h}{h}=0$$

Hence if can find some function $F(t)$ such that

$$c_{ab}(t+h)=c_{ab}(t)+hF(t)+o(h)$$

then we have

$$\begin{aligned}0 &= \lim_{h\to 0}\frac{c_{ab}(t+h)-c_{ab}t-hF(t)}{h}\\ &= \lim_{h\to 0}\frac{c_{ab}(t+h)-c_{ab}t}{h}-F(t)\\ &= \frac{d}{dt}c_{ab}(t)-F(t).\end{aligned}$$

Also note that if $P[\textit{Event } X_1] = \lambda_1 h + o(h)$ and $P[\textit{Event } X_2] = \lambda_2 h + o(h)$ then

$$P[\textit{Event } X_1] + P[\textit{Event } X_2] = \lambda_1 h + \lambda_2 h + o(h).$$

For any Poisson process with rate $\lambda$ the number of events occurring in the interval $[t, t+h]$ has a Poisson distribution

$$P[k \text{ events}] = e^{-\lambda h}\frac{(\lambda h)^k}{k!}.$$

If you expand out $e^{-\lambda h}$ into series form one gets

$$e^{-\lambda h} = 1-\lambda h+\frac{\lambda^2}{2!}h^2-\frac{\lambda^3}{3!}h^3+\ldots$$

The sum of the terms involving $h^2, h^3, \ldots$ is $o(h)$. We therefore get

$$P[1 \text{ event}] = \lambda h + o(h) \qquad (2)$$

$$P[2 \text{ or more events}] = 0 + o(h). \qquad (3)$$

*4.2. Setting up the ODE*

We now derive a formula for $c_{ab}(t + h)$ in terms of the probabilities at time $t$. Suppose that $t$ and $t + h$ are both in settlement phase $i$. As we have just seen, the probability of more than one event occurring between time $t$ and time $t + h$ is $o(h)$. This leaves four possible outcomes.

(i) *Exchange affecting this slot between islands* a *and* b. An exchange from island $a$ to island $b$ or from $b$ to $a$ affecting this slot occurs with probability $\tau(\mathbf{A}_{ab} + \mathbf{A}_{ba})h + o(h)$. If such a transfer occurs, the probability of $C_{ab}(t + h)$ equals one.

(ii) *Exchange affecting this slot from another settled island* x *to* a *or* b. For each settled island $x \in S^{(i)}$ there is an exchange from $x$ to $a$ affecting this slot with probability $\tau \mathbf{A}_{xa}h + o(h)$. If this transfer occurs the probability of $C_{ab}(t + h)$ is $c_{bx}(t)$. The formula for a transfer to $b$ is the same with $a$ and $b$ reversed. Note that we need to sum these probabilities over all $x \in S^{(i)}$ such that $x \neq a, b$.

(iii) *Innovation for this slot on island* a *or* b. A word innovation in this slot occurs on $a$ or $b$ with probability $2\mu h + o(h)$. If there is a word innovation then the probability $c_{ab}(t+h)$ of $a$ and $b$ having cognate words at time $t+h$ is 0.

(iv) *None of the above*. The probability of no transfers affecting $a$ or $b$ at this slot, and no innovations in $a$ or $b$ at this slot is simply 1 minus the probability of all of the above events, or

$$1-2\mu h-\tau(\mathbf{A}_{ab}+\mathbf{A}_{ba})h-\tau\sum_{x\in S^{(i)}-\{a,b\}}(\mathbf{A}_{xa}+\mathbf{A}_{xb})h+o(h)$$

$$=1-2\mu h-\tau\sum_{x\in S^{(i)}}(\mathbf{A}_{xa}+\mathbf{A}_{xb})h+o(h).$$

If none of these transfers or innovations do take place, then the probability, $c_{ab}(t+h)$, of identity at time $t+h$ is the same as the probability $c_{ab}(t)$ at time $t$.

Bringing everything together, we obtain

$$c_{ab}(t+h)=\tau(\mathbf{A}_{ab}+\mathbf{A}_{ba})h+\tau\sum_{x\in S^{(i)}-\{a,b\}}(\mathbf{A}_{xa}c_{bx}(t)+\mathbf{A}_{xb}c_{ax}(t))h$$
$$+\left(1-2\mu h-\tau\sum_{x\in S^{(i)}}(\mathbf{A}_{xa}+\mathbf{A}_{xb})h\right)c_{ab}(t)+o(h).$$

Subtracting $c_{ab}(t)$ from both sides, dividing by $h$ and taking the limit as $h\to 0$ gives the system of differential equations

$$\frac{d}{dt}c_{ab}(t)=\tau(\mathbf{A}_{ab}+\mathbf{A}_{ba})+\tau\sum_{x\in S^{(i)}-\{a,b\}}(\mathbf{A}_{xa}c_{bx}(t)+\mathbf{A}_{xb}c_{ax}(t))$$
$$-2\mu c_{ab}(t)-\tau\sum_{x\in S^{(i)}}(\mathbf{A}_{xa}+\mathbf{A}_{xb})c_{ab}(t) \qquad (4)$$

Here, $a,b$ ranges over all pairs in $S^{(i)}$.

Observe that the right-hand side is just a linear combination of the probabilities $c_{xy}(t)$. Hence we can re-express the entire system in one matrix equation. There are $11\times 10/2 = 55$ different pairs of islands $a,b$. Let $\mathbf{c}(t)$ be the vector with entries indexed by pairs of islands and

$$\mathbf{c}(t)_{ab} = c_{ab}(t).$$

Define the $55\times 55$ matrix $\mathbf{M}^{(i)}$ with rows and columns indexed by pairs of islands and entries given by

$$\mathbf{M}^{(i)}_{ab,cd}\begin{cases}0 & \text{if } a,b,c,d, \text{ are not all in } S^{(i)}\text{; else:}\\ -2\mu-\tau\sum_{z\in S^{(i)}}(\mathbf{A}_{za}+\mathbf{A}_{zb}) & \text{if } \{a,b\}=\{c,d\}\\ \tau\mathbf{A}_{bd} & \text{if } a=c;\\ \tau\mathbf{A}_{bc} & \text{if } a=d;\\ \tau\mathbf{A}_{ac} & \text{if } b=c;\\ 0 & \text{if } b=d;\\ & \text{otherwise.}\end{cases}$$

Let $\mathbf{x}^{(i)}$ denote the vector, also indexed by pairs of islands, with

$$x^{(i)}_{ab}=\begin{cases}\tau(\mathbf{A}_{ab}+\mathbf{A}_{ba}) & \text{if } a,b\in S^{(i)};\\ 0 & \text{otherwise.}\end{cases}$$

Let $t_i$ be the start of the current settlement phase. The system of equations (4) can be rewritten as

$$\frac{d}{dt}\mathbf{c}(t)=\mathbf{M}^{(i)}\mathbf{c}(t)+x^{(i)}$$

which has solution

$$\mathbf{c}(t) = e^{\mathbf{M}^{(i)}(t-t_i)}((\mathbf{M}^{(i)})^{-1}\mathbf{x}^{(i)}+\mathbf{c}(t_i)) - (\mathbf{M}^{(i)})^{-1}\mathbf{x}^{(i)}. \qquad (5)$$

Equation (5) gives the probabilities of languages having cognate words for a slot given the probabilities at the beginning of a phase. These probabilities can change *between* phases as well, due to the settlement process. Consider the settlement stage between phase $i$ and phase $i+1$. If $a$ is a settled island and $b$ is an island settled in this turn, then the probability that $b$ is settled from $a$ is

$$\frac{\mathbf{A}_{ab}}{\sum_{x\in S^{(i)}}\mathbf{A}_{xb}}$$

which we denote by $\sigma(a,b)$. This leads immediately to formulae for the probability $\mathbf{c}_{ab}$ that languages on islands $a$ and $b$ have cognate words in that slot after settlement:

*If* a,b *both already settled* then $\mathbf{c}_{ab}$ is unchanged.

*If* a *is already settled and* b *is newly settled* then for $b$ to have the same cognate as $a$ it must either have been settled from $a$ or from an island with a word that is cognate to the word used in $a$. Hence

$$\mathbf{c}_{ab}=\sigma(a,b)+\sum_{z\in S^{(i)}-\{a\}}\sigma(z,b)\mathbf{c}_{az}.$$

*If* a *and* b *are both newly settled* then the probability that they have cognate words in this slot equals the probability that they were settled from the same island, or from islands with words that are cognate. Hence in this case

$$\mathbf{c}_{ab} = \sum_{z \in S^{(i)}} \sigma(z,a)\sigma(,b) + \sum_{y \in S^{(i)}} \sum_{z \in S^{(i)}-\{y\}} \sigma(y,a)\sigma(z,b)\mathbf{c}_{yz}$$

Each of the above cases involves a linear combination of the elements in **c** and some constant terms. We can therefore construct a matrix $\mathbf{B}^{(i)}$ and vector $\mathbf{b}^{(i)}$ such that if **c** is the vector of probabilities before settlement then

$$\mathbf{B}^{(i)}\,\mathbf{c} + \mathbf{b}^{(i)}$$

is the vector of probabilities after settlement.

*4.3. Solution of the system: expected differences*

We now bring everything together and compute the expected proportion of semantic slots at which the current eleven languages have cognate words (given the values for the parameters $\tau,\mu$). For each phase $i$ we let $t_i$ denote the time just at the beginning of phase $i$ (after settlement). We also define $\mathbf{y}^{(i)} = -(\mathbf{M}^{(i)})^{-1}\mathbf{x}^{(i)}$. Then $\mathbf{y}^{(i)}$ contains the *equilibrium probabilities* for phase $i$, in the sense that if the system stayed in this phase for $t \to \infty$ then the limiting cognate probabilities would be $\mathbf{y}^{(i)}$. Generally, these are either all one or all zero, depending on the relative rate of innovations and exchanges.

Under our model, the initial conditions are that Samoa and Tonga were the first settled and, in the beginning, they shared the same language. Thus $\mathbf{c}(t_1)_{12} = 1$ and $\mathbf{c}(t_1)_{\mathrm{ab}} = 0$ for all other islands $a,b$.

From equation (5) the cognate probabilities are the end of phase 1 are

$$e^{(t_2 - t_1)\mathbf{M}^{(1)}}(\mathbf{c}(t_1) - \mathbf{y}^{(1)}) + \mathbf{y}^{(1)}$$

so the probabilities after settlement, at the beginning of phase 2, are

$$\mathbf{c}(t_2) = \mathbf{B}^{(1)}\left[e^{(t_2-t_1)\mathbf{M}^{(1)}}(\mathbf{c}(t_1) - \mathbf{y}^{(1)}) + \mathbf{y}^{(1)}\right] + \mathbf{b}^{(1)}.$$

In the same way

$$\mathbf{c}(t_3) = \mathbf{B}^{(2)}\left[e^{(t_3-t_2)\mathbf{M}^{(2)}}(\mathbf{c}(t_2) - \mathbf{y}^{(2)}) + \mathbf{y}^{(2)}\right] + \mathbf{b}^{(2)},$$

$$\mathbf{c}(t_4) = \mathbf{B}^{(3)}\left[e^{(t_4-t_3)\mathbf{M}^{(3)}}(\mathbf{c}(t_3) - \mathbf{y}^{(3)}) + \mathbf{y}^{(3)}\right] + \mathbf{b}^{(3)},$$

$$\mathbf{c}(t_5) = \mathbf{B}^{(4)}\left[e^{(t_5-t_4)\mathbf{M}^{(4)}}(\mathbf{c}(t_4) - \mathbf{y}^{(4)}) + \mathbf{y}^{(4)}\right] + \mathbf{b}^{(4)},$$

and the present-day probabilities are given by

$$\mathbf{c} = \mathbf{c}(3004) = e^{(3004-t_5)\mathbf{M}^{(5)}}(\mathbf{c}(t_5) - \mathbf{y}^{(5)}) + \mathbf{y}^{(5)}.$$

*4.4. Estimating the parameters*

For each pair of islands $a,b$ and each semantic slot we have that $\mathbf{c}_{ab}$ is the probability that both islands have words that are cognate. As the expectation of a sum is the sum of expectations, $1 - \mathbf{c}_{ab}$ equals the expected proportion of slots for which islands $a$ and $b$ have words that are not cognate. By comparing these expected differences with the observed differences, we can obtain rough estimates for the rate of innovations $\mu$ and the rate of exchanges $\tau$, as well as test whether our estimates of $\tau$ are large enough to reject the radiation model.

The values $\mathbf{c}_{ab}$ depend on $\mu$ and $\tau$ so we write them as a function $\mathbf{c}_{ab}(\mu,\tau)$. Let $\delta_{ab}$ denote the observed proportion of differences between the islands $a$ and $b$. We minimize the least squares residue

$$\sum_{a<b} (\mathbf{c}_{ab}(\mu,t) - \delta_{ab})^2.$$

We used the `fminsearch` routine in MATLAB to find values of $\mu$ and $\tau$ giving the smallest residue.

## 5. Results

Our model has two parameters, one determining the rate of innovation and the other determining the rate at which words are exchanged between islands. By fitting the model to the linguistic data, we can obtain estimates for these parameters and identify the extent to which linguistic differences between the Polynesian islands support a network-breaking or radiation model.

The residue (eqn. 6) is minimized when the rate of innovation $\mu$ is $9.09 \times 10^{-5}$ and the rate $\tau$ of transfers is $\tau = 0.0041$ words exchanged per year. All 100 random starting points converged to the same minimum. The value for $\mu$ corresponds to a rate of change of 9 per cent of slots per 1000 years, roughly in concordance with the rate obtained by Swadesh (1952). The value of $\tau$ corresponds to about 4 transfers between all islands per slot per thousand years.

Note that if we hold the transfer rate at $\tau = 0$ (no exchanges) as in the radiation model, the optimal value for $\mu$ is $\mu = 8.07 \times 10^{-5}$.

To test whether this is a significant amount of transfer, we generated random data under our model with parameters $\tau = 0$ (no exchanges) and $\mu = 8.07 \times 10^{-5}$. The goal was to test whether the high estimates of $\tau$ could be obtained randomly even when the true model had no transfers. The experiment was repeated 100 times. For each replicate we generated a simulated language data set and then determine the values of $\mu$ and $\tau$ that gave the best fit. We found that, out of the

100 runs, only 5 per cent gave estimates for $\tau$ that were greater than 0.0041 word exchanges per year. Hence, if our model is correct but there is no migration then we would expect to estimate the amount of migration we did get with probability at most 0.05. We can interpret this as a fairly significant indication that there were indeed non-trivial amounts of migration between the different Polynesian islands.

We stress that these results come with the obligatory warning that our statistical tests are only as good as our model. We have made a great number of simplifying assumptions when setting up our model, and these could well have misled our analysis. The long and arduous process of model validation, and detection of systematic biases, remains.

## 6. Discussion

We believe that this is the first explicit model for the effect of network breaking on linguistic patterns. There is, understandably, a lot of work remaining, and a lot of model assumptions that need testing. We have identified the most important directions for future research:

1. *Analysis of larger data sets.* In order to reduce the variance in our estimators, and properly compare different modes of language evolution, we need to increase both the number of semantic slots and the number of islands in the analysis. The POLLEX data base (Biggs 1998) is a rich source of linguistic data — but this needs to be complemented with accessibility data for a larger set of islands.
2. *Improved models of language change.* Following (Ringe *et al.* 2002) we have shoe-horned the linguistic data into a simple multi-state, infinite alleles, model. Unfortunately this model does not allow polymorphism in the data (more than one word for a concept), and any polymorphism will bias our estimates for mutation and transition rates.
3. *More sophisticated models for transfers.* There are several factors which should perhaps be incorporated into our model of exchange. For example, the varying population sizes on difference islands would influence the rate of language innovation and the rate of exchanges with neighbouring islands. As well, it is not clear that our naive use of the accessibility matrix really captures the relative ease of exchange between different islands.
4. *More efficient statistical techniques.* We have determined explicit formulae for the expected differences between islands. However to obtain really accurate estimates we also need to model variances and higher level joint probabilities. A full likelihood model would be ideal, possibly within a Bayesian framework.

With the appropriate statistical tools and enlarged data sets we can start testing and refining our model and, in the process, shed light on the features of Polynesian language evolution.

## References


Biggs, B., 1998. *POLLEX: Proto Polynesian Lexicon.*

Bryant, D. & V. Moulton, 2004. Neighbornet: an agglomerative algorithm for the construction of planar phylogenetic networks. *Molecular Biology and Evolution* 21, 255–65.

Bryant, D., F. Filimon & R. Gray, 2005. Untangling our past: languages, trees, splits and networks, in *The Evolution of Cultural Diversity: a Phylogenetic Approach,* eds. R. Mace, C. Holden, S. Shennan. London: UCL, 69–86.

Buja, A. & D.F. Swayne, 2002. Visualization methodology for multidimensional scaling. *Journal of Classification* 19(1), 7–43.

Goodenough, W.H., 1957. Oceania and the problem of controls in the study of cultural and human evolution. *Journal of the Polynesian Society* 66, 146–55.

Irwin, G.J., 1992. *The Prehistoric Exploration and Colonisation of the Pacific.* Cambridge: Cambridge University Press.

King, M., 2003. *The Penguin History of New Zealand.* Auckland: Penguin.

Kirch, P. & R. Green, 2001. *Hawaiki, Ancestral Polynesia.* Cambridge: Cambridge University Press.

Pawley, A. & R. Green, 1984. The Proto-Oceanic language community. *Journal of Pacific History* 19, 123–46.

Ringe, D., T. Warnow & A. Taylor, 2002. Indoeuropean and computational cladistics. *Transactions of the Philological Society* 100, 59–129.

Sharp, A., 1956. *Ancient Voyagers in the Pacific.* (Memoir 32.) Wellington: Polynesian Society

Stephens, M. & P. Donnelly, 2000. Inference in molecular population genetics. *Journal of the Royal Statistical Society* B62(4), 605–55.

Swadesh, M., 1952. Lexico-statistic dating of prehistoric ethnic contacts. *Proceedings of the American Philological Society* 96, 453–63.

Terrell, J.E., T. Hunt & C. Gosden, 1997. The dimensions of social life in the Pacific: human diversity and myth of the primitive isolate. *Current Anthropology* 38(2), 155–95.

# *Chapter 10*

# Inference of Divergence Times as a Statistical Inverse Problem

Steven N. Evans, Donald Ringe & Tandy Warnow

## 1. Introduction

A familiar complaint about statisticians and applied mathematicians is that they are the possessors of a relatively small number of rather elegant hammers with which they roam the world seeking convenient nails to pound, or at least screws they can pretend are nails. One all too often hears tales of scholars who have begun to describe the details of their particular research problem to a statistician, only to have the statistician latch on to a few phrases early in the conversation and then glibly announce that the problem is an exemplar of a standard one in statistics that has a convenient, pre-packaged solution — preferably one that uses some voguish, recently developed technique (bootstrap, wavelets, Markov chain Monte Carlo, hidden Markov models,...).

To some degree, this paper continues that fine tradition. We will observe that various facets of the inference of linguistic divergence times are indeed familiar nails to statisticians. However, we will depart from the tradition by being less than sanguine about whether statistics possesses, or can ever possess, the appropriate hammers to hit them. In particular, we find the assertion of (Forster & Toth 2003) that

> Phylogenetic time estimates ... are statistically feasible once the language tree has been correctly reconstructed, by uncovering any recurrent changes of the items.

and similar optimistic uses of statistical methodology for dating purposes elsewhere in the historical linguistics literature need much more justification before they can be accepted with any degree of confidence.

We begin with a discussion about inverse problems in section 2, and continue in section 3 with a description of stochastic models of evolution that have been proposed for biomolecular or linguistic characters. The critical issues involved in parameter estimation under these models are presented in section 4, while specific issues involving data selection are discussed in section 5. We then turn to the specific issues involved with estimating dates at internal nodes in section 6. We make some concluding remarks in section 7.

## 2. Inverse problems

It has been recognized for a long time that phylogenetic reconstruction in linguistics (and, of course, biology) can be viewed as a statistical inference problem: we have a collection of possible stochastic models for the past evolution of languages and we are trying to determine which of those models best fits some observed data. However, phylogeny is clearly rather different from the statistical problems that typically confront experimental scientists, such as determining from a long sequence of *independent and identical trials* what the mortality will be for mice that are injected with a particular toxin. Phylogeny raises issues of model complexity and adequacy of the data (both in terms of amount and structure) that are usually not so germane to standard experimental situations.

Phylogenetic inference is an instance of a *statistical inverse problem* (see Evans & Stark (2002) for a survey of this general area). This term doesn't have a clear, agreed-upon definition. Rather, it is a little like U.S. Chief Justice Potter Stewart's definition of obscenity, 'I know it when I see it'. It is therefore best to give a standard example that shares many features with phylogenetic inference, but for which those features are more immediately comprehensible. However, before we give an example of a statistical inverse problem, we give an example of a corresponding *forward* problem.

Consider monitoring earthquakes using seismographic apparatus. If we knew the detailed composition and structure of the earth, then we could, in principle, solve the relevant partial differential equations to compute what the measurements for amplitude, time-of-travel and so forth would be at a particular seismic monitoring station when an earthquake of a given magnitude occurs at some other location. This is an example of a *forward* problem: we know how a system is built and we want to calculate what the output of the system will be from a given input. In practice, an exact deterministic model of the earth's interior is often replaced by a stochastic model that attempts to mimic the finer details of the interior's heterogeneity using a random structure that is more tractable to compute with.

Of course, the forward problem is not the situation that actually confronts us. Based on seismographic observations we want to *reverse engineer* the earth and determine its internal structure from a knowledge of various inputs and outputs. In essence we have some universe of potential interiors for the earth; for each of these we can solve the forward problem, and we want to determine which of the potential interiors best fits our observed data.

We hope that the correspondence between this problem in geophysics and the problem of linguistic phylogeny is starting to form in the reader's mind. Instead of standing on the surface of the earth and attempting to infer the nature of its interior, we are standing at the present and attempting to infer the nature of the linguistic past. We will have an ensemble of models for the possible course of linguistic evolution. These models have a stochastic component because we believe that the *typical* outcome of an appropriate random process will somehow act as a suitable proxy for a detailed description of historical events and because it is usually rather straightforward to compute the predictions of these models for our data. We then wish to determine which model from our ensemble does the best job of explaining the data.

This reverse engineering process is fraught with difficulties in both seismology and phylogeny. We will go into more detail later, but we can give a brief overview of some of the difficulties as follows.

To begin with, the mathematics of wave propagation is such that the reconstruction of the earth's interior from seismographic observations is an *ill-posed* problem: there can be different structures for the interior that would lead to the same connection between inputs (that is, earthquake magnitudes and locations) and outputs (that is, seismographic measurements around the earth). This is as we might expect: it should be difficult to determine the conditions inside a country from just watching people entering and leaving its borders. Even if there wasn't this degeneracy, reasonable models for the interior can contain infinite dimensional or very high-dimensional features (for example, the boundary between the core and the mantle is some surface of potentially arbitrary *complexity*, whereas we only have a finite number of low-dimensional observations on which to base our inferences. In essence, we are trying to constrain a high-dimensional object with low-dimensional observations and, in essence, we run up against a basic mathematical problem of *too few equations in too many unknown variables*.

The counterpart of this issue in phylogeny is what statisticians usually call *lack of identifiability*. The most extreme instance of this difficulty is when two different models make the same predictions about the state of the present. However, even if different models do make different predictions about the present, our actual data might be too meager to notice the difference because of the too few equations in too many unknowns phenomenon. Thus two genuinely different historical processes simply may not be distinguishable on the basis of our data.

It should be stressed that this problem of inadequacy of data is rather different to what we usually encounter in experimental settings. There we repeat the 'same' experiment and the purpose of collecting more data is just to reduce variability in our inferences about nature. Whether we inject 10 mice or 1000, our estimate of mortality will be correct 'on average' in both cases, but injecting more mice means that the probability distribution of the estimated mortality will be more tightly clustered around its expected value.

In an inverse problem, we don't usually make repeated observations under the same conditions. New observations may enable us to probe the object we are interested in from different directions and hence have the dimensional coverage of our data set approach that of the object we are investigating. Simply repeating the 'same' observations may increase our certainty about what is present in the directions we probe, but this won't help in constraining the object in the 'perpendicular' directions. Furthermore, if our data are observational rather than experimental, then we don't have control of the directions in which such probing occurs, and so in certain directions we may never see data that will constrain the model. Earthquakes occur in a limited set of positions and their effects can only be measured at a sparse set of locations that, for example, only include places on dry land, and this prevents certain features of the earth's interior from being inferred unless we are willing to assume *a priori* a certain amount of smoothness or homogeneity. This does not mean that the inferential task is completely hopeless: there may still be facets of the model for which the data are adequate even if they are inadequate for others. For example, in historical linguistics we may be able to estimate the tree topology of the model with some confidence even if the data are not available which would enable us to resolve certain divergence times with any degree of accuracy.

In any use of statistics, great care needs to be taken to ensure valid sampling strategies and, in particular, that missing data are treated appropriately. The usual probabilistic models for linguistic evolution are meant to describe *generic* characters from some population that is being sampled, and inferences are only justified to the extent that this is a reasonable assumption. Essentially, we have the following *Gedankenexperiment*: there is a population of possible states for a character that are akin to tickets in a box, some states appear on more tickets than others in proportion to how *likely* the state is to be exhibited by the character, and we imagine that nature has somehow shaken up the box and chosen a ticket at random to give us the observed state of the character. If someone was allowed to rummage through the box and discard tickets before the drawing took place or we are able to look at a ticket after the drawing and can accept or reject it, then the proportions of tickets originally in the box no longer describe the experiment and we need to consider another, perhaps substantially more complex, box that somehow incorporates this *a priori* or *a posteriori* winnowing. In essence, if we have a model that describes the probability of a character exhibiting a particular value, then we need to be able to tell a reasonable story about why the state of the character can be seen as a draw from a box of possible states with a given composition and we have to be careful about any pre- or post-processing we do that may invalidate this story. This is a fundamental concern in statistics, and is usually covered early on in elementary courses under the rubrics of *random versus convenience samples*, *ascertainment bias*, or *selection bias*.

We can do no better than quote (Berk & Freedman 2003) on this point

> If the random-sampling assumptions do not apply, or the parameters are not clearly defined, or the inferences are to a population that is only vaguely defined, the calibration of uncertainty offered by contemporary statistical technique is in turn rather questionable. Thus, investigators who use conventional statistical technique turn out to be making, explicitly or implicitly, quite restrictive behavioral assumptions about their data collection process. By using apparently familiar arithmetic, they have made substantial empirical commitments; the research enterprise may be distorted by statistical technique, not helped.
>
> ... researchers may find themselves assuming that their sample is a random sample from an imaginary population. Such a population has no empirical existence, but is defined in an essentially circular way — as that population from which the sample may be assumed to be randomly drawn. At the risk of the obvious, inferences to imaginary populations are also imaginary.

One way in which a sampling strategy can violate the implicit assumptions of the model is via its treatment of missing data. For example, social scientists have long been aware that non-respondents to questionnaire items can't simply be scored as though they would have replied in the same proportions as respondents, the so-called *missing at random* assumption. A standard monitory example is a poll conducted just prior to the 1936 U.S. presidential election by *Literary Digest*. Based on 10,000,000 post card surveys, the magazine predicted that Republican Alfred Landon would win 57 per cent of the popular vote to convincingly defeat Franklin Delano Roosevelt, whereas Roosevelt actually polled 62.5 per cent of the vote. About 80 per cent of the people who received the mail-in questionnaires did not respond and the mailings went to people who, in the depths of the Great Depression, had current automobile registrations or were listed in telephone books — hardly a sampling scheme designed to fairly capture low-income supporters of Roosevelt's New Deal. The moral is that there is not much point having lots of data if they aren't the right data for the question we want to answer.

Linguistic data often undergo a great deal of processing. A character may be removed from a word list after it is discovered that certain languages don't have a representative in that lexical slot. Similarly, in methods based on estimated evolutionary distances, if a language is missing an item, then that item may be simply ignored in computations. The latter procedure seems to be recommended by (Embleton 2000)

> Some languages are missing a translation for a particular item on the Swadesh-list (e.g. 'ice' or 'swim' in some languages). Normally this is best dealt with just as a statistician would with any missing data, namely as a blank and reduce $N$ accordingly in relevant comparisons.

As we have remarked, the validity of this seemingly innocuous practice rests on definite assumptions and is not what a statistician would (or at least should) do without careful thought and justification.

Alternatively, a language is sometimes scored as exhibiting a fictitious unique state of the character if the character is not present for that language. This procedure is suspect, as it treats the 'missing' states in the same manner as observed states and, in particular, treats them as being the outcome of the same substitution mechanism. At the very least, this practice will typically inflate estimates of the variability of the substitution process (and hence effect estimates of divergence times) even if it doesn't have a significant effect on estimates of the tree topology.

Such matters of sampling adequacy and treatment of missing data do not seem to have been considered in the historical linguistics literature at the length they deserve to justify the subsequent use of statistical methodology. In short, statistical methods are often applied without any clear sense of the population that the data are meant to represent and whether they actually do so.

Lastly, we come to the question of producing probability models for our whole corpus of data from models for individual data points. The standard practice in both linguistic and biological phylogenetic inference has been to assume that successive characters behave statistically independently. For example, biologists will sometimes erroneously use each position in a stretch of DNA sequence and treat neighbouring positions as independent, even though this is generally not supportable in light of our understanding of the mechanisms by which DNA evolves, but if characters are chosen more carefully (for instance, from separated areas of the genome, or perhaps from non-coding regions), then the independence assumption is usually more tenable. The contrast with linguistic data is drawn by McMahon & McMahon (2000).

> Second, individual mutations in biology are generally independent, but this is not necessarily the case in linguistics. Sometimes the effects of contact can set up predisposing conditions for further influence; in other cases, one change in a system will cause knock-on effects in a classically structuralist fashion. These interdependencies cause extreme difficulty for our prospects for quantification.

If one wishes to treat characters as independent for the sake of inference, then one needs to argue that any common mechanisms can be satisfactorily captured by simply positing similar evolution dynamics (that is, by the operation of stochastic models with shared parameters but independent noise).

## 3. Models in phylogeny

We present a mathematical exposition of the basic ingredients of stochastic models of evolution. (Readers interested in obtaining a deeper or more extensive discussion about models should consult any standard textbook in the field; however, readable accounts with extensive bibliographies of probability models in biological phylogenetics and related inferential issues may be found in Felsenstein (2003), Kim & Warnow (1999) and Holmes (1999).) Most stochastic models in phylogeny consist of two ingredients — a putative phylogenetic tree (for the sake of simplicity we will not consider *reticulate* situations such as word borrowing) and various numerical parameters that describe the evolution of a given character through time.

The tree is a rooted directed tree, with edges directed away from the root. The leaves of the tree correspond to taxa for which we can observe character states, the interior nodes of the tree correspond to divergence events in lineages, and the root corresponds to the most recent common ancestor of the set of taxa. Given an edge in the tree connecting two nodes, we will refer to the node closer to the root as the *tail* of the edge and to the node further from the root as the *head* of the edge.

Each node has a time. If the node is a leaf, then the time is the date when the leaf was observed (so that if all of our taxa are contemporary, then all leaves will have the same time). For an interior node, the time is the date at which the corresponding divergence of lineages occurred. There is a significant amount of debate over this so-called *Stammbaum* structure, which views the divergence of lineages as a clear-cut event that can be localized in time, but we will not address these issues here. The assignment of times to nodes induces an assignment of durations to edges: the duration of an edge is the difference between the time of its head and the time of its tail. The duration of the edge $e$ is denoted by $t_e$.

Each character $c$ will have a state space $S_c$ that is the collection of possible values of the character. In biological models, the choice of $S_c$ is usually fairly straightforward. For example, it will be something like the set of four DNA nucleotides or twenty amino acids. For certain linguistic characters (for example, lexical characters), it is not clear how one delineates *a priori* the entire universe of possible states of the character. Using just the set of states observed in the data is insidiously self-referential and complicates the inference process because our model is implicitly conditional on certain features of the data and it is unclear how to interpret the results of statistical procedures within the usual frequentist or Bayesian paradigms. More importantly, such a choice of state-space rules out the possibility of ancestral forms that aren't present in the data, thereby placing quite severe constraints on the model.

Given a state-space, the next step is to build a model for the states observed at the taxa for a given character. This step is usually divided into two parts.

Firstly, one builds a model for both the observed states of the taxa and the unobserved states of the ancestral forms present at each interior node in the tree.

This model is usually of the *Markov random field* type, which simply means that the random states exhibited at two nodes (either leaf nodes or interior nodes) are conditionally independent given the random state exhibited at any node on the path through the tree joining the two nodes. Informally, this is the same as saying that the course of evolution on two lineages is independent after the lineages diverge.

Secondly, one obtains a model for the observed states of the taxa by taking the appropriate marginal distribution in the above notional model for both observed and unobserved forms. That is, we 'sum over' the possibilities for the unobserved ancestral states.

The specification of the Markov random field model is equivalent to specifying a probability distribution for the state exhibited at the root and specifying for each edge in the tree a conditional distribution for the state exhibited at the head of the edge given the state exhibited at the tail. If the state space $S_c$ of character $c$ is finite with $k$ states, this means that there is a probability vector $\pi_c$ of length $k$ giving the distribution of the state exhibited at the root and a $k \times k$ stochastic matrix (that is, a matrix with rows that are probability vectors) $P_{c,e}$ for each edge $e$ giving the family of conditional distributions for $e$. That is, $\pi_c(i)$ is the probability that the state $i$ is exhibited at the root, and $P_{c,e}(i, j)$ is the conditional probability that the state exhibited at the head of edge $e$ is $j$ given that the state exhibited at the tail is $i$.

Furthermore, it is usual to think of the matrix $P_{c,e}$ as arising from time-homogeneous Markovian dynamics. That is, there is a rate matrix $Q_{c,e}$ such that $P_{c,e}$ is the matrix exponential $\exp(t_e Q_{c,e})$. The matrix $Q_{c,e}$ has non-negative off-diagonal entries and rows that sum to 0. The interpretation is that $-Q_{c,e}(i, i)$ is the infinitesimal rate at which substitutions away from state $i$ occur and $-Q_{c,e}(i, j)/Q_{c,e}(i, i)$ is the probability that such a substitution will be to state $j$ for $i \neq j$.

This special form for $P_{c,e}$ is somewhat hard to justify, as it posits that the dynamics of substitution are constant throughout the edge of a tree, but may change discontinuously at a divergence time. However, some structure of this sort appears necessary if the edge durations $t_e$ are to appear explicitly in the model and hence for the model to be of use for dating purposes, but it is not necessary if one is primarily interested in obtaining the tree topology.

Note that, in general, the rate $-Q_{c,e}(i, i)$ may depend on $i$, and this should indeed be the case if there no reason to believe that all states of the character $c$ are equally mutable. When $-Q_{c,e}(i, i)$ takes the same value for all states $i$, say $r_{c,e}$, then we can say that 'character $c$ evolves at rate $r_{c,e}$ on edge $e$'. Otherwise, such a rate does not have any clear-cut meaning other than simply the expected number of substitutions of character $c$ on edge $e$ divided by the time duration $t_e$, but this quantity will then typically be a rather complicated function of the root distribution $\pi_c$ along with the edge durations $t_{e'}$ and rate matrices $Q_{c,e'}$ for all the edges $e'$ on the path through the tree from the root to $e$.

In biological settings, the choice of the rate matrices $Q_{c,e}$ is a mixture of mathematical convenience and biological insight about the *geometry* of the state space. For example, the four DNA nucleotides {A, G, C, T} come in two families, the purines {A, G} and the pyrimidines {C, T}. For biochemical reasons, substitutions that stay within a family, A ↔ G or C ↔ T, (so-called transitions) are easier than substitutions that move between families (transversions). Many commonly-used models of DNA nucleotide evolution incorporate this fact by allowing different rate parameters for transitions and transversions.

The geometry of linguistic state spaces doesn't seem to be understood as well and there don't appear to be models that incorporate structure inherent in the landscape of possible states for a character. Rather, existing models seem to be 'black boxes' that either adopt a 'one-size-fits-all' strategy by allowing the entries of the matrices $Q_{c,e}$ to be arbitrary, or adopt Procrustean solutions such as treating all character substitutions as being equally likely.

The issue of appropriate models of evolution has been addressed in McMahon & McMahon (2000).

> The difficulty for this point ... which requires that we understand the mechanisms of change and transmission, lies primarily in the relevant forces of selection. While, as with biological change, language change rests on the bedrock of mutation and consequent variation, the subsequent selection for language change is often under (at least subconscious) human control, since variants adopted frequently depend on the situation in which the speaker finds herself and the impression she wishes to make. In other words, although the initial processes of mutation may be random (and note that, at present, we understand the mechanisms creating variants much better in sound change than in any other area, and in semantic change, for instance, these are still particularly opaque), it is hard to conceive of randomness or neutrality when the shift from variation to incipient change often reflects the acquisition of social meaning to a variant, which then becomes manipulable in context.

Moreover, most of the models used in biology are *time-reversible* in the sense that the evolution of the model in equilibrium is the same whether time is run forwards or backwards (that is, we would be unable to distinguish between a videotape of the process on 'fast forward' or 'rewind'). Many processes in linguistic evolution don't have this feature. For example, phonemic mergers are irreversible, and though the exact reversal of a change in inflectional morphology is theoretically possible, actual examples are rare and confined to specific types of development. Thus, reversible models will not be appropriate for morphological and phonological characters.

In connection with our comments above about the choice of the state space $S_c$, it is worth pointing out that there are problems inherent in dodging the issue of just what the 'real' state space should be by simply scoring character states in terms of the presence or absence of one or more features (that is, by collapsing the state space down to a set of binary vectors, where each binary vector can represent several states of the original state space — a binary vector is just a sequence of zeros and ones representing the answers to a corresponding list of yes-or-no questions). The chief difficulty with this approach is that if a model of the form above with its concomitant, interpretable Markovian substitution dynamics holds for the original state space, then such a model will, in general, no longer hold for the collapsed model: when one clumps the states of a Markov random field together the resulting object is typically no longer a Markov random field. Thus taking a multi-state character and shoe-horning it into an off-the-shelf model from, say, biology by clumping states together will typically lead to a model that doesn't obey any sort of Markovian dynamics with attendant, understandable rate parameters.

Moreover, if one does code a multi-state character as a binary vector (or a collection of binary characters) and model the evolution of this vector with a Markov process, then it is critical that the Markovian dynamics reflect the fact that one is looking at the evolution of the answers to a number of related yes-or-no questions about the *same* object. For example, forcing the coordinates to evolve independently, as seems to be done for such a coding in (Gray & Atkinson 2003), is patently inappropriate: at the very least, such a model assigns positive probability to binary vectors that contain several ones, even though the coding procedure used to turn data into binary vectors will only produce binary vectors that contain a single one.

This point was made by Bill Poser (2004) in a *Language Log* posting where one can find some illustrative graphics, but is easily seen in the following example. Suppose one takes a lexical character $c$ with three states, indicated by $A$, $B$, and $C$. The binary encoding of this multi-state character produces three binary characters, $c_A$, $c_B$, $c_C$. Now suppose the character $c$ changes its state on an edge in the tree from $A$ to $B$. Then $c_A$ changes from 1 (indicating presence) to 0 (indicating absence), $c_B$ changes its state from 0 (indicating absence) to 1 (indicating presence), and $c_C$ doesn't change at all. Similarly, if one traces just the evolution of $c_A$ on the tree and observes that $c_A$ changes state from 0 to 1 on an edge $e$, then both $c_B$ and $c_C$ *must* both be 0 at the end of that edge. That is, it is *impossible* for two of the three binary characters to both be 1 at any node in the tree, since every node can have only one state of the character $c$. In other words, these characters are highly dependent.

While independence may not be absolutely a valid assumption for genuinely different linguistic characters (rather than the ersatz binary 'characters' produced by this encoding of a single multi-state character), extreme violations of the independence assumption that arise from this type of binary encoding need to be avoided unless thorough theoretical and/or simulation studies have been done to support a claim that there is enough data with a strong enough signal to overcome even such gross imperfections in the model.

Lastly, we come to the question of how such single character models may be combined into a model for a whole data set consisting of many characters. As we discussed in section 2, the only really feasible way of doing this is to justifiably assume that the evolution of different characters is stochastically independent. Any attempt to work with dependent characters would introduce another layer of complexity to the model and involve some hard thinking about how one could sensibly model any dependencies present. Moreover, any model that allows dependence would entail yet more parameters that must then be estimated from the relatively meager amount of data available in most linguistic settings.

## 4. Parameter estimation

Once one has a model of the form described in section 3, the next question that arises is how one goes about estimating the various parameters in the model, that is, the tree, the times of the nodes, the root distributions $\pi_c$, and the matrices $Q_{c,e}$.

In order to understand the issues involved, it is helpful to consider a generic statistical problem, that of non-parametric regression, where analogous issues arise.

Suppose that our data consist of pairs of real numbers

$$(x_1, y_1), \ldots, (x_n, y_n),$$

where the $x_i$ are thought of as inputs that are under an experimenter's control whilst the $y_i$ are the corresponding outputs and have a stochastic component to them (for example, measurement error may be present).

A reasonable model in such circumstances is that $y_1, \ldots, y_n$ are realizations of independent random variables $Y_1, \ldots, Y_n$, for $Y_i$ of the form

$$Y_i = f(x_i) + \varepsilon_i,$$

where $f$ is an unknown function (the *regression function*) that needs to be determined and the $\varepsilon_i$ are independent random variables with some known distribution (for example, the normal distribution with mean zero and variance $\sigma^2$ for a known value of $\sigma$). The function $f$ is the parameter in this model that must be estimated.

A standard procedure for constructing estimates of parameters in statistical models is that of *maximum likelihood* whereby one writes down the probability of the data under the model (or, more correctly in this continuous case, the probability density — the term likelihood subsumes both cases) and attempts to find the choice of parameters that maximizes the likelihood. Maximum likelihood is not the only method for constructing sensible estimates, but most of the difficulties we discuss are also present with other approaches, so we will confine our discussion to this approach.

The likelihood in this case is given by

$$L(y_1, \ldots, y_n; x_1, \ldots x_n, f) = \prod_{i=1}^{n} \frac{1}{\sqrt{2\pi\sigma^2}} \exp\left(-\frac{(y_i - f(x_i))^2}{2\sigma^2}\right).$$

Note first of all that there is a degeneracy problem with the likelihood function. Any two regression functions $f'$ and $f''$ that satisfy $f'(x_i) = f''(x_i)$ for $1 \le i \le n$ will have

$$L(y_1, \ldots, y_n; x_1, \ldots, x_n, f') = L(y_1, \ldots, y_n; x_1, \ldots, x_n, f'')$$

for all values of $y_1, \ldots, y_n$. Thus the probability model for the data is the same for $f'$ and $f''$ and we have no hope of deciding which of these two regression functions is behind the data. This is an instance of the problem of identifiability that we discussed in the Introduction.

In particular, we see that the likelihood will be maximized for any regression function $f$ such that $f(x_i) = y_i$ for $1 \le i \le n$. Rather than being a peak with a unique summit, the likelihood surface is a flat-topped mesa.

The problem here is one of dimensionality. The space of possible regression functions is infinite-dimensional, while we only have finite-dimensional data.

However, this is not simply a problem of infinite versus finite dimensions. Suppose that instead of allowing arbitrary regression functions we insisted that the regression function be a polynomial of degree at most $m$. That is, $f$ is of the form

$$f(x) = a_0 + a_1 x + a_2 x^2 + \ldots + a_m x^m$$

for some choice of real parameters $a_j$, $1 \le j \le m$. As soon as $m$ is larger than $n$ there are two distinct such polynomials $f'$ and $f''$ for which $f'(x_i) = f''(x_i) = z_i$ for any given choice of $z_i$, $1 \le i \le n$, and so the model is no longer identifiable and again there is no unique regression function that maximizes the likelihood. That is, we run into difficulties once the dimension $m$ of the parameter set is greater than the dimension $n$ of the data.

Even if $m \le n$ and the model is identifiable, the maximum likelihood estimate may not be a good estimate of $f$ if $m$ is large compared to $n$ because there is not enough *independent replication* present for a law of large numbers effect to take over and the noise in the data to become *averaged out*. That is, when the $n$ is not much greater than $m$, relatively small changes in the observations can have significant effects on the estimates of the parameters, and so the noise in the data leads to substantial variability in the estimates. In other words, the estimates are correct on average, but for any particular data set there is a substantial probability that the estimates are quite far from the true values. It may be comforting to the statistician to know that in a life-time of applying such procedures he/she will be correct on the average, but this is of little comfort to the practitioner who wants make substantially correct inferences for a particular data set.

These same issues arise in phylogeny: it would be nice to have maximal flexibility by allowing the matrices $Q_{c,e}$ to vary from character to character and edge to edge and for each $Q_{c,e}$ to be completely unconstrained within the class of rate matrices on the state space of the character $c$. However, even if such rich models are identifiable they may well have so little *replication per parameter* that parameter estimates are unacceptably variable. As (Embleton 2000) remarks with reference to the use of complex models in linguistic dating

> All those variables/parameters in those elegant models then have to be estimated, and that is where the problems begin. It is virtually impossible to do even with languages for which we are blessed with both extensive written records over a long time-span and an overwhelming amount of scholarly attention, for example, Germanic or Romance ... There will simply be too many parameters to estimate, making it either impossible to proceed or else only possible to proceed in a somewhat circular manner.

It should be stressed that the problem of insufficient

replication may not affect all parameters equally. For example, even in cases where the rate matrices $Q_{c,e}$ or edge durations $t_e$ can't be estimated that well, it may still be possible to estimate the tree topology quite accurately.

For example, in molecular phylogenetics, under even fairly complex models of evolution (such as the *General Markov model*: Steel 1994), the tree topology can be reconstructed with high probability from not that many characters; this is studied theoretically in (Erdös *et al.* 1999), and confirmed in simulation studies (Nakhleh *et al.* 2001). Therefore, for some models and some reconstruction methods, the tree topology can be estimated quite well, even though the other parameters (edge durations and substitution matrices) may be hard to estimate.

There are various options for dealing with this problem. The simplest is to restrict the class of regression functions to some low-dimensional subspace. For example, one could insist that $f$ is linear (that is, $m = 1$ in the above polynomial regression). The analogue in phylogeny problems would be to insist that the matrices $Q_{c,e}$ come from some low-dimensional class. Molecular or lexical clock hypotheses are of this form, in that they essentially posit that $Q_{c,e}$ is independent of the edge $e$. The problem with such approaches is that the low-dimensional class may simply not be rich enough to effectively capture the features of the data: in the regression example, a scatter plot of the pairs $(x_i, y_i)$ might have a pronounced U-shape and hence it is apparent that a linear choice of $f$ is simply not appropriate. The molecular and lexical clock hypotheses have been discredited for a wide range of biological and linguistic data (see, for example, Bergsland & Vogt (1962); Embleton (2000), Arbogast *et al.* (2002) and Felsenstein (2003)).

The next simplest option is, in statistical parlance, to replace *fixed effects* by *random effects*. In the polynomial regression example, one could, for instance, take the coefficients $a_0,\ldots,a_m$ to themselves be realizations of independent normal random variables with mean $\mu$ and variance $\tau^2$. The effect of this move is to turn a problem with $m + 1$ parameters into one with two parameters while not restricting $f$ to lie in a low-dimensional space. Analogous approaches have been tried in phylogeny where rate parameters (either across characters or edges) have been taken to be independent, identically distributed realizations of random variables with common distribution from some parametric family such as the gamma distributions or as the output of an unseen Markov random field on the tree (so we have a *hidden Markov model*). A discussion of these approaches with references to the literature may be found in Felsenstein (2003, chap. 16). Proponents of these models typically do not propose that this structure should be taken too literally. Rather, they assert informally that the range of 'proxy' parameter values that are likely to be produced by such a mechanism can match the heterogeneity seen in the 'actual' parameters. Hence this approach is essentially a somewhat *ad hoc* device for mathematical convenience in situations where the various numerical parameters are *nuisance parameters* that are not the chief focus of scientific interest and the practitioner is most interested in establishing the correct tree topology. Note that this sort of random-effects model is still effectively imposing something like a molecular or lexical clock: the independent, identically distributed rates model forces the now random rates to have the same distribution (and hence, for example, the same mean) on each branch of the tree, and hidden Markov models also force a great deal of homogeneity amongst branches.

Random-effects models implicitly replace the original likelihood function by one in which there is a penalty for the parameters being too heterogeneous: the parameters are forced to look like a typical realization of the random generating mechanism. An approach which tries to do the same thing more explicitly is that of *penalized likelihood*. In the regression example, one could look for functions that don't maximize the likelihood but rather a new function of the data and the regression function $f$ that incorporates both the likelihood and a *penalty* for functions that are too 'rough'. For example, one could index the data so that $x_1 < x_2 < \ldots < x_n$ and seek to maximize

$$\log L(y_1,\ldots,y_n;x_1,\ldots,x_n,f)-C\sum_{i=1}^{n-1}[(f(x_{i+1})-f(x_i))/(x_{i+1}-x_i)]^2,$$

where $C$ is a positive *tuning constant*. The larger $C$ is the more preference is given to 'smooth' functions $f$, and different choices of $C$ will typically lead to different estimates. There is no canonical choice of $C$ and the choice of this constant is essentially a matter of taste for the practitioner.

Analogous approaches have been proposed in phylogeny in (Sanderson 1997; 2002). There the logarithm of the likelihood is modified by the addition of a term that penalizes daughter branches for having rates that are far from the rate of their parent, so that that some sort of local smoothness of rates is rewarded. Such approaches are *ad hoc* in the extreme. To begin with, the object being maximized is no longer a likelihood for any probability model. Instead it is an apples-and-oranges hybrid that attempts to combine two incommensurable quantities, and the appealing rationalization of the maximum likelihood method is lost. Moreover, the choice of roughness penalty and the particular manner in which it is combined with the likelihood are arbitrary and there is no particularly convincing reasoning why one choice is better than another. Sanderson offers a somewhat heuristic explanation of his method by claiming that it is, in some vague sense, a proxy for maximum likelihood in a random-effects model in which there is local statistical dependence between the random rate parameters for adjoining branches, but this is not justified by actually proposing a formal random-effects model that incorporates such a dependence structure. As with a random-effects model, the penalized likelihood approach is a mathematical device rather than a procedure driven by a clear and convincing modelling rationale. Unlike random effects, however, penalized likelihood is not a model, but simply an inferential procedure applied to a model that one could fit to data in other ways. This point seems to be a cause of some confusion. For instance, Gray & Atkinson (2003) speak of the 'penalized-likelihood model'.

## 5. Data issues

The structures of the data sets that are typically used in linguistic cladistics are not obviously appropriate as a basis for statistical inferences. Most are based on the famous 'Swadesh list' of basic vocabulary. A brief examination of the Swadesh list will suggest where pitfalls can be expected to lie.

Morris Swadesh originally constructed his comparative list with several objects in mind (see e.g. Swadesh 1955). He attempted to include only lexical items which are psychologically 'basic' and culturally universal; he also hoped to include lexemes which are maximally resistant to replacement. The criterion of 'basicness' raises no clear issues for the statistician, but the others are clearly problematic for at least the following reasons.

It proves to be impossible to construct a list of even a hundred lexical meanings that are genuinely universal (Hoijer 1956). Languages not uncommonly use the same word for 'come' and 'go', or for 'yellow' and 'green'; 'who' and 'what' are often morphologically derived from the same root (e.g. in Indo-European languages); 'this' and 'that' are likewise often morphologically derived from the same root, or are not distinguished at all, or the language's system of demonstratives is more complex — and so on. These and similar problems virtually guarantee that there will be some duplication among the items of even the most basic word list, which will of course affect any statistical inferences based on the list. The alternative is to tailor the lists for individual languages or families; but in that case we no longer have a standard list to be used for all experiments.

This last outcome would not be a problem if the word lists used were in any sense representative random samples from an explicit, well-defined population; but a Swadesh list is anything but a random selection of lexical items from some *a priori* prescribed wider universe with an 'empirical existence' in the words of the quote from (Berk & Freedman 2003) given in section 2. Most importantly, the empirical distribution of rates of replacement of the items over time is heavily skewed toward the retentive end of the scale. Words that are fairly seldom or even very seldom replaced (such as pronouns, numerals, and body-part terms) are well represented on the list, while those that are replaced very often are scarcely represented at all. The consequences for statistical inferences of this skewness remain unclear.

Finally, there is the problem of sample size. Swadesh began with a list of 200 words, then reduced it to 100 in the hope of achieving maximal universality and a minimal average rate of replacement. But a glottochronological experiment by Johann Tischler has shown that the shorter list gives much more widely varying dates of divergence (Tischler 1973). This is *prima facie* evidence that sample size is a problem. Even the longer Swadesh list may not be substantial enough to give statistically reliable results; as of now we just don't know.

It would seem that experiments of a different kind, using lexical items selected randomly from a significantly larger 'universe', are needed.

## 6. Limitations with dating internal nodes

Much of what we have said has focused on two issues: one is formulating appropriate stochastic models of character evolution (by formally stating the properties of the stochastic processes operating on linguistic characters), and the other is inferring evolutionary history from character data under stochastic models.

As noted before, under some conditions it may be possible to infer highly accurate estimations of the tree topology for a given set of languages. In these cases, the problem of dating internal nodes can then be formulated as: *given the true tree topology, estimate the divergence times at each node in the tree.* This approach is implicit in the recent analyses in Gray & Atkinson (2003) and Forster & Toth (2003), although they used different techniques to obtain estimates of the true tree for their data sets.

The problems with estimating dates on a fixed tree are still substantial.

Firstly, dates do not make sense on unrooted trees, and so the tree must first be rooted, and this itself is an issue that presents quite significant difficulties.

Secondly, if the tree is wrong, the estimate of even the date of the root may have significant error.

Thirdly, and most importantly perhaps, except in highly constrained cases it simply may not be possible to estimate dates at nodes with any level of accuracy. Recall that it is usual to model the data for each character with a tree that is common to all characters plus stochastic evolution mechanisms on the edges of the tree that may be character and edge specific. The evolution mechanism for character $c$ on edge $e$ is described by a matrix $P_{c,e}$ of conditional probabilities for possible substitutions. Different characters are usually assumed to be independent. In order for such a model to be useful for dating, it is necessary that there is some connection between $P_{c,e}$ and the duration $t_e$ of the edge $e$: this is usually accomplished by positing the existence of a time-homogeneous Markov chain evolution with rate matrix $Q_{c,e}$ so that $P_{c,e} = \exp(t_e Q_{c,e})$. Note that there is some ambiguity in such a model because one can multiply $t_e$ by some number $r$ and divide each entry of $Q_{c,e}$ by $r$ to arrive at the same value of $P_{c,e}$. Thus the best we can hope for is to identify the *relative* values of the durations $t_e$; that is, we can only get at ratios $t_{e'}/t_{e''}$ for different edges $e'$ and $e''$. We need some external calibration of at least one *absolute* edge duration $t_e$ to estimate the remaining absolute edge durations. Moreover, if the rates $Q_{c,e}$ can vary arbitrarily, then the model may be too parameter-rich for the edge durations to be estimated successfully. Even supposing we could construct the true tree, in order to estimate the $t_e$ we would need to overcome this over-parameterization by placing constraints on how the rates $Q_{c,e}$ can vary across characters and across edges. All attempts we know of to estimate edge durations and so estimate times at nodes are based upon either some kind of explicit assumptions about how rates can vary (such as assuming that the $Q_{c,e}$ are independent of $c$ and $e$ or are the output of some further homogeneous stochastic mechanism), or else they try to minimize the variation of the estimated values of the $Q_{c,e}$ in some *ad hoc* way that is supposed to be justified by implicit assumptions about the degree to which rates vary. Currently, we just do not know that any of these assumptions are sufficiently valid to suggest that such attempts are reasonable.

Unlike biological phylogenetics, in historical linguistics the amount of data we have is rather meagre and we aren't going to get much more of it. It is thus unsatisfactory to cross one's fingers and hope for the best when using data, models, or inference procedures that have obvious imperfections in the hope that there is enough signal to overcome these flaws or that further data can be collected which will confirm or discredit conclusions made using questionable methods.

Therefore we propose that rather than attempting at this time to estimate times at internal nodes, it might be better for the historical linguistics community to seek to characterize evolutionary processes that operate on linguistic characters. Once we are able to work with good stochastic models that reflect this understanding of the evolutionary dynamics, we will be in a much better position to address the question of whether it is reasonable to try to estimate times at nodes. More generally, if we can formulate these models, then we will begin to understand what can be estimated with some level of accuracy and what seems beyond our reach. We will then have at least a rough idea of what we still don't know.

## 7. Conclusion

In this paper we have shown that phylogenetic estimation, and in particular the dating of divergence times in historical linguistics, are instances of a statistical inverse problem, and many of the issues that complicate the proper treatment of other inverse problems are also present there. We have also argued that development of better models in linguistic evolution are needed before the dating of internal nodes can be done with any degree of accuracy and/or reliability.

## 8. Epilogue

As we know,
There are known knowns.
There are things we know we know.
We also know
There are known unknowns.
That is to say
We know there are some things
We do not know.
But there are also unknown unknowns,
The ones we don't know
We don't know.

– Donald Rumsfeld, U.S. Secretary of Defense

## Acknowledgements

TW would like to acknowledge the Radcliffe Institute for Advanced Study and the Program in Evolutionary Dynamics at Harvard University, which provided generous support for this research. We also thank the McDonald Institute for inviting us to the conference, and to submit this paper. SNE was supported in part by NSF grants DMS-0071468 and DMS-0405778. DR was supported in part by NSF grant BCS-0312911. TW supported by NSF grant BCS-0312830.

## References


Arbogast, B.S., S.V., Edwards, J. Wakeley, P. Beerli & J.B. Slowinski, 2002. Estimating divergence times from molecular data on phylogenetic and population genetic timescales. *Annual Review of Ecology and Systematics* 33, 707–40.

Bergsland, K. & H. Vogt, 1962. On the validity of glottochronology. *Current Anthropology* 3, 115–53.

Berk, R.A. & D.A. Freedman, 2003. Statistical assumptions as empirical commitments, in *Punishment, and Social Control: Essays in Honor of Sheldon Messinger,* eds. T.G. Blomberg, & S. Cohen. 2nd edition. New York (NY): Aldine de Gruyter, 235–54.

Embleton, S., 2000. Lexicostatistics/glottochronology: from Swadesh to Sankoff to Starostin to future horizons, in *Time Depth in Historical Linguistics,* vol. 1, eds. C. Renfrew, A. McMahon & L. Trask. (Papers in the Prehistory of Languages.) Cambridge: The McDonald Institute for Archaeological Research, 143–65.

Erdös, P.L., M.A. Steel, L. Székély & T. Warnow, 1999. A few logs suffice to build almost all trees - I. *Random Structures and Algorithms* 14, 153–84.

Evans, S.N. & P.B. Stark, 2002. Inverse problems as statistics. *Inverse Problems* 18, R55–R97.

Felsenstein, J., 2003. *Inferring Phylogenies*. Sunderland (MA): Sinauer Associates.

Forster, P. & A. Toth, 2003. Toward a phylogenetic chronology of ancient Gaulish, Celtic, and Indo-European. *Proceedings of the National Academy of Sciences of the USA* 100, 9079–84.

Gray, R.D. & Q.D. Atkinson, 2003. Language-tree divergence times support the Anatolian theory of Indo-European origin. *Nature* 426, 435–9.

Hoijer, H., 1956. Lexicostatistics: a critique. *Language* 32, 49–60.

Holmes, S.-P. 1999. Phylogenies: an overview, in *Statistics in Genetics,* eds. M.E. Halloran & S. Geisser. (The IMA Volumes in Mathematics and its Applications 112.) New York (NY): Springer Verlag, 81–119.

Kim, J. & T. Warnow, 1999. Tutorial on Phylogenetic Tree Estimation. Presented at ISMB (Intelligent Systems for Molecular Biology) 1999, Heidelberg, Germany. Available electronically at http://kim.bio.upenn.edu/~jkim/media/ISMBtutorial.pdf.

McMahon, A. & R. McMahon, 2000. Problems of dating and time depth in linguistics and biology, in *Time Depth in Historical Linguistics,* eds. C. Renfrew, A. McMahon & L. Trask. (Papers in the Prehistory of Languages.) Cambridge: The McDonald Institute for Archaeological Research, 59–73.

Nakhleh, L., K. St John, U. Roshan, J. Sun & T. Warnow, 2001. Designing fast converging phylogenetic methods. *Bioinformatics* 17, S190–S198.

Poser, W., 2004. Gray and Atkinson – Use of Binary Characters. http://itre.cis.upenn.edu/~myl/languagelog/archives/000832.html.

Sanderson, M.J., 1997. A nonparametric approach to estimating divergence times in the absence of rate constancy. *Molecular Biology and Evolution* 14, 1218–31.

Sanderson, M.J., 2002. Estimating absolute rates of molecular evolution and divergence times: a penalized likelihood approach. *Molecular Biology and Evolution* 19, 101–9.

Steel, M., 1994. Recovering a tree from the leaf colourations it generates under a Markov model. *Applied Mathematics Letters* 7(2), 19–23.

Swadesh, M., 1955. Towards greater accuracy in lexicostatistic dating. *International Journal of American Linguistics* 21, 121–37.

Tischler, J., 1973. *Glottochronologie und Lexikostatistik.* Innsbruck: IBS.

# *Chapter 11*

# Evolution of English Basic Vocabulary within the Network of Germanic Languages

Peter Forster, Tobias Polzin & Arne Röhl

Within the Germanic languages (Fig. 11.1), English basic vocabulary appears to be an anomaly. The English language is thought, by some, to be closely related to Frisian on the basis of morphological and phonological considerations (for example Nielsen 1981), and on the basis of a fifth-century account by Procopius. However the postulated English–Frisian relationship is not reflected in shared lexical innovations. For example, Walter (1911) demonstrated that Old Frisian shares five times more innovations with German than with Old English. Alternatively, English lexicon might have been brought by immigrant Angles, Saxons and Jutes according to Beda's account, written around AD 730 (Fig. 11.2). From his account, it is often implied that Angles and Saxons spoke languages ancestral to existing northwestern German languages. But again, the Indo-European diagrams published by Dyen *et al.* (1992), Gray & Atkinson (2003) and McMahon & McMahon (2003) mostly reveal a deep branching of English within the other living Germanic languages, rather than English grouping with the German branch as might have been expected. A Scandinavian component in English must also be considered, which may even predate the traditional Norse invasions. In particular Gildas, writing approximately AD 500–600 on the Saxon raids of Britain two generations earlier (Sims-Williams 1983a,b), points out that the Saxons used the word 'cyul' for their longboats with sails, and it is not at all clear that a Scandinavian origin for this word can be ruled out (*OED* 1989). However, locating the Saxons geographically or linguistically with confidence is not straightforward (Fig. 11.2).

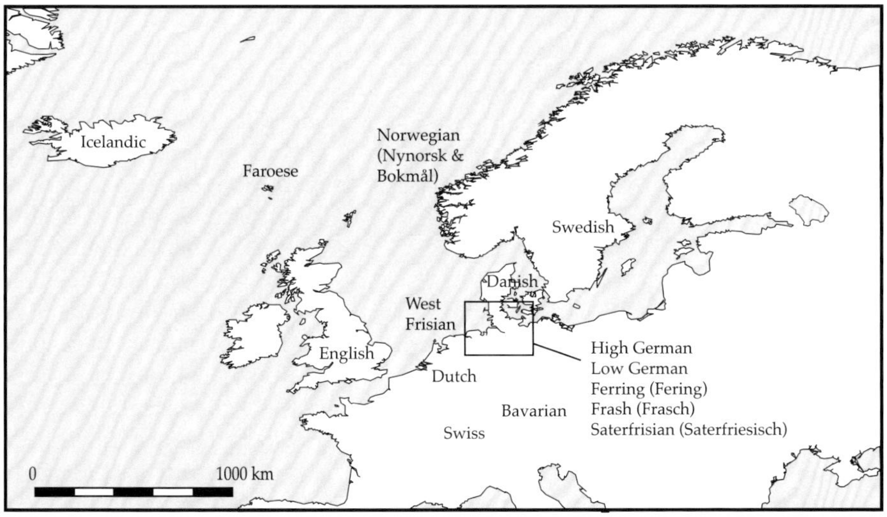


**Figure 11.1.** *Geographic locations of Germanic language samples. For the purposes of this paper, languages are defined as mutually unintelligible speech forms, as declared by the native speakers sampled here. This criterion was relaxed for some of the Scandinavian languages, among which a degree of mutual intelligibility was reported by the native speakers. For higher resolution of the sample locations of Saterfrisian (from the Saterland), Low German (from Husum and Land Wursten), Ferring (from the island of Föhr), Frash (from the mainland facing Föhr) and High German (from suburban Kiel), see Figure 11.2.*

In order to explore the evolution of English basic vocabulary, this paper applies a phylogenetic network approach to the basic lexica of 21 modern and ancient Germanic languages. Basic lexicon is represented here by the popular Swadesh 100-word list (Swadesh 1955), and for the sake of brevity, henceforth the terms 'English', 'German', etc. will be used when in fact reference is made to their basic vocabulary. We hope to make

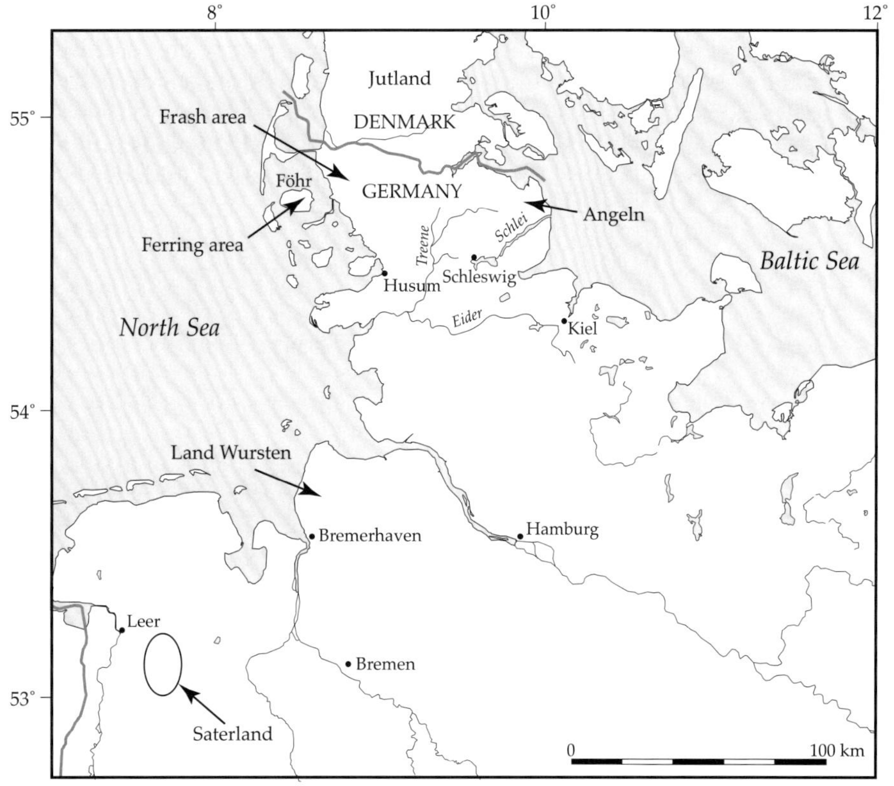


**Figure 11.2.** *Possible geographic and linguistic locations of Angles, Saxons and Jutes. Beda (writing in* AD *730) has the Angles based in Anglia (modern Angeln?) sandwiched between the Jutes and the Saxons. More specifically, Ptolemaios in* AD *150 locates the Saxons at the neck of the Cimbric peninsula, and additionally places three Saxon islands off the west coast of the peninsula at approximately latitude 55°N (taking into account his systematic shift by about 2°). The narrowest part of the peninsula is near Schleswig, where only a few kilometres of land separates the Baltic Schlei fjord from the river Treene flowing into the North Sea. According to historical accounts and place-name studies, this potential Saxon homeland north of the river Eider was largely Danish-speaking from at least medieval times until 1820 (Lammers 1981; Østergaard 1983).*

progress on the question of Germanic lexical evolution by introducing two new aspects into lexical analysis: firstly, the network diagram which our method generates (Bandelt *et al.* 1999) visualizes the changes of individual word use along the language branches, rather than providing only an abstract branch length or difference measure. This incidentally means that at its best, the network approach can reconstruct the lexicon, i.e. the specified word list, of a language which no longer exists. Moreover, our network method makes allowance for borrowing and convergent evolution by not forcing the data into a tree. Secondly, we have added four extinct lexical sources from the first millennium AD (*Beowulf*, Ælfred, *Heliand*, and the Gothic Bible) into the analysis along with modern Germanic languages to investigate whether their inclusion would change the deep branching of English reported by Dyen *et al.* (1992), Gray & Atkinson (2003) and McMahon & McMahon (2003).

### Methods

An evolutionary 'tree' of languages is an idealized concept that may not exist in reality. Throughout known history, language features such as lexical items have been borrowed from one language to another, violating the pure tree model of language evolution, and there is little evidence to assume that the situation was any different in prehistory. Hence, we merged the tree model (Schleicher 1863) with the wave model (Schmidt 1872) into a network model of language evolution (Forster *et al.* 1998), and advocate networks for reconstructing language evolution. Network approaches offer the advantage that they can visualize convergent evolutionary events (such as loan-word events, independent loss of inflectional morphological features, parallel and independent evolution of a sound change, and faulty or inappropriately coded data) as reticulations or parallelisms in the network. Two examples may illustrate the non-treelike information content of a network. In our network analysis of Alpine Romance languages (Forster *et al.* 1998), most branches were largely treelike, but the southern Ladin branch had degenerated into reticulations, evidently due to the influence of Italian loan words particularly in the southern Dolomites. In the Gaulish analysis (Forster & Toth 2003), loss of the grapheme 'ps' in Gaulish (and by implication, its phonetic quality) was found to be a feature of only limited phylogenetic value as this feature was involved in a network reticulation implying parallel change.

Nevertheless, for our two previously published network analyses no computer program was available at the time to generate the networks, and we had to resort to a manual approach. This is a potentially serious practical deficiency, which this manuscript begins to rectify. The manual approach was in the spirit of the reduced median network approach of Bandelt *et al.* (1995), by requiring binary data. However, lexical data are frequently multistate data rather than binary data, and the Celtic and Alpine Romance data were no exception. In those papers, a Procrustean data processing was employed to favour those items in the data table which were binary or nearly so. In this paper we explore network solutions for a data table in which all parts are initially treated as equal. On this basis the initial raw network reveals items prone to parallelisms or other problems, and in a subsequent analysis, the researcher may then choose to downweight or to omit problematic items, in order to reveal the underlying evolutionary tree free of convergence, if that tree exists at all.

With the release of the new version of our phylogenetic network program package, Network 4.106 (available free at www.fluxus-engineering.com), which includes advanced network streamlining procedures (Polzin & Daneshmand 2001; 2002; 2003), the analysis of non-binary (i.e. multistate) language data can now be attempted in their totality. The method used here within the Network 4.106 package is the median-joining (MJ) network algorithm (Bandelt *et al.* 1999) which identifies groups of closely related types, and introduces hypothesized ancestral types in order to unite the types into a parsimonious tree or network. A user-defined parameter $\varepsilon$ governs the initial grouping of closely related types and consequently the probability of recovering optimal trees. Optimal trees in this context are shortest trees, known as maximum parsimony trees or Steiner trees depending on the weighting. A low setting of $\varepsilon$ (typically zero) leads to rapid calculation times of seconds or minutes but can miss the best solutions, while higher settings of $\varepsilon$ (typically 10 or 20) are less likely to miss useful trees, but at the cost of much longer calculation times. After the MJ network has been generated, a subsequent and vital step is the streamlining of the MJ network using the new Steiner tree algorithm implemented in Network from version 4.1 onwards. Raw MJ networks of linguistic or genetic data generally contain numerous superfluous links. The Steiner procedure eliminates such links, considerably simplifying and indeed enabling for the first time the visual inspection of complex networks.

## Materials

Basic 100-word vocabulary lists (Swadesh 1955) were compiled for 21 samples of Germanic languages and ancient texts. The five ancient taxa are Old Norse (from various sources), Old English (the *Beowulf* epic poem and King Alfred's translations of three Latin texts), Gothic (the Bible translation by Ulfila) and a form of Old Low German (the *Heliand* epic poem). Old Norse was compiled from Bergsland & Vogt (1962) with minor modifications. The *Beowulf* Old English 100-word list was compiled from the *Beowulf* text as provided in the internet by the Online Book Initiative, with the assistance of the *Beowulf* translation of Gummere (1910) and Köbler's online Old English dictionary 'Neuhochdeutsch-Angelsächsisch' (http://homepage.uibk.ac.at/homepage/c303/c30310/publikat.html). King Alfred's Old English was compiled from the three translations ascribed with certainty to him, and written within the decades around AD 890, namely *Boethius* (Ælfred 890a), *Regula Pastoralis* (Ælfred 890b) and *Soliloquies* (Ælfred 890c); Köbler's online dictionary 'Neuhochdeutsch-Angelsächsisch' and the online Toronto Old English Corpus (http://ets.umdl.umich.edu/o/oec/) were used to determine translations and word frequencies. Gothic was compiled using the dictionary 'Neuhochdeutsch-Gotisch' provided by Köbler (1989). The Swadesh list for *Heliand* was compiled using the original text (http://www.artsci.wustl.edu/~bkessler/OS-Heliand), the translation by Genzmer (1955), and Köbler's online dictionary 'Neuhochdeutsch-Altsächsisch'. In the cases of Old English, Gothic and *Heliand*, the motivation behind choosing single sources rather than general compilations consisted in minimizing the risk of combining distinct language traditions into one hypothetical language which may never have existed. The word lists for the following living languages were compiled by native speakers and/or by linguists: Ferring (*Fering*), Frash (*Frasch*), West Frisian, Saterfrisian (*Saterfriesisch*), Low German from the Husum area (Low German from Land Wursten differed by only one cognate, see Table 11.1), Dutch, High German from Kiel, Bavarian from Prien am Chiemsee, Swiss German from Sankt Gallen, Danish from Copenhagen, Faroese, Icelandic and Swedish from Stockholm. For all languages, living and dead, Swadesh's criteria were followed, namely that only the most frequent and general word for a given semantic slot was chosen. For example, for the semantic slot 'neck', the specific German words 'Nacken' (nape) or 'Genick' (vertebrae within the neck) are disregarded and instead the general term 'Hals' (neck, internal throat) is entered in the data table. The frequency criterion comes into play particularly with the ancient languages, where potential semantic nuances (in the case of the Gothic bible) and alliterative style (in the cases of *Beowulf* and *Heliand*) sometimes hamper the choice of the most appropriate word. The resulting word lists are presented in Table 11.1.

For the phylogenetic analysis, the program package Network 4.106 (www.fluxus-engineering.com)

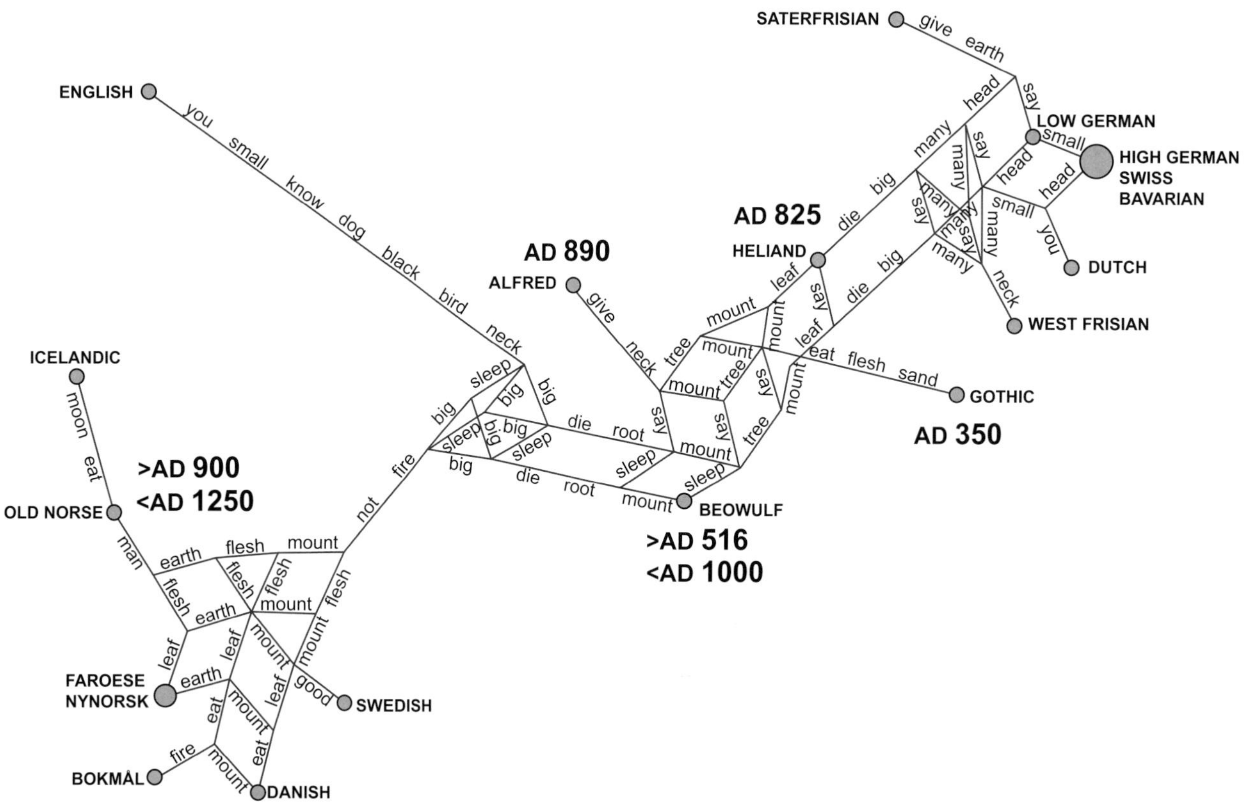


**Figure 11.3.** *Unrooted network of 19 Germanic language samples. The network was calculated from a list of 56 words using the Median-Joining-Steiner network method. The word changes are labelled along the links; for example, the label 'die' on the link next to Heliand delineates the change between 'sweltan' (in Heliand, Gothic, Ælfred and Beowulf) and 'sterben' (in German, Frisian, Dutch etc.), as can be deduced from Table 11.1. The character 'die' also changes its state on the links to English and Scandinavian; in this case, the languages to the left of 'die' (English and Scandinavian) have cognates of die. Thus, the network has split the multistate character 'die', which has the three states sweltan, sterben and die, into two distinct events. For some other multistate characters such as 'big' (with the four states groot, stor, micel and big), the network is unable to resolve each state into a distinct subtree, and triangular reticulations and prisms result. The position of 'Old Norse' should be interpreted with caution, as the Old Norse word list was compiled by Bergsland & Vogt (1962) from geographically and temporally diverse sources.*

was used as follows. The words were grouped into cognates and coded alphabetically as characters, but only in cases where there were no missing data, and where variation existed. Initially, 37 characters with missing data were omitted entirely from the analysis, as were 'this'/'that' and the concept 'person' which is not universal in Germanic. This left a list of 60 characters, of which 32 were variable. The variable words were coded etymologically and entered in Network 4.106 as amino-acid sequences, see the lettering A, B, C etc. in Table 11.1. Each word was initially given equal weight 10. Initial trial runs with the median-joining algorithm (the parameter $\varepsilon$ was set to zero or to 10) showed that 'kill', 'mouth', 'walk', and 'woman' caused considerable complication (i.e. chaotic reticulation) in the network. These four words were henceforth excluded. A further exploratory network analysis (not shown) of the Germanic data set then showed that two of the 21 Germanic languages contributed disproportionately to the network complexity (graphically evident as high-dimensional reticulations), namely Ferring and Frash. These two languages are spoken in the North Sea coastal region between Germany and Denmark, and this intermediate geographical location appears to be reflected in some of the words (compare the entries for 'fire', 'root' and 'not' in Table 11.1) which then caused the network reticulations. In a subsequent analysis we therefore omitted Ferring and Frash. The $\varepsilon$-10 network contained numerous non-optimal links which were purged by running the Steiner algorithm. The resulting Steiner network is shown in Figure 11.3.

**Table 11.1.** *Swadesh lists for 21 Germanic language samples. Note: capital letters A, B, C etc. indicate cognation coding, performed only for variable words and words without missing entries.*

**Notes**

13 Dutch: klauw is used in the context of scratching and refers to the paw and its nails, while nagel refers only to the nail but is less likely to be used.

14 Gothic: milhma is possibly cognate to Swedish moln, according to Lehmann (1986).

17 Gothic: gaswiltan is the most frequent word for 'to die', occurring 44 times, as opposed to only 27 occurrences for the next most frequent synonym, gadauthnan. Gaswiltan appears mainly in the context of the speaker or of an acquaintance dying, typically Jesus. I found only three exceptions to this rule. Gadauthnan is generally used for third parties dying.

28 Gothic: fon is cognate to fire etc. according to Lehmann (1986).

35 Beowulf: the term for single hair is absent if the conjectural translation of 'bundenheorde' as 'with hair upbound' is disregarded.

38 Beowulf: hafola is cognate with head according to Holthausen (1934).

58 Dutch: hals is more commonly used than nek, according to uit den Boogaart (1975).

67 English: road is hardly synonymous with path as suggested in the Swadesh specification, hence the new specification here.

71 Heliand: quethan occurs 259 times, seggian 161 times.

76 Beowulf: swefan is cognate with sove according to Pokorny (1959).

82 Scandinavian: sol and sun are cognate according to the *Oxford English Dictionary* (1989).

85/86 Gothic: the demonstrative sense of þata is weak according to Krause (1953).

87 Dutch: jij cognate with English according to the *Oxford English Dictionary* (1989).

95 Bavarian/Swiss: mia/miir is derived from postverbal wir, according to Ochs *et al.* (1997).

98 Low German: weer in Flensburg, wokeen or keen in Land Wursten.

Low German phonetic spelling here is given as in standard High German, except: oo (as in standard British English 'stoke'), initial s- voiceless, e (as in standard High German 'fett'), ee (as in standard High German 'See'), ch ambiguous (in 'dröch' as High German 'ich', but in 'Barch' as in High German 'Dach'), and å as in standard Danish.

Bavarian and Swiss were written phonetically based largely on standard High German, except: initial s- voiceless, and final -a reduced.

| High German | Bavarian | Swiss | Danish | Faroese | Old Norse | Icelandic | Nynorsk | Bokmål | Swedish | Gothic |
|---|---|---|---|---|---|---|---|---|---|---|
| alle | alle | alli | alle | øll | öll | öll | alle | alle | alla | alla |
| Asche | Aschn | Äsche | aske | øska | aska | aska | åske | aske | aska | azgo |
| Rinde | Rindn | Rinde | bark | børkur | borkr | börkur | bark | bark | bark | ? |
| Bauch | Bauch | Buuch | mave | búkur | magi | magi | mage | mage | mage/buk | wamba |
| C groß | C grooss | C grooss | D stor | D stórur | D stórr | D stór | D stor | D stor | D stor | B mikils |
| B Vogel | B Foogl | B Foogel | B fugl | B fuglur | B fugl | B fugl | B fugl | B fugl | B fågel | B fugls |
| beißen | baissen | biisse | bide | bíta | bíta | bíta | bita | bite | bita | beitan |
| B schwarz | B schwaaz | B schvaarz | B sort | B svartur | B svartr | B svartur | B svart | B sort/svart | B svart | B swarts |
| Blut | Bluad | Bluet | blod | blóð | blóð | blóð | blod | blod | blod | bloÞ |
| Knochen | Knocha | Chnochä | knogle | bein | bein | bein | bein | ben/bein | ben | ? |
| A Brust | A Brust | A Bruscht | A bryst | A bróst | A brjóst | A brjóst | A brøst | A bryst | A bröst | A brusts |
| brennen | brenna | brenne | brænde | brenna | brenna | brenna | brenna | brenne | brinna | brinnan |
| Kralle | Kroin | Kralle | klo | klógv | kló | kló | klo | klo | klo | ? |
| Wolke | Woikn | Wukkä | sky | skýggj | ský | ský | sky | sky | moln | milhma |
| kalt | koid | chalt | kold | kaldur | kaldr | kaldur | kald | kald | kall | kalds |
| kommen | kemma | choo | komme | koma | koma | koma | koma | komme | komma | qiman |
| C sterben | C schteam | C schtäärbe | A dø | A doyggja | A deyja | A deyja | A døy | A dø | A dö | B (ga)swiltan |
| B Hund | B Hund | B Hund | B hund | B hundur | B hundr | B hundur | B hund | B hund | B hund | B hunds |
| trinken | dringa | trinke | drikke | drekka | drekka | drekka | drikka | drikke | dricka | drigkan |
| trocken | druckad | trocke | tør | turrur | Þurr | Þurr | torr/tørr | tørr | torr | ? |
| Ohr | Ooa | Oor | øre | oyra | eyra | eyra | øyre | øre | öra | auso |
| A Erde | A Erdn | A Erde | A jord | C mold | C mold | C mold | C mold | A jord | A jord | A airÞa |
| A essen | A essn | A ässe | B spise | A eta | A eta | C borða | A eta | B spise | A äta | D matjan |
| Ei | Oa | Ai | æg | egg | egg | egg | egg | egg | ägg | ? |
| Auge | Aug | Aug | øje | eyga | auga | auga | auge | øye | öga | augo |
| Fett | Fett | Fett | fedt | feitt | fita | fita | feitt | fett | fett | ? |
| Feder | Feeda | Fäädre | fjer | fjøður | fjọðr | fjöður | fjør | fjær | fjäder | ? |
| A Feuer | A Faia | A Füür | B ild | B eldur | B eldr | B eldur | B eld | C varme/brann/ bål/flamme | B eld | A fon |
| Fisch | Fiisch | Fisch | fisk | fiskur | fiskr | fiskur | fisk | fisk | fisk | fisks |
| fliegen | fliang | fliege | flyve | flúgva | fljúga | fljúga | flyga | fly | flyga | ? |
| Fuß | Fuass | Fuess | fod | fótur | fótr | fótur | fot | fot | fot | fotus |
| voll | foi | foll | fuld | fullur | fullr | fullur | full | full | full | fulls |
| A geben | A gebm | A gee | A give | A geva | A gefa | A gefa | A gje | A gi | A ge/giva | A giban |
| A gut | A guad | A guät | A god | A góður | A góðr | A góður | A god | A god | B bra | A goÞs |
| grün | grea | grüen | grøn | grønur | grœnn | grænn | grøn | grønn | grön | ? |
| Haar | Haar | Hòòr | hår | hár | hár | hár | hår | hår | hårstrå | tagl |
| Hand | Hant | Hand | hånd | hond | họnd | hönd | hand | hånd | hand | handus |
| B Kopf | B Koopf | B Kopf | A hoved | A høvd | A họfuð | A höfuð/haus | A hovud | A hode | A huvud | A haubiÞ |
| hören | hearn | khööre | høre | hoyra | heyra | heyra | høyra | høre | höra | hausjan |
| Herz | Heaz | Herz | hjerte | hjarta | hjarta | hjarta | hjarte | hjerte | hjärta | hairto |
| Horn | Hoan | Horn | horn | horn | horn | horn | horn | horn | horn | haurn |
| ich | I | iich | jeg | eg | ek | ég | eg | jeg | jag | ik |
| D töten | E umbringa/hiimocha | D tööte | F dræbe | F drepa | F drepa | F drepa | F drepa | F drepe | D döda | G usqiman |
| Knie | Knia | Knoi | knæ | knæ | kné | hné | kne | kne | knä | kniu |
| B wissen | B wissn | B wüsse | B vide | B vita | B vita | B vita | B vita | B vite | B veta | B witan |
| B Blatt | B Blaadl/Blatt | B Blatt | B blad | B blað | A lauf | A laufblað | B blad | B blad | A löv | A lauf(s) |
| liegen | liang | ligge | ligge | liggja | liggja | liggja | liggja | ligge | ligga | ligan |
| Leber | Leeba | Lääbere | lever | livur | lifr | lifur | lever | lever | lever | ? |
| lang | lang | lang | lang | langur | langr | langur | lang | lang | lång | ? |
| Laus | Laus | Luus | lus | lús | lús | lús | lus | lus | lus | ? |
| A Mann | A Moo | A Maa | A mand | A maður | B karl | B karl/maður | A mann | A mann | A man | A manna |
| B viele | B fui | B fili | A mange | A mangir | A margir | A margir | A mange | A mange | A många | A managa |
| A Fleisch | A Flaisch | A Flaisch | B kød | B kjøt | C hold | C hold | B kjøt | B kjøtt | B kött | D leik |
| A Mond | A Moond | A Mond | A måne | A máni | A máni | B tungl | A måne | A måne | A måne | A mena |
| C Berg | C Beag | C Berg | C bjerg | D fjall | D fjall | D fjall | D fjell | D fjell | C berg | B fairguni |
| A Mund | B Mai | B Muul | A mund | A muður | A munnr | A munnur | A munn | A munn | A mun | A munÞs |
| Name | Naama | Naame | navn | navn | nafn | nafn | namn | navn | namn | namo |
| B Hals | B Hois | B Hals | B hals | B hálsur | B hals | B háls | B hals | B hals | B hals | B hals |
| neu | nai | nòi | ny | nýggjur | nýr | nýr | ny | ny | ny | niujis |
| Nacht | Nacht | Nacht | nat | nátt | nótt | nótt | natt | natt | natt | nahts |
| Nase | Naasn | Naase | næse | nøs | nef | nef | nase | nese | näsa | ? |
| A nicht | A ned | A nit | B ikke | B ikki | B eigi | B ekki | B ikkje | B ikke | B inte | A ni |
| eins | oans | ains | en | ein | einn | einn | ein | en | en | ains |
| Person | - | - | person | persónur | maðr | maður | menneske | menneske | person/mäniska | andwairÞi |
| Regen | Reng | Rääge | regn | regn | regn | regn | regn | regn | regn | rign |
| rot | rood | root | rød | reyður | rauðr | rauður | raud | rød | röd | rauÞs |
| Straße | Schtraassn | Schtrooss | vej | vegur | vegr | vegur | veg | vei | väg | ? |
| B Wurzel | B Wurzl | B Wurzle | A rod | A rót | A rót | A rót | A rot | A rot | A rot | B waurts |
| rund | rund | rund | rund | rundur | kringlóttr | kringlóttur | rund | rund | rund | ? |
| A Sand | A Sand | A Sand | A sand | A sandur | A sandr | A sandur | A sand | A sand | A sand | B malma |
| A sagen | A sang | A saage | A sige | A siga | A segja | A segja | A seia | A si | A säga | B qiÞan |
| sehen | seeng | ksee | se | síggja | séa | sjá | sjå | se | se | (ga)saihwan |
| Samen | Saama | Saame | sæd | sáð | frjó | fræ | frø | frø | frö | fraiw |
| sitzen | sitzn/hockä | sitze/hocke | sidde | sita | sitja | sitja | sittja | sitte | sitta | sitan |
| Haut | Haut | Hut | hud | húð | skinn/húð | húð | skinn | hud | hud/skinn | ? |
| A schlafen | A schlaffa | A schloofe | B sove | B sova | B sofa | B sofa | B sova | B sove | B sova | A slepan |
| C klein | C gloa | C chlai | B lille | B lítil | B lítill | B lítill | B liten | B liten | B liten | B leitels |
| Rauch | Rauch | Rauch | røg | roykur | reykr | reykur | røyk | røyk/røk | rök | ? |
| stehen | schtee | schtoo | stå | standa | standa | standa | stå | stå | stå | standan |
| Stern | Schtean | Schtern | stjerne | stjørna | stjarna | stjarna | stjerne | stjerne | stjärna | stairno |
| Stein | Schtoa | Schtei | sten | steinur | steinn | steinn | stein | stein/sten | sten | stains |
| Sonne | Sonn | Sunne | sol | sól | sól | sól | sol | sol | sol | sunno |
| schwimmen | schwimma | schwimme | svømme | svimja | svima | synda | symja | svømme | simma | ? |
| Schwanz | Schwanz | Schwanz | hale | hali | hali | hali | hale | hale | svans | ? |
| das | des | säb | det | hatta | Þat | Þetta | det | det | det | Þata? |
| dieses | dees | da | dette | hetta | Þetta | Þetta | dette | dette | detta | Þata? |
| B Du | B duu | B duu | B du | B tú | B Þú | B Þú | B du | B du | B du | B Þu |
| Zunge | Zunga | Zunge | tunge | tunga | tunga | tunga | tunge | tunge | tunga | tuggo |
| Zahn | Zaan | Zaa | tand | tonn | tonn | tönn | tann | tann | tand | tunÞus |
| B Baum | B Baam | B Baum | A træ | A træ | A tré | A tré | A tre | A tre | A träd | B bagms |
| zwei | zwoa | zwai | to | tvey | tveir | tveir | to | to | två | twai |
| B gehen | C laafa | C laufe | B gå | B ganga | B ganga | B ganga | B gå | B gå | B gå | B gaggan |
| warm | waam | warm | varm | heitur | varmr | hlýr | varm | varm | varm | ? |
| Wasser | wassa | Wasser | vand | vatn | vatn | vatn | vatn | vann | vatten | wato |
| wir | mia | miir | vi | vit | vér | við | vi/me | vi | vi | weis |
| was | was | waas | hvad | hvat | hvat | hvað | kva | hva | vad | hwa |
| weiß | waiss | wiss | hvid | hvítur | hvítr | hvítur | kvit | hvit | vit | hweits |
| wer | wea | wèèr | hvem | hvør | hverr | hver | kven | hvem | vem | hwas |
| B Frau | A/B Weiberz/Frau | B Frau | C kvinde | C kvinna | C kona | C kona | C kvinnfolk | C kvinne | C kvinna | C qino |
| gelb | geib | gääl | gul | gulur | gulr | gulur | gul | gul | gul | ? |

| | English | Beowulf | Alfred | Heliand | Ferring | Frash | West Frisian | Saterfrisian | Low German | Dutch |
|---|---|---|---|---|---|---|---|---|---|---|
| 1 | all (adjective, plural neuter) | eal | eall | all | ale/aal | åle/åål | al | aal/alle | aal | alle |
| 2 | ashes | ? | ? | ? | eesk | eesch | jiske | Ääske | Asch | as |
| 3 | bark | ? | rind | ? | riinj/buark | rin | bast | Boa(r)ke | Bork | schors |
| 4 | stomach (belly, e.g. stomach is full) | ? | wamb | ? | bük | bük/buuke/lif | liif | Buuk | Buuk | buik |
| 5 | A big | B micel | B micel | B mikil | C grat | C grut | C grut | C groot | C groot | C groot |
| 6 | A bird | B fugol | B fugol | B fugal | B fögel | B föögel | B fûgel | B Fúgel | B Vågel | B vogel |
| 7 | to bite | bitan | ? | bitan | bitj | bite | bite | biete | biten | bijten |
| 8 | A black | B sweart | B sweart | B swart | B suart | B suurt | B swart | B swot/swoot | B schwatt | B zwart |
| 9 | blood | blod | blod | blod | blud | blödj | bloed | Bloud | Blood | bloed |
| 10 | bone | ban | ban | ben | knook | knooke | bonke | Knoke | Knocken | been |
| 11 | A breast (chest, male & female) | A breost | A breost | A briost | A brast | A burst | A boarst | A Brust | A Boss | A borst |
| 12 | to burn (intransitive, e.g. the fire is burning) | ? | ? | brinnan | braan | bråne | baarne | baanje/bad(d)enje | brenn | branden |
| 13 | claw (non-avian nail) | egl | ? | ? | kral | kral/klau/klaa | klau | Klaue | Krall | klauw |
| 14 | cloud | ? | wolcen | wolkan | wolk | woolken/wulk | wolk | Wulke | Wulk | wolk |
| 15 | cold | ceald | ceald | kald | kuul | kölj | kâld | koold | koold | koud |
| 16 | to come | cuman | cuman | kuman | kem | kaame | komme | kume | kåm | komen |
| 17 | A to die | B sweltan | B sweltan | B sweltan | C sterev | C stärwe | C stjerre | C stierve | C schtarbm | C sterven |
| 18 | A dog | B hund | B hund | B hund | B hünj | B hün | B hûn | B Huund | B Hund | B hond |
| 19 | to drink | drincan | drincan | drinkan | drank | drainke | drinke | drinke | drinkn | drinken |
| 20 | dry | ? | dryge | drokno | drüg/drööch | dröög | droech | druug | dröch | droog |
| 21 | ear | ? | eare | ora | uar | uur | ear | Oor | Ohr | oor |
| 22 | A earth (soil as in flower pot) | A eorÞe | A eorÞe | A ertha | A eerd | A jard | A ierde | B Gruund(e) | A Eer | A aarde |
| 23 | A to eat | A etan | A etan | A etan | A iitj | A ääse | A ite | A iete | A edden | A eten |
| 24 | egg | ? | æg | ? | ai | oi | aai | Oai/Ai | Ei | ei |
| 25 | eye | eage | eage | oga | uug | uug | each | Oog/Oge | Ooch | oog |
| 26 | fat (noun) | ? | ? | ? | feet | smeer | fet | Fat | Fett | vet |
| 27 | feather | feÞer | feÞer | fethera | feeler | fääder | fear | Fugge | Feller | veer |
| 28 | A fire | A fyr | A fyr | A fiur | B ial | B iilj | A fjoer | A Fjúur | A Füer | A vuur |
| 29 | fish | fisc | fisc | fisk | fask | fasch | fisk | Fisk | Fisch | vis |
| 30 | to fly | fleogan | fleogan | faran | flä | fliinj | fleane | fljoge | fleegn | vliegen |
| 31 | foot | fot | fot | fot | fut | fötj | foet | Fout | Foot | voet |
| 32 | full | full | full | ful | fol | ful | fol | ful | full | vol |
| 33 | A to give | A gifan | B sellan | A gevan | C du | C düünj | A jaan | D reke | A gebm | A geven |
| 34 | A good | A god | A god | A god | A gud | A gödj | A goed | A goud | A good | A goed |
| 35 | green | ? | grene | groni | green | gräin | grien | gräin | grön | groen |
| 36 | (single) hair | ? | ? | har | hiar | häär | hier | Híer/Häier | Hohr | haar |
| 37 | hand | hand | hand | hand | hun | hönj | hân | Hounde | Hant | hand |
| 38 | A head | A hafola | A heafod | A hovid | A hood | A hood | A holle | B Kop/Haud | B Kopp | A hoofd |
| 39 | to hear | hieran | hieran | (gi-)horian | hiar | hiire | hearre | here | hörn | horen |
| 40 | heart | heorte/hreÞer | heorte | herta | hart | hart | hert | Haat | Hart | hart |
| 41 | horn | horn | horn | ? | hurn | horn | hoarn | Houden/Hudden | Hurn | hoorn |
| 42 | I | ic | ic | ik | ik | ik | ik | iek | ick | ik |
| 43 | A kill | B (a)cwellan | C ofslean | C slahan | D duadmaage | D düüdj mååge | D deadzje | D doodmoakje | D dood moken | D doden |
| 44 | knee | ? | cneo | knio | knöbian | knäibling | knibbel | Kniebel | Knee | knie |
| 45 | A to know | B witan | B witan | B witan | B ved | B waase | B witte | B wiete | B weetn | B weten |
| 46 | A leaf | A leaf | A leaf | B blad | B bleed | B blees | B blêd | B Blääd | B Blatt | B blad |
| 47 | to lie (on the side) | licgan | licgan | liggian | lai | lade | lizze | läze | lingn | liggen |
| 48 | liver | ? | lifer | ? | liver | liwer | lever | Lieuwer | Lever | lever |
| 49 | long (spatial) | lang | lang | lang | lung | lung | lang | long/loang | lang | lang |
| 50 | louse | ? | ? | ? | lüs | lüs | lûs | Lúus | Lus | luis |
| 51 | A man | A mann | A mann | A man | A maan | A moon | A man | A Mon | A Mann | A man |
| 52 | A many | A manig | A manig | A manag | A/B manigen/fölen | A maning | C in soad | B fúul | B vel | B veel |
| 53 | A flesh (e.g. flesh wound; not meat) | A flæsc | A flæsc | A flesk | A fleesk | A flååsch | A fleis | A Flaask | A Fleesch | A vlees |
| 54 | A moon | A mona | A mona | A mano | A muun | A moune | A moanne | A Moune | A Moond | A maan |
| 55 | A mountain | B fyrg- | A munt | C berg | C berig | C bärj | C berch | C Bíerig/Bäierg | C Barch | C berg |
| 56 | A mouth | A muÞ | A muÞ | A muth | A mös | A müs | B mûle | B Mule | A Munt | A mond |
| 57 | name | nama | nama | namo | nööm | noome | namme | Nome | Nåm | naam |
| 58 | A neck | B heals | C suira | B hals | B hals | B hals | A nekke | B Hoals/Haals | B Hals | B hals |
| 59 | new | niw- | niwe | niuwi | nei | nai | nij | näi | ni | nieuw |
| 60 | night | niht | niht | naht | naacht | nåcht | nacht | Noacht/Naacht | Nach | nacht |
| 61 | nose | ? | nosu | ? | nöös | noos | noas | Noze | Nääs | neus |
| 62 | A not | A ne | A na | A ne/ni | B ei | B ai | A net | A nit | A nich | A niet |
| 63 | one (numeral) | an | an | ên | ian | iinj | ien | een | een | een |
| 64 | person (e.g. room for one person only) | guma | ? | gumo | persuun | persoon | persoan | - | Persoon | persoon |
| 65 | rain | ? | ren | regin | rin | rin | rein | Rien | Reng | regen |
| 66 | red | *read? | read | rod | ruad | rüüdj | read | rood | root | rood |
| 67 | road (outside settlements, hard surface optional) | stræt | weg | weg | struat | stroote | dyk | Sträite/Dom | Schtråt | weg |
| 68 | A root | B wyrt | B wyrtruma | B wurt | A rut | A rötj | B woartel | B Wuttel | B Wuddel | B wortel |
| 69 | round | ? | ? | ? | trinj | trin | rûn | rund | runt | rond |
| 70 | A sand | A sand | A sand | A sand | A sun | A sönj | A sân | A Sound | A Sant | A zand |
| 71 | A to say | A secgan | B cweÞan | B kwethan | A sai | A seede | A sizze | B kwede | A seng | A zeggen |
| 72 | to see | seon | geseon | (gi-)sehan | sä | siinj | sjen | sjo | seen | zien |
| 73 | seed (single seed for germination) | ? | sæd | ? | siad | sädj | sie(d) | Säid | Såt | zaadje |
| 74 | to sit | sittan | sittan | sittian | sat | sate | sitte | sitte | siddn | zitten |
| 75 | skin (human) | ? | hyd | fel | hedj | hüd/schan | hûd/fel | Häid | Huut | huid |
| 76 | A to sleep | B swefan | A slæpan | A slapan | A sliap | A släipe | A sliepe | A släipe | A schlåpm | A slapen |
| 77 | A small | B lytel | B lytel | B luttil | B letj | B latj | B lyts | B litje/litjet | B lütt | C klein |
| 78 | smoke | rec | rec | rok | riik | riik | reek | Rook | Rook | rook |
| 79 | to stand | standan | standan | standan | stun | stönje | stean | stounde | schtån | staan |
| 80 | star | ? | steorra | sterro | stäär | stäär | stjer | Stiern | Schtirn | ster |
| 81 | stone | stan | stan | sten | stian | stiinj | stien | Steen | Schteen | steen |
| 82 | sun | sunna | sunne | sunna | san | san | sinne | Sunne | Sunn | zon |
| 83 | to swim | swymman/fleotan | ? | ? | sweem | swume | swimme | swimme | schwimm | zwemmen |
| 84 | tail | ? | steort | ? | stöört | stjart | sturt | Stäit/Stit | Schteert | staart |
| 85 | that (adjective, neuter) | Þæt | Þæt | that | detdiar | dåt(deer) | dat | dät | dat | dat |
| 86 | this (adjective, neuter) | Þis | Þis | thit | detheer | dåtheer | dit | dut | dit | dit |
| 87 | A you (thou) | B Þu | B Þu | B thu | B dü | B dü | B do/dû | B du | B Du | A jij |
| 88 | tongue | ? | tunge | tunga | tong | tung | tonge | Tunge | Tung | tong |
| 89 | tooth | toÞ | ? | tand | tus | täis | tosk | Tusk | Tään | tand |
| 90 | A tree | A/B treo/beam | A treo | B bom | B buum | B buum | B beam | B Boom | B Boom | B boom |
| 91 | two (numeral) | twegen | twegen | twene | taav | tou | twa | two | twee | twee |
| 92 | A to walk | B gangan | B gangan | B gangan | B gung | C luupe | D rinne | C lope | B gån | C lopen |
| 93 | warm | ? | wearm | warm | warem | wurm | waarm | woorm | warm | warm |
| 94 | water | wæter | wæter | watar | weeder | wååder | wetter | Woater/Water | Wåter | water |
| 95 | we | we | we | wi | wi | we | wy | wie | wi | wij |
| 96 | what (interrogative) | hwæt | hwæt | hwat | wat | wat | wat | wät | watt | wat |
| 97 | white | hwit | hwit | hwît | witj | wit | wyt | wiet | witt | wit |
| 98 | who (interrogative) | ? | hwa | hwe | hoker | huum | wa | wäl | weer, wokeen/keen | wie |
| 99 | A woman | A wif | A wif | A wif | A wüv | A wüset | B frou | A Wieuw(moanske) | B Fru | B vrouw |
| 100 | yellow | geolu | ? | gelu | güül | gööl | giel | jeel | chääl | geel |

## Results

*1. Evolution of Germanic*

The unrooted network of Germanic languages in Figure 11.3 contains reticulations, which indicates uncertainty as to the existence of a historical lexical tree; nevertheless the network algorithm has successfully clustered the oldest languages near the centre of the network and placed the living languages on the peripheries. One of the intermediate nodes at the centre of the network probably represents the Common Germanic basic word list, spoken at some point in prehistory; the precise identification of the Common Germanic node must, however, await a more detailed network analysis based on longer word lists.

In the network of Germanic languages, four branches can be discerned, defined here as Gothic, Scandinavian, English and German (the latter including Frisian and Dutch). Hence the network only partly matches the traditional classification scheme of Germanic into North, East and West Germanic, but agrees with the recent results by Dyen *et al.* (1992), Gray & Atkinson (2003) and McMahon & McMahon (2003). Furthermore, in the network analysis the four Frisian word lists do not form a distinct branch of their own but show reticulate relationships with the languages to which they are geographically proximal. Specifically, Ferring and Frash (not included in the displayed network; see Methods) are spoken in areas close to the Danish border and show lexical relationships to the Scandinavian branch, while the Saterfrisian and West Frisian languages show lexical relationships to Low German and Dutch, which are spoken in the surrounding areas. It must be emphasized at this point that there is no *a priori* reason to suppose that this evolutionary reconstruction, based on frequencies of words in semantic slots, should match precisely other classifications, which may be based on morphology and phonology.

*2. Evolution of English*

The isolated and deep position of the English branch merits attention. Neither the modern English nor the Old English word lists are closely related with the German branch, as might have been expected if one interpreted Beda's account, written three centuries after the Saxon raids, to mean that the English population in Britain, and by implication the English language, are largely descended from German-speaking tribes (compare Fig. 11.2).

Looking at the detail in Figure 11.3, modern English emerges from a rather complicated reticulate phylogenetic relationship with *Beowulf* and Ælfred. In the network, this is due to the branching of modern English from an intermediate node, the precise location of which is not clear at the present resolution. In any case, neither King Alfred's English nor *Beowulf* appear to be directly ancestral to modern English vocabulary. Specifically, the network postulates that Ælfred's Wessex English does not lie on the branch to modern English but differs by at least the autapomorphies 'suira' for 'neck' and 'sellan' for 'give'. *Beowulf* differs by 'swefan' for 'sleep', a word related to the Scandinavian forms. Thus, the network shows a noticeable lexical diversity within Britain at the time of *Beowulf* and Ælfred, i.e. more than 1000 years ago. The lexical diversity which formerly existed in Britain was comparable to the present diversity within mainland Scandinavia, or within the present Dutch/German language area. Turning our attention to the relationship between English and Scandinavian, the network displays some common evolution or convergence between the two (compare the words for 'die' and 'root'). Interestingly, the Scandinavian relationship may date back at least as far as *Beowulf* if the word for 'sleep' is taken as an indicator. It is of note in this context that the story of *Beowulf* is located in Scandinavia, and that Britain is never mentioned in the narrative. The network thus offers evidence for a Scandinavian influence on the modern English ancestor, but not on Ælfred. The deep branching of Ælfred seems to indicate an archaic component in English; this possibility should be investigated with networks based on longer word lists.

*3. Timescales*

At best we can hope only to estimate approximate boundaries for the age of Common Germanic, because it is not clear that it is possible to apply a universal lexical clock to our phylogeny. Within the past 1000 years, basic vocabulary in the English branch seems to have evolved more rapidly than in other Germanic branches. The three texts by Ælfred were written just before AD 900. The exact date for the language of *Beowulf* is unknown but must be within the period AD 516 to AD 1000 (Bjork & Obermeier 1997) and is postulated by some to be approximately AD 800 (Whitelock 1951; Haywood 1991). Thus, in a time span of around 1200 years, English seems to have changed about ten words within the shortened 56-word list used for the network (for example, 'hund' has changed to 'dog', see Fig. 11.2 and Table 11.1). Moreover, according to the *Oxford English Dictionary* (1989), which documents the earliest appearances for each of these words, all ten changes originated before AD 1300. This compares with only five changes in the 1200 years between *Heliand* (approximately AD 825) and modern Low German, and two changes in around

1000 years between Icelandic and 'Old Norse'. Next, we presume Common Germanic to be an empty node located somewhere in the central reticulation of the network, and apply these rates of change to estimate the time when Common Germanic was last spoken. However, it is unclear how to form a reliable overall rate estimate, as a test of the clock hypothesis based on these few numbers would have little power. Also it is unclear where the precise location of the node of Common Germanic is in the network. Nevertheless, at one extreme, Common Germanic can be no younger than the Gothic bible (approximately AD 350). At the other extreme, we can apply the slow Icelandic mutation rate (two words in 1000 years) to the Gothic branch assuming that Gothic is at most eight words distant from the root node yielding a conservative point estimate for Common Germanic at 3600 BC. The real range of uncertainty might become even broader if we considered two further sources of error, namely the shape of the phylogeny and the small sample sizes. Clearly there is ample potential for constraining this time bracket of 3950 years, but first, the priority must be to identify reliably the root node for Germanic, ideally using an outgroup such as Latin or Sanskrit.

## Conclusions

Our preliminary network of Germanic word lists differs from the classical subdivision of Germanic into North, East and West Germanic by classifying English as a deep, fourth Germanic branch. The network analysis furthermore reveals a Scandinavian influence on English and apparently a pre-Scandinavian archaic component in Old English. The Germanic word lists spoken today appear to converge in the network on an ancestral Common Germanic lexicon spoken at an unknown time, but constrained to before AD 350 and probably after 3600 BC.

## Future directions

The results presented in this study are based on only 56 words and must be considered preliminary pending more detailed networks using longer word lists, to resolve potential parallelisms.

Furthermore, Old Norse as compiled by Bergsland & Vogt (1962) looks like an Icelandic speech variant in the network of Figure 11.2, rather than representing the ancestral consensus lexicon of the modern Scandinavian branch. Those authors compiled the list for Old Norse from a variety of sources, and it may be worthwhile to enter each source as a separate taxon in future analyses. Generally, to confirm or adjust the branching pattern within ancient Germanic, more lists for ancient Germanic texts should be added to the network to compare known evolution with phylogenetically reconstructed evolution. Meanwhile, it would be desirable for linguists to compile morphological and phonological character lists suitable for phylogenetic analysis, as suggested during this conference. Ideally, such lists would be as globally applicable as is the Swadesh 100-word list. Lexical evolution could then be compared with phonological and morphological evolution, and observed differences and similarities between the three phylogenies would contribute to a clearer picture of Germanic language prehistory as a whole.

## Acknowledgements

We are grateful to Antje Arfsten, Morten Broberg, Jon Eysturoy, Marron C. Fort, Angela Gründemann, Agnar Helgason, Marco Hermann, Wiebke Meyer, Adeline Petersen, Kari Anne Rand, Eva Reyment, Marie-Louise Sørensen, Charity Scott-Stokes, Thomas Sternsdorf, Elsa Strietman, and Alfred Toth for assistance with compiling the word lists, Diane Lister, Stephen Oppenheimer and Chau Pak-Lee for improving the manuscript, Catherine Hills for discussion, and Paul Forster for suggesting the glossary.

## References

Ælfred, 890a (1899). *De consolatione philosophiae. King Alfred's Old English Version of Boethius, from the Manuscripts, with Introduction, Critical Notes and Glossary,* ed. W.J. Sedgefield. Oxford: The Clarendon Press.

Ælfred, 890b (1871). *Regula Pastoralis. King Alfred's West-Saxon Version of Gregory's Pastoral Care: with an English translation, the Latin text, notes, and an Introduction,* ed. H. Sweet. London: Trübner.

Ælfred, 890c (1902). *Soliloquies. King Alfred's Old English Version of St Augustine's Soliloquies, with Introduction, Notes and Glossary,* ed. H.L. Hargrove. New York (NY): Holt.

Bandelt, H.-J., P. Forster, B.C. Sykes & M.B. Richards 1995. Mitochondrial portraits of human populations using median networks. *Genetics* 141, 743–53.

Bandelt, H.-J., P. Forster & A. Röhl 1999. Median-joining networks for inferring intraspecific phylogenies. *Molecular Biology and Evolution* 16, 37–48.

Bergsland, K. & H. Vogt 1962. On the validity of glottochronology. *Current Anthropology* 3, 115–53.

Bjork, R.E. & A. Obermeier, 1997. Date provenance, author, audiences, in *A Beowulf Handbook,* eds. R.E. Bjork & J.D. Niles. Lincoln (NE): University of Nebraska Press, 13–34.

Dyen, I., J.B. Kruskal & B. Black, 1992. An Indoeuropean classification: a lexicostatistical experiment. *Transactions of the American Philosophical Society* 82, 1–132.

Forster, P. & A. Toth, 2003. Toward a phylogenetic chronology of ancient Gaulish, Celtic, and Indo-European. *Proceedings of the National Academy of Sciences of the USA* 100, 9079–84.

Forster, P., A. Toth & H.-J. Bandelt, 1998. Evolutionary network analysis of word lists: visualising the relationships between Alpine Romance languages. *Journal of Quantitative Linguistics* 5, 174–87.

Genzmer, F., 1955 (1982). *Heliand und die Bruchstücke der Genesis*. Stuttgart: Reclam.

Gray, R.D. & Q.D. Atkinson, 2003. Language-tree divergence times support the Anatolian theory of Indo-European origin. *Nature* 426, 435–9.

Gummere, F.B., 1910. *Beowulf*. (The Harvard Classics 49.) New York (NY): P.F. Collier & Sons.

Haywood, J., 1991. *Dark Age Naval Power: a Reassessment of Frankish and Anglo-Saxon Seafaring Activity*. London: Routledge.

Holthausen, F., 1934. *Altenglisches etymologisches Wörterbuch*. Heidelberg: Carl Winters Universitätsbuchhandlung.

Köbler, G., 1989. *Gotisches Wörterbuch*. Leiden: EJ Brill Verlag.

Krause, W., 1953. *Handbuch des Gotischen*. Munich: C.H. Beck.

Lammers, W., 1981. *Geschichte Schleswig-Holsteins*, vol. 4, part 1, ed. Olaf Klose. Neumünster: Wachholtz.

Lehmann, W.P., 1986. *A Gothic Etymological Dictionary*. Leiden: Brill.

McMahon, A. & R. McMahon, 2003. Finding families: quantitative methods in language classification. *Transactions of the Philological Society* 101, 7–55.

Nielsen, H.F., 1981. *Old English and the Continental Germanic languages: a Survey of Morphological and Phonological Interrelations*. (Innsbrucker Beiträge zur Sprachwissenschaft 33.) Innsbruck: Universität Innsbruck, Institut für Sprachwissenschaft.

Ochs, E., K.F. Müller & G.W. Baur, 1997. *Badisches Wörterbuch*, vol. 3. Lahr im Schwarzwald: Moritz Schauenburg.

Østergaard, B., 1983. *Indvandrernes danmarkshistorie*. Copenhagen: Gad.

*Oxford English Dictionary*, 1989. http://dictionary.oed.com/entrance.dtl.

Pokorny, J., 1959. *Indogermanisches etymologisches Wörterbuch*. Bern: Francke.

Polzin, T. & S.V. Daneshmand, 2001. A comparison of (Steiner) tree relaxations. *Discrete Applied Mathematics* 112, 241–61.

Polzin, T. & S.V. Daneshmand, 2002. Extending reduction techniques for the (Steiner) tree problem, in *Algorithms – ESA 2002: 10th Annual Symposium, Rome, Italy*, eds. R.H. Möhring & R. Raman. Berlin: Springer, 795–807.

Polzin, T. & S.V. Daneshmand, 2003. On Steiner trees and minimum spanning trees in hypergraphs. *Operations Research Letters* 31, 12–20.

Schleicher, A., 1863. *Die Darwinsche Theorie und die Sprachwissenschaft*. Offenes Sendschreiben an Herrn Dr. Ernst Haeckel, o. Professor der Zoologie und Direktor des zoologischen Museums an der Universität Jena. Weimar: Böhlau.

Schmidt, J., 1872. *Die Verwantschaftsverhältnisse der Indogermanischen Sprachen*. Weimar: Böhlau.

Sims-Williams, P., 1983a. Gildas and the Anglo-Saxons. *Cambridge Medieval Celtic Studies* 6, 1–30.

Sims-Williams, P., 1983b. The settlement of England in Bede and the Chronicle. *Anglo-Saxon England* 12, 1–41.

Swadesh, M., 1955. Towards greater accuracy in lexicostatistic dating. *International Journal of American Linguistics* 21, 121–37.

uit den Boogaart, P.C., 1975. *Woordfrequenties in geschreven en gesproken Nederlands. Werkgroep Frequentie-Onderzoek van het Nederlands*. Utrecht: Oosthoek, Scheltema & Holkema.

Walter, G., 1911. Der Wortschatz des Altfriesischen. *Münchener Beiträge zur romanischen und englischen Philologie* 53.

Whitelock, D., 1951. *The Audience of Beowulf*. Oxford: Clarendon Press.

# *Chapter 12*

# Convergence in the Formation of Indo-European Subgroups: Phylogeny and Chronology

Andrew Garrett

## 1. Introduction

In this chapter I address two interrelated problems. The first is the problem of Indo-European (IE) phylogeny: How is the early filiation of the IE language family best modelled, and if our models are tree-like what should the trees look like? I will suggest that conventional models of IE phylogeny are wrong. Their basic presupposition is that IE has a set of ten or more familiar subgroups — Anatolian, Indo-Iranian, Greek, etc. — which can in turn perhaps be organized into higher-order subgroups such as 'Italo-Celtic' or the non-Anatolian subgroup I will call *Nuclear IE* (NIE). The latter is now widely accepted (Melchert 1998; Ringe *et al.* 2002; Jasanoff 2003), but most higher-order subgrouping proposals are controversial, because the shared innovations said to justify them are far less robust than those defining the well-established subgroups. There is, in short, an essential difference in linguistic profile between the familiar IE subgroups and proposed higher-order subgroups. No model whose sole mechanism of filiation is simple branching seems well suited to capture this basic difference.

I will suggest an alternative model: the familiar branches arose not by the differentiation of earlier higher-order subgroups — from 'Italo-Celtic' to Italic and Celtic, and so on — but by convergence among neighbouring dialects in a continuum. Dialect continua are typical in shallow-time-depth language families; in its early history, I will suggest, there were also IE continua from which the familiar branches emerged by mutual assimilation as adjacent dialects came to occupy and define new linguistic and sociocultural areas (Celtic, Germanic, etc.). The adjacent dialects from which new groups emerged may not have formed subgroups within an earlier continuum; dialects may even have shared innovations with neighbours that eventually fell into other linguistic groups. Convergence, together with loss of intermediate dialects in the prehistoric continuum, has created the historical mirage of a branchy IE family with its many distinctive subgroups.

If this model is right, it also has ramifications for the problem of IE chronology: When (and where) was Proto-IE spoken, and what processes led to its spread across a wide Eurasian territory by 1000 BC? I will suggest in section 3 that a convergence model of IE phylogeny adds to the dossier of evidence against the early chronology proposed by Renfrew (1987), and in favour of the traditional view. I should add as a caveat that what follows is in part speculative and programmatic; further linguistic work is certainly needed. One reason the convergence processes I describe have eluded discovery is that their nature is to erase the evidence for earlier dialect continua. Our evidence for the IE languages mostly begins with the results of the processes I describe here; only in rare cases, like that of Linear B and Mycenaean Greek, do the accidents of archaeological discovery offer a clear window on the formation of an IE branch.

## 2. Phylogeny: the formation of Greek

Work by Alice Kober, Michael Ventris, and John Chadwick led fifty years ago to the discovery that the Linear B writing system, used on Crete and the Greek mainland in the second millennium BC, was a system of writing Greek. It is now well established that the dialect of the Linear B texts, Mycenaean, though documented over four centuries prior to the first significant attestation of other Greek dialects, must be treated as a Greek dialect and not as Proto-Greek or a separate IE dialect. This is because Mycenaean shares innovations with individual Greek dialects, such as the assibilation of **-ti* > *-si* (as in *ehensi* 'they are'), shared with Arcado-Cyprian, East Aeolic, and Attic-Ionic (vs West Greek *entí*). Based on shared innovation patterns, the scholarly consensus is that Mycenaean is most closely affiliated with Arcado-Cyprian (Morpurgo Davies 1992).

It is also well established that there are linguistic changes found in all first-millennium Greek dialects, including Arcado-Cyprian, that are not found in Mycenaean. Before the decipherment of Linear B such changes were assumed to be Proto-Greek, but now it is clear that they reflect areal diffusion across the Greek-speaking area. The masculine-neuter active perfect participle presents a typical case. All first-millennium dialects reflect a suffix **-wot-*, as in Homeric *arērót-* 'fashioned' < **arār-wot-*, but this is a Greek development; the corresponding NIE suffix was **-wos-*. Yet Mycenaean has forms like neuter plural *arārwoha* < **arār-wos-* and none with *-wot-*. An apparent Proto-Greek innovation is unreconstructible for the ancestor of all Greek dialects. How general is this pattern, and does it affect our overall view of Proto-Greek? In this context Morpurgo Davies (1988, 102n4) writes that 'it would be a useful exercise to collect all the features which we would have attributed to Common Greek before the decipherment of Linear B'.

*2.1. The evidence for Proto-Greek*

This is not the place to present in detail the results of the exercise Morpurgo Davies advocates, but I can summarize its findings. I have examined features attributed to Proto-Greek by Meillet (1913), well before the decipherment of Linear B, excluding those that are not unique to Greek. It turns out that little remains of Meillet's Proto-Greek; excluding post-Mycenaean innovations, few unique changes distinguish Greek phonologically or morphologically from NIE.[1]

In inflectional morphology it is well known that the Greek verb system is quite archaic, but the first-millennium system of noun inflection has undergone significant change. Meillet (1913) stressed the loss of the spatial (ablative, instrumental, and locative) cases, which he called 'one of the traits that characterize Common Greek' (1913 [1975], 46); these categories survived in no Greek dialect known in 1913. While the Mycenaean case system is still controversial in part, Hajnal (1995) argues that the instrumental and locative cases both survived and that in a major inflectional class, animate athematic consonant-stem nouns, the only case-marking change from PNIE to Mycenaean was a dative-locative plural syncretism. The new ending *-si* (vs earlier loc. pl. **-su*) shows the only clear nominal form-change that is both unique to Greek and pan-Greek, but it is a trivial adaptation based on loc. sg. *-i* and instr. pl. *-p*$^h$*i* with final *i*. The loss of the ablative had begun in IE inasmuch as its forms were parasitic on the genitive in the singular and on the dative in the plural; since the Greek genitive expresses ablative functions, the loss of the ablative can be viewed as an extension of the singular syncretism into the plural. The inflectional system of the Proto-Greek noun thus differed only marginally from that of its PNIE ancestor.

In phonology, the discussion is usefully divided into three areas: segment inventory, syllable structure, and word structure. In the area of segment inventory, the question is what the sounds of PIE were and how they have changed. Since the Greek vowel system is famously conservative, this amounts to examining the consonants and syllabic sonorants. To begin with the latter, it is well known that PIE **l̥*, **r̥*, **m̥*, and **n̥* mainly did not survive in IE languages; their loss is a major cause of the collapse of the inherited morphological ablaut system. In Greek, reflexes of **l̥* and **r̥* show *a* and *o* vocalism varying across dialects; no pan-Greek development can be reconstructed. The nasals **m̥* and **n̥* become *a* in first-millennium dialects but instead often show *o* in Mycenaean when preceded by labial consonants, as in **sper**mn̥*** > *sper**mo*** 'seed'. The IE syllabic sonorants would therefore still have been distinct phonological categories in the ancestor of Mycenaean and other Greek dialects.

Among other segment types, Mycenaean also retains the labiovelar stops $k^w$, $g^w$, $k^{wh}$, as well as *y* and *w* in most positions; indeed, the change of *y* > *h* before sonorants is recent and ongoing in Mycenaean. Associated with the general loss of *y* is palatalization of many consonant types in *Cy* clusters; the First Palatalization affecting $*t^{(h)}y$ occurred before Mycenaean, but the Second Palatalization affecting a broader range of *Cy* clusters was arguably at least still ongoing.

In segmental terms, then, any Proto-Greek ancestral to Mycenaean and the first-millennium dialects must have had the relatively archaic segment types $k^w$, $g^w$, $k^{wh}$, *y*, *w*, *l̥*, *r̥*, *m̥*, and *n̥*. In fact the only IE segment types missing in Proto-Greek would have been the laryngeals $*h_1$, $*h_2$, and $*h_3$, segments lost in all NIE languages and probably already at least partly in PNIE. On a purely segmental level, the most significant changes to have preceded Mycenaean seem to have been the First Palatalization and the conditioned change of **y* and **s* to *h*. The segmental changes that distinguish PNIE and Proto-Greek look less substantial than those differentiating English, French, or German dialects (not all of which are always mutually intelligible, of course).

Under the syllable-structure rubric can be grouped various changes simplifying original *CsC* and obstruent-sonorant clusters in first-millennium dialects. As shown by Mycenaean forms like ***aiksmā*** 'spear', *hehrap*$^h$***menā*** 'sewn', and ***dl****eukos* 'sweet wine', these innovations cannot be reconstructed for Proto-

Greek even where they affect all later dialects. Steriade (1993) has shown that such cluster changes reflect a basic change in syllable structure: Mycenaean retained an IE syllable structure canon allowing many more onset types than the relatively impoverished set of clusters (such as stop + liquid) of later Greek dialects.

Finally, under the word-structure rubric I consider a set of changes not often seen as related. With characteristic insight, Meillet (1913) wrote that 'the end of the word is distinct; without presenting any constant particularity it was felt in a precise manner' (1913 [1975], 26). He meant by this that several Greek changes conspired to demarcate word ends: the accentual *Dreimorengesetz*, the loss of final stops, and the merger of the nasals. I would extend this approach, and suggest that it is an organizing feature of a number of Greek innovations that they serve to demarcate prosodic words both at the left and the right edge.

At the left word-edge, two Greek changes can be seen as by-products of the development of aspiration as an initial-syllable prosody. One is aspiration metathesis, by which an *h* in a second-syllable onset sometimes migrated to the beginning of the word, as in **euhō* > *héuō* 'singe' (Lejeune 1982, 95–6, 137–8). This is clearly post-Mycenaean, since 'wheel' is spelled <a-mo> in Linear B and must be interpreted as *arhmo*, not †*harmo*, which would be spelled <a$_2$-mo>; aspiration metathesis is seen in later *hárma*.

The second left-edge change is Grassmann's Law, by which an initial aspirated stop is deaspirated when an aspirate follows in the word, as in gen. sg. ***$t^h$*rik*$^h$*os* > *trik*$^h$*ós* 'hair'. The Linear B script does not distinguish aspiration, but Grassmann's Law must postdate Mycenaean because it must postdate the post-Mycenaean ***$p^h$*m* > *mm* change (compare *hehrap*$^h$*menā* 'sewn' above). This in turn is shown by later forms like *tet*$^h$*ramménos* 'having been nourished' without Grassmann's Law, from the root ***$t^h$*rep*$^h$- (*tréph*$^h$*ō* 'nourish'). If Grassmann's Law preceded Mycenaean we would expect †*tetrap*$^h$*ménos* > †*tetramménos*, like Homeric *epépit*$^h$*men* 'we had been persuaded' from the root ***$p^h$*eit*$^h$- (*péit*$^h$*ō* 'persuade').

Underlying both aspiration metathesis and Grassmann's Law is a single pattern: aspiration is a temporally extended phonetic feature stretching across the entire first syllable. A dissimilatory loss of aspiration of this type occurs when aspiration associated with the first stop is reinterpreted (due to its extended duration) as a coarticulatory effect of the second stop, while a metathesis as seen in *héuō* or *hárma* arises when the phonological source of extended-duration aspiration is phonetically obscure (Blevins & Garrett 1998; 2004).

At the right word-edge, a set of changes occurred that can be related not just phonologically as demarcative but phonetically via the inverse of initial aspiration: final laryngealization. These changes are a shift of the position of the accent, which originally could occupy any syllable of the word but in Greek is restricted to the last three syllables; the loss of all final stops; and the merger of word-final **m* and **n* as *n*. The defects of Linear B, which writes neither accent nor coda consonants, make it hard to tell whether these changes had occurred in Mycenaean. But an indirect suggestion can be made that the final nasal merger may not have taken place, since the transfer of historical *m*-stem nouns into the class of *n*-stems had not happened, as shown by the dative singular *hemei* 'one'.[2] That transfer is in turn a consequence of the merger of word-final **m* and **n* as *n*. If it is plausible that the three right-edge sound changes are interrelated, it is also plausible that none had taken place in Mycenaean. Note that the tradition in Mycenaean studies is to interpret Mycenaean so as to be as similar as possible to first-millennium Greek, even where Linear B gives us no evidence. The opposite strategy may be as appropriate even if to some extent speculative.

The relationship among the three right-edge changes can be understood as follows. It is likely in Greek, as in many languages, that final stop loss had an intermediate stage with glottalized stops ([͡ʔp],etc.). The retention of stops before word-final *s* (as in *t*$^h$*ríks* 'hair') supports this view, since stops before *s* would articulatorily have a spread glottis, preventing glottalization. I suggest that the Greek accent shift regularized falling pitch at the right edge of the word; previously there was no correlation between the right word-edge and postaccentual falling pitch. This facilitated word-final stop glottalization, perhaps as a reinterpretation of the ambient laryngealization often associated with falling pitch. Merger of word-final stops as [ʔ] > ∅ and neutralization of word-final nasal place contrasts may then have been the same change: loss of distinctions cued by final VC transitions. As I have suggested, it is reasonable to speculate that these changes all occurred in the centuries after Mycenaean.

In sum, especially if we allow that at least a few post-Proto-Greek changes must already have affected Mycenaean before its attestation (it is after all a Greek dialect), detailed analysis reduces the dossier of demonstrable and uniquely Proto-Greek innovations in phonology and inflectional morphology to nearly zero. Proto-Greek retained the basic NIE noun system, verb system, segment inventory, syllable structure, and arguably phonological word structure. In all these areas of linguistic structure, Greek was not yet Greek early in the second millennium. But if so, it hardly makes sense to reconstruct Proto-Greek as such: a coherent IE dialect, spoken by some IE speech community, ancestral to all the later Greek dialects. It is just as likely that Greek was formed by the coalescence of dialects that originally formed part of a continuum with other NIE dialects, including some that went on to participate in the formation of other IE branches. With this in mind it is possible to see external links for some Greek dialect patterns. For example, the first-person plural endings *-mes* and *-men* are distributed such that *-mes* occurs in West Greek, across the Adriatic from Italic (with *s* in Latin *-mus*), while *-men* occurs elsewhere, across the Aegean from Anatolian (with *n* in Hittite *-wen*). The isogloss separating prepositional variants *protí* (as in Homer) and *potí* (West Greek) likewise corresponds to the Indo-Iranian isogloss separating Sanskrit *práti* and Avestan *paiti*.

If Proto-Greek did not exist as such and Mycenaean phonology and inflection are minimally 'Greek', what makes Mycenaean Greek? Chadwick, seeing the essence of the problem, has written that 'there must have been a time when the ancestral language could not fairly be described as Greek', adding that the best evidence that Mycenaean is Greek 'comes from the vocabulary, which contains numerous words which are ... specific to Greek' (1998, 27). In short, Greek in the second millennium already had a distinctive derivational, lexical, and onomastic profile. It might not overstate the case to say that Mycenaean was a late NIE dialect with Greek vocabulary; a distinctively Greek phonological and inflectional profile was largely a development of post-Mycenaean history.

### 2.2. *Systems collapse and linguistic innovation*

The finding that numerous linguistic innovations spread across the Greek dialect area in the centuries after Mycenaean makes sense both historically and sociolinguistically. Two points are key. First, archaeological evidence points to massive population shift and economic change during the Greek Dark Age *c.* 1200–800 BC. Morris (2000, 195–6) writes of 'gigantic upheavals all across the east Mediterranean around 1200', including the destruction of the Mycenaean palaces, migration, famine, disease, 'economic disaster', and massive depopulation. The archaeological data, according to Dickinson (1994, 87), 'surely reflect considerable social changes'. The linguistic effects of these changes have been noted before; for example, during the Dark Age, nearly 'the whole of the terminology connected with the systems of land-tenure seems to have disintegrated' (Morpurgo Davies 1979, 98).

Second, toward the end of the Dark Age and subsequently there is a wealth of evidence for emerging systems of interaction that linked the Greek world economically, socially, and politically. In this context Snodgrass (1980) mentions arable farming, metallurgy, colonization, panhellenic sanctuaries, ship-building and navigation, *polis* rivalries (in architecture, athletics, etc.), and writing and literacy, though it must be said that some at least of these systems emerged only later in the relevant period.

In short, prototypical examples of two patterns are seen between the Mycenaean period and the re-emergence of Greek writing in the first millennium: a systems collapse (Tainter 1988, 10–11) and the emergence of a new system also based on peer-polity interaction (Renfrew & Cherry 1986). A salient feature of the new system is the well-known sense of Greek ethnic identity, which by defining the boundaries of a Greek dialect area must have favoured the diffusion of innovations across that area and no farther.

These historical phenomena are important sociolinguistically because they let us fit Greek into a broader picture of language change. Linguists studying social structure have found that tight social networks are

> an important mechanism of language maintenance, in that speakers are able to form a cohesive group capable of resisting pressure, linguistic and social, from outside the group ... One important corollary to the link between language maintenance and a close-knit territorially-based network structure is that linguistic change will be associated with a break-up of such a structure (L. Milroy 1987, 182–90).

By contrast, loose social networks, those with many ties outside their networks, 'are likely to be generally more susceptible to innovation' (J. Milroy 1992, 181).

Ethnographic sociolinguists mainly study local social contexts, but extrapolating to a broader scale and *longue durée* few historical settings could more aptly be called 'the break-up of a close-knit territorially-based network structure' than the Greek Dark Age. Complex systems collapse should yield rapid linguistic change; citing the well-known case of the Algonquian languages Arapaho and Gros Ventre, Bakker (2000, 586) writes that '[i]n situations of great social upheaval and changes one can witness phonological change which takes place much faster than otherwise'. For Greek, the period between the end of Linear B documentation and the re-emergence of writing in the first millennium should have been a period of relatively rapid linguistic innovation. This change, I submit, was the formation of Greek as we know it.

### 2.3. *The origin of Indo-European phylogeny*

Does the model presented above apply only to Greek, or can it be generalized? In an earlier article (Garrett

1999) I suggested that Greek may be typical of IE subgroups, and that the reason we see the pattern clearly in Greek is that we have Mycenaean.[3] For no other IE branch do we have comparable data — an Italic dialect of 1000 BC, or an Indo-Iranian variety documented early in the second millennium. But the coherence of other IE branches can be doubted too. The question of Italic unity has been debated by linguists for at least 75 years. Even for Indo-Iranian, not a long-standing problem like Italic, the Nuristani languages show that the RUKI sound change postdated Proto-Indo-Iranian, and the patterning of early loans into Uralic has suggested that Indo-Iranian was already dialectally differentiated *c.* 2000 BC (Carpelan *et al.* 2001).

If the formation of Greek was a local event facilitated by local interaction patterns and ethnic identity, it is also relevant that IE branches like Indo-Iranian, Slavic, Celtic, and even the poorly attested Venetic show evidence of a collective sense of ethnic identity. In such cases, as Nichols (1998, 240) puts it, 'a complex native theory of ethnicity and a strong sense of ethnic identity can be reconstructed, and both the theory and the identity were based on language'.

I have argued that a Mycenaean systems collapse precipitated a period of rapid innovation in Greek dialects and the creation of a characteristic Greek phonological and morphological profile, but the collapse was no mere parochial event of the eastern Mediterranean. According to Cunliffe (1997, 41),

> [t]he impact of the Aegean systems-collapse on the European hinterland was considerable. Existing exchange systems broke down or were transformed. Some communities, once part of European-wide networks, found themselves isolated and new configurations emerged.

It is thus possible that the dynamics behind the emergence of Celtic, Italic, and other IE branches of Europe refract the same history as those behind the emergence of Greek. In Asia, though there can hardly be direct evidence, we may imagine similar processes at play in the formation of Indo-Iranian after the collapse of the Bactria-Margiana Archaeological Complex *c.* 1750 BC (Parpola 2002, 91–2).

If this framework is appropriate for IE branches generally, we cannot regard IE 'subgroups' as subgroups in a classical sense. Rather, the loss or 'pruning' of intermediate dialects, together with convergence *in situ* among the dialects that were to become Greek, Italic, Celtic, and so on, have in tandem created the appearance of a tree with discrete branches. But the true historical filiation of the IE family is unknown, and it may be unknowable.

I conclude section 2 by noting a pattern in need of an explanation. Early in the second millennium, I have suggested, IE branches such as Greek had acquired much of their lexical and derivational profile, while their grammatical apparatus continued to have its basic NIE character. Speaking in the broadest terms, early IE language spread was thus a two-phase process. In the first phase, local IE dialects acquired their specific lexical, derivational, and onomastic features; in the second phase, late in the second millennium in some cases, changes that gave dialect areas their characteristic phonology and morphology swept across those areas. What sociolinguistically plausible scenario could give rise to such effects?

## 3. Chronology: the dispersal of Indo-European

Phylogenetic reconstructions may also contribute to the debate between the two chronological frameworks posited for the initial IE dispersal. In what I will call the *first-agriculturalists* framework (Renfrew 1987), PIE was spoken around 7000 BC and IE spread with the diffusion of agriculture from Anatolia into Europe in the seventh millennium. On this view the modern IE languages have diverged for about 9000 years. In what I will call the *secondary-products* framework, the time depth of IE is some three millennia shallower: PIE was spoken and IE language dispersal began in the fourth millennium. This chronological framework is traditional; general presentations from this point of view include that of Mallory (1989). The name I use alludes to the *secondary products complex*. Under this rubric Sherratt (1981; 1983; 1997) has identified several emergent uses of domesticated animals — ploughing, carting, wool, and dairy — that arose in Europe in the late fourth and early third millennia; he refers to a 'revolution' that 'marked the birth of the kinds of society characteristic of modern Eurasia' (1981 [1997, 161]). New property transmission systems, land-use practices, and social network patterns are said to be aspects of the transition.

### *3.1. Implications of convergence*

Insofar as the formation of IE branches was a local process, and their characteristic innovations took place later than usually supposed, their phonological and morphological structures must have been closer in the centuries around 2000 BC than has been thought. Table 12.1 shows reflexes of five PNIE numerals in three intermediate protolanguages and representative modern descendants: Greek; Spanish; and Waigali (Nuristani, Indo-Iranian: Turner 1962–6).

The similarity of the intermediate protolanguages is obvious, and clearly also fewer changes occurred *en route* to each intermediate protolanguage than subsequently. Modern Greek is the most phonologi-

**Table 12.1.** *Five numerals in PNIE and three NIE branches.*

| | 'three' | 'five' | 'seven' | 'eight' | 'nine' |
|---|---|---|---|---|---|
| **PNIE** | ***treyes** | ***peŋk$^w$e** | ***septm̥** | ***oḱtō** | ***$h_1$newn̥** |
| **Proto-Greek** | ***treyes** | ***peŋk$^w$e** | ***heptm̥** | ***oktō** | ***ennewn̥** |
| Modern Greek | tris | pente | efta | oxto | eñja |
| **Proto-Indo-Iranian** | ***trayas** | ***pañča** | ***sapta** | ***aćtā** | ***nawa** |
| Waigali | tre | pũč | sot | oṣṭ | nũ |
| **Proto-Italic** | ***trēs** | ***k$^w$eŋk$^w$e** | ***septm̥** | ***oktō** | ***newn̥** |
| Spanish | tres | siŋko | sjete | očo | nweve |

cally conservative language in the sample of Heggarty (2000), and even for Greek Table 12.1 shows only four sound changes *en route* to the intermediate protolanguage ($h_1 > e$, $\acute{k} > k$, $s > h$, irregular *nn* in 'nine') but at least eleven historically distinct later sound changes: syllabic nasals > *a*; $k^w > t$ before *e*; losses of *y*, *w*, and *h*; *ee* > *ē*; *ē* > *ī*; *ea* > *ja*; loss of vowel length; stops > fricatives before stops; and a shift from pitch to stress accent (not shown). In the other languages the later changes are plainly numerous, also including pitch-to-stress shifts, while Proto-Italic and Proto-Indo-Iranian each show only four changes.[4] The Greek reconstructions follow §2.1, and it is worth adding that the Indo-Iranian and Italic forms may be too innovatory precisely because we do not have the equivalent of Mycenaean Greek proving the presence of areally diffused changes. If anything, the extent of phonological changes in the modern languages is understated.

The time depth from the intermediate protolanguages to their modern descendants is on the order of 4000 years (Proto-Italic may be somewhat younger), and during this period significantly more phonological change has taken place than occurred en route from PNIE.[5] Note that all three intermediate protolanguages retain the basic PNIE system of nominal cases and inflection, and in the verbal system the three-way PNIE aspect contrast among present, aorist, and perfect (Meiser 2003). None of this survives in the modern languages.

The first-agriculturalists model posits a span of 3000–4000 years between PNIE and 2000 BC. This means assuming two typologically incomparable periods, each three or four millennia long: a period marked by less phonological or inflectional change than is observed in any documented language, followed by a period when all IE languages were transformed by accumulating waves of phonological and morphological change. That is, the model requires the unscientific assumption that linguistic change in the period for which we have no direct evidence was radically different from change we can study directly.[6]

There is nothing new in a conclusion that linguistic evidence favours the secondary-products chronology over than the first-agriculturalists chronology (Nichols 1998, 254–5; Darden 2001), though I hope new light is shed on the question if IE subgroups are products of secondary convergence. Other types of relevant linguistic evidence include especially the evidence of linguistic palaeontology, a method with well-known pitfalls whose results in this case have been challenged; I will consider this issue in section 3.2. Most importantly, as Renfrew (1987) has reminded us, it behooves a proponent of any view of IE dispersal to situate that view in a plausible model of ancient social dynamics. The central questions have always been: What caused the spread of Indo-European, and why did it spread over its broad Eurasian territory? I will sketch an approach to these questions in section 3.3.

### *3.2. Linguistic palaeontology*

In essence, the argument from linguistic palaeontology is that IE is reconstructed with words for secondary products (plough, wool, yoke) and wheeled transport (axle, nave, thill, wagon, wheel); since these technologies did not arise before 4000 BC, the IE dispersal cannot be associated with the diffusion of agriculture several millennia earlier. In the first-agriculturalists framework, PIE and even PNIE date from before 5000 BC, neither language could have had secondary-products or wheeled-transport terms, and the entire terminological ensemble must be a linguistic mirage if it seems reconstructible to PIE or PNIE.[7] How then are the data explained? Even the advocates of linguistic palaeontology recognize that the method has general pitfalls, but the specific data must be scrutinized critically.[8]

One alternative account is independent formation: apparent cognates do not reflect common inheritance from a single ancestral prototype, but were separately formed in several languages. For example, perhaps the apparent PIE **$h_2$wr̥gis* 'wheel' (based on **$h_2$werg-* 'turn around') reflects independent formation in Hittite and Tocharian. But such an account is hardly possible for PNIE **$k^w$ek$^w$los* 'wheel' (in Germanic, Greek, Indo-Iranian, Tocharian, also borrowed early into Uralic): though derived from **$k^w$elh$_1$-* 'turn', a reduplicated $C_1e$-$C_1C_2$-*o*- noun is so unusual morphologically that parallel independent formation is excluded. Likewise, for PIE **yuǵom* 'yoke' (**yeuǵ-* 'harness, join, yoke'), with reflexes in Anatolian and almost all other branches, while neuter thematic nouns are common in some IE languages, they are quite rare in Anatolian and it has long been known that the category was not very productive in PIE. It is unlikely that **yugom* was independently created in Anatolian and other branches, all the more so because the form is morphologically invariant; had it been created independently we might expect other formations in some cases. Other words pose a different problem: PIE **$h_2$erh$_3$-* 'plough' (everywhere but Albanian and Indo-Iranian) is a root and PNIE **aḱs-* 'axle' (in Baltic, Celtic, Germanic, Greek, Indo-Iranian, Italic, Slavic) is not transparently based on a root; therefore neither can be the result of any re-formation. In almost all cases, the forms of secondary-products and wheeled-transport terms must be reconstructed for PIE or PNIE.

For their meanings, secondary semantic shift is a possible alternative account. Thus Renfrew (2001, 46) suggests that PIE **$h_{2/3}$wl̥h$_1$neh$_2$* 'wool' (in Anatolian, Baltic, Celtic, Germanic, Greek, Indo-Iranian, Italic, Slavic) might originally have referred to 'the fiber from the sheep', perhaps used for rugs, clothing, or felt, shifting its meaning later as sheep were bred for wool. Indeed, for morphological reasons, it is clear that the word referred originally to fiber that was used in some way: **$h_{2/3}$wl̥h$_1$neh$_2$* is derived via the suffix **-neh$_2$* from the root **$h_{2/3}$welh$_1$-* 'to pluck or pull hair' (Latin *vellere*). The word cannot simply have referred to hair; it must have arisen at a time when sheep had coats whose hairs were plucked. But there is no reason to believe that such a practice existed before the breeding of woolly sheep: the earliest uses of the sheep's coat were in felting, for which there is no evidence before the third millennium, and spinning into thread for weaving, known for wool from the fourth millennium in the Near East and later in Europe.[9] In short, *wool* makes no morphological sense on the first-agriculturalists IE chronology.

Arguments involving secondary semantic shift can be envisioned for other terms, like those for 'nave' and 'thill', which refer generally to poles in some languages; the shift to a vehicular context could be independent (Specht 1947, 100–102). But in other cases it is hard to see how secondary semantic shift can explain the data. Perhaps **yuǵom* 'yoke' originally referred to another joining result, but what? and why was the original meaning lost throughout IE? In the case of words for 'wheel', what did they originally designate if not wheels? A semantic shift from concrete 'wheel' to abstract 'circle, cycle' is plausible but the reverse shift (abstract > concrete) is unusual at best (Sweetser 1990; Traugott & Dasher 2001).

It remains to comment on the possibility of vocabulary diffusion or borrowing after the relevant technology arose. Borrowing ordinarily betrays itself phonologically; if 'yoke' had been borrowed from Indo-Iranian into other IE branches, it would have taken the form **yuǵam* after the Indo-Iranian change of *o* to *a*. One could suggest that vocabulary diffusion took place before the phonological changes of individual branches, but given the overall requirements of the first-agriculturalists chronology this would mean that IE history first had a period of several thousand years with just vocabulary change and diffusion, and that linguistic change as it occurs in clearly documented languages would only have begun with the secondary-products complex; as noted in section 3.1, this idea is unrealistic. A possible alternative account invoking 'etymological nativization' (Hock 1991, 392–3) would founder on the divergent profiles of that process and the IE data.

It is worth adding in conclusion that linguistic reconstruction yields not just isolated words but a terminological ensemble in a coherent semantic field. The explanatory strategy forced by the first-agriculturalists framework misses the big picture by invoking an unsystematic jumble of *ad hoc* alternatives.

### *3.3. The dispersal of Indo-European*

Renfrew (1987) originally articulated the first-agriculturalists framework using the mechanism of demic diffusion, the slow movement of peoples over many centuries as one farmer after another moves a few miles to clear new farmland. This means of language spread is clearly documented in many cases (Bellwood & Renfrew 2002; Diamond & Bellwood 2003). For IE itself Renfrew (2000) has largely abandoned the idea, allowing in response to critics that demic diffusion was not the mechanism of IE language spread in western and northern Europe and instead invoking language shift (a term that labels a phenomenon without offering a sociolinguistic mechanism or model to explain it). For Indo-Iranian, a connection between the spread of farming and language dispersal in an area comparable in size to Europe has been abandoned altogether (Renfrew 2000, 423–4).

As recently as 2001 Renfrew has written that 'the only process or event of sufficiently general significance for the whole of Europe to account for the Indo-Europeanization of almost an entire continent was the coming of farming' (Renfrew 2001, 37). Such a statement hides two misleading assumptions. First, Sherratt and others contend that the secondary products 'revolution' was a watershed in European social history; the difference between a chronology based on farming and one based on secondary products is just what is at stake. Second, in this context calling Europe 'an entire continent' is distractingly Eurocentric. Europe is also 'a small peninsula of the Eurasian landmass' (Richards 2003, 142), and the IE spread is a broad Eurasian phenomenon that should be seen as such. An interpretation that sets aside half the IE area, offers an explanatory model of language spread (demic diffusion) only for part of Europe, and mainly dismisses linguistic evidence cannot be regarded as a satisfactory account of what is after all a linguistic process: the dispersal of IE languages across Europe and Asia.

I take it that PIE was spoken *c.* 3500 BC, perhaps somewhat earlier, in a part of what Mallory (1989, 239) calls the 'circum-Pontic interaction sphere'; the PIE area could not have been larger than that of ecologically comparable languages, for example the size of Spain (Anthony 1995). It is traditional to situate PIE in the Pontic-Caspian steppe, though a western Pontic PIE may suit dialect geography better (Sherratt & Sherratt 1988 propose a circum-Pontic PIE not long before 4000 BC). It is important to bear in mind that PIE may have had linguistically related neighbours; we cannot know how the ensemble would appear in the archaeological record.

The oldest IE split, between Anatolian and NIE, may have begun as a small-scale collapse of the PIE speech community with a sociocultural reorientation of its northern and southern halves. Perhaps the southern half of the community was drawn into the interactional sphere of the late fourth-millennium Aegean, or the northern half was drawn into the Balkans. In any case, Pontic IE speakers came to be oriented towards the Balkans and the steppe, while others were oriented socioculturally towards the Aegean and Anatolia.

In the Pontic area NIE began to differentiate, with Tocharian its easternmost dialect along the Black Sea and the first known IE language to make its way to Central Asia. The second was Indo-Iranian, whose spread on the steppe and *c.* 2000 BC to Bactria-Margiana is widely accepted (Mallory 1998; 2002; Parpola 1988; 1998; 2002; Renfrew 2000, 423–4). Tocharian had perhaps separated from the NIE area by *c.* 3000 BC, with Indo-Iranian spreading eastward on the steppe during the third millennium.

The European expansion, even if it represents only part of IE dispersal, is a crucial problem. Renfrew (1999; 2000; 2001) suggests that NIE dialects had a long episode of mutual convergence in what he calls 'Old Europe', following Gimbutas (1973) — a Balkan and East-central European interactional sphere that flourished in the fifth and fourth millennia before fragmenting. In his view this period was marked by diffusion across most NIE dialects; at its end 'the strong cultural interactions marking the "Old Europe" episode discussed by Gimbutas came to an end, and the various sub-regions tended to go their own separate ways' (Renfrew 2001, 42).

Renfrew (1979) has strongly emphasized the consequences of systems collapse. These include linguistic diffusion as in post-Mycenaean Greek (section 2.1), or linguistic replacement as discussed by Renfrew (1987, 133–7) for several state collapses. But not all complex societies subject to systems collapse are states; some are networks of the Old Europe type. In his analysis of the collapse of complex societies, including societies of several organizational types, a general pattern emphasized by Tainter (1988, 191) is that '[i]n each case, peoples on the periphery ... rose to prominence after the older society had collapsed'.

In the scenario I have sketched NIE dialects were spoken on the periphery of Old Europe, and I suggest, in what I hope is not an unholy alliance of the doctrines of Gimbutas and Renfrew, that it was the *collapse* of the Old Europe interactional system that facilitated the initial spread into Europe. Like Gimbutas, I see IE dispersal as related to what Mallory (1989, 238) summarizes as mid-fourth millennium 'cultural chaos' and 'something of a Balkan 'dark age'. But I agree with Renfrew that it is not necessary or desirable to imagine invasions by warrior Indo-Europeans; systems collapse naturally led to rapid dispersal of the speech of its periphery.[10] In a complex system IE speakers must already have interacted with more central participants in roles we cannot know (perhaps some were specialist wainwrights, weavers, or herders). The point is that an IE spread into the Balkans and East-central Europe, in the late fourth and early third millennia, would be a natural aspect of the collapse of Old Europe. As argued in section 2.3, the later emergence of European IE languages that were distinctively Celtic, Italic, and so on may have followed the Aegean systems collapse of the late second millennium.

Viewing the IE dispersals broadly, it is possible to discern three major patterns. One is the steppe spread that led to the dispersal of Tocharian and Indo-Iranian. A second pattern is characteristic of the IE spread into Europe and linguistic changes that took place there: dispersal was associated with systems collapse (Old Europe, the late-second-millennium Aegean) and the social reorganizations of the secondary products complex. The Indo-Iranian spread into Iran and South Asia after the collapse of the Bactria-Margiana Archaeological Complex can also perhaps be assimilated to this pattern.

The third pattern is not widely noted but seems quite robust: a north–south spread into the interactional spheres of the urbanized zone that runs from the Aegean through Anatolia and the Near East to Bactria-Margiana. This significant Eurasian pattern has at least four instantiations:

- the initial split of PIE, insofar as it was associated with a reorientation of Proto-Anatolian towards the Aegean and Anatolia, with the subsequent eastward spread of Hittite;
- the spread of Greek dialects into Greece and the Minoan sociocultural world;
- the Indo-Iranian spread into the oasis citadels of Bactria-Margiana;
- the spread of the Mitanni Indo-Iranian dialect into Syria.

In each case the resulting sociocultural profile shows significant continuity with indigenous patterns, respectively Hattic (in the case of Hittite), Minoan, Bactria-Margiana, and Hurrian.

Mallory's analysis of the Indo-Iranian spread may be broadly applicable here. Mallory & Mair (2000, 267) comment as follows on the interaction of Andronovo-culture steppe Indo-Iranians and the urban oasis dwellers of Bactria-Margiana *c.* 2000 BC:

> [T]he Andronovans would have come into contact with the oasis-dwellers, adopted items of their material culture, some of their religious beliefs and cultural practices (such as the fire cult and consumption of the hallucinogenic **sauma*), but not the language of the oasis-dwellers. Rather, the language of the steppe-dwellers would have operated as the *lingua franca* of exchange between regions, then perhaps within the settlements themselves until some variety of Indo-Iranian had become the main language of West Central Asia ....

Mallory (2002, 39) writes further:

> Indo-Iranian tribes from the steppelands entered into the political sphere of the BMAC [Bactria-Margiana Archaeological Complex] and absorbed from it a suite of religious institutions and their names as well as the concept of a superordinate tier within their social organisation. This tier ... provided a system of coordination between the different elements both within the BMAC and the mobile units outside. It linked oasis dwellers and steppe nomads in Central Asia and ... it could also bring together people practising different settlement and economic strategies on the northern steppe.

For Greece, Palaima (1995, 127) describes

> a process whereby the established Helladic/Aegean and Indo-European features of mainland culture were transformed and made part of the Late Helladic palatial culture through a strong, selective adaptation of diverse elements of Minoan material culture and Minoan social, political and religious ideology.

Across Eurasia generally, I suggest, IE language spread may be interpreted partly as a result of such interactions between a northern periphery and a southern urban zone.

To speculate further, the same pattern of interaction may well lie behind the two-stage process identified in section 2. The first stage of IE language spread is characterized by a distinctive lexical, derivational, and onomastic profile; this corresponds to urbanization and the use of indigenous sociocultural traditions by speakers of IE languages. In Anatolia, Greece, and Bactria-Margiana respectively, compare the 'dominant role of Hattic elements in Old Hittite religion and cult and ideology of kingship' (Melchert 2003, 17), including Hattic loanwords like *halmaššuitt-* 'throne'; the elite semantic profile of 'Minoan' loans in Greek (Renfrew 1998), including the vocabulary of kingship (Mycenaean *wanaks* > *ánaks*, perhaps $g^{w}$*asileus* > *basiléus*); and the dossier of borrowed Indo-Iranian social and religious vocabulary, including important terms like **indra-* 'Indra' and **dāsa-* '(hostile) people' (Lubotsky 2001).[11] In such circumstances, we expect significant lexical change as well as changes in more socioculturally embedded aspects of morphology, such as onomastics and ways of deriving occupational terms, ethnic adjectives, and the like. What is responsible for this first stage of IE dispersal is thus the sociocultural continuity we see in Anatolia, Greece, and Bactria-Margiana as IE languages arrive.

The second stage with its phonological and inflectional transformations corresponds, on this view, to the emergence of local ethnic identities and networks. In some cases this may have been a long, gradual process; in others a systems collapse may have facilitated rapid innovation, as in Greek, Indo-Iranian (if a Bactria-Margiana collapse *c.* 1750 BC played a role in the emergence of distinctive Indo-Iranian phonology and morphology), and perhaps some European IE languages.

## 4. Conclusion

I have made two main arguments in this chapter. In section 2, based on a new analysis of Mycenaean, I argued that the apparent features of Proto-Greek mainly diffused throughout Greece during and after the Mycenaean period. It follows that Proto-Greek — or if this did not exist, IE speech of *c.* 2000 BC that was to become Greek — was linguistically closer to IE than has been supposed. I suggest more generally that we should contemplate models of IE phylogeny that assign a greater role in the formation of IE branches to convergence *in situ*.

In section 3, I explored the chronological consequences of this view of IE phylogeny. If the linguistic changes in various IE branches took place relatively late in their histories, then it is unlikely that PIE was spoken *c.* 7000 BC as in the first-agriculturalists framework. Speculatively but I hope constructively, I briefly sketched a scenario for IE dispersal that fits the linguistic facts and may perhaps answer what Renfrew rightly asks of Indo-Europeanists, that any account be situated in a plausible model of linguistic change and social dynamics.

## Acknowledgements

Thanks to James Clackson, Peter Forster, and Colin Renfrew for inviting me to participate in the Cambridge symposium and to other participants for useful discussion. For valuable comments on a written draft of this chapter, which have saved me from many errors, I am grateful to Juliette Blevins, Peter Forster, Jay Jasanoff, Leslie Kurke, Nino Luraghi, Craig Melchert, Anna Morpurgo Davies, Colin Renfrew, and Michael Weiss (few if any of whom agree with all my conclusions).

## Notes

1. For information about Mycenaean Greek readers may consult the handbook of Bartoněk (2003) and the lexicon of Aura Jorro (1993), both with full references to other literature. A change in the verb system that should be noted because it is seen in Mycenaean is the development of thematic 3 sg. **-eti* > *-ei* (which, I would argue, is indirectly related to the First Palatalization mentioned below).
2. On this view <ko-to-na-no-no> (PY Ea 922) cannot be interpreted as haplography for <ko-to-na-na-no-no> with acc. sg. ***ktoinōn*** (Morpurgo 1963 s.v.), and the epigraphically uncertain form at PY Eq 146.11 cannot be interpreted as <ị-qọ-na-to-mo> with gen. pl. ***hik$^w$k$^w$ōn*** 'horses' (Chadwick 1979, 25). As far as I know, unambiguous Mycenaean forms where a final nasal is written in sandhi have not yet been found.
3. See Zimmer (2002) for discussion of related perspectives.
4. The Indo-Iranian changes are laryngeal loss, palatal stop affrication, the Law of Palatals, and the merger of non-high vowels and syllabic nasals as *a*. The Italic changes are laryngeal loss, *y* loss, *ee* > *ē*, and the *p* > *k$^w$* change in 'five'. For Proto-Italic I follow Meiser (2003, 30–31) except that I take *ew* > *ow* as a secondary development in light of early Latin forms like *neuna*. In any case, among the Italic changes only laryngeal loss is secure: *y* loss is precisely a change formerly reconstructed for Proto-Greek before the decipherment of Linear B, *ee* > *ē* contraction is dependent on *y* loss, and the *p* > *k$^w$* change is only weakly reconstructible.
5. Note that the Reader (referee) of this volume objected that if we had additional information from otherwise unknown languages descended from PNIE (and such languages certainly existed), our changed PNIE reconstructions might amplify the changes en route to the attested daughter languages; the relative closeness of PNIE and the intermediate proto-languages might represent a mirage. In principle, of course, this is a fair point. However, on the one hand, something of this general sort did indeed happen with the discovery of Anatolian, and by now a major effect has been the widely accepted redrawing of the IE family tree; on the other hand, it is just as true that newly discovered languages or dialects (like Mycenaean Greek) can change one's reconstructions of the intermediate proto-languages and there would be no *a priori* reason for these new discoveries to have a systematic effect on the overall differences under discussion.
6. To be sure, in a widely publicized study, Gray & Atkinson (2003) have suggested that computational phylogenetic analysis may support the first-agriculturalists chronology. But even setting aside methodological questions, and doubts about linguistic reconstruction from lexical data, the specific results of Gray & Atkinson's research are likely to be in error as a result of a bias in the underlying data (Dyen *et al.* 1997). Modern IE branches show examples where, in a particular semantic slot, their known common ancestor (Latin, Sanskrit, etc.) has one word which has been replaced by a different word in all or most descendant languages. Thus Latin *ignis* 'fire' has been replaced by reflexes of Latin *focus* 'hearth' throughout Romance, and archaic Sanskrit *hanti* 'kills' has been replaced by reflexes of a younger Sanskrit form *mārayati* throughout Indo-Aryan. This process especially targets words of IE antiquity, which are more often irregular and therefore prone to replacement. This pattern creates the illusion of a slower rate of change in the internal histories of modern branches: it seems in retrospect (say) that Latin *focus* replaced an IE word for 'fire' in the prehistory of Latin and not later in Romance. Because the overall rates of change posited in Gray & Atkinson's model are based on apparent rate of change in modern branches with known histories, the overall rates of change assumed will be too slow. Over the evolution from PIE to Proto-Italic, Proto-Indo-Iranian, etc., the time depth calculated will thus be too long. I cannot assess the precise effects of this bias, but to speculate, if 5 per cent of the data is like *focus* a 'true' average lexical retention rate of 80 per cent over 1000 years will instead look like 85 per cent; this is equivalent to 23 per cent retention over 9000 years, while an 80 per cent rate is equivalent to a similar figure (26 per cent) over 6000 years. Precisely this 3000-year difference distinguishes the first-agriculturalists and secondary-products models.
7. It is not true, as alleged by Renfrew (2000, 432–4; 2001, 45), that the morphology of such vocabulary shows that it is post-PIE, nor is this suggested by Specht (1947) or Lehmann (1993), whom he cites. Rather, the argument is that because athematic nouns are older than thematic nouns *within the prehistory of PIE*, wheeled-transport terms were relatively new *in PIE*.
8. For an excellent review of the evidence see now Darden (2001). The sensibly skeptical assessment of Clackson (2000) treats mainly the weakest evidence in the dossier,

and in a crucial case he offers an inconsistent analysis, rightly noting that 'thill' and 'yoke' terms 'do not need the reconstruction of a chariot, but could also apply to a plough' (445), but then suggesting that 'claims linking Indo-European to ... the "secondary products revolution" ... can also be challenged in much the same way' (447). If the apparent secondary-products vocabulary is illusory then it should not be used to explain other vocabulary.

9. See Barber (1991, 24–5, 221) and Sherratt (1983 [1997, 203]). According to Barber (1991, 24n8), 'the kempier type of wild sheep' have 'virtually unspinnable' coats. Because wool was plucked or torn before it was shorn (Barber 1991, 21), $*h_{2/3}welh_2$- gives the right sense where a verb root 'cut' would not. Outside Latin the verbal forms of this root are harder to judge; for relevant material see now Rix (2001, 674–9), and see Darden (2001, 196–204) on the archaeological evidence.
10. For a review of archaeological data see Whittle (1996), who notes 'extensive and profound changes throughout south-east Europe' *c.* 4000–3500 BC and suggests that IE languages 'may have spread *after* these changes were underway, not as their primary cause' (126–7).
11. It is important to emphasize that Hattic linguistic influence on Hittite has been overstated in the past and that the case is stronger for Luvian linguistic influence (Melchert 2003). For Greek, Renfrew's (1998) otherwise lucid treatment is marred by a failure to distinguish two processes of contact-induced language change, borrowing via maintenance and interference via shift (Thomason & Kaufman 1988; Thomason 2001); the two leave distinct linguistic 'footprints', and the Greek data show borrowing.

## References


Anthony, D., 1995. Horse, wagon, and chariot: Indo-European languages and archaeology. *Antiquity* 69, 554–65.

Aura Jorro, F., 1993. *Diccionario Micénico*, 2 vols. Madrid: Consejo Superior de Investigaciones Científicas.

Bakker, P., 2000. Rapid language change: Creolization, intertwining, convergence, in Renfrew *et al.* (eds.), 585–620.

Barber, E.J.W., 1991. *Prehistoric Textiles.* Princeton (NJ): Princeton University Press.

Bartoněk, A., 2003. *Handbuch des mykenischen Griechisch.* Heidelberg: C. Winter.

Bellwood, P. & C. Renfrew (ed.), 2002. *Examining the Farming/Language Dispersal Hypothesis.* (McDonald Institute Monographs.) Cambridge: McDonald Institute for Archaeological Research.

Blevins, J. & A. Garrett, 1998. The origins of consonant-vowel metathesis. *Language* 74, 508–56.

Blevins, J. & A. Garrett, 2004. The evolution of metathesis, in *Phonetically based phonology*, ed. B. Hayes, R. Kirchner & D. Steriade. Cambridge: Cambridge University Press, 117–56.

Carpelan, C., A. Parpola & P. Koskikallio (eds.), 2001. *Early Contacts between Uralic and Indo-European: Linguistic and Archaeological Considerations.* (Mémoires de la Société Finno-Ougrienne 242.) Helsinki: Suomalais-Ugrilainen Seura.

Chadwick, J., 1979. The use of Mycenaean documents as historical evidence, in *Colloquium Mycenaeum: Actes du Sixième Colloque International sur les Textes Mycéniens et Egéens tenu à Chaumont sur Neuchâtel du 7 au 13 septembre 1975*, eds. E. Risch & H. Mühlestein. Genève: Droz, 21–32.

Chadwick, J., 1998. The Greekness of Mycenaean. *Aevum* 72, 25–8.

Clackson, J., 2000. Time depth in Indo-European, in Renfrew *et al.* 2000, 441–54.

Cunliffe, B., 1997. *The Ancient Celts.* Oxford: Oxford University Press.

Darden, B., 2001. On the question of the Anatolian origin of Indo-Hittite, in Drews (ed.), 184–228.

Diamond, J. & P. Bellwood, 2003. Farmers and their languages: the first expansions. *Science* 300, 597–603.

Dickinson, O., 1994. *The Aegean Bronze Age.* Cambridge: Cambridge University Press.

Drews, R. (ed.), 2001. *Greater Anatolia and the Indo-Hittite Language Family: Papers Presented at a Colloquium hosted by the University of Richmond, March 18–19, 2000.* Washington (DC): Journal of Indo-European Studies.

Dyen, I., J.B. Kruskal & P. Black, 1997. Comparative Indo-European database. Downloaded on 3 July 2004 from http://www.ntu.edu.au/education/langs/ielex/IE-DATA1.

Garrett, A., 1999. A new model of Indo-European subgrouping and dispersal, in *Proceedings of the Twenty-Fifth Annual Meeting of the Berkeley Linguistics Society, February 12–15, 1999*, eds. S.S. Chang, L. Liaw & J. Ruppenhofer. Berkeley (CA): Berkeley Linguistics Society, 146–56.

Gimbutas, M., 1973. Old Europe *c.* 7000–3500 BC: the earliest European civilization before the infiltration of the Indo-European peoples. *Journal of Indo-European Studies* 1, 1–21.

Gray, R.D. & Q.D. Atkinson, 2003. Language-tree divergence times support the Anatolian theory of Indo-European origins. *Nature* 426, 435–9.

Hajnal, I., 1995. *Studien zum mykenischen Kasussystem.* Berlin: Walter de Gruyter.

Heggarty, P., 2000. Quantifying change over time in phonetics, in Renfrew *et al.* (eds.), 531–62.

Hock, H.H., 1991. *Principles of Historical Linguistics.* 2nd edition. Berlin: Mouton de Gruyter.

Jasanoff, J.H., 2003. *Hittite and the Indo-European Verb.* Oxford: Oxford University Press.

Lehmann, W.P., 1993. *Theoretical Bases of Indo-European Linguistics.* London: Routledge.

Lejeune, M., 1982. *Phonétique historique du mycénien et du grec ancien.* 2nd edition. Paris: Klincksieck.

Lubotsky, A., 2001. The Indo-Iranian substratum, in Carpelan *et al.* (eds.), 301–17.

Mair, V.H. (ed.), 1998. *The Bronze Age and Early Iron Age Peoples of Eastern Central Asia*, 2 vols. (*Journal of Indo-European Studies* Monograph 26.) Washington (DC): Journal of Indo-European Studies.

Mallory, J.P., 1989. *In Search of the Indo-Europeans: Language, Archaeology and Myth.* London: Thames & Hudson.

Mallory, J.P., 1998. A European perspective on Indo-Europeans in Asia, in Mair (ed.), 175–201.
Mallory, J.P., 2002. Archaeological models and Asian Indo-Europeans, in Sims-Williams (ed.), 19–42.
Mallory, J.P. & V.H. Mair, 2000. *The Tarim Mummies: Ancient China and the Mystery of the Earliest Peoples from the West.* London: Thames & Hudson.
Meillet, A., 1913 [1975]. *Aperçu d'une histoire de la langue grecque.* 8th edition. Paris: Klincksieck.
Meiser, G., 2003. *Veni vidi vici: die Vorgeschichte des lateinischen Perfektsystems.* München: C.H. Beck.
Melchert, H.C., 1998. The dialectal position of Anatolian within Indo-European, in *Proceedings of the Twenty-Fourth Annual Meeting of the Berkeley Linguistics Society, February 14–16, 1998: Special Session on Indo-European Subgrouping and Internal Relations*, eds. B.K. Bergen, M.C. Plauché & A.C. Bailey. Berkeley (CA): Berkeley Linguistics Society, 24–31.
Melchert, H.C., 2003. Prehistory, in *The Luwians*, ed. H.C. Melchert. Leiden: Brill, 8–26.
Milroy, J., 1992. *Linguistic Variation and Change: On the Historical Sociolinguistics of English.* Oxford: Blackwell.
Milroy, L., 1987. *Language and Social Networks.* 2nd edition. Oxford: Blackwell.
Morpurgo, A, 1963. *Mycenaeae Graecitatis Lexicon.* Rome: Ed. dell'Ateneo.
Morpurgo Davies, A., 1979. Terminology of power and terminology of work in Greek and Linear B, in *Colloquium mycenaeum: Actes du sixième Colloque international sur les textes mycéniens et égéens tenu à Chaumont sur Neuchâtel du 7 au 13 septembre 1975*, eds. E. Risch & H. Mühlestein. Geneva: Droz, 87–108.
Morpurgo Davies, A., 1988. Mycenaean and Greek language, in *Linear B: a 1984 Survey*, eds. A. Morpurgo Davies & Y. Duhoux. Louvain-la-Neuve: Peeters, 75–125.
Morpurgo Davies, A., 1992. Mycenaean, Arcadian, Cyprian and some questions of method in dialectology, in *Mykenaïka*, ed. J.-P. Olivier. (*Bulletin de Correspondance Hellénique*, Supplément 25.) Paris: Boccard, 415–32.
Morris, I., 2000. *Archaeology as Cultural History: Words and Things in Iron Age Greece.* Malden (MA): Blackwell.
Nichols, J., 1998. The Eurasian spread zone and the Indo-European dispersal, in *Archaeology and Language II: Correlating Archaeological and Linguistic Hypotheses*, eds. R. Blench & M. Spriggs. London: Routledge, 220–66.
Palaima, T.G., 1995. The nature of the Mycenaean *wanax*: non-Indo-European origins and priestly functions, in *The Role of the Ruler in the Prehistoric Aegean*, ed. P. Rehak. (Aegaeum, 11.) Liège: Université de Liège, 119–39.
Parpola, A., 1988. The coming of the Aryans to India and the cultural and ethnic identity of the Dāsas. *Studia Orientalia* 64, 195–302.
Parpola, A., 1998. Aryan languages, archaeological cultures, and Sinkiang: Where did Proto-Iranian come into being, and how did it spread?, in Mair (ed.), vol. 1, 114–47.
Parpola, A., 2002. From the dialects of Old Indo-Aryan to Proto-Indo-Aryan and Proto-Iranian, in Sims-Williams (ed.), 43–102.
Renfrew, C., 1979. Systems collapse as social transformation, in *Transformations, Mathematical Approaches to Culture Change*, eds. C. Renfrew & K.L. Cooke. New York (NY): Academic Press, 275–94.
Renfrew, C., 1987. *Archaeology and Language: the Puzzle of Indo-European Origins.* London: Cape.
Renfrew, C., 1998. Word of Minos: The Minoan contribution to Mycenaean Greek and the linguistic geography of the Bronze Age Aegean. *Cambridge Archaeological Journal* 8(2), 239–64.
Renfrew, C., 1999. Time depth, convergence theory and innovation in Proto-Indo-European: 'Old Europe' as a PIE linguistic area. *Journal of Indo-European Studies* 27, 257–93.
Renfrew, C., 2000. 10,000 or 5000 years ago? — Questions of time depth, in Renfrew *et al.* (eds.), 413–39.
Renfrew, C., 2001. The Anatolian origins of Proto-Indo-European and the autochthony of the Hittites, in Drews (ed.), 36–63.
Renfrew, C. & J.F. Cherry (eds.), 1986. *Peer Polity Interaction and Socio-political Change.* Cambridge: Cambridge University Press.
Renfrew, C., A. McMahon & L. Trask (eds.), 2000. *Time Depth in Historical Linguistics*, 2 vols. (Papers in the Prehistory of Languages.) Cambridge: McDonald Institute for Archaeological Research.
Richards, M., 2003. The Neolithic invasion of Europe. *Annual Review of Anthropology* 32, 135–62.
Ringe, D., T. Warnow & A. Taylor, 2002. Indo-European and computational cladistics. *Transactions of the Philological Society* 100, 59–129.
Rix, H. (ed.), 2001. *LIV: Lexikon der indogermanischen Verben: die Wurzeln und ihre Primärstammbildungen.* 2nd edition. Wiesbaden: Reichert.
Sherratt, A., 1981. Plough and pastoralism: aspects of the secondary products revolution, in *Patterns of the Past: Studies in Honour of David Clarke*, eds. I. Hodder, G. Isaac & N. Hammond. Cambridge: Cambridge University Press, 261–305 (reprinted in Sherratt 1997, 158–98).
Sherratt, A., 1983. The secondary exploitation of animals in the Old World. *World Archaeology* 15, 90–104 (revised in Sherratt 1997, 199–228).
Sherratt, A., 1997. *Economy and Society in Prehistoric Europe: Changing Perspectives.* Princeton (NJ): Princeton University Press.
Sherratt, A. & E.S. Sherratt, 1988. The archaeology of Indo-European: an alternative view. *Antiquity* 62, 584–95 (reprinted in Sherratt 1997, 471–85).
Sims-Williams, N. (ed.), 2002. *Indo-Iranian Languages and Peoples.* (Proceedings of the British Academy 116.) Oxford: Oxford University Press.
Snodgrass, A., 1980. *Archaic Greece: the Age of Experiment.* London: J.M. Dent and Sons.
Specht, F., 1947. *Der Ursprung der indogermanischen Deklination.* Göttingen: Vandenhoeck & Ruprecht.
Steriade, D., 1993. *Greek Prosodies and the Nature of Syllabification Processes.* New York (NY): Garland.
Sweetser, E. 1990. *From Etymology to Pragmatics: Metaphorical and Cultural Aspects of Semantic Structure.* Cambridge:

Cambridge University Press.
Tainter, J.A., 1988. *The Collapse of Complex Societies.* Cambridge: Cambridge University Press.
Thomason, S.G., 2001. *Language Contact.* Washington (DC): Georgetown University Press.
Thomason, S.G. & T. Kaufman, 1988. *Language Contact, Creolization and Genetic Linguistics.* Berkeley (CA): University of California Press.
Traugott, E.C. & R.B. Dasher, 2001. *Regularity in Semantic Change.* Cambridge: Cambridge University Press.
Turner, R.L., 1962–6. *A Comparative Dictionary of the Indo-Aryan Languages.* London: Oxford University Press.
Whittle, A., 1996. *Europe in the Neolithic: the Creation of New Worlds.* Cambridge: Cambridge University Press.
Zimmer, S., 2002. The problem of Indo-European glottogenesis. *General Linguistics* 39, 25–55.

# Chapter 13

# Why Linguists Don't Do Dates: Evidence from Indo-European and Australian Languages

April McMahon & Robert McMahon

The use of phylogenetic methods and models for linguistic data has contributed considerably to the current development of quantitative comparative linguistics, and on any measure is therefore a step forward. Our view is that any replacement of arguments from authority with repeatable, testable methods must be a force for good. However, just as many historical linguists accept and see the value in lexicostatistics while rejecting its application to dating language splits in glottochronology, so we might embrace the development of tree-based or network-based quantitative methods (Ringe *et al.* 2002; McMahon & McMahon 2003; 2004; 2005) without accepting dating here either. The main difficulty in dating is that certain assumptions of general independence of rates and direction of change are invalid for language: more precisely, they may be invalid for some languages all the time, and are certainly invalid for all languages some of the time. Consequently, any calculated dates for splits within the best tree (strictly speaking, the collection of best splits) constructed using Monte-Carlo simulation Maximum Likelihood estimates will be subject to a degree of error depending on the vagaries of linguistic and external history. We here critically compare the merits of phylogenetic reconstruction and classification versus the pitfalls of phylogenetic dating.

## Phylogenetic methods and language contact

The apparent success of the network approach for Ladin languages (Forster *et al.* 1998), and of tree-based dating for Polynesian and Indo-European (Gray & Jordan 2000; Gray & Atkinson 2003) reflect the power of phylogenetic approaches applied to simple word-list data. These phylogenetic approaches are of immense value in themselves: they do not go beyond the normally accepted analyses of historical linguists (most notably in assessing items as cognate or not), and nor do they require the collection or construction of complex data sets, since they are based on straightforward and readily collectable Swadesh-type lists. Furthermore, the use of Network3.0 (Bandelt *et al.* 1995; 1999), and of more recent network-type programs which are designed for distance-based data (for instance Neighbor-Net, Bryant & Moulton 2004, as implemented in SplitsTree4.0), offer the possibility of visualizing complex connections among languages, due not only to common ancestry but also reflecting contact. However, similar data can also be used to indicate the limitations of such phylogenetic approaches under different conditions. The central difficulty is that recent work in contact linguistics (see Thomason 2001) has revealed the multiplicity of linguistic consequences which multilingualism or population interactions can occasion, from lexical borrowing (which can in itself present significant problems, as we show below), through structural borrowing and convergence, to pidginization, creolization, and the development of mixed languages like Media Lengua or Michif. Contact can produce outcomes indistinguishable, without significant linguistic detective work or prior knowledge of the external and linguistic history, from common ancestry with subsequent divergence; moreover, there is no longer any real option of excluding contact, since we now know there are languages which would not exist at all without it.

Dixon (1997) has expressed the essential problem in his punctuated equilibrium approach; but even leaving aside this particular model, we can see that linguistic conditions need not be even relatively consistent over time. In certain periods, settled, geographically close and interacting populations may be the norm, resulting in their languages growing closer together, whether or not they share a common ancestor. Recovered relationships for such convergence areas may be very un-tree-like, and may be best approximated by a balance between geographical and historical connectedness, with geography being the dominant reason for

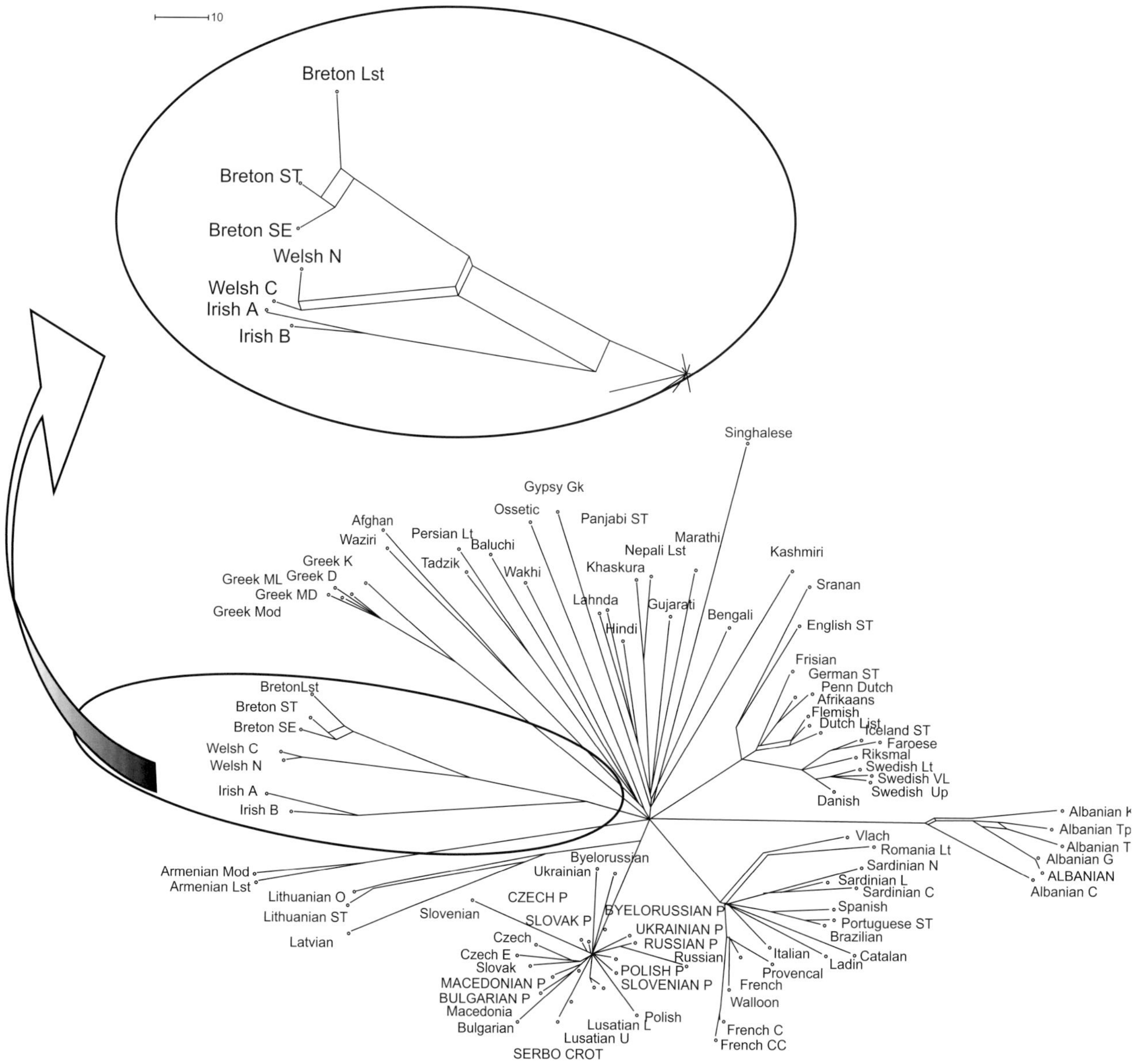


**Figure 13.1.** *Indo-European data (from Dyen* et al. *1992), analyzed using SplitsTree (Huson 1998); inset shows reticulations, and hence suspected borrowings, within Celtic.*

similarity, rather than phylogeny. However, in other periods of geographical spread (or indeed simply for other kinds of languages), with rapid population expansion and diversification from an originally discrete and localised ancestor group speaking a single language or closely related languages, we may find a history reflected accurately and appropriately in a tree model showing the order of divergence.

## Convergence in Australia: a worst-case scenario?

To test the significance of these effects, it seems apposite to turn to the classic Dixonian case of Australian languages and potential convergence situations, and we have therefore considered a range of data from southeastern Western Australia analyzed and published by David Nash (2002). These data come from a group of languages whose interrelationships are poorly understood, and where the available data frequently consist of an incomplete, modified Swadesh list, collected in most cases from a single speaker. These data possibly represent a worst-case test for phylogenetic methods: we can neither select our data, since the sources are intrinsically limited, nor do we have the advantage of previous Comparative Method work to inform judgements on likely cognate relationships, which instead are necessarily based simply on recurrent similarity without reconstruction. We have compared the results for these Australian data with analyses of Indo-European data from previous work. In a comparison of networks (based on percentage lexical cognacy scores) drawn using the SplitsTree algorithm (Huson 1998), a strong tree-like signal is present in the Indo-European data (Fig. 13.1), and indeed this dominates the limited, but still significant signal of contact, which is manifested in reticulations at a higher magnification, as shown in the inset for Celtic.

In the Australian data, however, the phylogenetic signal is much weaker. If only a subset of data is included, involving those lists with more than 70 items each, and one list only from each region, an approximately tree-like signal can be discerned; but if all the data are included, this signal is completely swamped by the contact-induced similarities. The result is that, as shown in Figure 13.2, only five nodes are distinguished, one of which comprises 20 of the 26 languages: no phylogenetic structure can be discerned. The problem for dating is a stark one. Splits Tree4.0 is a network-based phylogenetic method, and therefore has the considerable advantage over solely tree-based methods of being able to accommodate contact phenomena as well as indicators of common ancestry. If the order of splitting cannot be determined using a relatively sensitive phylogenetic method of this kind, there is clearly no prospect at all of generating reasonable dates, or indeed any dates at all, for the divergence of these sister systems.

Using Neighbor-Net (Bryant & Moulton 2004), we do see vestiges of tree-like structure emerging, as shown in Figure 13.3; but the volume of reticulations we find is very considerable, and suggests that the effects of contact have been the most significant factor in the development of these groupings.

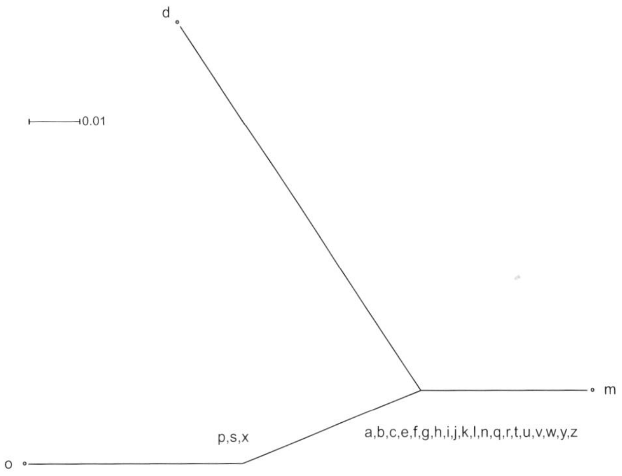


**Figure 13.2.** *Australian data from Nash (2002) analyzed using SplitsTree4.0 (Huson 1998). (For key see Nash 2002, table 1). Languages are labelled 'a' through 'z' and represented by nodes shown as small black dots. 0.01 distance is equivalent to 1 per cent lexical distance; the number of words in 1 per cent will depend on the lengths of the individual word lists.*

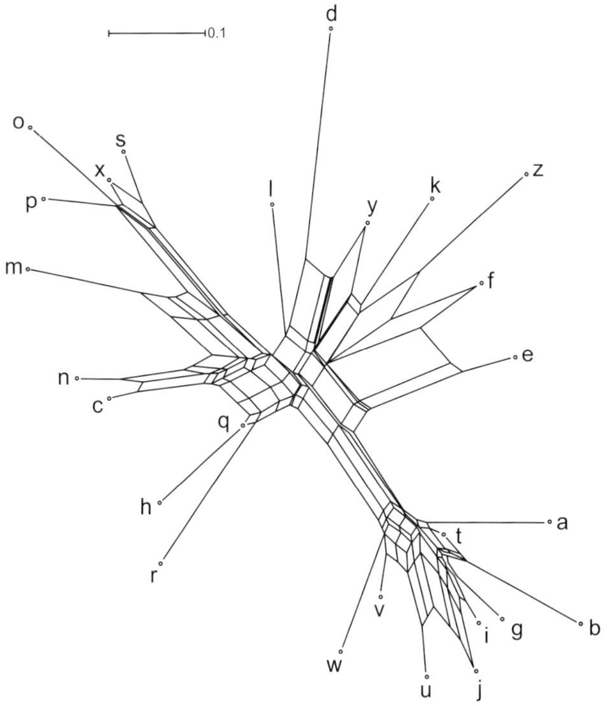


**Figure 13.3.** *Australian data from Nash (2002) analyzed using Neighbor-Net (Bryant & Moulton 2004). (For key see Nash 2002, table 1). The scale is as for Figure 13.2 above; so, 0.1 represents 10 per cent lexical distance.*

## Implications for Indo-European

One possible conclusion to be drawn from these Australian data is that we should simply exclude certain problematic languages, or linguistic areas, from analysis using phylogenetic methods, and from the dating mechanisms consequent on such analyses. However, this is to assume, quite counterfactually, that we always know when languages have had a particularly contact-prone history, and also that most languages are 'non-contact languages' without such un-tree-like characteristics. On the contrary, we argue that when examining a group of languages to determine historical relatedness and the timing of cultural events, the success of any phylogenetic model will depend critically on the balance between the two opposing trends towards convergence and divergence respectively: and even limited lexical borrowing can have a discernible and problematic influence, at least on the dating part of the equation. In this sense, the phylogenetics

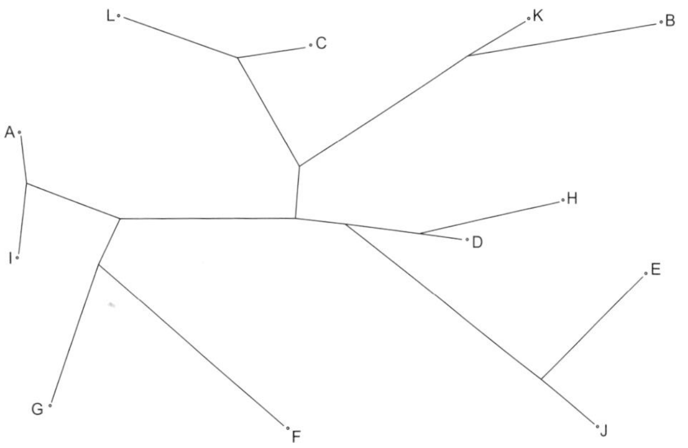


**Figure 13.4a.** *Network for simulated hihi list (25 items), from full list with 10 per cent borrowing.*

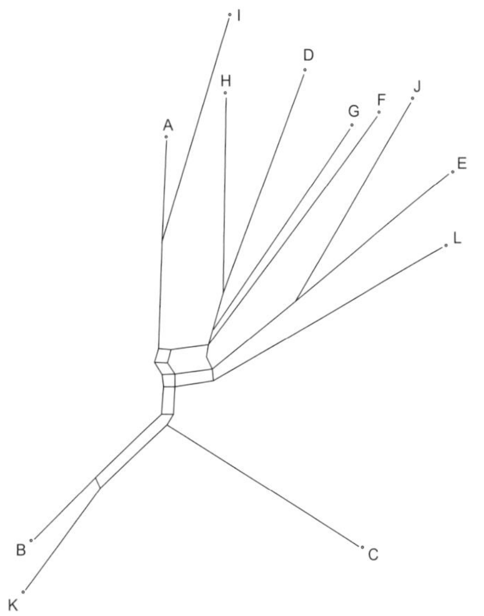


**Figure 13.4b.** *Network for simulated lolo list (25 items), from full list with 10 per cent borrowing.*

of language change, based for example on word-list data, is more akin to morphological or phenotypic than to molecular genetic evolution. This follows from the fact that the selection pressure, as it were, driving the fixation of the random variation in lexical usage, is variable for any particular group of speakers, and is at least in part dependent on extra-linguistic factors such as population contact and prestige. Since these effects are likely to affect subsets of the linguistic data differently and in non-independent ways (think, to take a slightly frivolous example, of all the French culinary terms in English), it is difficult to see how these can be modelled in stochastically meaningful ways so as to estimate the time depth involved, certainly in cases where the contact relationships have not been well characterised. Trees drawn using data which are more amenable to borrowing generally, or which have a high frequency of culinary vocabulary specifically, would be more likely to characterize English as a Romance language than a Germanic one.

We argue that, if contact-induced change is not uncommon in the history and prehistory of languages, any dating based on phylogenetic approaches where we do not know the contact history involved must be treated with caution, as even low levels of linguistic interchange could seriously disrupt the proposed dates. In support of this conclusion, we have carried out extensive computer simulations, reported in McMahon & McMahon (2005) using the MJ algorithm in the program package Network3.0. If borrowing of particular types and intensities creates a typical signal for Network3.0, we can look for just that signal, or variants of it, when we apply Network3.0 to real data.

Our simulations involve an Excel spreadsheet starting from a single ancestral 'language' consisting of a 200-item list. We modelled the emergence of 12 daughter languages, over 220 generations, with each bifurcation taking place at a specific, set time point. Each run (consisting of 220 generations) involves the same history of bifurcations, but the location of mutations in the 200 items is stochastic.

In our earlier work (McMahon & McMahon 2003; 2004), we have worked with so-called 'hihi' and 'lolo' lists; these are short subsets of approximately 25 items each from the 200-meaning Swadesh lists, which contrast in their retentiveness and reconstructability, constructed using methodologies pioneered by Lohr (1999). Essentially, the hihi list is maximally conservative and resistant to borrowing, and the lolo list maximally changeable and borrowable, within the limits of a Swadesh list.

For the present paper, we simulated 25-item equivalents of our hihi list, mutating at one item per run, and of our lolo list, mutating at double that rate. At the end of each run, we calculated the cognate frequencies, created a distance matrix, and applied PHYLIP3.6 tree-drawing and tree-selection programs (Felsenstein 2001). Essentially, full-list trees first became disrupted at the 5 per cent borrowing level, with the branch containing an affected language noticeably shifting away from its sister group and towards the root, in about 15 per cent of runs. This effect is clearer with 10 per cent borrowing, where branching order is also clearly counterhistorical for the borrowing language in more than 80 per cent of runs. At 20 per cent borrowing, the affected language is consistently displaced into a cluster with the 'lending' language, despite the fact that these do not, in our known history, belong to the same branch.

In addition, we carried out a median-joining analysis using Network3.0 (http://www.fluxus-engineering.com: Bandelt *et al.* 1999) with $\varepsilon$ set to zero, and found strongly similar patterns, though Network3.0 is advantageous in terms of visual representation, since it typically includes reticulations in cases of borrowing. We cannot illustrate all these trends here, but Figure 13.4 shows the output of Network3.0 for simulated hihi and lolo sublists, over a full 200-item list with a variable mutation rate and borrowing set at 10 per cent. In Figure 13.4a, there is in fact no borrowing from B to A, as befits the character of the hihi items modelled; the result is therefore a very straightforward tree, strongly congruent with the real history.

Figure 13.4b shows the lolo list, which changes at twice the rate, and here Network3.0 has clearly had insuperable problems in constructing a tree. Network3.0 has the advantage of listing the items which cause problems of this kind, showing that there are 4 loans from B into A, out of the 25 items in the lolo sublist; 3 of those are included in the reticulations towards the root of the tree, which clearly link A and B.

These simulations are strongly relevant to our analyses of Indo-European data, based on the Dyen *et al.* (1992) data base. Each data point in this data base is a cognacy judgement, with a code of 0 where there is no data, a specific shared code for each cognate set, and, crucially, another, unique coding for each loan or unclear form. This should ensure that lending and borrowing languages never share a code for any loan, which is instead effectively removed from further calculations. Our methods, however, have revealed that there are in fact some cases (very few, for a data base of 95 × 200 items) where loans have been coded erroneously as cognates. Runs of Network3.0 reveal that certain languages appear in different positions for hihi and lolo sublists; since Network3.0 also lists the problematic items which are inconsistent with any tree, it is possible to check the database codings for these items specifically. For example, 'wing' turns out to be erroneously coded by Dyen, Kruskal and Black as a cognate between English and North Germanic, giving the result in Figure 13.5, where English appears as a North Germanic language. If 'wing' is correctly recoded as a loan, English appears outside North Germanic.

The preceding discussion rests on two assumptions: first, that the hihi and lolo lists we have been comparing are really discernibly different; and second, that we can confidently categorize the items Network3.0 picks up as problematic and non-tree-like as loans. Much more detail on each point is provided in McMahon & McMahon (forthcoming), but the answers in both cases are positive.

One indirect assessment of the difference in borrowability between the hihi and lolo lists involves investigating the Swadesh 100- and 200-meaning lists

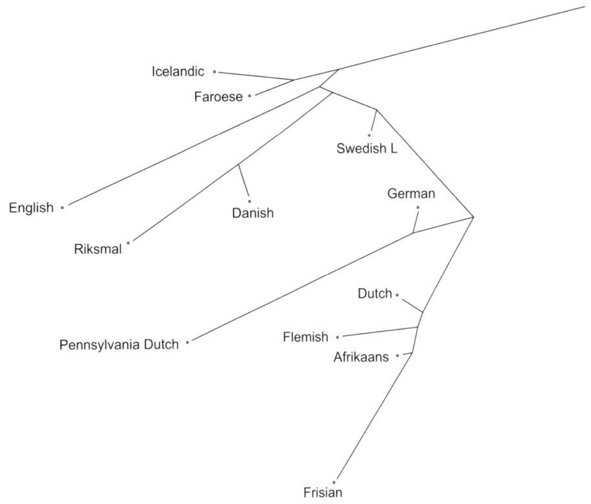


**Figure 13.5.** *Germanic as drawn by Network3.0, with 'wing' incorrectly coded as cognate between English and North Germanic.*

for languages with fairly high levels of borrowing: we worked here with data from Kessler (2001), selecting Albanian, French, English, German and Turkish. We calculated the proportions of loans (which Kessler marks very carefully in his data) for both lists, and found an overall borrowing rate across these 5 languages of 12.3 per cent, unevenly distributed as 8.6 per cent in the 100-meaning list, and 15.7 per cent in the 107 items in the 200-meaning list which are not included in the shorter list. This difference is highly significant ($\chi^2 = 10.7$; $p < 0.001$). The majority of our hihi items (20 out of 30) are from the 100-meaning list, and the majority of the lolo items (16 out of 23) from the part of the 200-meaning list which does not overlap with the shorter list, so that these calculations would also lead us to expect a greater frequency of borrowing in the lolo sublist. In addition, at least six items recorded by Embleton (1986) as borrowed within Germanic fall within our lolo list, while none at all are in the hihi sublist.

As for the problematic items diagnosed by Network3.0, these again correspond with borrowings identified by Kessler (2001) and Embleton (1986) within Indo-European. We cannot *a priori* rule out the possibility that forms listed as non-tree-like may be shared retentions rather than loans; it was for this reason that we embarked on our simulations, since understanding the signals borrowing produces with a known and controlled history should help us interpret patterns we may find in languages where the history is altogether less clear. In addition, the fact that trees were seriously disrupted only with at least 5 per cent borrowing, and more usually with 10 per cent, in our simulations, is helpful since it seems highly unlikely that we would expect this frequency of shared retentions for a language pair — though this is an assumption which strictly requires further testing.

**Implications for dating**

On the basis of this combination of simulations and analyses of real linguistic data, we arrive at two conclusions for attempts to date split points in language family trees. The first is that, in cases like the Australian one, such attempts cannot conceivably be successful: if contact-induced change has been sufficiently extensive, then it will outweigh any signal of common ancestry, so that branching will be minimal or non-existent — and if clear branching points do not arise from phylogenetic methods, no amount of ingenuity can date them. Although Neighbor-Net (implemented in Splits Tree4.0) did provide a minimally tree-like signal for the Australian data, it must be remembered that it produced, by its distance-based nature, a phenogram rather than a phylogram. In other words, the graph gives an indication of relative similarity between systems, but assigning a historical interpretation to in terms of contact or common ancestry is a separate stage of the enterprise.

Initially, we might assume that existing attempts at constructing datable networks (Forster *et al.* 1998; Forster & Toth 2003; also Gray & Atkinson 2003, using MCML) are as far away from such problematic convergence situations as possible, and this may indeed have informed the choice of languages for comparison: in the case of Ladin, we have relatively isolated populations speaking transparently related languages and varieties, while in Indo-European we have the best-researched and most plentifully attested language family on the planet. However, we have seen that even relatively low-level lexical borrowing can disrupt trees and networks, both for simulated and real data (see Figs. 13.3 & 13.4). What, then, is the impact of these findings for recent attempts at dating within Indo-European?

In the case of Gray & Atkinson's (2003) Indo-European dating, the effect will not necessarily be overly problematic, since individual contact events are likely to be localized to relatively few branches, and will therefore be smoothed out, resulting only in a minor increase in the variance around the estimated Maximum Likelihood dates. These effects are also minimised by Gray & Atkinson's use of a carefully prepared data set, based on the best available linguistic knowledge, in the shape of Dyen *et al.* (1992) — though even here, as we have shown and as Gray & Atkinson (2003) suspected, there are individual miscodings which are mainly internal to subgroups, but which could again have a foreshortening effect on individual branch lengths.

What this means is that the quality of the linguistic data used is vitally important; indeed, this factor cannot be overstated. In less well-studied or smaller families, or where the data are poorly characterized, the effects of admixture may completely mask the phylogenetic signal, particularly when this is weak since the time depth involved is relatively great, as in the Australian case. Forster & Toth's (2003) attempt at dating in Celtic may well fall into this problematic category. The central problem here, as highlighted for example by Trask and others in recent electronic list discussions, is the lack of cognacy judgements or objective measurements of similarity. Whereas Gray & Atkinson (2003; and see also Gray & Jordan (2000), who used equally carefully prepared data from Blust's Austronesian dictionary), used codings developed on the basis of the Comparative Method, Forster & Toth (2003) base their analyses on face-value similarity. An accumulation of minor errors due to borrowing, misclassification, or poor selection of meanings may have resulted in significant deviation between their calculated dates (8100±1900 BC years for Indo-European and 3200±1500 BC years for Celtic) and those expected from historical evidence, or obtained from other dating methods.

Turning to specific aspects of Forster & Toth's (2003) method, the inset in Figure 13.1 above showed our analysis of relevant data from Dyen *et al.* (1992). Despite a generally strong phylogenetic signal, there is clearly sufficient interborrowing within Celtic for Splitstree to generate reticulations. Since Forster & Toth's (2003) work is situated only within a single sub-family, the effect of such interborrowing may be disproportionately important: we cannot assume, as with Gray & Atkinson's (2003) larger-scale dating, that these effects will be smoothed out higher up the tree. Again, the picture is made more complex by the likely interfering effects of external history: Insular Celtic and Continental Celtic may have developed differently partly because the latter had more possible contacts with other languages than the former, being situated in a more complex and variable linguistic landscape. If any such contacts are undiagnosed (and recall that some of the languages and varieties with which these surviving languages might have been in contact have disappeared, making accurate diagnosis that much more of a challenge), the time depth of the family will have been artificially extended, pushing the original split of Celtic earlier than was in fact the case.

Turning to just one specific example, dating for any event depends on the mutation rate assumed, as well as a suitable range of calibrations, which allow the conversion of number of changes of state into time. Forster & Toth's (2003, 5) calculations reveal that their mutation rate is one change per 1350 years (with no confidence interval) in a list of 21 lexemes; our calculation, based on our hihi list of 25 items (the most conservative meanings) and the Dyen *et al.* (1992) data base, suggests one lexical substitution per 470 years ±50 years. Forster & Toth's rate is so surprisingly low because they have excluded 7 of their original 28 lexemes, on the grounds that these are multistate characters which 'contribute disproportionately to network complexity' (2003, 2), thereby prioritizing those characters which have changed relatively little, though not by any objective or generalizable prior criteria. However, prioritizing those characters with very low mutation rates will also increase the negative effect of individual coding errors, with each such error potentially contributing 1000 years to the dating estimates. As shown above, we cannot be sure, even for the best understood, most carefully collected, and most thoroughly analyzed linguistic data, that no such errors have crept in; and Forster & Toth are dealing with relatively recent splits.

This combination of general limitations and local errors is not likely to tempt historical linguists to accept proposed dates. However, we wish to focus here on those general limitations, rather than listing further local errors: we are not so much concerned about the way the dating game might be being played, as keen to make the case for not playing the game at all. Our conclusion is that dating divergence will always be inherently problematic for language. Whatever we might believe about the basis of language in human evolution and in our contemporary genes, languages are human behaviour too, and inevitably subject to the unmodellable vagaries of culture, prestige, external history and pure, blind chance. This will affect not only the variants chosen, but also the speed of change. That we can capture patterns of split and descent convincingly using phylogenetic methods is in itself a candidate for a minor miracle. That we can begin to isolate some of the contact events which make the patterns more complex and less clear-cut, using those same methods, is even better. But by trying to attach dates to these (perhaps specious) events, we are just unacceptably pushing our luck. It is hard enough to convince historical linguists of the benefits of quantitative and computational approaches as things stand; allowing such phylogenetic methods to become automatically associated with dating simply increases the chance that both will be rejected out of hand. If we persist in attempts at dating now, we are intrinsically restricted in what can be achieved: we will have to limit ourselves to very specific, well-researched cases where borrowing can be analyzed out, and even here, as shown in the Indo-European cases, we will find error and inclarity. Extending dating to cases where the data are less plentiful and more problematic, or where contact is likely to have had a more significant effect, simply compounds that error. Moreover, while the phylogenetic methods themselves are increasingly promising in isolating family-specific problems which might provide insights for the histories of particular groups, these are exactly the interesting and unorthodox details which have to be submerged in the interests of the one-size-fits all, simplified approach required for generalizable dating.

This does not, of course, mean relative chronologies can never be established. It is entirely feasible to say that First Fronting in Germanic preceded the Great Vowel Shift in English without placing absolute dates on either. Likewise, we can say that Proto-Germanic existed earlier than Modern Dutch without dating — and indeed, this kind of relative temporal information is implicit in the family tree. The order of events is not the same as their timing, and we can establish one without being able to say anything convincing about the other. There is a relevant analogy here in human pedigrees. It is one thing to know who is whose mother, or grandfather, or sibling, but quite another to date earlier lives in family trees, in the absence of documentary evidence. We are able to go some way towards this because we have an approximate idea of the human generation interval, and how this changes over time and space. Nonetheless, we are at risk of drawing quite the wrong conclusions for specific families or groups, since in one there may be a generation interval of 16 years, and in another something closer to 30. For language, we are in an even worse position, since the equivalent of the generation interval is not at all clear, and we cannot be sure, yet, how it may vary across space and time. This means, crucially, that we cannot generalize across families: if we draw particular conclusions about the dating of Proto-Germanic relative to Modern Dutch, we cannot then assume a similar period will obtain wherever we find two degrees of branching. Until we have more and better data, more extensive and structured cross-linguistic data bases available for quantitative study, more sophisticated simulations, and hence a clearer idea of the signals we can expect under particular social and linguistic circumstances, we cannot hope to provide accurate and generalizable dates. It might be argued that this is to advocate an unscientific approach: science, after all, involves getting it partly wrong, and refining methods until we get it righter. We do not accept this view: it seems to us quite unscientific to persist in attempting to date language splits when we do not have enough information to know whether and how far we are wrong. Any attempts to refine our methods and measurements in those circumstances can be no more than stabs in the dark.

## Conclusion

We are, in short, at a crossroads. We can choose, as a community of population historians with an interest in language, to repeat the catastrophic history which equated lexicostatistics with glottochronology: the result of that confusion, which was not at all an inevitable one, has been more than 30 years spent trying to rehabilitate aspects of the former, while distancing ourselves from the latter. Or we can call a halt to attempts at dating now, until we have established what we can and cannot validly do with our phylogenetic methods, under assumptions which are reasonable to language rather than to any other, ostensibly similar systems. We can concentrate on getting the quality of the data as right as we can, and on formulating methods which help us discern and interpret different patterns. Until then, attempts at dating will be unfalsifiable, ungeneralizable, and counterproductive.

## Acknowledgements

The work reported here, as part of the project 'Quantitative Methods for Language Classification' (2001–2004) is funded by the UK Arts and Humanities Research Board (award number AN6720/APN12536); we gratefully acknowledge their support. We also thank the other members of the project team, Paul Heggarty and Natalia Slaska, for their comments and contributions, and gratefully acknowledge the contribution of the volume editors and reviewers in improving the final version of this chapter. All remaining misapprehensions and infelicities are, of course, our own: we undertake only to blame these on each other, and not on any third party whatsoever.

## References

Bandelt, H.-J., P. Forster, B.C. Sykes & M.B. Richards, 1995. Mitochondrial portraits of human populations using median networks. *Genetics* 141, 743–53.

Bandelt, H.-J., P. Forster & A. Röhl, 1999. Median-joining networks for inferring intraspecific phylogenies. *Molecular Biology and Evolution* 16, 37–48.

Bryant, D. & V. Moulton, 2004. NeighborNet: an agglomerative algorithm for the construction of planar phylogenetic networks. *Molecular Biology and Evolution* 21, 255–65.

Dixon, R.M.W., 1997. *The Rise and Fall of Languages*. Cambridge: Cambridge University Press.

Dyen, I., J.B. Kruskal & P. Black, 1992. An Indoeuropean classification: a lexicostatistical experiment. *Transactions of the American Philosophical Society* 82, part 5. Data available at http://www.ldc.upenn.edu.

Embleton, S.M., 1986. *Statistics in Historical Linguistics*. Bochum: Brockmeyer.

Felsenstein, J., 2001. *PHYLIP: Phylogeny Inference Package. Version 3.6*. Seattle (WA): Department of Genome Sciences, University of Washington, Seattle.

Forster, P. & A. Toth, 2003. Toward a phylogenetic chronology of ancient Gaulish, Celtic, and Indo-European. *Proceedings of the National Academy of Sciences of the USA* 100, 9079–84.

Forster, P., A. Toth & H.-J. Bandelt, 1998. Evolutionary network analysis of word lists: visualising the relationships between Alpine Romance languages. *Journal of Quantitative Linguistics* 5, 174–87.

Gray, R. & Q. Atkinson, 2003. Language-tree divergence times support the Anatolian theory of Indo-European origin. *Nature* 426, 435–9.

Gray, R. & F. Jordan, 2000. Language trees support the express-train sequence of Austronesian expansion. *Nature* 405, 1052–5.

Huson, D.H., 1998. Splitstree: a program for analysing and visualizing evolutionary data. *Bioinformatics* 14, 68–73.

Kessler, B., 2001. *The Significance of Word Lists*. Stanford (CA): CSLI Publications.

Lohr, M., 1999. Methods for the Genetic Classification of Languages. Unpublished PhD thesis, University of Cambridge.

McMahon, A. & R. McMahon, 2003. Finding families: quantitative methods in language classification. *Transactions of the Philological Society* 101, 7–55.

McMahon, A. & R. McMahon, 2004. Family values, in *New Perspectives on English Historical Linguistics*, vol. 1: *Syntax and Morphology*, eds. C. Kay, S. Horobin & Je. Smith. Amsterdam and Philadelphia: Benjamins, 103–23.

McMahon, A. & R. McMahon, 2005. *Language Classification by Numbers*. Oxford: Oxford University Press.

Nash, D., 2002. Historical linguistic geography of South-East Western Australia, in *Language in Native Title*, eds. J. Henderson & D. Nash. Canberra: Aboriginal Studies Press, 205–30.

Ringe, D., T. Warnow & A. Taylor, 2002. Indo-European and computational cladistics. *Transactions of the Philological Society* 100, 59–129.

Thomason, S.G., 2001. *An Introduction to Language Contact*. Edinburgh: Edinburgh University Press.

# *Chapter 14*

# Quantifying Uncertainty in a Stochastic Model of Vocabulary Evolution

Geoff K. Nicholls & Russell D. Gray

## 1. Introduction

This paper makes a statistical exploration of certain human vocabulary data. We would like to know whether the data in question can be used to infer language ancestry. The data we treat is a representation due to Gray & Atkinson (2003) of the Dyen *et al.* (1997) Indo-European lexical corpus. Gray & Atkinson (2003) supplement the lexical data with a small but important collection of historical constraints. Can we infer the pattern and timing of events in the history of the Indo-European language group from these data? We reformulate this question in something like statistical terms. For the processes which shaped the data, can we construct a mathematical model with the following properties: the symbols of the mathematical model are in one to one correspondence with elements of the real-world system; the data is a likely outcome of the model; the model has predictive power?

We provide evidence that progress has been made. We studied the data to look for clues as to what sort of model was needed (section 3). We then wrote down the simplest model we could think of for vocabulary evolution (section 4 preamble). We fit the model to the data (section 4.3 through to section 4.5) using Monte-Carlo simulation to quantify systematic error. We then divide the data into subsets in several different ways and check for consistency between subsets (section 5) as a means of displaying model mis-specification error. The results are encouraging.

The purpose-built model we develop in this paper lacks certain features likely to be a part of human vocabulary evolution. These include missing data in poorly reconstructed languages such as Hittite, rate heterogeneity in time and space and between meaning classes, word transfer between languages, constraints due to structure by meaning class, and polymorphism within meaning class. Our consistency checks (section 5) show that some aspects of the reconstruction are not confounded by these complex effects; we can recover language ancestry from data synthesized under processes which model some of these effects. The results presented remain preliminary.

## 2. Background

In this section we introduce the data, discuss a recent attempt to reconstruct the ancestry of languages in the data, and introduce some basic assumptions which will be important in our analysis.

What is the data, and how was it gathered? Dyen *et al.* (1997) group the words of a number of human languages into equivalence classes called cognate classes. Words in a cognate class have two important things in common. First, they have (in their respective languages) roughly the same meaning. Secondly, words in a cognate class are descended from a common ancestor, so that they constitute homologous language traits. Cognate classes are generated by starting with 200 meaning categories, and collecting together all words in all languages under study which fall in one of the meaning categories. These categories are then further subdivided into homologous groupings. In Gray & Atkinson (2003) each cognate class (labels $j = 1, 2 \ldots N$) generates a binary valued trait ($D_{i,j}$ say) for each language (labels $i = 1, 2 \ldots L$). Language $i$ either possesses ($D_{i,j} = 1$) or lacks ($D_{i,j} = 0$) a word in cognate class $j$. The data analyzed by Gray & Atkinson (2003) and here contain $N = 2398$ cognate classes observed in $L = 87$ Indo-European languages and $K = 200$ meaning categories.

Cognate classes present in the data are a subset of the cognate classes which existed in the history of the languages represented in the data. Cognate classes which existed in the past, but survived into no recorded language are of course absent from the data. However, in the course of building the Gray &

Atkinson (2003) data from the Dyen *et al.* (1997) corpus, cognate classes represented by a single word in a single data language were dropped from the data. It follows that words generating cognate classes in the data are those words with descendants in two or more of the observed languages. Cognate classes which existed in the past, and are present in just one data language are absent from the data. We refer to cognate classes present in the data as data-cognates. We refer in contrast to those cognate classes which existed at some point in the collective history of the languages in this study, but are not represented in the data, as tree-cognates. The class of tree-cognates is infinite in number (at least in our model) since it includes cognates born in the distant past in languages ancestral to Indo-European itself.

A great deal is known about the recent history of the languages in our study. We use the information summarized in the addendum to Gray & Atkinson (2003). Those authors imposed 16 language clades, and corresponding constraints on clade-root times. The clade information adds little to the cognate data which is already very informative on that score. However the clade root age constraints are important, in particular the few upper bounds which are available for clade root times. It is this historical knowledge which sets the clock throughout the tree. For example, the Brythonic clade is made up of two Welsh and three Breton languages and we impose $1450 \leq t_{\texttt{Brythonic}} \leq 1600$ years for the age of the root of this clade. The Italic clade contains Romanian, Vlach, Italian, Ladin, Provencal, French, Walloon, two French creole languages, three Sardinian languages, Spanish, Portuguese, Brazilian and Catalan, and $1700 \leq t_{\texttt{Italic}} \leq 1850$ years.

How do we interpret the data? We assume that language 'speciation' is fundamentally tree-like. We specify a model of cognate birth and death in which any given cognate class is born exactly once in the language phylogeny. It has two parameters, representing the birth rate for cognate classes and the per capita death rate for each word in a cognate class. We do not impose the constraint that all meaning categories of all ancient languages are filled at all times by words from data-cognate classes, since those meaning categories may have been filled by instances of tree-cognates — words belonging to cognate classes which are not represented in the data. Our model predicts that there are about two such tree-cognate classes for each data-cognate class (ignoring tree-cognates on the tree-branch ancestral to Indo-European). Words from tree-cognate classes filled meaning categories not occupied by words belonging to data-cognate classes. We extend our model to account for lateral cognate transfer (word 'borrowing'). This second model has an additional parameter, the per capita borrowing rate (which it is natural to express relative to the per capita death rate).

The models we describe are of a simple but novel kind, and there is therefore some value in our model specification itself. They are the simplest instances of a new class of models for trait-based phylogenetic inference. However, it is very easy to come up with new models of language evolution. It is typically much harder to fit models to data, that is, it is difficult to find model parameters which make the data a relatively likely outcome of the model. We have set up analytical tools and software for model fitting for our cognate birth–death model. We simulate the cognate birth-borrowing-death model as part of our model mis-specification analysis in section 5.

The model which Gray & Atkinson (2003) fit has certain weaknesses. Gray & Atkinson (2003) adapt finite-sites Markov mutation models of the kind proposed by Felsenstein (1981) to fit these data. In the class of models Gray & Atkinson (2003) consider, the number of sites is fixed, and corresponds to the number of distinct cognate classes in the data. In their model, a cognate class can come into existence independently in more than one language. It might be observed that this allows the model to fit lateral word transfer events. However, two parameters are doing the work of three. The two rate parameters for cognate birth and death must be chosen to fit the borrowing rate, the equilibrium probability to find a cognate at any given site, and the cognate loss rate. We accept that some model mis-specification is inevitable for a large and complex data set of the kind Gray & Atkinson (2003) treat. However, we would like to begin with a model which is at least a mathematical description of idealized cognate evolution.

## 3. Data exploration

In this section we explore the data without assuming any particular model. We are looking both for qualitative features of the data which will inform our choice of model, and also for any unusual or striking features of the data which our model must be able to reproduce.

We begin by considering convenient representations of the data. There is a representation of the data as a list of sets. Suppose language $i$ has words in $N_i$ data-cognate classes, so $N_i = \sum_{j=1}^{N} D_{i,j}$. Suppose words from data-cognate class $c$ are found in $M_c$ languages. For cognate $c = 1, 2 \ldots N$, let the set $C_c$ contain a list of the $M_c$ language-labels in which cognate $c$ was present. Let $C = (C_1, C_2 \ldots C_N)$. $C$ and $D$ are equivalent representations of the data.

We now plot histograms for the distributions of $M_c$ ('languages per cognate') and $N_i$ ('cognates per language'). Figure 14.1a shows the distribution of $N_i$ in the data. The distribution is centred around the 200 cognate mark, the number of meaning catagories in the Swadesh (1952) word list. It has a tail skewed toward smaller values. Hittite has relatively few cognates. This need not indicate lost vocabulary. Hittite would share relatively few words with other IE languages (and therefore possess less data-cognates) if it was the first to branch. Figure 14.1b shows the $M_c$-distribution in the data. The number of cognates present in one language and no others is zero. This absence could explain the direction of the skew in the $N_i$-distribution at top. Returning to Figure 14.1b, most cognates are present in just a few languages. However there is a shoulder which extends out to 16 languages and a flat tail running the full extent of the graph, ending with three cognates present in all 87 languages. The shoulder is caused by language selection: the dense sampling of the Germanic and Italic clades gives two large clades of relatively closely related languages. The long tail suggests rate heterogeneity among words. A small fraction of data-cognates are evolving at a distinctly slower pace.

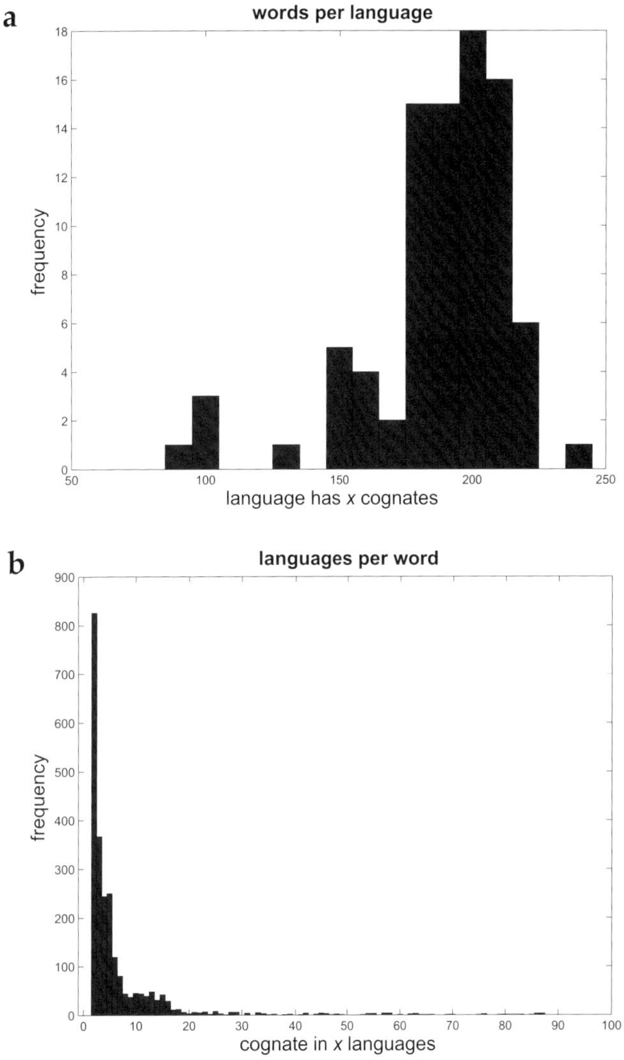


**Figure 14.1.** *(a) The distribution of the number of cognates per language. Each language has around 200 cognates. Hittite has 94 cognates, the least in the data. Nepali has 236, the most. (b) The distribution of the number of languages to which cognates belong. Cognates are typically shared by just a few languages. However, no data-cognates are in just one language, while 11 are in 80 or more of the 87 languages.*

## 4. A cognate-birth and word-death model

In this section we define the basic terms of the inference in the context of a simple model. This is a key section for readers who wish to familiarize themselves with our model assumptions.

We begin by giving a simple summary of the model we will analyze. First of all, a language is summarized by a set of words. The number of words in such a set fluctuates. When a word is born a new cognate class is created. Each word carries a label indicating its cognate class. Indeed, cognate class is the only property our words possess. In the following the term 'language' is used to mean a set of words each of which carries a cognate class label. We suppose a 'raw' cognate-class-creation process generates words (and therefore cognate classes) at a rate $\lambda$ constant in all languages at all times (as we explain below it is necessary to modify this raw process — also, the process acts at constant rate, but the number of word births is a Poisson distributed random variable). Secondly, each language evolves according to a set-branching process to form a language tree. At a branching, the language entering the branch point is copied to yield two identical sets of words. That is, each word in the parent language is copied to give two sibling words, one in each of the offspring languages. Sibling words belong to the same cognate class. Thirdly, each word in each language dies independently of any event occurring to any other word in any languages in the process at constant per capita rate $\mu$. The number of words in a language is randomly variable over time. A cognate class is born exactly once (so that realizations of the process respect the Dollo-parsimony condition). The first word in a cognate class reproduces as the language-set branching process generates new language sets. Its descendants may die in the distinct languages into which they are copied. The full history of a word is a

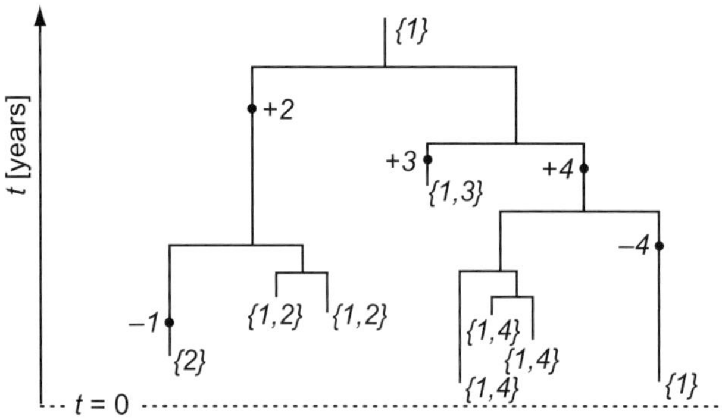


**Figure 14.2.** *An example of the modelled cognate birth word death process. The ancestral language has a single word in cognate class 1. As time advances new cognate class 2 is born. Words in cognate class 2 propagate into three of the observed languages. The word in cognate class 1 in the leftmost language is lost. Cognate class 3 would not be represented in the data as it is present in just one observed language.*

subtree of the language-set tree. A simple illustration is given in Figure 14.2.

The languages at the leaves of the tree in Figure 14.2 would give rise to the data matrix

$$\begin{pmatrix} 0 & 1 & 0 \\ 1 & 1 & 0 \\ 1 & 1 & 0 \\ 1 & 0 & 0 \\ 1 & 0 & 1 \\ 1 & 0 & 1 \\ 1 & 0 & 1 \\ 1 & 0 & 0 \end{pmatrix}.$$

In this matrix the rows correspond to the leaves from left to right. The columns correspond to cognates 1, 2 and 4. Cognate 3 is omitted from the data.

We next consider the details of the data-gathering process itself. Languages extant in some fixed time slice of the evolution are observed. Homologous words are grouped into cognate classes. In the data-gathering process, cognate classes with just one extant modern word are dropped from the data. While every word birth is associated with the birth of a cognate class, just a subset of all word births are associated with the birth of one of the cognate classes observed at the leaves of the tree. As a consequence of this heavy word thinning, a language, ancient or modern, may at any given time possess no data-cognates in any given meaning class. Because data-cognates are selected by the observation process on the basis that they survive to the leaves, the birth times of data-cognates are biased towards the leaves. The birth rate for data-cognates declines towards the root, and goes to zero on the edge leading away from the root into the depths of the past.

*4.1. Model details*

This section may be omitted at a first reading. It reiterates in technical terms the model description given in the previous section.

Let **g** be a binary tree graph with $L + 1$ nodes of edge-degree one and $L - 1$ nodes of degree three. Let $V$ denote the set of language-tree node labels. Let $t_i$ denote the time associated with node $i \in V$. Time is measured in years before the present. Node labels are ordered by increasing age, so that $j > i \Rightarrow t_j \geq t_i$. Let $t = (t_1, t_2, \ldots t_{2L})$. Of the degree one nodes, $L$ are leaf nodes, corresponding to data-languages, and one is ancestral to the root node, labelled $A \in V$ with $A = 2L$ and assigned age $t_A = \infty$. One degree three node is identified as the root node and labelled $R \in V$ with $R = 2L - 1$. Suppose $i, j \in V$ are two nodes of **g** connected by an edge. Let $\langle i, j\rangle$ denote the corresponding edge, ordered so that $i < j$, and $E$ the set of all edges of **g**. Let $E^- = E \setminus \{\langle R, A\rangle\}$. We define $\mathbf{g} = (E, t)$.

If $\theta$ denotes the branching rate for languages, and

$$l(g) = \sum_{(i,j)\in E-} (t_j - t_i)$$

gives the tree length $l(\mathbf{g})$ excluding edge $\langle R, A\rangle$, then $\mathbf{g} \sim f_G(\mathbf{g} \mid \theta)$ with

$$f_G(\mathbf{g}|\theta) = \theta^{L-1} \exp(\theta \ell(\mathbf{g})).$$

Consider data-cognate $c = 1, 2 \ldots N$ born on **g** in edge $\langle i, j\rangle \in E$ at time $\tau$. The edge is identified by the node $i$ at its base. Let $x_c = (\tau, i)$ denote a point on **g**. The set of birth points for all data-cognates is $x = \{x_1, \ldots x_N\}$. Denote by [**g**] the set of all points $(\tau, i)$ in **g**, by $\Omega_g^{(n)}$ the space of all regular subsets of [**g**] containing $n$ distinct points, and let

$$\Omega_g = \bigcup_{n=0}^{\infty} \Omega_g^{(n)}$$

so that $x \in \Omega_g$. Let $Y \in \Omega_g$ be the point process of 'raw' tree-cognate births, including those which fail to survive into two or more leaves. Denote by $\lambda$ the raw cognate birth rate and suppose that each copy of each cognate dies out with instantaneous per capita death rate $\mu$ per year.

Let $f_X(x \mid \mathbf{g}, \mu, \lambda)$ denote the point-process density for data-cognate birth times $x$ on a given tree, for known birth and death rates. The measure $dx = dx_1 \ldots d_{xN}$ of the point process distribution $F(dx \mid \mathbf{g}, \mu, \lambda)$ is a product measure of sets in $\Omega_g$ defined in terms of the element of length $d\tau$ on the random set [**g**]. We take the counting measure over the edges of **g**, including $\langle R, A\rangle$. The point process $X$ generating data-cognates is derived from the 'raw' point process $Y$ of tree-cognate births by thinning. A birth at $y \in [\mathbf{g}]$ is included in the data-cognate process $X$ if it generates descendants in two or more languages. The intensity $\lambda(y)$ of the thinned process is a function of position on the tree. The distribution function for the inhomogeneous point-process of data-cognate births is

$$(4.1)\quad F(dx \mid \mathbf{g}, \mu, \lambda) = f_X(x \mid \mathbf{g}, \mu, \lambda)dx = \exp\left(-\int_{[g]} \lambda(y)dy\right)\prod_{c=1}^{N}\lambda(x_c)dx_c.$$

The number of leaf languages, $M(y)$ say, in which a generic tree-cognate born at $y$ appears is a discrete random variable. If $\Pr(M(y) > 1 \mid y, \mathbf{g}, \mu)$ is the probability that $M$ exceeds one then

$$\lambda(y) = \lambda \times \Pr(M(y) > 1 \mid y, \mathbf{g}, \mu)$$

is the instantaneous birth rate for data-cognates at $y \in [\mathbf{g}]$. The total rate is

$$\int_{[g]} \lambda(y)dy \equiv \sum_{\langle i,j\rangle \in E} \int_{t_i}^{t_j} \lambda \Pr(M(y) > 1 \mid y = (\tau, i), \mathbf{g}, \mu)d\tau.$$

This is evaluated by observing that

$$\Pr(M(y) > 1 \mid y = (\tau, i), \mathbf{g}, \mu) = \Pr(M(y) > 1 \mid y = (t_i, i), \mathbf{g}, \mu)e^{-\mu(\tau - t_i)}$$

so that

$$(4.2)\quad \int_{[g]} \lambda(y)dy = \frac{\lambda}{\mu}\sum_{\langle i,j\rangle \in E(g)} \Pr(M(y) > 1 \mid (t_i, i), \mathbf{g}, \mu)(1 - e^{-\mu(t_j - t_i)}).$$

Notice that the contribution to Equation (4.2) from $\langle R, A\rangle$ is finite, as births in the distant past are killed off by the thinning inherent in the data cognate-collection process.

In order to compute $\int_{[g]} l(y)dy$ in Equation (4.2), we need only evaluate $\Pr(M(y) > 1 \mid y, \mathbf{g}, \mu)$ for $y$ at nodes of **g**, and this can be done using a pruning recursion of the kind described in Felsenstein (1981). Let $u_i^{(0)} = \Pr(M(y) = 0 \mid y = (t_i, i), \mathbf{g}, \mu)$ denote the probability for zero offspring at the leaves descended from node $i$, and let $u_i^{(1)} = \Pr(M(y) = 1 \mid y = (t_i, i), \mathbf{g}, \mu)$ denote the corresponding probability for one offspring. Notice that $u_i^{(0)} = 0$ and $u_i^{(1)} = 1$ if $i$ is a leaf. Since $\Pr(M(y) > 1 \mid y = (t_i, i), \mathbf{g}, \mu) = 1 - u_i^{(0)} - u_i^{(1)}$, the quantity of interest can be computed once we have $u_i^{(0)}$ and $u_i^{(1)}$ at each $i \in V$. Suppose $\langle j, i\rangle$ and $\langle k, i\rangle$ are edges of **g**, so that $j$ and $k$ are child nodes of $i$, and let $p_{i,j} = \exp(-\mu(t_i - t_j))$. The tree recursions

$$u_i^{(0)} = (1 - p_{i,j}(1 - u_j^{(0)})) \times (1 - p_{i,k}(1 - u_k^{(0)})),$$

$$u_i^{(1)} = u_i^{(1)} = (1 - p_{i,j}(1 - u_j^{(0)}))p_{i,k}u_k^{(1)} + (1 - p_{i,k}(1 - u_k^{(0)}))p_{i,j}u_j^{(1)},$$

are easily evaluated.

The model we have described provides a stochastic process realizing histories which satisfy the constraint of Dollo parsimony. Other parsimony schemes, such as Wagner parsimony, might be given a similar treatment. See Hillis *et al.* (1996, chap. 11) for a discussion of these parsimony schemes. Among existing stochastic process models, the infinite-sites model introduced in Watterson (1975) is similar. In that model, mutations generate new segregating sites (sites at which a character substitution has occurred) at constant rate. However word death corresponds to back-mutation at a segregating site. The absence of back mutation in the infinite sites model follows from its definition as a limit model of the finite-sites model, and is fundamental to the infinite-sites model. In the infinite alleles model of Kimura & Crow (1964) the setup is again similar. However new allele types are generated by mutation of existing alleles so the total number of alleles in each individual is constant. The model we have described does not appear to be related to existing models by conditioning or taking limits. We welcome comment on this point.

### *4.2. Borrowing model*

We specify but do not fit a model which accounts for word-transfer events, events in which a word is taken from some language into another. In the model above, cognates generated by the 'raw' tree-cognate process evolve subject to an instantaneous per capita death rate $\mu$ (applied to each copy of the cognate independently at each instant in each language). It is straightforward to allow each copy of the cognate to be subject to instantaneous per capita borrowing at rate $b\mu$, where $b \geq 0$ and we expect values between $b = 0$ and $b = 1$ are of practical interest. When a borrowing event occurs to an instance of a cognate, a target language-set is chosen uniformly at random from the languages existing at the time of the event, and a copy of the cognate is dropped into that set. If the language already possesses the cognate in question, there is no change. Otherwise, the target language adds a cognate in a new class.

*4.3. Inferential framework*

This section may be omitted at a first reading. It describes the statistical techniques used to fit the model to the data. We ask, what choices of ancestral language tree, and what choices of cognate birth and death rates, make the data a likely outcome of the vocabulary evolution model we have specified?

The aim of the inference is to reconstruct the unknown true tree $\mathbf{g}$, and the birth, death and branching rates $\lambda$, $\mu$ and $\theta$ from the cognate data $D$ (or equivalently $C$). Let $h(x, \mathbf{g}, \mu, \lambda, \theta \mid D)$ denote the joint posterior probability density for the unknown data-cognate birth times, $x$, and $\mathbf{g}$, $\lambda$, $\mu$ and $\theta$. The $x$ are to some extent nuisance parameters. We may not be interested in reconstructing these birth times. However, the observation model cannot be defined without them.

The likelihood $P(D \mid \mathbf{g}, \mu, \lambda)$ is given in terms of the point process density $f_X$ for data-cognates and $P(D \mid x, \mathbf{g}, \mu, M(x_c) > 1)$ (the probability to realize data $D$ given the tree, the data-cognate birth times, the death rate, and the requirement that each realized point $x_c$ generates two or more data-cognates) by

$$P(D \mid \mathbf{g}, \mu, \lambda) = \int_{\Omega_{\mathbf{g}}} P(D \mid x, \mathbf{g}, \mu, M(x_c) > 1) f_X(x \mid \mathbf{g}, \mu, \lambda)dx.$$

The evolution of cognate $c$ into the languages $C_c$ is conditionally independent of the evolution of all other cognates given $x_c$, $\mathbf{g}$ and $\mu$, hence

$$P(D|x, \mathbf{g}, \mu, M(x_c) > 1) = \prod_{c=1}^{N} P(C_c|x_c, \mathbf{g}, \mu, M(x_c) > 1).$$

It is not feasible to carry out Monte-Carlo inference for all 2398 data-cognate birth times $x_c$, $c = 1, 2, \ldots, N$. However it is feasible to integrate $x$ explicitly, by a combination of hand integration and a recursion like the one used to evaluate Equation (4.2). We have

$$h(\mathbf{g}, \mu, \lambda, \theta|D) \propto f_G(\mathbf{g}|\theta)p(\mu, \lambda, \theta)$$

$$\int_{\Omega_{\mathbf{g}}} P(D \mid x, \mathbf{g}, \mu, M(x_c) > 1) f_X(x \mid \mathbf{g}, \mu, \lambda)dx$$

$$= \frac{\lambda^N}{N!} \exp\left( \int_{[\mathbf{g}]} \lambda(y)dy \right) f_G(\mathbf{g}|\theta)p(\mu, \lambda, \theta) \times$$

$$\text{(4.3)} \quad \prod_{c=1}^{N} \int_{[\mathbf{g}]} P(C_c|x_c, \mathbf{g}, \mu, M(x_c) > 1) \Pr(M(x_c) > 1|x_c, \mathbf{g}, \mu)dx_c.$$

When we carry out MCMC for $h$, we must evaluate the right-hand side of Equation (4.3) thousands or even millions of times. The difficulty is that we must compute the probability $P(C_c \mid x_c, \mathbf{g}, \mu, M(x_c) > 1)$ to generate the cognate distribution pattern $C_c$ given cognate $c$ was born at $x_c \in [\mathbf{g}]$ and given (this is the difficult part) that the cognate survived into two or more languages. However the inconvenient condition cancels out of the expression because

$$P(C_c \mid x_c, \mathbf{g}, \mu) = P(C_c \mid x_c, \mathbf{g}, \mu, M(x_c) > 1) \Pr(M(x_s) > 1 \mid x_c, \mathbf{g}, \mu),$$

(using the fact that the outcome $\{C_c, M(x_c) > 1\}$ is trivially equivalent to the outcome $\{C_c\}$ whenever $C_c$ has at least two members, which it has, precisely because each data-cognate is present in at least two languages). We have only to calculate the probability to realize $C_c$ given a birth in the unconditioned 'raw' tree-cognate process $Y$, at $x_c$, rather than a birth in $X$, the data-cognate process.

We have now to evaluate $\int_{[\mathbf{g}]} P(C_c \mid x_c, \mathbf{g}, \mu)dx_c$ for each $c = 1, 2, \ldots, N$. For any two vertices $i, k \in V$ define the path $\mathrm{Path}(i, k)$ connecting $i$ and $k$ on $\mathbf{g}$ as the sequence of $p$ edges

$$\mathrm{Path}(i, k) = (\langle i, j_1 \rangle, \langle j_1, j_2 \rangle, \ldots \langle j_{p-2}, j_{p-1} \rangle \langle j_{p-1}, k \rangle)$$

running from $i$ to $k$ in $\mathbf{g}$ without backtracking. Recall that $A \in V$ is the node above the root, located in the distant past. For cognate $c = 1, 2, \ldots, N$ let

$$E^{(c)} = \bigcap_{i \in C_c} \mathrm{Path}(i, A)$$

denote the 'covering' edge set for cognate $c$, that is, $E^{(c)}$ is the set of edges ancestral to every language-leaf-node containing the $c$'th cognate. Clearly $P(C_c \mid x_c, \mathbf{g}, \mu) = 0$ whenever $x_c$ is not on an edge in $E^{(c)}$ so

$$\int_{[\mathbf{g}]} P(C_c \mid x_c, \mathbf{g}, \mu)dx_c = \sum_{\langle i,j \rangle \in E^{(c)}} \int_{t_i}^{t_j} P(C_c|x_c, \mathbf{g}, \mu)dx_c.$$

The integral $\int_{t_i}^{t_j} \Pr(C_c|x_c, \mathbf{g}, \mu)dx_c$ is evaluated in much the same way as the total rate (Equation(4.2)). We omit the details. Explicitly, for $h$,

$$h(\mathbf{g}, \mu, \lambda, \theta|D) \propto \left(\frac{\lambda}{\mu}\right)^N f_G(\mathbf{g}|\theta)p(\mu, \lambda, \theta) \times$$

$$\exp\left( -\frac{\lambda}{\mu} \sum_{\langle i,j \rangle \in E} \Pr(M(y) > 1|(t_i, i), \mathbf{g}, \mu)\left(1 - e^{-\mu(t_j - t_i)}\right) \right)$$

$$\text{(4.4)} \quad \times \prod_{c=1}^{N} \left( \sum_{\langle i,j \rangle \in E^{(c)}} P(C_c|(t_i, i), \mathbf{g}, \mu)\left(1 - e^{-\mu(t_j - t_i)}\right) \right)$$

with $\Pr(M(y) > 1 \mid (t_i, i), \mathbf{g}, \mu)$ and $P(C_c \mid (t_i, i), \mathbf{g}, \mu)$ given by three recursions.

*4.4. Priors*

In this section we summarize our prior knowledge of the ancestry of the languages in the data. Besides the historical constraints discussed in section 2 little is known, so we need to make a mathematical representation of a state ignorance about ancestry.

The space $\Gamma$ of trees $\mathbf{g}$ is restricted to those trees which satisfy the clade constraints discussed in section 2 and detailed in Gray & Atkinson (2003). The time-scale would be unresolved without this data. This is apparent in the expression for $h$ we have written above. The rate parameters appear only in dimensionless multiples $\lambda/\mu$, $\theta t_i$ and $\mu t_i$ for $t_i$ a tree node (language branching) time.

For simple $\theta$ and $\lambda$ priors, we can integrate $\lambda$ and $\theta$ out of the formulae above. We are left with a posterior density $h = h(\mathbf{g}, \mu \mid D)$. We imposed Jeffreys's priors $p(\mu, \lambda, \theta) = (\mu\lambda\theta)^{-1}$, a choice which is non-informative with respect to the time scale of $\mathbf{g}$. The bulk of our simulations were carried out with a tree prior which was not the exponential branching process prior $f_G(\mathbf{g} \mid \theta)$ described above, but a distribution in which the root time is uniformly distributed between 0 and a conservative maximum $T_{\max}$, and all trees with a given root time have equal prior probability density. The expression is

$$f_G(\mathbf{g}|T_{\max}) \propto \mathrm{I}_{0 \le t_R \le T_{\max}}\, t_R^{-L+2},$$

with $\mathrm{I}_{0 \le t_R \le T_{\max}}$ the indicator function for $0 \le t_R \le T_{\max}$. We used $T_{\max} = 16{,}000$ years before the present, which is intended to be uncontroversial. This prior is uninformative with respect the root time, which is the sensitive statistic. In the presence of clade constraints it is necessary to revise the formula for $f_G$ above to get uniform marginal prior $t_R$, and carry out prior simulations to check imposed priors are non-informative with respect to the hypotheses of scientific interest.

*4.5. Markov chain Monte Carlo*

This section may be omitted at a first reading. We describe the computer algorithm we designed and implemented in order to quantify uncertainty in our reconstruction of language ancestry. Of course, if the model assumptions we set out in section 4.1 are wrong, this measure of confidence may be quite unreliable.

We designed our own Markov chain Monte Carlo simulation algorithms and implemented them ourselves in the MatLab programming language. We summarize $h(\mathbf{g}, \mu \mid D)$ using samples

$$(\mathbf{g}^{(s)}, \mu^{(s)}) \sim h,\ s = 1, 2 \ldots S.$$

Using these samples we can quantify support from the data and prior for any particular hypothesis. For example the probability that the unknown true root time (branching of Indo-European) was smaller than some time $T$ is estimated directly from the proportion of sampled $\mathbf{g}^{(s)}$ in which $t_R^{(s)} < T$. These samples are drawn via MCMC. The software used to carry out these simulations is available from the authors. A user-friendly interface has been implemented by David Welch of Auckland University and a user manual, Nicholls & Welch (2004), is in preparation. MCMC for simulation over a space of trees is now fairly standard. Our MCMC updates are for the most part identical to those of Drummond *et al.* (2002). The main novelty in our implementation is in the rapid evaluation of $h$ itself, using Equation (4.4) and careful implementation of the defining recursions. Our code has been tested on a number of control problems. One non-trivial test, for the likelihood of a point process density, is the requirement that the likelihood function should sum to one over the data. We fix a tree, and fix birth and death rates, then enumerate all possible data sets with $N = 0, 1, 2, \ldots$ cognates from the empty data set with $N = 0$ up. For each data set we compute $P(D \mid \mathbf{g}, \mu, \lambda)$. When $\lambda/\mu$ is small (around one or smaller) and the number of leaves is small (up to five), the likelihood for data sets at $N > 7$ is tiny, and we find that $\sum_D P(D \mid \mathbf{g}, \mu, \lambda)$ converges to one rapidly with $N$ increasing. We checked we could reconstruct synthetic data also. The MCMC convergence analysis depended principally on the visual inspection of graphical output.

## 5. Sample results

In this section we present the results we obtained when we fit the model of section 4.1 to the data of Gray & Atkinson (2003). We then make two kinds of model mis-specification checks. We check that subsets of the data are in agreement with each other and with the full data set. We simulate synthetic data from a model with borrowing and check that the presence of such borrowing does not bias the inference.

We begin by presenting results from a straightforward analysis of the data, assuming constant death-rate at all times and in all languages and no borrowing. A tree sampled from the posterior is presented in Figure 14.3. It must be understood that no one tree can summarize the information available in such a complex data set, in particular the uncertainty. The figure is included simply for illustration, to give readers a feeling for the kind of analysis which was undertaken. We would like to move people away from summarizing a complex data set like Dyen *et al.* (1997) with a consensus tree with bootstrap confidence labels. The

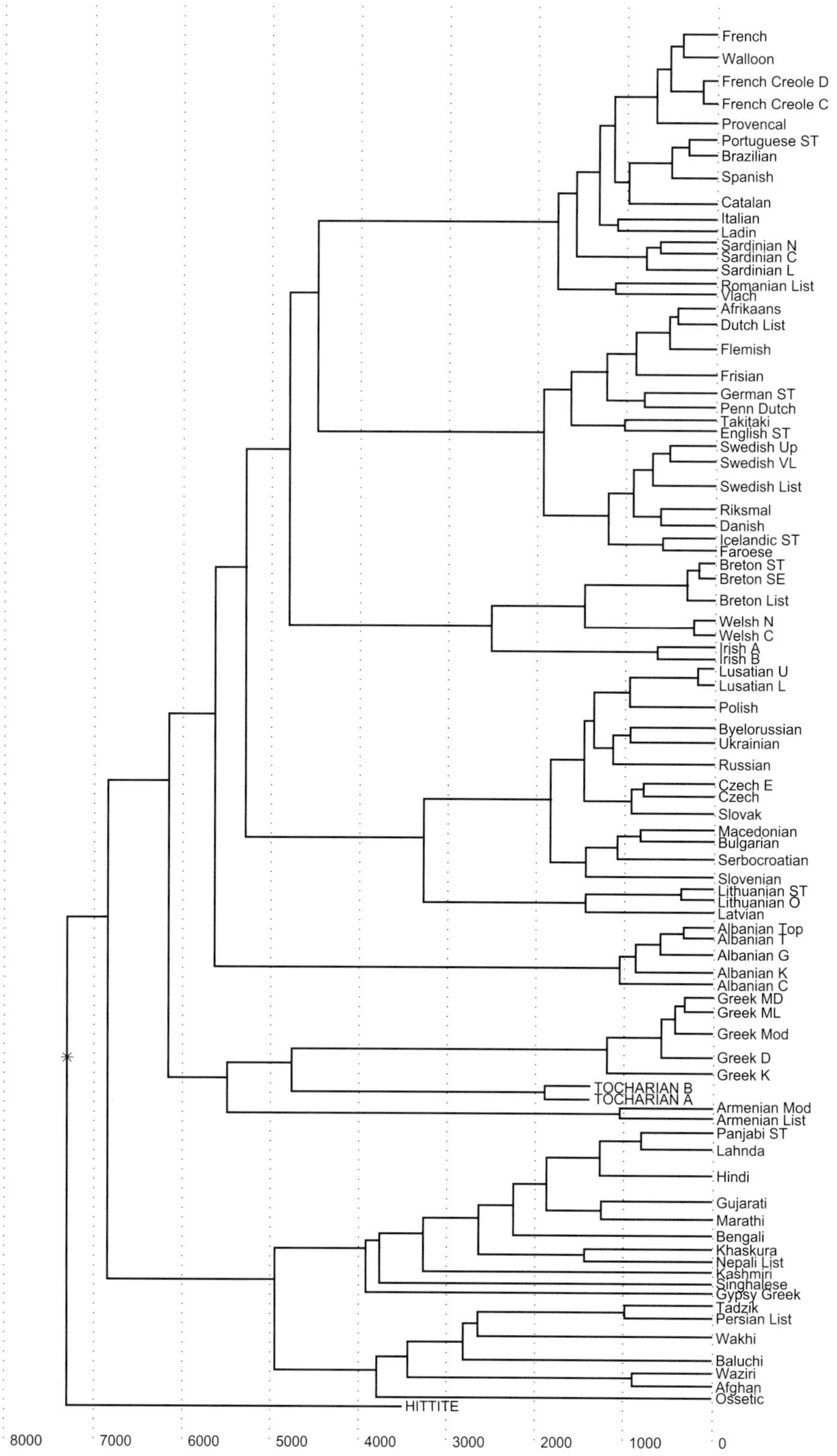


**Figure 14.3.** *One Indo-European language tree sampled from the posterior distribution of the data. The tree was generated using a prior with a uniform marginal tree root time, and is otherwise uniform over trees. It must be understood that no one tree can summarize the information available in the Dyen* et al. *(1997) data. The tree above does not constitute our 'result'.*

confidence interval for the root time was [6880, 8170] years ago at $3\sigma$ (in a normal approximation to the distribution, which was reasonable).

We would like to know how important model misspecification is for these data. We ask the following questions. To what extent is rate heterogeneity from one language group to another important? How about rate heterogeneity from one word to another? Is word borrowing important? In order to answer the first question we estimate the death-rate parameter $\mu$ from each of the constrained clades independently. The two-taxon Tocharian clade is omitted from this analysis. When cognates present in just one language are removed, a two-taxon clade with root time $t$ provides just a single integer datum, the number, $n$ say, of shared cognates. The likelihood for $\mu$ and $\lambda$ in this case is the probability to draw $n$ from a Poisson distribution with mean $(\lambda/\mu)\exp(-2\mu t)$. This likelihood has its maximum on a ridge $\lambda^* = n\mu^* \exp(\mu^* t)$. The confidence intervals for $\mu$ and $\lambda$ under a flat prior are both $(0,\infty)$. Even weak prior knowledge dominates the inference. Results for clades of size three and larger are presented in Table 14.1.

Root-time estimates are insensitive to mild rate heterogeneity (30 per cent in one of 6 clades) of the kind displayed in Table 14.1. It is possible that more evidence for rate heterogeneity would appear if constraints were available for the Indo-Persian languages. These languages are sampled at a lower density than the western European languages. If there is cladogenic loss of words (causing a spike in the

**Table 14.1.** *The per capita death rate (deaths per year per word), estimated from each of the age constrained clades in turn. There is rate constancy, with the exception of the Brythonic clade. The convention 'Italic 0.000268(11)' reports an Italic word death rate estimated at $\hat{\mu}$ = 0.000268 with standard error $\hat{\sigma}_{\hat{\mu}}$ = 0.000011. *We are grateful for input at the meeting enabling us to fix an extra rate. We have not otherwise incorporated that information in the analysis presented in this paper.*

| Clade | $\hat{\mu}$ | std($\hat{\mu}$) |
|---|---|---|
| Italic | 0.000268 | (11) |
| Iberian-French | 0.000224 | (21) |
| Germanic | 0.000246 | (13) |
| Balto-Slav | 0.000260 | (36) |
| Brythonic | 0.000176 | (16) |
| Celtic | 0.000299* | (24) |

**Table 14.2.** *Effect of borrowing on reliability of root-time estimates using synthetic data simulated on a tree like that in Figure 14.3 with true root time 6900 years ago.*

| $b$ | $\hat{t}_R$ | $\hat{\sigma}_{t_R}$ |
|---|---|---|
| 0 | 6720 | 250 |
| 0.1 | 6925 | 225 |
| 0.2 | 6282 | 184 |

rate of word loss at branching events associated for example with the founder effect) in this data then more rapidly branching languages should show more rapid evolution.

There is some evidence for rate heterogeneity from one word to another. In Figure 14.4 we simulate synthetic data from the model on a typical tree drawn from the posterior, and plot a histogram showing the distribution of $M_c$, the number of languages containing a given synthetic data-cognate. Compare this graph with Figure 14.1b. The synthetic data does not typically include values of $M_c$ close to $L$. In other respects the distribution mimics that of the real data reasonably well. Most cognates are in just a few languages, the shoulder extending to 16 cognates is visible and there is a tail of cognates present in many languages. However, the synthetic data has no cognates present in more than about half the 87 languages, in contrast to the real data.

In order to study the effect of borrowing, we simulate synthetic data from our model with borrowing, the birth-borrow-death model, and then ask, what do we estimate when we fit the model without borrowing, the birth-death model? We find that borrowing of the kind described in our model causes us to underestimate the root age. We simulated data with no borrowing, ($b$ = 0) and mild borrowing ($b$ = 0.1 and

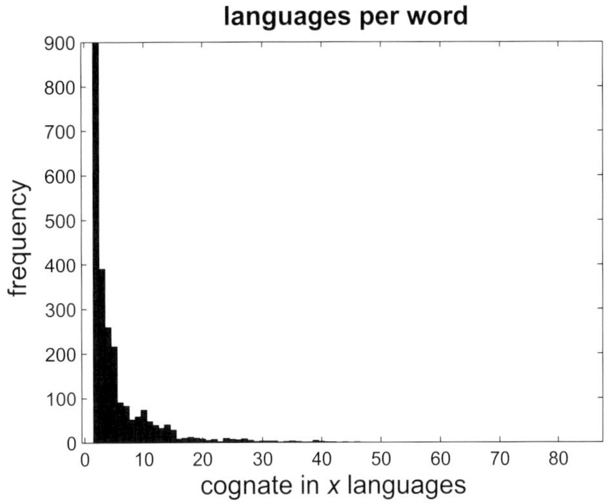


**Figure 14.4.** *The distribution of the number of languages* $M_c$ *which possess a given synthetic data-cognate. Data simulated on tree sampled from posterior. Compare Figure 14.1.*

$b$ = 0.2) on a tree drawn from the posterior distribution (like the tree in Fig. 14.3) which happened to have true root age 6900 years ago. We wish to explain what we mean by mild borrowing. In the birth-borrow-death model, $b$ is the mean number of times an instance of any particular cognate evolving in a given language, is copied into other languages before it dies in the given language. For small $b$ this is roughly the probability a cognate is borrowed before it dies. Results are shown in Table 14.2. When there is no borrowing in the synthetic data, and we simulate and fit the same model, the posterior distribution of the root time covers the true root time. The same applies if there is a little ($b$ = 0.1) borrowing. At $b$ = 0.2 the borrowing is sufficiently strong to distort the estimate. The estimated root age is too low. The direction of the bias may depend on the details of the borrowing model, see section 4.2 and the comments associated with Figure 14.5.

Estimates are robust to some model mis-specification. Rates are estimated from the same data we are extrapolating. If the nature of the model mis-specification is the same in both the later and earlier time intervals then rate estimates from the later interval can correctly predict time intervals in the early period. This observation applies in particular to mild rate heterogeneity from one cognate to another, if this difference is constant across time and language, and to borrowing. Rate estimates distorted to fit the language evolution where it is given can be good rate estimates for prediction. Mild model mis-specification does not typically cause catastrophic loss of predictive power. Evidence for this is seen in analysis of subsets of languages. Analyzed languages are selected so that the clade time

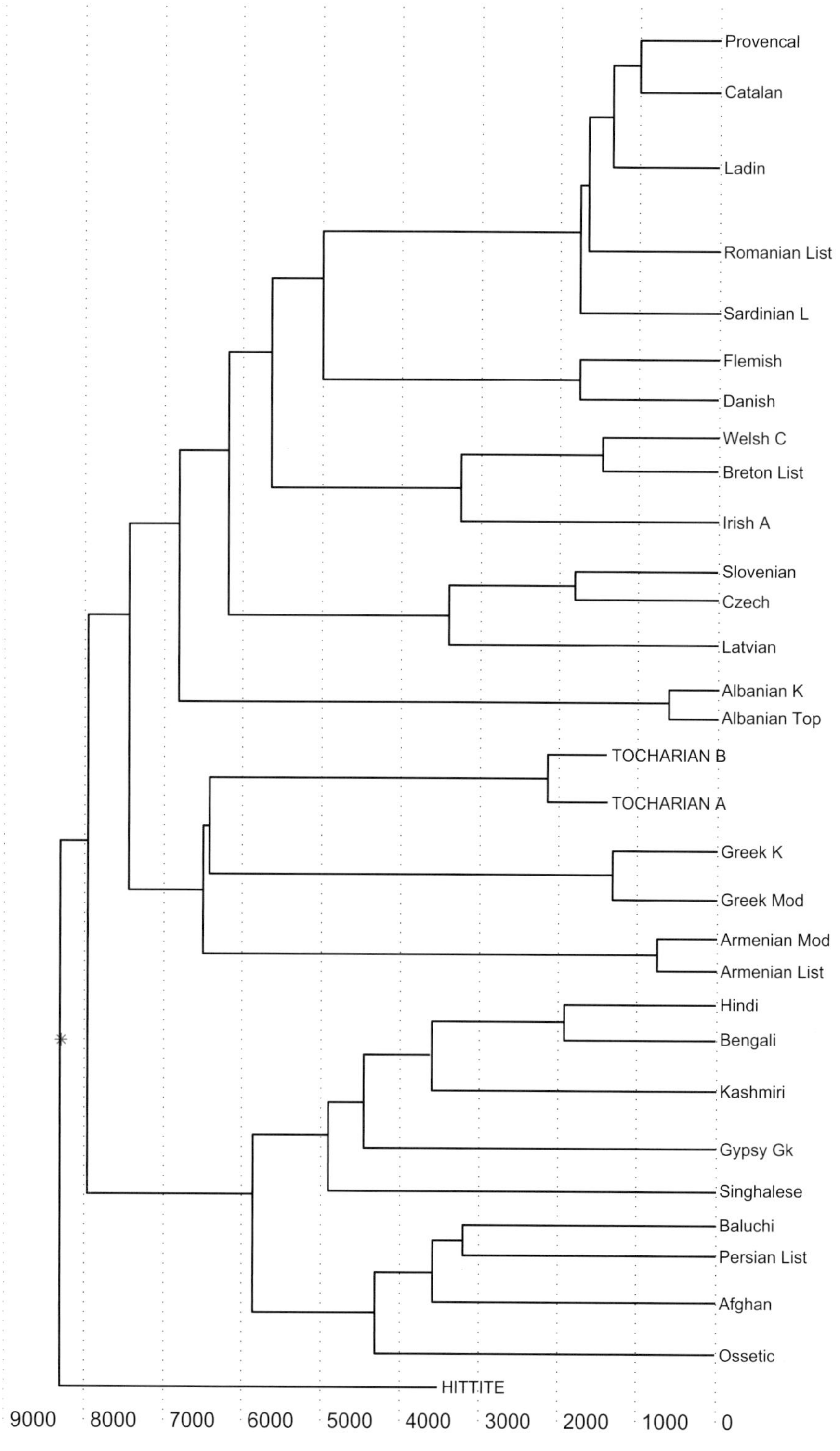


**Figure 14.5.** *One language tree sampled from the posterior distribution of a subsample of 31 languages from the 87 in the data is shown. The analysis of a subset of languages gave results (not shown) consistent with those on the full data set. It must be understood that no one tree can summarize the information available in the Dyen* et al. *(1997) data. The tree above does not constitute our 'result'.*

constraints remain appropriate. When we carry out this exercise on synthetic data we find, as we expect, that we recover similar results to those obtained on the full set of languages, but with greater uncertainty. When we make the same study for the real Indo-European data set we see a similar picture. A tree sampled from the posterior of such a reduced run is shown in Figure 14.5. Of the 87 languages in the full data set, 31 are selected for this analysis.

The new range is [6970, 9140] at $3\sigma$, double the interval obtained on the full data ([6880, 8170]) but in good agreement. However the deathrate parameter $\mu$ is in the range [0.00017, 0.00024] for the reduced data but [0.00024, 0.00028] for the full data, a conflict. The impact of borrowing is weakened by sub-selection of languages (borrowing from words which are no longer in the analysis is not a model violation, it is subsumed in the birth rate $\lambda$). However the estimated root time is insensitive to the reduced model mis-specification as we move from the full to the small data set, because the rate parameters must adjust to accommodate the new picture in the part of the tree where the language evolution is given.

## 6. Conclusions

We have described a stochastic generalization of Dollo parsimony. Although the model is a simple and natural model for cognate data, no model of this type has been considered in the past. Because of the technical difficulty of fitting models, authors have tended to avoid *ab initio* model specification and fitting.

We have taken into account in our analysis the fact that cognates present in zero or just one of the languages in the data are dropped from the analysis. We have found, in simulation studies which we do not report, that substantial biases can result if this property of the observation process is ignored.

We have summarized our model mis-specification analysis. We find evidence for mild model violation. We have presented evidence that our estimates are robust to violations of the type and degree detected. Our somewhat simplified analysis does tend to support the results presented in Gray & Atkinson (2003).

## Acknowledgements

We thank Alexei Drummond for his comments on the manuscript. The authors acknowledge advice and assistance from Quentin Atkinson and David Welch of the University of Auckland.

## References

Drummond, A.J., G.K. Nicholls, A.G. Rodrigo & W. Solomon, 2002. Estimating mutation parameters, population history and genealogy simultaneously from temporally spaced sequence data. *Genetics* 161, 1307–20.

Dyen, I., J. Kruskal & P. Black, 1997. FILE IE-DATA1, Available at http://www.ntu.edu.au/education/langs/ielex/IE-DATA1.

Felsenstein, J., 1981. Evolutionary trees from DNA sequences: a maximum likelihood approach. *Journal of Molecular Evolution* 17, 368–76.

Gray, R. & Q. Atkinson, 2003. Language-tree divergence times support the Anatolian theory of Indo-European origin. *Nature* 426, 435–9.

Hillis, D., C. Moritz & B. Mable, 1996. *Molecular Systematics.* 2nd edition. Sunderland (MA): Sinauer Associates.

Kimura, M. & J. Crow, 1964. The number of alleles that can be maintained in a finite population. *Genetics* 49, 725–38.

Nicholls, G. & D. Welch, 2004. Software manual for MCMC fitting a stochastic Dollo-model to binary character data.

Swadesh, M., 1952. Lexico-statistic dating of prehistoric ethnic contacts. *Proceedings of the American Philosophical Society* 96, 453–63.

Watterson, G., 1975. On the number of segregating sites in genetical models without recombination. *Theoretical Population Biology* 7, 256–76.

# Chapter 15

# Estimating Rates of Lexical Replacement on Phylogenetic Trees of Languages

Mark Pagel & Andrew Meade

Phylogenetic trees of human languages derived from word lists make it possible to study features of word or language evolution, just as phylogenetic trees of species are used to study aspects of biological trait evolution and adaptation. Words or vocabulary, grammar and syntax are conspicuous and fundamental traits of languages that can be studied phylogenetically. Understanding their rates of evolution and the causes of their diversification across languages has applied and theoretical interest.

Words are, in most cases, an arbitrary sound corresponding to a meaning. At a fundamental level, a theory of linguistic diversity would attempt to explain why some meanings are represented across languages by more different words than others. Is the diversity of words related to the frequency of usage, to phonological features, to some measure of cultural 'importance', to ecological factors, or to some deeper cognitive aspect of the concept itself? What is the upper limit to the rate at which lexical items are replaced for a given meaning? In a practical setting, the rate of lexical replacement determines a meaning's value for reconstructing relationships among languages; meanings for which the rate of lexical replacement is low are potentially useful for identifying very distant relationships.

In this chapter we use statistical models of word evolution in combination with linguistic phylogenies, to estimate rates of lexical replacement for 200 different meanings in the Indo-European and Bantu language families. Our chapter extends Kruskal *et al.*'s (1971) and Pagel's (2000a,b) investigations of rates of lexical evolution. In those studies, replacement rates were inferred from a mathematical model describing the relationship between linguistic divergence and time, and without knowledge of the phylogenetic relationships among the languages. Here we estimate lexical replacement rates directly by studying how words evolve along the branches of phylogenetic trees. By investigating rates of evolution in two language families, we can separate the influence of the meaning or concept on the rate of lexical evolution, from its actual spoken representation (the word).

**Phylogenetic inference with linguistic data**

To reconstruct linguistic phylogenetic trees, and to investigate questions of lexical evolution, we use Swadesh's (1952) fundamental vocabulary word list compiled for two language families (Ruhlen 1994): 87 languages from the Indo-European family (Kruskal *et al.* 1971; Atkinson & Gray, Chapter 8 this volume), and 95 languages from the Bantu language family (Holden 2002; Chapter 2 this volume). We are grateful to Russell Gray for making available his vocabulary data set for the Indo-European languages and to Clare Holden for allowing us to use her vocabulary data for the Bantu languages.

A data set of meanings for use in linguistic phylogenetic inference can be arrayed in an $n$ ] $m$ matrix such as in **M**:

$$\begin{array}{ccc} & & \text{meanings} \\ \mathbf{M} = & \begin{matrix} \text{language } 1 \\ \text{language } 2 \\ \cdot \\ \cdot \\ \text{language } n \end{matrix} & \begin{pmatrix} 1 & 1 & 0 & . & 0 \\ 1 & 0 & 1 & . & 0 \\ . & . & . & . & . \\ . & . & . & . & . \\ 0 & 2 & 2 & . & 0 \end{pmatrix} \end{array}$$

Each element of the matrix assigns a numerical code to the word in $n^{th}$ language that conveys the meaning in its column. Any given pair of languages may use cognate or non-cognate words to describe the same meaning. Two words are cognate if they are judged to have arisen from a common ancestral word. 'Father' and 'pater' are cognates whereas the English 'cheese' and the French 'fromage' are not. The analogous concept in biology is homology: two genes are homologous if they evolved from a common ancestral gene. Cognate words are assigned the same numerical code. The number of 'states' for a given linguistic meaning corresponds to the number of distinct cognate sets observed in a collection of languages. For example, the second meaning in **M** above has three different forms, whereas a single cognate set describes the $m^{\text{th}}$ meaning.

Statistical inference of phylogeny is based upon calculating the probability of observing the data in **M**, given the phylogenetic tree and a model of word evolution. The model of word evolution describes how various states (words) change over time within a specified meaning. For any given meaning with $k$ states or cognate sets, we can write a matrix **Q** describing these possible transitions:

$$\mathbf{Q} = \begin{array}{c} \\ 0 \\ 1 \\ . \\ . \\ k \end{array} \begin{array}{c} \begin{array}{cccccc} 0 & 1 & . & . & . & k \end{array} \\ \begin{pmatrix} - & q_{01} & \cdot & \cdot & q_{0k} \\ q_{10} & - & \cdot & \cdot & q_{1k} \\ \cdot & \cdot & \cdot & \cdot & \cdot \\ \cdot & \cdot & \cdot & \cdot & \cdot \\ q_{k0} & q_{k1} & \cdot & \cdot & - \end{pmatrix} \end{array}$$

Each $q_{ij}$ term in this matrix describes the instantaneous rate of change from state $i$ to state $j$ over short interval $dt$. These are the rates of lexical replacement. The main diagonal elements are always set equal to minus the sum of the remaining elements in the row, such that the elements in each row always sum to 0.0. Given this representation of lexical evolution, the probability of observing over longer time interval $t$, each of the changes implied in **Q**, is found by exponentiating the **Q** matrix: $\mathbf{P}(t) = e^{\mathbf{Q}t}$, where **P** is a matrix of the same order as **Q**.

The model we use assumes that each state can change to each other state, and there is no restriction on the number of times a given state (cognate set) arises in the tree. In fact, it is unlikely that the same word ever arises twice independently in different groups. On the other hand, words may be borrowed from other languages giving the appearance of having arisen more than once, and this is allowed under the model we use. Geoff Nicholls (Chapter 14 this volume) reports a model of word evolution that restricts each word to arise just once on the tree.

The likelihood that the set of meanings in **M** evolved on a given phylogenetic tree $T$, can be written as $P(\mathbf{M} \mid \mathbf{Q}, T)$ and is calculated as in Felsenstein (1981). The likelihood of the data in **M** is found as the product over meanings of the individual likelihoods of each meaning, reflecting our assumption that meanings are independent of one another:

$$P(\mathbf{M} \mid \mathbf{Q}, T) = \prod_i P(\mathbf{M}_i \mid \mathbf{Q}, T).$$

This is often called the likelihood of the data, and can be found by assigning numerical values to the $q_{ij}$. We allowed the rate of evolution to vary among the meanings in **M** according to a gamma probability distribution. We implemented gamma-rate heterogeneity in the standard way (Yang 1994).

The maximum likelihood approach to inferring phylogenetic trees tries out combinations of the rate parameters, and different tree topologies and branch lengths, until the likelihood cannot be improved. The branch lengths of this tree record the expected numbers of transitions per meaning in that branch and are estimated from the data as part of the phylogenetic inference step; longer branches indicate greater divergence between two languages. Pagel (2000a) describes models of language evolution in more detail, and Holden (Chapter 2 this volume), Pagel and Meade (this chapter) and Gray & Atkinson (2003; Chapter 8 this volume) use them to infer linguistic phylogenies of the Bantu and Indo-Europeans, respectively.

*Transforming linguistic data to a common rate matrix*

Word lists as data for inferring phylogenies differ in two fundamental respects from gene-sequence data. In gene sequences the same four different states (the nucleotides *A*, *C*, *G*, and *T*) are available to each site. A given meaning in a word list can adopt between 1 and $k$ different states (see definition of **M** above), and these different states are not comparable across sites; for example, two different meanings may each be represented by four different cognate sets, but these four 'states' are not comparable between the two meanings.

The word-list data can be transformed into a series of binary vectors to form a common basis across meanings. Each vector assigns a '1' to all the languages that share a given cognate word for that meaning, and a '0' to the rest. A meaning with $k$ different cognate sets is defined by $k$ binary vectors; each one providing a means to estimate the single rate of evolution between the cognate and collectively non-cognate forms.

## Bayesian inference of phylogenetic trees

The statistical approach in the previous section can be used to calculate the likelihood of the data for any given tree. The maximum-likelihood tree is the single tree that makes the observed data most probable, given the model of evolution. However, the maximum-likelihood tree ignores the many other trees that can arise under the model of evolution.

Bayesian methods offer a formal statistical procedure for calculating what is known as the posterior-probability distribution of phylogenetic trees. Bayesian methods begin with prior beliefs and then modify those beliefs on the basis of data to produce posterior beliefs. Given a set of meanings such as in **M**, Bayes' rule as applied to phylogenetic inference states that the posterior probability of tree $T_i$ is

$$p(T_i \mid \mathbf{M}) = \frac{p(\mathbf{M} \mid T_i)p(T_i)}{\sum_T p(\mathbf{M} \mid T_i)p(T_i)}, \qquad (1)$$

where $p(T_i \mid \mathbf{M})$ is the probability of tree $T_i$ given the sequence data **M**, $p(\mathbf{M} \mid T_i)$ is the probability or likelihood of the data given tree $T_i$ and $p(T_i)$ is the prior probability of $T_i$. The denominator sums the probabilities over all possible trees. Thus, the posterior probability of a tree is just that tree's portion of the total probability accounted for by all trees, weighted by the tree's prior probability. Finding $p(T_i \mid \mathbf{M})$ for a large number of different trees makes it possible to define the (posterior) probability distribution of phylogenetic trees.

Equation 1 usefully defines the probability of any given tree but can be difficult to put into practice. The number of possible different unrooted topologies for $n$ languages is $(2n-5)!/(2^{n-3}(n-3)!)$ meaning that the summation in the denominator is over a large number of topologies for all but the smallest data sets. In turn, for each of these possible topologies the quantity $p(\mathbf{M} \mid T_i)$ must be integrated over all possible values of the lengths of the branches of the phylogenetic tree and over the parameters of the model of evolution that describes the word data.

Letting **t** be the branch lengths of the tree and **Q** the parameters of the model of word evolution, then

$$p(\mathbf{M} \mid T_i) = \int_{\mathbf{t}} \int_{\mathbf{Q}} p(\mathbf{M} \mid T_i, \mathbf{t}, \mathbf{Q}) p(\mathbf{t}) p(\mathbf{Q}) d\mathbf{t} d\mathbf{Q}, \qquad (2)$$

where $p(\mathbf{t})$ and $p(\mathbf{Q})$ are the prior probabilities of the branch lengths and the parameters of the model.

### Markov chain Monte Carlo

Markov chain Monte Carlo (MCMC) methods (e.g. Geyer 1992; Gilks *et al.* 1996) as applied to phylogenetic inference provide a computationally efficient way to estimate the posterior probability distribution of trees. A Markov chain is a mathematical device that jumps from one state to another. It has the property that the probability of jumping to a new state, is a function only of the current state, and not of states that existed prior to the current state. In a phylogenetic context, a Markov chain is constructed, the states of which are different phylogenetic trees (Rannala & Yang 1996; Wilson & Balding 1998; Larget & Simon 1999; Lutzoni *et al.* 2001; Pagel & Lutzoni 2002). At each step in the chain a new tree is proposed by altering the topology, or by changing branch lengths, or the parameters of the model of word evolution. Successive trees are sampled by the Metropolis-Hastings algorithm (Metropolis *et al.* 1953; Hastings 1970). A newly proposed tree that improves upon the previous tree in the chain is always accepted (sampled), otherwise it is accepted with probability proportional to the ratio of its likelihood to that of the previous tree in the chain.

If such a Markov chain is allowed to run long enough, it reaches what is known as its stationary distribution. At stationarity, a properly constructed chain 'wanders' through the universe of trees, visiting better and worse trees, rather than inexorably moving towards 'better' trees, as an optimizing approach would do. The chain has the property of visiting trees in proportion to their frequency of occurrence in the universe of trees, allowing it to produce a random sample of trees.

By allowing the chain to run for a very long time — perhaps hundreds of thousands or millions of trees, the continuously varying posterior distribution of trees can be approximated to whatever degree of precision is desired. The stationary distribution simultaneously samples not only the posterior distribution of trees, but also the posterior distributions of the branch lengths and the parameters of the model of word evolution.

We applied the MCMC approach to the binary-transformed data, by using a model of lexical evolution (**Q**, as defined above) that allowed for just two states: presence of a particular cognate and its absence. Two problems may arise from using the binary-coded data in place of the 'multistate' data. One is that binary coding returns shorter total inferred tree lengths than the untransformed or multistate data. This is because binary coding implies fewer transitions; each binary code represents a given word versus all the rest. By comparison, a full multistate model calculates transition rates among all possible pairs of states (words), even though few of these possible transitions are actually observed in the data. It can be shown that a tree derived from characters that can take $k$ states, is expected to be longer by a constant of proportionality than a tree based on binary coding of the same data (Appendix A). Our (unpublished) investigations indicate that, apart from being shorter, binary and multistate coded trees have the same or similar topology.

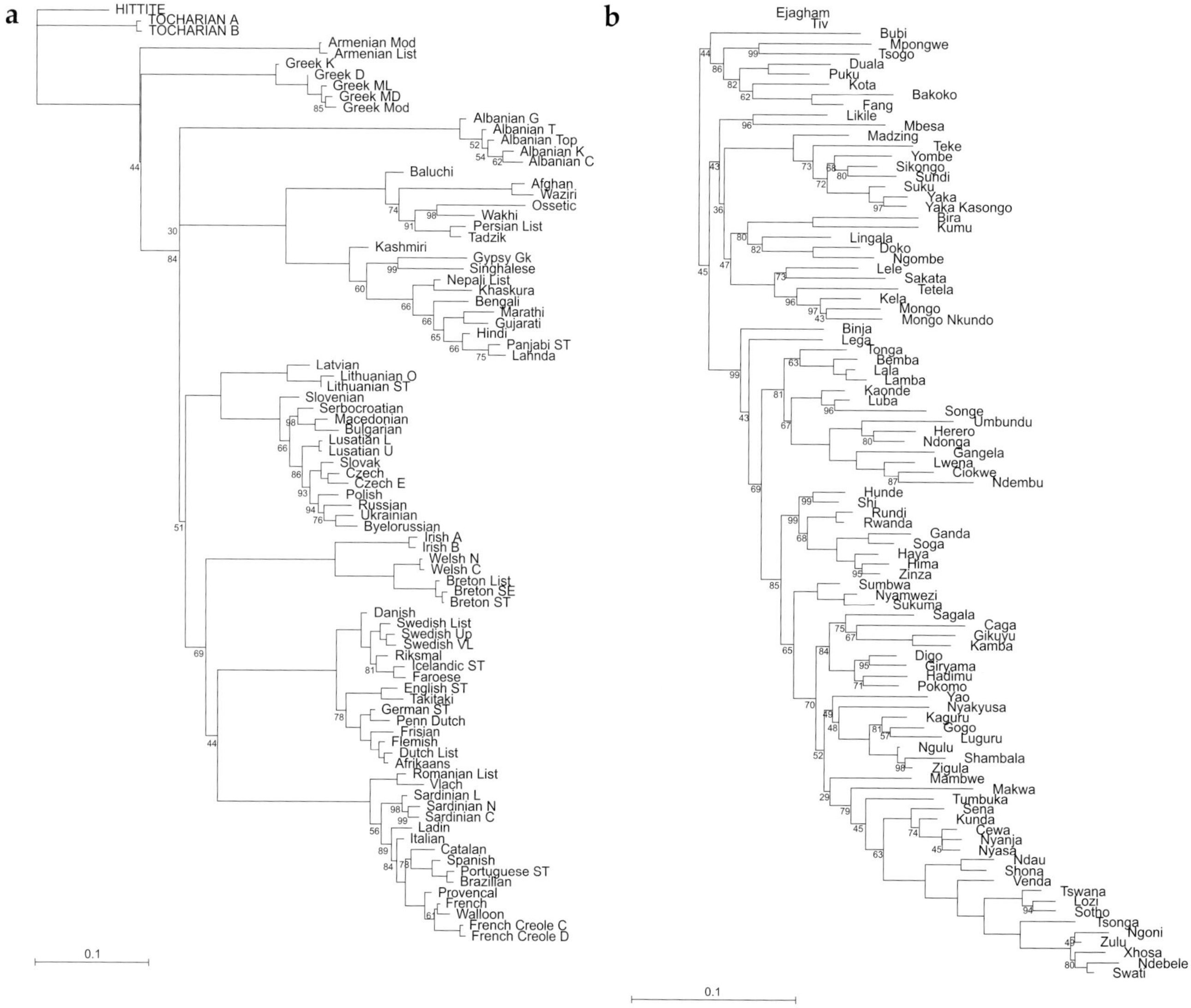


**Figure 15.1.** *Indo-European and Bantu trees: a) consensus phylogenetic tree of the 87 Indo-European languages derived from 500 trees sampled from a converged Markov chain; b) consensus phylogenetic tree of the 95 Bantu languages derived from 500 trees sampled from a converged Markov chain. In both trees, the numbers adjacent to each node are the posterior probabilities of the nodes, found as the number of times a given node appeared in the MCMC sample.*

Another problem that may arise from using binary-coded data derived from the multistate characters, is that the $k$ binary codes for a given meaning with $k$ states are not mutually independent. Under a phylogenetic likelihood model, the successive columns of **M** are treated as statistically independent. Non-independence may inflate the apparent confidence that one can place in the tree that is derived from the binary data. We show in Appendix B that the effect of non-independence on the likelihood can be estimated by raising the likelihood to a power less than 1.0. This is algebraically identical to a technique known as '*heating*'.

We allowed the Markov chain to run through many iterations until it reached convergence, and then sampled 500 trees at widely spaced intervals to ensure they were independent of one another (see Pagel & Lutzoni 2002; Pagel & Meade 2004 for examples of using MCMC methods in comparative studies).

### Estimating rates of meaning evolution on phylogenies

Given a phylogenetic tree it is straightforward to use the same likelihood-based statistical methods to estimate a unique rate of lexical replacement for each of the meanings in the Swadesh list. Unlike the phylogenetic inference step for which we used the binary-coded data, in estimating rates of evolution we allowed each meaning to adopt its $k$ different states on the tree. The transition from any state $i$ to any state $j$, can be written as $q\pi_j$, where $q$ is the instantaneous rate of change over short interval of time $dt$, and $\pi_j$ is the frequency of state $j$ in the observed data. Here, $j$, corresponds to the number of languages that use a particular word to express a given meaning.

$$\mathbf{Q} = \begin{array}{c} \\ 0 \\ 1 \\ . \\ . \\ \mathbf{s} \end{array} \begin{array}{c} \begin{array}{cccc} 0 & 1 & \ldots & s \end{array} \\ \left( \begin{array}{ccccc} - & q\pi_1 & . & . & q\pi_s \\ q\pi_0 & - & . & . & q\pi_s \\ . & . & . & . & . \\ . & . & . & . & . \\ q\pi_0 & q\pi_1 & . & . & - \end{array} \right) \end{array}$$

The probability of observing the $k$ lexical terms corresponding to meaning $i$ on any given tree can be written as $P(m_i|\mathbf{Q},T)$, and $q$ is estimated by maximum likelihood. Repeating this in each tree in the MCMC sample, we find the rate of lexical replacement for a given meaning as the average value of the instantaneous rate parameter across trees.

## Results

*Phylogenetic trees*

Figures 15.1a,b show the consensus phylogenetic trees for the Bantu and Indo-European language families as derived from the 500 trees in the MCMC sample. We sampled these trees after allowing the Markov chain to run through many iterations until it reached convergence. These trees are broadly similar to those published previously for these data (Gray & Atkinson 2003; Chapter 8 this volume; Holden 2002; Chapter 2 this volume). The number of times that a given monophyletic group appears in the MCMC sample of trees estimates the Bayesian posterior probability that that node defining that group actually exists, given the data and the model of evolution.

The posterior probabilities are labelled at each node, and reveal regions of relative certainty and uncertainty about the tree topology. The posterior probabilities emphasize the large number of different tree topologies that are consistent with the data. This underscores the importance of accounting for phylogenetic uncertainty in developing estimates of the rates, as rates will vary for a given meaning from tree to tree.

*Rates of meaning evolution*

For each meaning in **M**, we estimated $q$ across 500 trees obtained from MCMC sampling and calculated

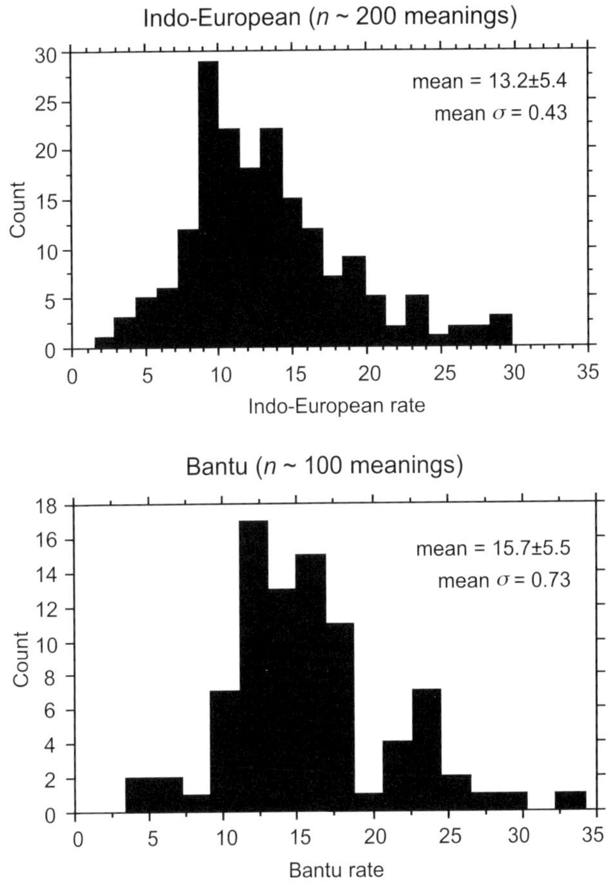


**Figure 15.2**. *Rates of meaning evolution. Histograms of the rates of lexical evolution for two-hundred Indo-European meanings and ninety Bantu meanings. The histograms record the average value of the instantaneous rate parameter,* q, *averaged over the* n = *500 trees in the MCMC sample. Each rate parameter's variation among trees is expressed by its standard deviation, and the average of these standard deviations across the 200 and 100 meanings respectively is shown.*

its mean and standard deviation. This gave us a set of estimated rates of lexical evolution that do not depend upon any one phylogenetic hypothesis.

Figures 15.2a,b display the frequency histogram of the average values of the instantaneous rate parameter $q$, for Indo-European and Bantu. The absolute values of these rates are arbitrary, depending upon the branch lengths, but their relative values are meaningful.

The histograms indicate that the rate of lexical evolution is relatively slow for most meanings, but that a small number of meanings have more rapid rates of lexical replacement. Within each language family there is at least a five to six-fold range in the rate of lexical evolution. The standard deviations for most meanings, calculated across the 500 trees, are

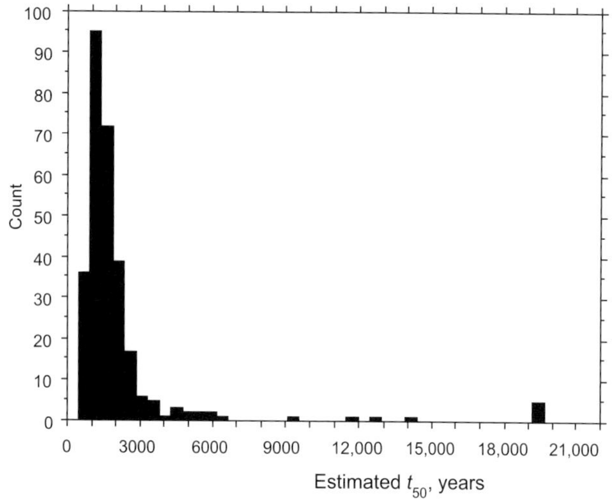


**Figure 15.3.** *Frequency histogram of lexical half-lives derived from the data in Figure 15.2. The quantity* $t_{50}$ *records the amount of time for a word to have a 50 per cent chance of being replaced by a new non-cognate word. These half-lives assume that Indo-European is 8000 years old and that Bantu is 4000 years old. These ages are based upon published information about these two families and are subject to other views. See Gray & Atkinson (2003), for a discussion of ages that have been suggested for Indo-European.*

small, and thus we can confidently conclude that different meanings vary dramatically in their rates of lexical replacement.

To give an idea of the magnitude of these rates, in Swadesh's (1952) original work he derived the rule that two languages will diverge about 20 per cent in their fundamental vocabulary in 500 years. At the average rates shown in Figure 15.2, the Indo-European meanings would require 479 years to accumulate changes to 20 per cent of the words, whereas the Bantu meanings would achieve this degree of lexical divergence in 360 years. The difference might be even greater if we accept Swadesh's statement that his 100-word list (used for Bantu here) changes more slowly than his 200-word list (used for Indo-European).

*Distribution of lexical half-lives*

An additional sense of the rates of evolution implied from Figure 15.2 can be obtained from calculating a lexical half-life for each meaning. This records the amount of time required for there to be a 50 per cent chance that the word will be replaced by a new non-cognate word for that meaning.

Figure 15.3 plots the distribution of lexical half-lives for all of the meanings combined across the two language families. The average half-life is 2343 years with a median of 1449 years. The meaning with the most rapid lexical evolution is the meaning 'warm' in Bantu, represented by 33 different words and with a lexical half-life of only 660 years. The slowest half-lives correspond to the five Indo-European meanings that are represented by only a single cognate for the entire family: *two, three, five, I,* and *who*. In this collection of languages their observed rate of change is zero. Presuming they can evolve, we can conservatively estimate their half-lives by interpolating the rate of change as lying between zero and the average rate of change for meanings with two cognate sets. This yields a half-life of 19,600 years. It is a conservative estimate because if the five meanings all had that rate of change it is very probable that at least one of them would have shown a change over the 8000 years the tree is assumed to represent.

Even a word with a 6000-year lexical half-life has a 25 per cent chance of not changing in 11,500 years. This shows that despite the fast average pace of language evolution, some meanings, like highly conserved genes, have lexical terms that evolve at a slow rate. Pagel (2000a,b) estimated that some words could have half-lives that allow them to identify ancient linguistic relationships, of 20,000 years or more separation, and the IE results reported here support that view. These words deserve far more investigation as possible sources of information for identifying very deep relationships among distantly related language families.

Why languages should in general evolve at relatively high rates is not obvious; it is apparent from some words that much slower rates of evolution are possible. Genetic systems can evolve to have optimal mutation rates; some viruses, for example, are selected to have high error rates as a strategy for evading the host's immune system. Is it somehow adaptive for lexical terms to evolve rapidly? Languages may evolve rapidly because there is little disadvantage in doing so and it would be costly to reduce the copying errors in human language learning and transmission systems. Nevertheless, there must be some upper limit to language evolution set by the need for more than one generation within the same language to understand each other, and so culturally or naturally selected processes must regulate this upper limit. The most rapidly evolving word has a lexical half-life well below the three-generation time-span that might typically arise in human societies.

*Rate of lexical evolution and the production of new cognate sets*

What are the consequences of varying rates of evolution on the production of linguistic diversity? Figures

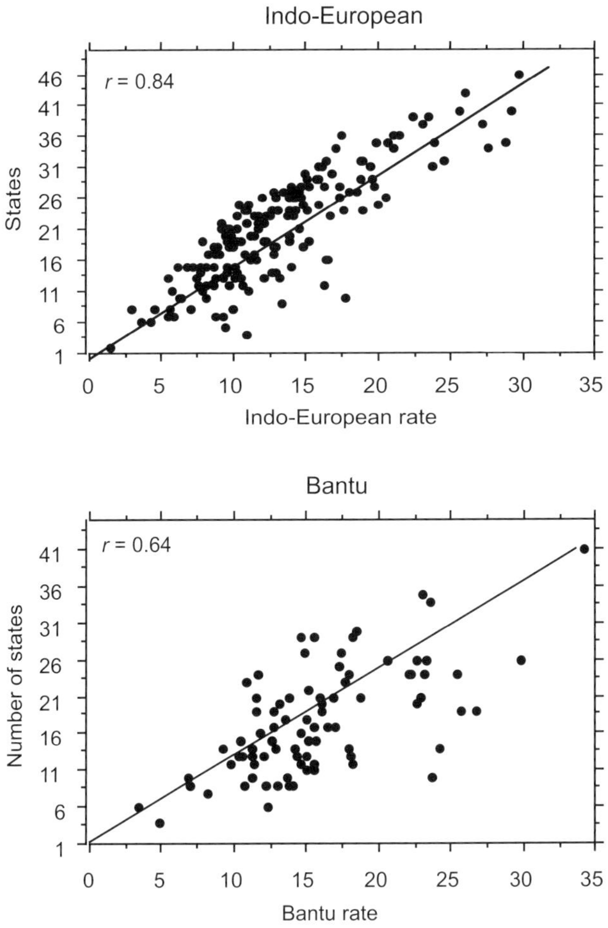


**Figure 15.4.** *Plot of the instantaneous rate of evolution,* q, *versus the number of distinct cognate sets for a meaning, labelled as the number of different 'states' of a meaning. The plots show that as the instantaneous rate increases, there is a greater diversity of words observed across the languages that make up each family. The statistic* r *is the correlation between the two sets of scores, and* b *records the slope of the line.*

15.4a,b plot a meaning's number of distinct cognate sets against the rate of lexical replacement. In both language families, meanings with higher instantaneous rates of lexical replacement yield a greater diversity of words or 'states' across their language family. The slopes of the lines relating rate to number of states are similar in the two languages families but the Bantu languages, with higher overall rates, have produced a greater diversity of words, despite their younger age.

The relationship between rates and numbers of states or cognate sets may seem obvious, even necessary. However, the wide variability in number of cognate sets for any given rate of lexical evolution shows that the two phenomena are not interchangeable. These data emphasize the importance of estimating rates from a phylogeny, rather than from merely tallying the number of states; the number of eventual states being a function of gains and losses of particular words and their distribution on the phylogenetic tree (see also Mace & Pagel 1994).

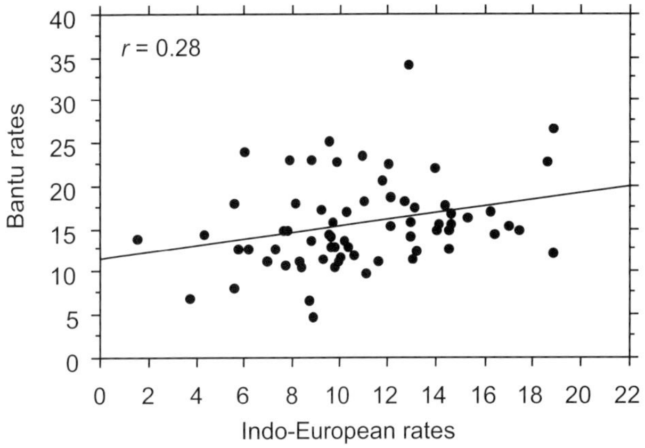


**Figure 15.5.** *Plot of the instantaneous rate of evolution,* q, *for the IE meanings versus the* q *obtained for the same Bantu meaning. The positive correlation (denoted by* r*) is modest but statistically significant, suggesting that some meanings have inherently higher (or lower) rates of evolution independently of the languages in which they are expressed.*

*Correlated rates of lexical evolution*

The wide range of different rates of lexical replacement raises the question of why some meaning are associated with a greater turnover of lexical items than others. Are rates of lexical evolution linked to a particular meaning? Figure 15.5 tests the hypothesis that rates of lexical evolution are correlated across language families. The IE and Bantu show a weak but significant ($p < 0.03$) correlation. We find it striking to consider that in two independent language families, separated in space and time, the underlying meaning somehow influences that rate of lexical evolution in a similar way.

**Discussion and conclusions**

We have demonstrated the feasibility of using phylogenies in combination with a statistical model to estimate rates of lexical replacement for meanings. We find that the rate of evolution varies considerably among meanings such that most meanings acquire new lexical terms relatively slowly but a few gain new words at a much more rapid pace. Bantu meanings seem to have a higher rate of lexical replacement than Indo-European meanings and produce a greater diversity of lexical items. Meanings with higher rates of lexical evolution in general produce a larger number of different words within a language family, but the relationship admits large amounts of variability. For a given number of different cognate sets, the estimated rate of lexical evolution often varies 3- to 5-fold.

Why some meanings should have higher rates of lexical evolution and why language families or even individual languages should vary in their overall rates of change are important questions for understanding linguistic diversity. A partial answer to the question of variation in rates of evolution may reside in the meaning itself: rates of lexical evolution correlate between Bantu and Indo-European despite the two language families being widely separated in space and time, and in the particular phonological representations. Some preliminary evidence (ms in preparation) suggests that the underlying correlation arises from frequency of use, with more frequently used forms being less likely to change.

A general theory of the rate of lexical evolution and of the production of linguistic diversity may also need to consider external or ecological influences. At the level of whole language evolution, Nichols (1990; 1995) has documented the greater density of language groups in coastal areas, and Mace & Pagel (1995) showed that linguistic density varies with latitude, and the richness of the habitat. What is not yet known is whether these ecological factors influence lexical evolution in a uniform way, or whether aspects of the environment influence the rate of evolution of specific classes of meanings.

## Acknowledgements

We thank Clare Holden for making available her Bantu data set and Russell Gray for providing his Indo-European data.

## Appendix A. Binary and Multistate coded data return phylogenetic trees that differ in total length by a constant of proportionality

We assume that the phylogenetic tree has been inferred from a likelihood model based upon the transition rate matrix, **Q** (see text). We further assume that **Q** has been normalized to have a mean rate of change of 1.0. Given these assumptions, branch lengths in a phylogenetic tree inferred from a likelihood model record the expected number of transitions per site. Here a 'site' is a column in **M** (see text) with one piece of information per tip (species or language group) in the tree. More generally, a site might correspond to the nucleotides at a particular position of a gene, or to morphological or other information. A transition represents an inferred change from one character state to the next. A branch length of 0.5 suggests that on average we expect a 50 per cent probability of a change along that branch in each character in the data matrix.

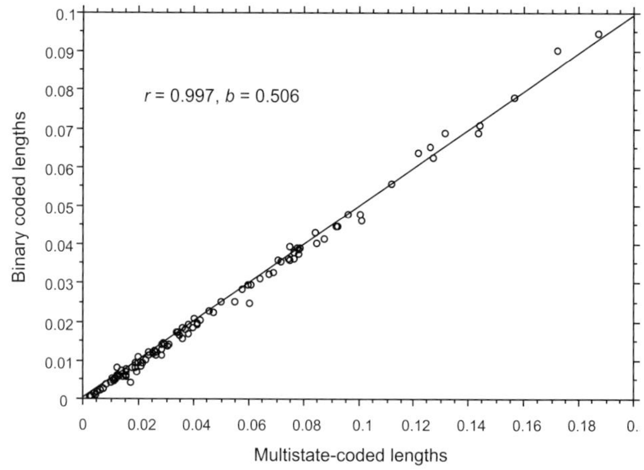


**Figure 15.6.** *Plot of the branch lengths as estimated from binary-transformed data versus the branch lengths obtained from untransformed gene-sequence data, for a tree of 54 species (Lutzoni* et al. *2001). The two sets of branch lengths are nearly perfectly related and fall along a line of slope* b = 2/k = *0.5.*

We wish to make statements about the total number of changes inferred from the same data in two different forms: (i) multistate coded linguistic data in which a given meaning is assigned *k* different states, one for each distinct cognate set; and (ii) binary coded data formed by writing each *k*-state vector of the multistate data as *k* distinct 0/1 vectors, each one coding a different cognate set as 1, and the remaining cognate sets as 0.

Assume that the rate matrix **Q** is reversible, such that $\pi_i q_{ij} \pi_j = \pi_j q_{ji} \pi_i$ for all *i*, *j*; where $\pi_i$ stands for the frequency of state *i* in the data and and $q_{ij}$ is the rate of change from state *i* to state *j*. For simplicity, assume that all $q_{ij}$ are equal. A multistate character with *k* states defines a $k \times k$ transition rate matrix, recording the rates of change among all possible pairs of states. The matrix contains $k^2$ elements, $k(k-1)$ of which record a transition from state *i* to state *j* ($i \neq j$), and the remaining *k* correspond to no change or stasis.

Binary coding of a multistate character creates *k* separate vectors, one for each of the multistate states. Each binary vector assigns 1s to a particular state from the multistate character and 0s to all other states. Thus, a given binary vector records the transitions to and from the state assigned a 1 and the remaining $k-1$ states (assigned 0s). There can be up to $k-1$ transitions to the state assigned a 1, and up to $k-1$ transitions away from this state. On average, then, a given binary vector will estimate the rate of change for up to $2(k-1)$ transitions per site of the multistate data.

This forms the basis for the expected difference in branch lengths between multistate and binary coded data. Recalling the interpretation of a branch length, a given binary vector stands in for $2(k-1)$ transitions of the $k(k-1)$ transitions in the multistate **Q** matrix. The ratio $2(k-1)/k(k-1) = 2/k$ is the expected ratio of branch lengths for binary versus multistate coded data.

For $k = 2$ (i.e., binary data) the ratio is 1.0 as it should be. For nucleotide data, we predict that the binary coded data will return a tree that is half the length of the usual coding for these data. Figure 15.6 plots the branch lengths obtained from nucleotide data ($x$-axis) versus binary coded nucleotide data ($y$-axis), for a tree of 54 species (data from Lutzoni *et al.* 2001). The strong linear relationship between the two sets of branch lengths has the predicted slope of 0.5.

We have assumed here that $k$ is a constant across sites. In practice $k$ will vary from site to site in linguistic multistate data. The relationship described here will hold separately for each different site, but the combined effect on the branch lengths averaged across sites may depend upon the goodness of fit of different sites to the tree. That is, the obtained tree length may be some composite weighted average of the $2/k$ scalar and the relative likelihood of a given site.

## Appendix B. Non-independence of sites can be approximated by 'heating' the likelihood

As described in the text, the likelihood of the data in **M** is found as the product over meanings of the individual likelihoods of each meaning, given the model of evolution, **Q**, and the phylogenetic tree, **T**. This equation reflects our assumption that meanings are independent of one another:

$$P(\mathbf{M}|\mathbf{Q}, T) = \prod_i P(\mathbf{M}_i|\mathbf{Q}, T) \quad \text{(B1)}$$

We denote the likelihood of the data in B1 as $L$. Because $L$ is the product over $k$ sites (here a site is a meaning in **M**) we can write

$$L^{1/k} = \tilde{p}$$

and thus, $\tilde{p}$ is the $k^{\text{th}}$ root of $L$. Assume that some proportion of the $k$ sites $k_I$ are independent of one another. Then, the true likelihood of the data is given by the product of the individual likelihoods of these $k_I$ sites:

$$L_I = \prod_I P(\mathbf{M}_{i \in 1}|\mathbf{Q}, \mathbf{T})$$

What is the relationship of $L_I$ to $L$? Assume that the $k_I$ sites are a random subset of $k$. Then, it follows that $\tilde{p}^{k_I} \approx L_I$. But we can write $L_I$ as:

$$L_I = (L^{1/k})^{k_I} = L^{k_I/k}$$

This shows that including non-independent sites in the calculation of the likelihood of the data, tends to underestimate the true likelihood by an amount equal to $L^{k_I/k} - L$. The effect of non-independence can therefore be removed by raising $L$ to the $k_I/k^{\text{th}}$ power. Given that $k_I < k$ this is equivalent to 'heating' the likelihood (let $k_I = {}^1/_{2k}$ for example).

This leads to the prediction that non-independence should have only a small effect on the best topology that is retrieved from an MCMC sample, but it will tend to yield higher posterior probabilities than would a data set in which sites are mutually independent.

## References


Geyer, C.J., 1992. Practical Markov chain Monte Carlo. *Statistical Science* 7, 473–511.

Gilks, W.R., S. Richardson & D.J. Spiegelhalter, 1996. Introducing Markov chain Monte Carlo, in *Markov Chain Monte Carlo in Practice,* eds. W.R. Gilks, S. Richardson & D.J. Spiegelhalter. Boca Raton (FL): Chapman & Hall/CRC Press, 1–19.

Gray, R. & Q. Atkinson, 2003. Language-tree divergence times support the Anatolian theory of Indo-European origin. *Nature* 426, 435–9.

Felsenstein, J.P., 1981. Evolutionary trees from DNA sequences: a maximum likelihood approach. *Journal of Molecular Evolution* 17, 368–76.

Hastings, W., 1970. Monte Carlo sampling methods using Markov chains and their applications. *Biometrika* 57, 97–109.

Holden, C., 2002. Bantu language trees reflect the spread of farming across sub-Saharan Africa: a maximum-parsimony analysis. *Proceedings of the Royal Society of London* Series B 269, 793–9.

Kruskal, J., I. Dyen & P. Black, 1971. The vocabulary method of reconstructing family trees: innovations and large scale applications, in *Mathematics in the Archeological and Historical Sciences,* eds. F.R. Hodson, D.G. Kendall & P. Tautu. Edinburgh: Edinburgh University Press, 30–55.

Larget, B. & D.L. Simon, 1999. Markov chain monte carlo algorithms for the Bayesian analysis of phylogenetic trees. *Molecular Biology and Evolution* 16, 750–59.

Lutzoni, F., M. Pagel & V. Reeb, 2001. Major fungal lineages derived from lichen-symbiotic ancestors. *Nature* 411, 937–40.

Mace, R. & M. Pagel, 1994. The comparative method in anthropology. *Current Anthropology* 35, 549–64.

Mace, R. & M. Pagel, 1995. A latitudinal gradient in the density of human languages in North America. *Proceedings of the Royal Society of London* Series B 261, 117–21.

Metropolis, N., A.W. Rosenbluth, M.N. Rosenbluth, A.H. Teller & E. Teller, 1953. Equation of state calculations by fast computing machines. *Journal of Chemical Physics* 21, 1087–92.

Nichols, J., 1990. Linguistic diversity and the first settlement of the New World. *Language* 66, 475–521.

Nichols, J., 1995. The spread of language around the Pacific Rim. *Evolutionary Anthropology* 3, 206–15.

Pagel, M., 1994. Detecting correlated evolution on phylogenies: a general method for the comparative analysis of discrete characters. *Proceedings of the Royal Society* Series B 255, 37–45.

Pagel, M., 2000a. Maximum likelihood models for glottochronology and for reconstructing linguistic phylogenies, in *Time Depth in Historical Linguistics,* eds. C. Renfrew, A. MacMahon & L. Trask. (Papers in the Prehistory of Languages.) Cambridge: McDonald Institute for Archaeological Rsearch, 189–207.

Pagel, M., 2000b. The history, rate, and pattern of world linguistic evolution, in *The Evolutionary Emergence of Language,* eds. C Knight, M. Studdert-Kennedy & J. Hurford. Cambridge: Cambridge University Press, 391–416.

Pagel, M. & F. Lutzoni, 2002. Accounting for phylogenetic uncertainty in comparative studies of evolution and adaptation, in *Biological Evolution and Statistical Physics,* eds. M. Lässig & A. Valleriani. Berlin: Springer-Verlag, 148–61

Pagel, M. & A. Meade, 2004. A phylogenetic mixture model for detecting pattern-heterogeneity in gene sequence or character-state data. *Systematic Biology* 53, 571–81.

Rannala, B. & Z. Yang, 1996. Probability distributions of molecular evolutionary trees: a new method of phylogenetic inference. *Journal of Molecular Evolution* 43, 304–11.

Ruhlen, M., 1994. *The Origin of Language: Tracing the Evolution of the Mother Tongue.* New York (NY): Wiley.

Swadesh, M., 1952. Lexico-statistic dating of prehistoric ethnic contacts. *Proceedings of the American Philosophical Society* 96, 452–63.

Wilson, I. & D. Balding, 1998.Genealogical inference from microsatellite data. *Genetics* 150, 499–510.

Yang, Z., 1994. Maximum likelihood phylogenetic estimation from DNA sequences with variable rates over sites: approximate methods. *Journal of Molecular Evolution* 39, 306–14.

# Chapter 16

# Interdisciplinary Indiscipline? Can Phylogenetic Methods Meaningfully be Applied to Language Data — and to Dating Language?

Paul Heggarty

A number of recent papers have sought to apply to language data various phylogenetic 'tree-drawing' techniques initially developed for uses outside linguistics. The reaction from many historical linguists, however, has typically been critical, if not outright hostile. This paper explores, and aims to explain, why it is that there has been such a long-running failure to reach a consensus between linguists and specialists from other disciplines, notably genetics and archaeology.

We consider linguists' fundamental concerns as to how non-linguists go about using language data; especially whether (and if so, how) one can meaningfully use such phylogenetic analyses on language data, interpret their results, and attempt to put dates on particular nodes in the trees. We look into certain aspects of the very nature of language that it is crucial to bear in mind in order to handle language data appropriately for these purposes, but which many linguists feel are not truly appreciated by non-linguists. These aspects are: language's inherent susceptibility to powerful external forces which vary tremendously through history; the nature of language data, and what it entails for how those data can meaningfully be compared and measured; and finally the nature of change and historical development in language, critical to how we are to interpret any parallels we observe between languages, not least for the purposes of dating.

It emerges, moreover, that these same characteristics of language change also challenge linguists' own 'established' dating of Proto-Indo-European by means of the so-called 'linguistic palaeontology', and that this issue is in truth much more open than Indo-Europeanist linguists generally admit.

## An inter-disciplinary problem – Why?

Few articles in recent years have provoked such controversy in historical linguistics as Gray & Atkinson (2003) and Forster & Toth (2003). We do not propose here to give detailed or specific critiques of these, which are available elsewhere, but look at the broader problem behind the failure to achieve an inter-disciplinary consensus on how phylogenetic methods, initially developed for applications outside linguistics, can be applied to language data, and particularly to dating languages.

The tone of commentaries from some historical linguistics circles on papers such as the above has ranged from the sceptical or bemused to the outright hostile, disparaging and dismissive, as if there were a few home truths that specialists from outside linguistics have yet to take fully on board. Their detailed criticisms revolve around two general aspects of language that are frequently poorly grasped.

The first is the nature of language as a **social phenomenon**. If languages can be so informative of history, then this is only because language in general, and all languages individually, are inherently susceptible to being moulded by the forces of history. What makes languages a function of the history of their speakers are certain social, cultural and political factors: contact, isolation, population size and density, conquest, and so on; and all the forces that influence those in turn. Such forces are themselves anything but stable over time; necessarily then, nor is their impact on language change and divergence. This is the key principle behind the rejection by mainstream linguistics of any dating mechanism that assumes that the rate of change is constant.

It has sometimes been claimed that Embleton (1986) 'rehabilitated' glottochronology to some extent. Despite her other improvements, however, her key innovation of 'borrowing rates' simply continues the original and flawed glottochronological assumption. For while she allows her borrowing factor *b* to vary from one language pair to the next, for the dating method to work it still cannot be allowed to vary over time. Embleton (1986, 102–3) works with a borrowing rate of '8.16% per millennium' for English from Danish, for instance. The problematic assumption remains, then: that change, specifically in this case borrowing under contact influence, is necessarily steady over time. This is plainly at odds with known historical and linguistic fact. There clearly never was even a single millennium throughout which Danish had any significant impact on English. A huge impact it did have, to be sure; but this was everything but constant 'per millennium'. It had precious little impact at all until the short age of Viking expansion, then a huge impact over a period of just some three centuries, when half of England was the Danelaw, before that intense influence then faded rapidly, to end pretty much abruptly and for good. Far from being an atypical case, this punctuality has been pretty much the normal scenario for contact influence between European languages, not least that of many of the Romance and Germanic languages on each other, (Norman) French and English being another case in point.

Language as a 'social animal' also determines the processes and patterns by which languages *diverge*, particularly into dialect continua by the wave model and other processes. Despite the lip-service paid to them, these are still all too often overlooked and their true nature misconstrued. Speciation in particular is a very poor analogy for these processes. And even if it were not, the idealized assumption that splits are punctual is more problematic in linguistics because its time-scales are so different to those of genetics: margins of error in estimating split-dates are consequently much greater. All this has led to confusion as to exactly what the abstract concept of a language 'split' actually corresponds to in real languages — yet this 'event' is exactly what phylogenetic models both aspire to put dates on, and use to calibrate their dating mechanisms in the first place.

The other main grounds on which linguists have rejected given applications of phylogenetic methods as plain 'bad science' have to do with the general approach to language **data** as input: how they are analyzed and processed, and what they are claimed to demonstrate.

The onus still appears to be on linguists to explain adequately these two key aspects of language to specialists from other disciplines. Unfortunately there is not space here to do so fully for both, and this paper has had to choose to focus on the second. We consider and illustrate a number of aspects of the very nature of language data and language change that have critical consequences for the use of phylogenetic methods. We shall also see, however, that among these same inescapable characteristics of language are some that also question the grounds on which some historical linguists have based their own estimates for the date of the first Proto-Indo-European split, specifically the claim that it must necessarily have occurred *after* the emergence of certain technologies such as wheeled vehicles.

## Applying phylogenetic methods to language: a multi-stage process

Applying phylogenetic methods to language is a process that it is helpful to see as a series of discrete stages.

(a) The *encoding* stage: getting from real languages to some expression of the relationships between them in the form of numerical or state data, so that those data can then be used as input to phylogenetic methods.

(b) The *representation* stage: applying phylogenetic analysis methods to extract from those numerical and/or state data a signal that is converted into some useful form of representation, usually two-dimensional graphical ones such as trees or networks, which synthesize and 'collapse' what are often highly complex multi-dimensional relationships in the signal.

(c) The *interpretation* stage: assessing those tree and network representations to extract from them what they actually mean for real languages and their relationships through time.

As Embleton (1986, 3) makes clear, we first have to confirm that this whole process is viable, by testing it against cases for which we already know the answers, where we are fortunate enough to have copious historical knowledge available. Once we can trust the process, we can then progress to the ultimate point, to make use of it in cases where we do *not* have sufficient knowledge to find out the answers by other more traditional means.

The need for the different disciplines to work together in this 'new synthesis' is clear from how these different stages implicate specialists from the respective fields. Encoding, certainly, cannot be successful without a deep understanding of the nature of language data and change. Interpretation, likewise, needs an awareness of how real languages behave through time, and of the processes and scenarios by which they diverge and converge. Yet it is equally crucial for interpretation, and for the representation stage that precedes it, to understand in detail precisely how the phylogenetic methods work. This calls for a particularly sound grasp of statistics, significance, and the various alternative configurations possible in the methods that can effect important adjustments to the trees and networks they produce, suited to a range of different applications and data sets.

And what of dating, and its place in this process? Dating is not just an interpretation, but an extra stage in that it adds further assumptions, about rates of change over time. Glottochronology's assumption of a constant rate of change in core vocabulary has been demonstrated to be fundamentally flawed; it remains to be established whether Gray & Atkinson's calibration and rate-smoothing can give us a viable alternative, or whether their assumptions too are invalid.

### The nature of language data

Linguists have objected to what they characterize as an undisciplined, unscientific approach to using language data, ignoring key characteristics that limit the suitability of those data as input to phylogenetic methods designed for what are actually very different data from other disciplines. A tacit assumption is often made that language offers data that can be used just like many data from the natural sciences.

The most fundamental point to bear in mind here is that language is not a creation of the natural world, but of the human mind. There may exist some high-level 'universal grammar' type constraints, but these are not of concern at the level of the language data used as input to phylogenetic methods. In such data, the human mind can be perfectly happy with gradations, irregularities, and a whole host of complex and indirect relationships. As any linguist who has sought to quantify data from any field of language knows all too well, real language data are by no means always amenable to clear-cut representation either in numerical terms, or as oppositions between two or more discrete states all 'equally different' from each other. Analyses and measurements of language data, even in a single feature, are typically nothing like as precise, unequivocal and reliable as a carbon-14 reading, for instance. True, carbon datings are not quite as simple as was first thought, and it was soon realized that they need to be adjusted in order to take certain other environmental variables into account. Yet the point, and the qualitative difference with language data, remains: these data too are nonetheless such that they can be measured and processed to a degree of accuracy and reliability *sufficient to achieve a consensus among specialists* as to the robustness of the results thus 'corrected'.

Since language data are often not reliably clear-cut, it follows too that *changes* in language from one state to another are not discrete either, but eminently gradual questions of degree. All these difficulties increase exponentially when one tries to match up multiple different systems in different languages in order to quantify precisely how different they are to each other.

Of course, language data will always need to be simplified to some extent to make them suitable for numerical processing. Yet on many occasions this simplification is taken so far, in order to fit data into far too rigid a mathematically-led model, as to render the whole process meaningless. The data end up so distorted and correspond so indirectly to the linguistic reality that as 'features' or quantifications they misrepresent it completely, and are actually worse than no data at all. For a stark illustration, see the critiques in Heggarty *et al.* (2005) and Heggarty (forthcoming, §2.2.1) of Nerbonne *et al.*'s (1999) dialect phylogenies based on comparing word strings by 'edit distance', on the model of applications in the natural sciences. For computational convenience their simplistic adaptation ends up treating the least change in sound quality as a 'mutation' rated as twice as significant as the loss of the whole sound. Every sound is effectively rated as more similar to silence than to any other speech sound. Take the example of RP English *mother* against Standard German *Mutter*, where there are certain differences in the pronunciations of the last three of the four sounds: ['mʌðə] vs ['mʊtɐ]. A 'mutation' approach like that of Nerbonne *et al.* would end up measuring these words as *more* different to each other than either is to a sound sequence such as [im]. Such results are all but meaningless as measures and representations of the linguistic reality — not that this comes as a surprise, because an analysis model in terms of mutations and edit distance so completely misrepresents the nature of language differences and processes.

The term 'mutation' is often heard misapplied by proponents of tree-drawing models too, presumably because it fits with the applications in genetics that they were originally designed for. The superficial analogy is a dangerously misleading one. Language data are by no means all made up of discrete slots and states, all equally different from one another. Sounds, affixes, words, meanings, grammatical contexts, and no end of other linguistic variables, are not carbon isotopes, nor the distinct A, C, G and T bases of DNA. Likewise, the real linguistic processes that bring about change and determine our language data at any given time are not at all sudden 'mutations' or discrete switches from one state to another, but typically subtle, gradual shifts in the relationships between multiple different variables on various levels.

Linguists' countless objections to particular lexicostatistical data are all just instances of this general principle as it applies to lexical semantics. The types of change that result in the meaning-cognacy mismatches that form lexicostatistical data are not 'mutations', the sudden complete 'loss' or 'replacement' of a given word. The cognate is often not lost at all in the language, but just drifts to a very closely related meaning slot, as with German *Hund* (*dog*) vs English *hound*. Had Swadesh (1952) not drawn up his list in English in the first place, it would be a close call between *small* and *little* as the word that best corresponds to the intended meaning-slot. Such debatable calls in multiple languages at the same time can have serious repercussions for the 'matches' between them. How should English really be matched up with Danish, for instance, which has singular *lille* but a plural *små*? Indeed this case is even more complex than meets the eye, and only serves to illustrate how even a yes/no cognacy judgement between two superficially similar-looking forms can be far from a clear-cut question. According to the *Oxford English Dictionary*'s (*c*. 2000–) etymologies, the true relationship between *small* and *små* is 'doubtful'; and while in principle *little* and *lille* actually go back to *different* roots, they also raise strong suspicions of contact influence.

Contact and borrowing are critical problems for lexicostatistics, whose proponents take highly inconsistent approaches to them — another instance of a rather undisciplined approach to using and interpreting language data, even by linguists. Gray & Atkinson (2003), at least, cannot be faulted for relying on data analyzed not by themselves but by linguists, albeit advocates of lexicostatistics: Dyen *et al.* (1992). Yet this hardly means that all linguists are convinced of how meaningful and reliable such data are for producing precise phylogenies, given the troublesome nature of language data. For the *small* meaning slot, for instance, Dyen's data and cognacy choices put English not with any other Germanic language, but alone with Slavic. For the *Oxford English Dictionary* (*OED*), however, the relationship with Slavic is 'somewhat uncertain'. And even if the Slavic words *are* cognates with *small*, it is unclear whether this modern meaning match might actually be the result of parallel meaning shifts that happened *independently* in each branch, rather than the preservation of the original form-to-meaning relationship. Indeed, in the *OED*'s earliest records for *small*, in Old English it originally had a more specific sense of *narrow*, as still in German *schmal* (one form that we can say is definitely cognate).

Linguists' protestations that there is something particularly awkward about language data are often met with scepticism from specialists in other disciplines. Geneticists may retort that in trees based on language data, the phylogenetic signal is typically extremely strong by the usual standards of genetics, and can be frustrated at linguists' hesitation in venturing claims about real language histories on the basis of such clear phylogenies.

In fact there is truth in the claims from both sides, but importantly because each focuses on a very different aspect of what constitutes 'messy' data. The messiness in genetics is not so much in getting from the DNA to an encoding of it; it is simply that the picture the DNA gives is messy in the sense that the phylogenetic signal it contains is often weak, and can be hard to interpret conclusively. In linguistics, the opposite holds: the messiness in language data is not so much in the picture we get once we have encoded the data, it's in deciding what is a meaningful encoding of them in the first place. The signal may be stronger, but we are less confident that it actually does necessarily mean what we would like it to mean (such as a period of shared ancestry). Linguists' experience leaves them acutely conscious that language data are inherently open to multiple different analyses and interpretations, and it is this that has undermined and frustrated efforts to come up with workable encoding methods. Those proposed so far, such as lexicostatistics, force on language data what we know to be a seriously simplistic characterization, and we are left in doubt as to whether this encoding really is a particularly meaningful representation of the actual relationships between the real languages that we are hoping it will help us investigate.

### What does an apparent correspondence mean?

For the particular task of working out the phylogeny (and from that the datings?) inherent in a set of data features, it goes without saying that however sophisticated and potentially useful an analysis tool may be, unless correspondences in the data features really *are* valid indicators of common origin, its output can have no meaning as a true genealogy.

At times some linguists too have not been immune to the temptation of granting themselves great leeway with their data and their interpretations of them, Greenberg's (1987) 'multilateral comparison' technique being the most notorious case. Abandoning due scientific rigour may offer a way of claiming discoveries novel and significant enough as to make big waves outside one's discipline; it is also a way to question if not discredit one's work and reputation amongst colleagues in the know.

How is one to know how much phylogeny can safely be read into a particular correspondence that at first sight may seem particularly striking? For a parallel in archaeology, take the issue of whether other civilizations or cultures had contact with and/or settled South America before Columbus. Granted, certain parallels can be found in various cultural attributes such as pottery technologies and styles, or the construction of reed boats, but they are hardly enough to convince us of a necessary link with Oceania or Egypt; independent and parallel development offers an alternative explanation. Or in biology, as McMahon & McMahon (1995, 158) point out, just because a mammalian mole and a marsupial mole have many morphological similarities does not mean it is correct to assume they are closely related genealogically.

There are a number of inherent characteristics of language that conspire to produce a great many apparent correspondences of this type in language data, arguably to a degree far more misleading than in other disciplines. Certainly, a linguist's training is a long experience of constantly realizing how much more complex language data are than meets the untrained eye. A non-specialist — in some cases, even a linguist who is not a specialist in the particular languages concerned — cannot simply 'eyeball' the data and reliably tell apart which correspondences do or do not necessarily go back to a time of shared history before a split. To have any value, phylogenies drawn from feature-based comparisons *must* be based on features that are powerfully diagnostic of shared origin, as opposed to the many others which, despite appearances, do not necessarily mean anything of the sort. Such are the complexities and pitfalls of language data that the only way to be sure is through informed, painstaking research.

Four key characteristics of language data to consider here are that many features of language:

- tend to proceed along the same typical steps or *pathways of change* in any language;
- offer precious *few alternative states*;
- involve simply *re-interpreting* in new ways *existing resources* already available to a language;
- are not fully independent of each other, because of the *systemic* nature of language structure.

Among other problems they raise, these characteristics entail that changes often occur *independently* and *in parallel* in different languages, especially when they are tipped into a relatively sudden whole-system change. Superficial correspondences in features of language that are subject to these characteristics are therefore of very limited significance as evidence of a period of common history during which they arose, since they fail to exclude convincingly chance and systemic reasons as alternative explanations. We shall now look at each characteristic in more depth.

### Typical paths of change

A common misapprehension about language change is that the changes are by their nature random, on the model of mutations. This is correct only in part. It is true that, other than in known cases of direct contact influence, we usually cannot explain why in any particular language a given change occurred when it did, nor why that change did while other possible ones did not. However, the changes a language undergoes are not so much random as just a randomly 'selected' subset of a larger number of well-known, typical steps of change. These changes *do* follow clear types, and contrast with a vast number of others which in principle are highly unnatural, and in practice do not occur. Indeed it is only this predictable aspect of language change that enables us to 'reverse' it so as to make reconstruction possible at all.

It is essentially random, for example, whether a language allows words to end in the [l] sound; and if so, whether that sound in this position does or does not change during a particular period. What is not random is that if its pronunciation *does* change, then it is overwhelmingly likely to change along a particular known path, for there are very few natural directions for a word-final [l] sound to change in. The first step is typically from clear [l] as in German, to dark [ɫ] as in most varieties of English, and independently in European Portuguese. Next this dark [ɫ] typically turns into [w] or [u], as occurred independently in Cockney, Glaswegian, Brazilian Portuguese, Polish and some varieties of Bulgarian. This can then even change to [o], as happened in French (*cheval~chevaux*) and in Serbo-Croat (*Belgrad→Beograd*). That a sound change like this occurs in two or more language varieties is no necessary indicator whatsoever that it happened during a period of common history, for the innovation so often occurs independently anyway, as all these known cases show.

There are similar 'typical paths of change' in the grammatical system too. In *I saw a cat today; the cat was black*, reversing the articles would be a grammatical mistake. This is because English 'grammaticalizes' definiteness: i.e. it is compulsory to make the *a* vs *the* distinction where appropriate. Other languages, including Latin and most Slav languages, simply do not bother to make this distinction, and have no words to perform the functions of English *a* vs *the*. The historical process of acquiring or 'grammaticalizing' such a distinction from a previous state of not having it has occurred repeatedly and independently in many European languages: in modern Romance, Germanic and Bulgarian, for instance. Again, definiteness marking is no sound evidence for historical relationships.

### A limited number of states and re-interpreting existing resources in a language

Moreover, whether a language does or does not grammaticalize definiteness is a variable with only two basic states (though the details are actually much more complex), either of which is entirely natural for a language. So this simple feature alone can hardly be taken as a reliable or statistically significant indicator of the relatedness of any two languages. Likewise for the *position* of definite articles: either in front of the noun they refer to, or after it (or both). French and English share the former, Romanian and Danish (with some complications) the latter, but these correspondences do not in themselves prove that they arose during a period of shared history — indeed, again we know full well that the *opposite* genealogical relationships hold between these languages.

Furthermore, with the exception of the borrowing of a specific loanword, in any change (including many other contact-induced changes such as calques) the new form or arrangement can only come about by using in a new way resources *already available* in that language. Normally this means that there is only a very limited range of existing resources with a meaning suitable to be put to the new use. For indefinite articles, a typical source is the numeral *one*, while for definite articles it is demonstratives like *this* and *that*. Not only have multiple languages grammaticalized definiteness; in most cases they have even grammaticalized exactly the 'same' words in this use, again entirely independently.

This means also that superficial correspondences can be even more deceptive when languages that change in parallel are ones that have previously diverged from a common origin, for they can thus end up not just with similar systems but with specific *forms* that are ultimately related too, such as English *a(n)* and French *un*. Even this form-to-meaning correspondence is no evidence that they actually arose *as articles* before the languages split; again, on the contrary, we know they did not.

### Whole-system change

Many instances of language change are not isolated and independent of each other, but have knock-on and cumulative effects that together can help tip a language into a more general transformation, as when a language switches the whole character of its sound or grammatical system from one type to another. This typically occurs as per a 'punctuated equilibrium' model (see Dixon 1997), in bursts of faster change in that area of language structure, separated by periods of relative system stability, or at least much slower change. Here we have another factor causing instability in rates of change through history, only this time not an external but essentially a language-internal one.

What is more, wholesale system change in one area of language structure may accelerate change in other areas too. Generalized *phonetic* attrition of word endings, for instance, can accelerate the collapse of *grammatical* case systems (or vice versa), as in the development of Vulgar Latin into the early stages of the Western Romance languages. And by causing originally distinct words all to end up pronounced the same, *phonetic* attrition can also accelerate *lexical* replacements, in order to disambiguate the new homonyms.

Again, it is with languages related at an earlier stage that such whole-system changes can be particularly misleading. Related languages not only share many form-to-meaning correspondences, but they are also likely still to be at a similar stage in many typological characteristics, all just 'waiting' for some trigger to set them off along the next typical stretch of accelerated cyclical change. Despite all their immediate ancestors being highly inflectional and fusional languages, for instance, most modern Indo-European languages have become much less so, all but entirely independently of each other down each branch.

### Dating by linguistic palaeontology?

One proposed linguistic method for locating and dating the origin of languages is the so-called 'linguistic palaeontology', the one on which the proposed date of *c.* 6500 BP is largely founded. To start with, it is well to remind readers that linguistic palaeontology as a method has never attained any status as linguistic orthodoxy as a dating mechanism, for just like glottochronology, it reposes on assumptions about language change in lexical semantics that the majority of historical linguists do not consider tenable.

For Dixon (1997, 49), for example: 'What has always filled me with wonder is the assurance with which many historical linguists assign a date to their reconstructed proto-language ... it does seem to be a house of cards'. Sims-Williams (1998, 510), meanwhile, considers linguistic palaeontology specifically in the case of Indo-European, only to find that its arguments rely on 'unprovable assumptions about the absolute chronology of the prehistoric IE sound changes'. He is bound to conclude that

> To sum up, then, there seems to be no reliable way of establishing the upper limit for the breakup of PIE. If Renfrew were able convince his fellow archaeologists that the first farmers were the only possible bearers of PIE, then philologists could probably explain away all the shared vocabulary that has seemed to imply later phases of civilization.

How is it, though, that linguists could 'explain away'

shared vocabulary like the *axle* or the *wheel*? Again, it is typical paths of change that provide the alternative explanations. We have looked at examples of these paths, and of the many resulting cases of independent parallel change, so far only in the grammatical and sound systems of languages; it is often overlooked that in lexical semantics too there are a number of typical paths along which word-to-meaning relationships shift over time. Almost all changes fall into one of a number of types well known to linguists: extension, specialization, pejoration, and so on.

Underlying all of these is that when one word comes to replace another in a particular meaning, that new word (unless it is a loanword) has not simply been generated out of nowhere, but was a word that either already existed in the language in a very similar meaning, or was coined from an original word by adding an affix. The word for *tomorrow* in various languages (including German and Spanish) has independently come by extension from the existing word for *morning*; likewise the *money* word has been repeatedly taken from *silver* (French, Latin American Spanish); *drink* from *take*; and so on. This matters not just for the lexical data for many phylogenetic studies, but also for linguistic palaeontology.

Firstly as a means of locating the Indo-European homeland, the key weakness of the method is that peoples who move into new areas frequently apply their existing lexical roots to any similar-looking species in the new environment, so a Proto-Indo-European root for a species name such as *beech (tree)* is by no means conclusive for locating the PIE environment.

For dating, meanwhile, linguistic palaeontologists appeal to the roots that it has been possible to reconstruct for certain technologies, in particular wheeled transport, as proof that the PIE split cannot be dated before those cultural developments. Again though, this is by no means the only, inescapable conclusion from such language data. Once more, the spanner in the works is language's tendency to base new meanings, lexical as well as grammatical, on new interpretations of resources already present within the language, simply extending them to new senses.

First consider a modern example: the new sense acquired by English *mouse* in computing. That the German equivalent is *Maus* and the Dutch *muis* is most plausibly attributable to contact of some sort, on the model of the initial meaning extension in English (quite how best to analyze the contact process is debatable). This new *sense* was acquired first in one language, English, then 'borrowed' into others, at least fifteen hundred years after the languages 'split'. Yet since the two languages still have cognates that are phonetically similar, the result is indistinguishable from shared origin.

New cultural items are well-known to be eminently susceptible to contact influence, indeed none more so than technological terminology for transport (examples are legion with seafaring terms borrowed between the languages of maritime western European peoples). There is every reason to suppose that terms for wheeled transport could indeed have spread through some form of contact — and this too could have been just by calquing new senses and meaning extensions, not necessarily borrowing new words. An entirely plausible linguistic scenario would run as follows. Many centuries after Proto-Indo-European first split and began diverging into dialects and languages, an existing Indo-European root for some meaning like *pole* or *post* acquires the additional sense of *axle*, initially in one dialect or language whose speakers are the first to use the new technology. Other early Indo-European dialects or closely related languages still have cognate forms either identical or instantly recognizable as just dialectal variants of this *pole* word, that now also means *axle* in one dialect. So there simply is no 'new word' to borrow, only a new sense — *axle* as well as *pole* — to extend their existing cognate lexemes to. As the innovation spreads, every dialect starts using its own variant of the *pole* word also to mean *axle*. Another typical path of language change in lexical semantics, specialization, may well then narrow the meaning of this term to *axle* only, with the original *pole* meaning taken over by a near-synonym (*stick*, *post*, etc.) to disambiguate the now unhelpfully broad meaning of the original *pole/axle* word.

When one recalls how change in lexical semantics typically proceeds, the supposed proofs of linguistic palaeontology soon begin to seem highly speculative. *Bronze* might have referred originally perhaps to a colour, or to the rock that was first used as bronze ore, or to a number of other related meanings. Linguistic palaeontologists themselves are very happy to envisage such well-known types of semantic changes when it suits them (i.e. when they happen to have been able to reconstruct forms that look like possible more remote cognates), as per Beekes's (1995, 37) suggestion: '"Gold", *$\acute{g}^{h}$(o)l(H)-* … perhaps derived from the word for "yellow"'. Indeed Beekes (1995, 37) not only takes care to specify two forms for *wheel* **Hrot-*$h_2$ and ***$k^{w}$*e-*$k^{w}$*l-os*, but immediately goes on to explain 'The root **Hret-* meant "walk", **kWel-* "turning"'. We know that these words are derivations of some sort. Even if we have indications in the data of how far back the derivation happened in the history of particular sub-branches of Indo-European, or indeed back at the Proto-Indo-European stage, we do not know the precise meaning the derivation had at the time. Indeed, it is indicative that Beekes's example languages that preserved reflexes of *$Hrot$-$h_2$ vary in the precise meanings: *wheel*, *wagon*, and '*wheel, circle*'. And just as they can borrow and calque long after they split, languages can also make derivations that are still cognate even after many centuries of divergence.

Indo-Europeanists certainly did excellent detective work to reconstruct the words. But reconstruction takes us back only to assumed *forms* (in the linguistic sense of a word seen only on the level of sound), not necessarily their *exact meanings* in the proto-language. Indeed, reconstruction in so many cases is specifically compelled to allow explicitly for indirect meaning matches. We can reconstruct an ancient *form* whose modern reflexes now occupy the meaning slot of a current technological term; but this does not of itself necessarily entail that the proto-form already had that technical *sense* at the time of the proto-language, nor thereby that the language split can only have happened after the technological innovation. With Proto-Indo-European we are working at such a depth in time that the exact meanings of the reconstructed forms are by no means certain, particularly in areas of the lexicon subject to very significant technological and cultural changes over the millennia.

Nor are our reconstructed forms reliable to any great phonetic precision either, at such a great remove. While reconstructions may appear fairly sound to a more abstract phonemic level, precious little *phonetic* detail at all is absolutely certain. What this means is that we are unlikely indeed to have enough phonetic resolution to distinguish clear signals of either one of the two possible scenarios by which early Indo-European languages could have ended up with terms for new technologies that now appear shared, even though those meanings arose only long after the initial PIE split. Firstly, as discussed so far, there could have been a calque only of the extension of the meaning of a particular word, whose cognate forms were still clearly recognizable as such in the early Indo-European languages, despite some regular sound changes since an initial PIE split possibly many centuries earlier. Alternatively, a wordform itself could have been borrowed, either from an outside language, or from one early Indo-European language in which it still survived while others had lost its cognates. In each Indo-European language that borrowed this word, it would undergo different phonetic adaptations, and these are largely determined by precisely the same characteristics of its individual sound system that lie behind the historic sound changes that differentiated it from its sister languages in the first place. When modern Romance languages borrow a word from a language either within or outside the family, whatever the precise pronunciation of any r-sounds in the lender language, each borrowing language will adapt it to pronounce it precisely as per its normal modern reflex of Latin r-sounds: a uvular fricative in French, a tap in Spanish, an [h] sound in many accents of Brazilian Portuguese, and so on. That is, much phonetic adaptation mimics precisely the effects of regular sound changes.

Whichever of these two scenarios happened, the output can look confusingly similar. For the natural phonetic adaptation of a loanword into a borrower language's phonological system can further muddy the waters, not least at the time depth of PIE. And in highlighting this, again the scenario we propose hardly has to appeal to some one-off that can be dismissed by linguistic palaeontologists as relatively unlikely to have actually happened. Quite on the contrary, linguists are bound to recognize that such phonetic adaptation of loanwords is an entirely automatic process, and absolutely what we should expect by default.

Only if a language has undergone particularly significant change in the phonological status of the sounds concerned, or lost all traces of the cognate root in any related meanings, is a borrowing likely to enter in a different form to an existing cognate. Between languages that are still closely related, most cognate roots, and derivations from them, remain immediately recognizable as such, wherever any sort of meaning connection can be made. Alongside the *mouse* words in Germanic, Romance words for *train* illustrate an even more involved mix of borrowing, meaning extension, regular sound change and phonetic adaptation. Moreover, these are languages which we have good reason to imagine have been diverging at perhaps an abnormally rapid pace over the tumultuous last two millennia. So we can well imagine similar borrowing processes occurring between early Indo-European languages for at least as long after they first began to diverge.

In such cases where recognizable cognates still exist, rather than a true borrowing of the wordform itself, it is an entirely normal scenario for only the meaning extension to be borrowed, and such calques can be all but impossible to distinguish from true common origin at the depth of Proto-Indo-European. For the phonetic signal left in the data, calque processes are a shortcut that reproduces or 'inherits' in one fell swoop many of the relevant sound changes between the lender and borrower languages since they diverged, such as the two millennia of sound changes in the *mouse* word in the various Germanic languages.

Linguistic palaeontologists sometimes try to object that the *mouse* example is not pertinent, and insist on a case-by-case scrutiny of their reconstructions, but this misses the point. It is not the details of a reconstructed Proto-Indo-European form that are in question, any more than they are for the Proto-Germanic form of *mouse*. What *is* in question is the series of assumptions that linguistic palaeontologists make: about what a given proto-form does or does not necessarily entail for the culture and date of the proto-language — by virtue, in their view, of the simple fact that they have been able to reconstruct it; and about how and when that form acquired the meaning that they now read for it. The Germanic *mouse* and Romance *train* words are just two examples of general and completely normal processes of borrowing and calque. The *mouse* example is relevant particularly as an illustration of how it is in the very nature of those processes that they conspire to render their output 'reconstructible' too, indeed indistinguishable from common origin. This applies *a fortiori* where all the output we have left to go on is whatever imperfect signal of it we can reconstruct many millennia later.

Advocates of linguistic palaeontology tend to present the alternative scenarios to theirs as unlikely one-offs that require a special justification; whereas in reality, in the specific case of coining words for new technology, those scenarios are precisely what we should *expect* to apply by default. All the processes we have cited as offering alternative explanations — derivation, borrowing, phonetic adaptation, extension, specialization, and so on — are the classic 'typical paths of change' in lexical semantics. Far more than that: the one class of words most subject to precisely those processes is none other than terms for new technologies. And the one scenario where it is most difficult to distinguish them from common origin is when they operate between closely related languages, still at a fairly early stage of divergence.

As soon as one abandons preconceived ideas about Proto-Indo-European necessarily being dated no earlier than 6500 BP, and envisages an alternative scenario in which terms for new technologies became necessary at a time when the family was already in the early stages of breaking up into a dialect continuum and/or still closely related languages, the boot is on the other foot. The terms for the new technology can hardly just be plucked out of nowhere: they *must* come either from borrowing (with automatic phonetic adaptation); or from the existing resources within the languages, whether by derivation or by some realignment between existing lexemes and related meanings. In both cases, the trace we would be left with now, many thousands of years down the line, will look temptingly reconstructible and dangerously indistinguishable from true common origin.

On whom does the onus of proof rest, then? Linguists who reject linguistic palaeontology as a reliable dating method are making no claims either way about what these particular language data — the terms for new technologies found in Proto-Indo-European — can be used to prove. They exclude neither scenario; on the contrary they recognize that the nature of the evidence is not such as to demonstrate conclusively either Renfrew's long chronology or the traditional shorter one. It is the linguistic palaeontologists who are making assumptions about what the mere fact that we can reconstruct a given lexeme means for the culture that spoke it. If they wish to use given reconstructions to argue for a particular chronology, the onus is on them to prove why their assumptions are valid. More specifically, the onus is those who hold that earlier dates are unacceptable to prove why the assumptions of linguistic palaeontology are so *uniquely* valid, and why other explanations — which moreover are perfectly in line with typical paths of change in coining terms for new technologies — are not plausible. For many historical linguists, linguistic palaeontologists have signally failed to provide such proofs, as attested by the above citations from Dixon and Sims-Williams. So while linguistic palaeontology can offer one possible historical scenario that can explain given patterns in the linguistic data, it has certainly not been able convincingly to exclude other linguistically and historically plausible scenarios that could have left us with exactly the same patterns in the data.

Now of course there may be other 'non-chronological' arguments in the linguistic data — in the network of relationships between the early Indo-European languages, for instance — which may not be neatly compatible with the geography of Renfrew's scenario. It is certainly not linguistic palaeontology, though, that can offer any conclusive linguistic evidence for why we may not put the first Indo-European split before the *wheel*, the *cart*, and the *horse*.

Quite how many lexemes and how much certainty in their reconstruction are enough to tip the balance between linguistic palaeontology's explanation for the shared terms, and the alternative scenario that the split came after the inventions, is another question open to our interpretation of language data and how languages change. Certainly, many linguists' objections to the earlier dates of the proposed long chronology tend to be expressed very subjectively: they are simply too 'hard to believe' for that writer's personal, unquantified impressions of how much change is feasible over how long a time-span. Yet if we have no certain dating mechanism, and no reliable quantifications of degrees of change over time, then there is no objective basis for deciding at which particular date one crosses from the plausible to the 'hard to believe'. Maximum and minimum observed rates of change offer a possible yardstick for a *bracket* of plausible dates, as suggested for change in phonetics by Heggarty (2000). One of Gray & Atkinson's (2003) steps in the right direction is also to deal in terms of spans of dates. Both of those very different studies leave open broad spans of dates compatible with the Neolithic farming hypothesis.

With two scenarios imaginable, in weighing up the overall balance of probabilities between them we should do well to take into account other relevant questions. In particular, recalling how language is a function of social forces, a plausible scenario also needs to offer a sufficiently powerful socio-cultural factor to account convincingly for the astonishing spread of the Indo-European language family, and the completeness of its territorial domination, as Renfrew (1989, 124–31, 150–52) points out. Is 'elite dominance' really so realistic an explanation, when historical linguists know of endless examples of very powerful elites signally *failing* to impose their language: the Romans in Britain, Germanic tribes throughout the Romance area, the Normans in England, the Turks in the Balkans...

## Dangers in the data for feature-based phylogenetic methods

The consequences of our four characteristics of language data are equally important for phylogenetic methods whose input consists of feature-based language data. For together they conspire to make even distantly related languages inevitably show parallels that in fact do *not* go back to their period of common descent, and so say nothing conclusive about *when* they split.

No analysis model magically produces a true phylogeny: they only convert patterns of correspondences in a data set into the tree or network diagrams that best fit those patterns. It goes without saying that for such an output to stand as a phylogeny, the features in the data much be such that correspondences in them do point unequivocally to shared innovation at a moment of common history before a split, rather than parallel change after it. It is crucial to take great care to identify how much diagnostic power can or cannot be read into a given feature: this is necessarily a task that requires much specific linguistic knowledge and experience.

We close with an illustration, taken from Heggarty *et al.* (2005), of the dangers for otherwise valuable phylogenetic methods, when applied to selective feature-based language data. The phenogram in Figure 16.1 is the output of FITCH, one of the PHYLIP suite of programs (Felsenstein 2001), from input in the form of quantifications of phonetic similarity between the cognates of the numerals *one* to *ten* in a number of Romance varieties. These data and quantifications are effectively equivalent to a feature-based analysis of all the phonetic features responsible for the key differences between the pronunciations of these cognates in these languages, with all differences weighted against each other for their relative phonetic significance, and for their frequency in this data set.

The resulting phenogram immediately strikes linguists as 'wrong' at first glance. It is at odds with the phylogeny commonly proposed for Romance, which has an Iberian sub-branch in which Portuguese and Spanish are more closely related to each other than either is to French. Given the historical reality of the origins of Romance as a dialect continuum, that phylogeny is not necessarily accepted here without many provisos; but by the same token the aim here is certainly not to argue for the tree in Figure 16.1 either. Rather, it serves to illustrate just how easily a certain selection of language data can give a *similarity* or *correspondences* phenogram out of line with the true *phylogeny*. (There are more examples within the Spanish and Portuguese dialect tree structures here.)

Figure 16.1 is put forward here for illustrative purposes only, and there is no space here to go into the details of the methods used to produce the phenogram — for a fuller discussion see Heggarty *et al.* (2005). It should be pointed out that with bigger data sets the method does give trees more consistent with 'consensus' genealogies for Romance, Germanic and Indo-European. Moreover, its quantifications are closely in line with perceptions among linguists of the phonetic similarity between cognates. In fact this turns out to be true for these numerals too, as we shall now see on closer inspection, despite the different relationships between the languages in other fields.

Firstly, part of the branching in Figure 16.1 is due to Spanish having innovated in ways that neither French nor Portuguese have: changing certain vowels to diphthongs, for instance, as in *siete* vs *sept*, *sete*. A shared *retention* like this is of course completely uninformative as to branching — a reminder of how crucial it is, in order to arrive at a correct phylogeny, to identify which state of a feature is an innovation and which the original form. (See Landerman (1991) for a detailed discussion of this, but also Heggarty (2005) for a critique.)

Other features, however, warn that working this out is not always easy and unequivocal. From the original Latin cluster [kt] in *octō*, both French *huit* and Portuguese *oito* simplified to [t], while Spanish has ended up with [tʃ] in *ocho*. Here it is a more debatable call as to which is most innovative, since all languages have changed radically from the original [kt].

Moreover, even with shared retentions filtered out, there are still a host of features in which French and Portuguese together share what is indeed an *innovated* value, while Spanish has either a retention or a different innovation. Even in this tiny data set, further instances of French and Portuguese changing independently in parallel include: syllable-final nasalization (as in the numerals for *one* and *five*); original [k$^{(w)}$] before high front vowels becoming [s] in French *cinq* and Portuguese *cinco*, as opposed to [θ] in Spanish *cinco* (any similarity in modern spelling is irrelevant!); and devoicing and/or loss of unstressed final vowels, complete in French and well underway in European Portuguese (as in *four, five, seven, eight* and *nine*).

Taking this battery of sound changes together, the phenogram they produce no longer appears at all surprising. It so happens that of all the phonetic features in this small data sample, those that are consistent with a separate Iberian branch within Romance are outweighed by a number of other features in which French and Portuguese have shared retentions, and particularly parallel innovations, not found in Spanish. This serves as a warning of just how common parallel changes can be, and how many of a set of randomly chosen features can be entirely unreliable for representing, quantifying and diagnosing language relatedness.

Much depends, then, on one's particular selection of features. Given the arbitrariness of the form-to-meaning relationship in language, the numerals *one* to *ten* do form a *phonetically* random sample of dozens of phonetic differences, selected with no expectation of the 'accidental' result in Figure 16.1. When looking at very poorly attested languages there is a particular danger, then, for the selection is made for us by the limited records available. Where only a very small sample happens to have survived, nothing guarantees that these few data will necessarily contain enough diagnostically powerful features, nor a balanced set of them. This applies not just to phonetics: with grammatical features too, the limited subset contained in a random short text could easily be biased towards features in which that language has either innovated, or been particularly conservative while other related languages have changed in parallel. When branching structure is based on very few distinctive states, and on correspondences in features that are not diagnostic and actually go back to independent changes, phylogenetic methods can all too easily produce erroneous trees, and datings.

We can be confident in rejecting the tree in Figure 16.1 as a genealogy, and in accepting others as correct, only because we are able to confirm both which states are innovations, and which among these are shared ones predating a split as opposed independent parallel changes postdating it. This knowledge can come only from a careful, linguistically informed analysis of the features; in this case supported by our good fortune in still having evidence of intermediate data, both through history and from a large number of other extant regional varieties. In cases where such information is lacking, and the data set contains too few features truly diagnostic of shared history, it is clearly methodologically unsound to trust any phylogenetic method, however refined, to uncover from such data the true historical tree, let alone date the nodes.

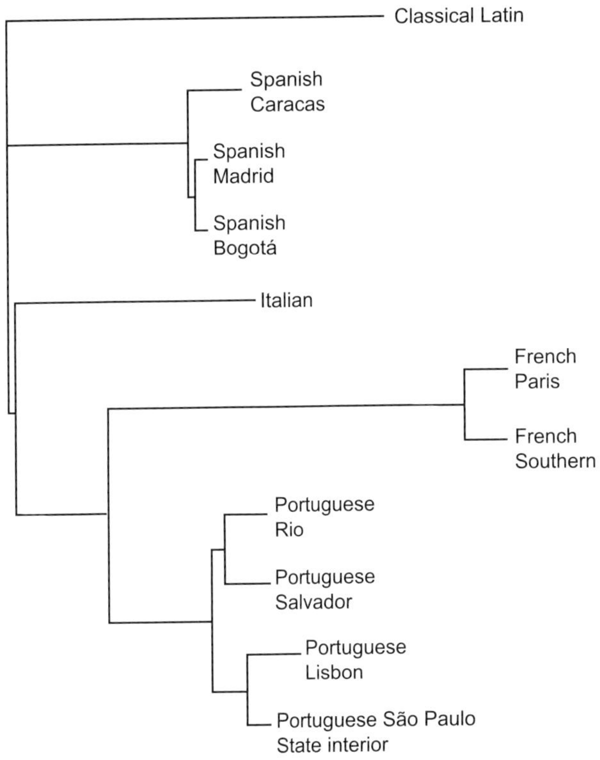


**Figure 16.1.** *Rooted* FITCH *tree for Romance varieties using the results for phonetic similarity for the numerals one to ten.*

## Conclusions

So however applicable and promising phylogenetic methods might appear to be at first sight as tools for investigating language histories, even a cursory look at how language behaves in reality shows just how problematic their application to language data can be. The analysis of those data has to be alive to the myriad ways in which the nature of language, and how it changes, can so readily render language data immeasurably less straightforward than meets the eye. It is self-evident that unless the encodings we feed into phylogenetic methods are informed by such linguistic awareness, we cannot place any great faith in their output as meaningful enough to be of any real use.

The facets of language that we have looked at here, and more generally its inherent susceptibility to being moulded by external socio-cultural forces, conspire to make the attempt to use language data to extrapolate back into an unknown past an enterprise fraught with pitfalls. The unhappy history of methods proposed by linguists themselves serves as a cautionary tale: multilateral comparison and glottochronology raised grand edifices founded upon sweeping inferences from data that are in truth quite equivocal between various possible explanations. Linguistic palaeontology, too, has failed to convince many linguists that it escapes a similar trap. That the dating question remains more open than even many linguists like to admit is simply a function of the nature of language itself.

There is undoubted potential for linguistic purposes in phylogenetic methods, not least the more recent network-type representations that are more sensitive to the reality that relationships between languages by no means always go back to neatly branching histories (*Neighbor-Net* by Bryant & Moulton (2002), *Network* by Bandelt *et al.* (1999)). Long before we push phylogenetic methods so far as to hail them as miraculous new language-dating techniques, however, the first step in unlocking their potential is to ensure that their input, and thus also their output, is truly *linguistically* meaningful. Likewise for our historical interpretations of those outputs, which must accept the reality that certain configurations that we observe in surviving language data may go back to any of a number of different possible linguistic histories, all of them consistent with those same end results, as we saw for the shared terms for technological innovations like the axle. Telling which scenario among them was what actually happened is not a task to be taken lightly on the basis of questionable assumptions that we already know do not always hold in real language history. From all disciplines in the new synthesis, there is a need for closer co-operation, and for a careful and deeply linguistically-informed approach to the inherent complexities of language data, change, divergence and dating.

## References


Bandelt, H.-J., P. Forster & A. Röhl, 1999. Median-joining networks for inferring intraspecific phylogenies. *Molecular Biology and Evolution* 16, 37–48. Programme available at: http://www.fluxus-engineering.com.

Beekes, R.S.P., 1995. *Comparative Indo-European Linguistics: an Introduction.* Amsterdam: John Benjamins Publishing Company.

Bryant, D. & V. Moulton, 2002. NeighborNet: an agglomerative method for the construction of planar phylogenetic networks. *Proceedings of the Workshop in Algorithms for Bioinformatics.* Programme available at: http://www-ab.informatik.uni-tuebingen.de/software/jsplits/welcome_en.html.

Dixon, R.M.W., 1997. *The Rise and Fall of Languages.* Cambridge: Cambridge University Press.

Dyen, I., J.B. Kruskal & P. Black, 1992. An Indoeuropean classification: a lexicostatistical experiment. *Transactions of the American Philosophical Society* 82(5). Full data available at: http://www.ntu.edu.au/education/langs/ielex/HEADPAGE.html.

Embleton, S.M., 1986. *Statistics in Historical Linguistics.* Bochum: Brockmeyer.

Felsenstein, J., 2001. *PHYLIP: Phylogeny Inference Package. Vers. 3.6.* Department of Genetics, Univ. of Washington.

Forster, P. & A. Toth, 2003. Toward a phylogenetic chronology of ancient Gaulish, Celtic, and Indo-European. *Proceedings of the National Academy of Sciences of the USA* 100(15), 9079–84.

Gray, R.D. & Q.D. Atkinson, 2003. Language-tree divergence times support the Anatolian theory of Indo-European origin. *Nature* 426, 435–9.

Greenberg, J.H., 1987. *Language in the Americas.* Stanford (CA): Stanford University Press.

Heggarty, P.A., 2000. Quantifying change over time in phonetics, in *Time Depth in Historical Linguistics*, eds. C. Renfrew, A. McMahon & L. Trask. (Papers in the Prehistory of Languages.) Cambridge: McDonald Institute for Archaeological Research, 531–62.

Heggarty, P.A., 2005. Enigmas en el origen de las lenguas andinas: aplicando nuevas técnicas a las incógnitas por resolver. *Revista Andina*, 40, 9–57.

Heggarty, P.A., forthcoming. *Measured Language: From First Principles to New Techniques for Putting Numbers on Language Similarity.* Oxford: Blackwell.

Heggarty, P.A., A. McMahon & R. McMahon, 2005. From phonetic similarity to dialect classification: a principled approach, in *Perspectives on Variation*, eds. N. Delbecque, J. van der Auwera & D. Geeraerts. Amsterdam: Mouton de Gruyter, 43–91.

Landerman, P., 1991. *Quechua Dialects and their Classification.* Ann Arbor (MI): U.M.I. Dissertation Services.

McMahon, A.M.S. & R. McMahon, 1995. Linguistics, genetics and archaeology: internal and external evidence in the Amerind controversy. *Transactions of the Philological Society* 93(2), 125–225.

Nerbonne, J., with W. Heeringa & P. Kleiwig, 1999. Edit distance and dialect proximity, in *Time Warps, String Edits and Macromolecules: the Theory and Practice of Sequence Comparison*: eds. D. Sankoff & J. Kruskal. Stanford (CA): CSLI, v–xv.

*Oxford English Dictionary, c.* 2000– (web edition: www.oed.com) Oxford: Oxford University Press.

Renfrew, C., 1989. *Archaeology and Language.* London: Penguin.

Sims-Williams, P., 1998. Genetics, linguistics, and prehistory: thinking big and thinking straight. *Antiquity* 277, 505–27.

Swadesh, M., 1952. Lexico-statistical dating of prehistoric ethnic contacts: with special reference to North American Indians and Eskimos. *Proceedings of the American Philosophical Society* 96, 452–63.

# Glossary

*Occurrences are indicated by the first author of a chapter; implied use of a glossary term in a chapter is indicated by the author's name in parentheses.*

**Autapomorphy.** A derived character state found only in one taxon. For example, *suira* for 'neck' is found only in King Ælfred's English, among the 21 Germanic taxa analyzed in Forster (Chapter 11 this volume). Forster

**Basic vocabulary.** Standardized list of meanings that is intended to be cross-culturally applicable. Examples: 'man', 'tongue', 'drink' and 'sun'. Advocated by Morris Swadesh, such lists are intended to be less prone to borrowing than lists of other areas of vocabulary, and less liable to change through innovation. Atkinson, Evans, Forster, Holden, Marten

**Bayesian inference.** Statistical inference in which probabilities are interpreted not as frequencies, but rather as degrees of belief. It uses a **prior probability** (or **prior** for short), i.e. an estimate of the degree of belief in a hypothesis before the advent of some evidence, applied to give a **posterior probability** (**posterior** for short), i.e. a numerical value to the degree of belief in the hypothesis after the advent of the evidence. Example: the prior probability for fine weather tomorrow in the absence of any information might be set at 50/50; given a red sunset, the posterior probability for fine weather tomorrow may increase to a higher value. Atkinson, Bryant, Evans, Holden, Pagel, Spencer

**Branch.** In a phylogeny, a set of linked nodes distinguished from the rest of a tree by a shared link. The term is thus completely analogous to a branch in a botanical tree. The term is also often used for referring to the complete bipartition, not only one side of it.

**Branch(ing) point** is a synonym for **node** (see entry). Atkinson, Dewar, Evans, Forster, Garrett, Heggarty, Holden, Kessler, Marten, McMahon, Nicholls, Nichols, Pagel, Spencer

**Calque.** Loan translation. Example: English *skyscraper* and French *gratte-ciel*. Heggarty, Nichols

**Character.** General term for an item, a feature, a semantic slot, or a position in a DNA molecule etc. Atkinson, Bryant, Evans, Forster, Holden, McMahon, Nicholls, Nichols, Pagel, Spencer, Warnow

**Character state.** The actual realization of a character. For example, the state for the character 'big' in German is *groß*. Atkinson, Evans, Forster, Pagel, Spencer, Warnow

**Clock.** Device for measuring the passage of time. Two types of clocks are variously implied in this volume: the hourglass (corresponding for example to radioactive decay or the molecular clock of cumulative DNA mutations), and the metronome (corresponding for example to astronomical clocks). Atkinson, Evans, Forster, (Heggarty), (McMahon), Nicholls, (Nichols), (Pagel)

**Cognates.** Words whose form has a common root in two or more languages. Atkinson, Bryant, Dewar, Forster, Heggarty, Holden, Kessler, Marten, McMahon, Nicholls, Nichols, Pagel, Warnow

**Consistency index.** The consistency index for a single character on a given tree is the minimum possible number of changes $m$ on any tree divided by the minimum number $s$ on the given tree. The ensemble consistency index over a set of characters is then (sum of $m$ over all characters)/(sum of $s$ over all characters). Example: from a table with four binary variable characters, we calculate a tree with five mutations (i.e. the tree postulates one parallel mutation). The consistency index is hence 4/5 = 0.8. A perfect value of 1.0 would indicate that parallelisms (i.e. homoplasy) are absent in the data. Holden

**CVC.** Consonant-Vowel-Consonant. This shorthand is used to describe **syllable structure** (see entry), e.g. *limit* as an English word consists of two syllables, of types CV and CVC. Kessler, Marten

**Derivational.** Pertaining to the formation of a word from another word or root. Garrett, Nichols

**Distance.** A measure of the level of difference between two taxa. For phylogenetic purposes, the distance often is an estimate of the expected number of changes per character. In its simplest form, distance between languages is estimated by counting the number of words with different states. Example: standard British English and American English differ in their words for spanner/wrench, pupil/student, and autumn/fall. In this short word list, British and American English are at a distance of 3 lexemes to each other. Atkinson, Bryant, Evans, Heggarty, Holden, Kessler, McMahon, Nichols, Spencer, Warnow

**Dollo parsimony.** Assumption that mutated characters cannot revert to their original state. Example: phonemic mergers are considered irreversible. Nicholls

**Dreimorengesetz.** Rule by which the accent in ancient Greek is restricted to fall within the final three syllables of a word. Garrett

**Edge.** Synonym for **link** (see entry). Evans, Holden, Nicholls, Spencer, Warnow

**Homoplasy.** Parallel independent evolution or reversal of the same trait. Example: Spanish *mucho* and English *much*. Synonym: **homoplasmy**. Adjective: homoplasious, homoplastic, or homoplasmic. Holden, Nichols, Warnow

**Leaf.** Synonym for **tip** (see entry). Evans, Nicholls, Warnow

**Lexical.** Pertaining to the words **(lexemes)** or vocabulary **(lexicon)** of a language. Atkinson, Bryant, Dewar, Evans, Forster, Garrett, Heggarty, Holden, Kessler, Marten, McMahon, Nicholls, Nichols, Pagel, Warnow

**Likelihood.** In technical usage, a shorthand for **likelihood function**. (In colloquial language, 'likelihood' is a synonym for 'probability'.) In a sense, likelihood works backwards from probability. The likelihood function $L(D|H)$ is the probability of some data $D$ given some hypothesis $H$. Example: in Snowland, it snows for 10 per cent of the time in November and 30 per cent of the time in December. We have an undated photograph of falling snow taken in Snowland (the data). The likelihood is $L(D|H1) = 0.1$ under the hypothesis $H1$ that the photograph was taken in November, and $L(D|H2) = 0.3$ under the hypothesis $H2$ that it was taken in December. The data are three times more likely under the hypothesis that the photograph was taken in December than under the hypothesis that the photograph was taken in November. If we furthermore know that the owner of the camera had the habit of taking one picture every month, then the photograph is three times more likely to have been taken in December than November. Atkinson, Bryant, Evans, Holden, McMahon, Nicholls, Pagel, Spencer, Warnow

**Link.** In a phylogeny, the connection between two nodes. A link graphically symbolizes a character which distinguishes the two nodes. A link is necessarily part of a branch or of a reticulation. The synonym **edge** is often used. Forster

**Long-range comparison.** Deep-time comparison between well-established language families, such as between Indo-European and Uralic. Kessler, Nichols

**Markov Chain process.** Process in which the distant past is irrelevant given knowledge of the recent past. Or, as Bryant (Chapter 9 this volume) puts it, only the current state of the system affects what happens next. Atkinson, Bryant, Evans, Holden, Nicholls, Pagel, Spencer, Warnow

**Mass comparison.** Synonym for **multilateral comparison** (see entry). Marten

**Matrix (1)** Set of mathematical equation coefficients displayed as a parenthesized table of columns and rows. More generally an ordered rectangular array of numbers. The display of equations in matrix format is for visual and thus conceptual convenience. Atkinson, Bryant, Evans, Pagel, Warnow

**Matrix (2)** Data table. In genetic statistics, the term is usually used in connection with distance data rather than character data. Atkinson, Bryant, Holden, McMahon, Nicholls, Pagel

**Maximum parsimony (MP) tree.** The shortest possible tree linking the given taxa. See also entry for MP. Forster, Holden, Marten, Nicholls, Spencer

**MCMC.** Abbreviation for Markov Chain Monte Carlo (see the two separate entries). A computationally intensive method used in Bayesian statistics to estimate the posterior distribution of parameters. Atkinson, Holden, Nicholls, Pagel

**Median-joining (MJ) network.** A network produced by a network algorithm for multistate data. The method was published by Bandelt and colleagues in 1999 and available in the program package Network 4.109. The MJ method complements the **Reduced median** method (see entry) which can only accept binary data. Language data are typically multistate data (e.g. in the multistate set English-Danish-German, more than two cognates for 'cloud' occur, i.e. cloud-sky-Wolke) rather than binary data (e.g. in the binary set English-Danish-German, only two cognates occur for 'neck', i.e. neck-hals-Hals). Forster, Heggarty, McMahon

**Monte Carlo method.** Random sampling of numbers to estimate the solution to a numerical problem. The name is taken from the Mediterranean gambling resort. Atkinson, Evans, Holden, Kessler, McMahon, Pagel

**Morphological (1).** Pertaining to the study of physical features of a human or other organism. Atkinson, Heggarty, McMahon, Pagel, Spencer

**Morphological (2).** Pertaining to the study of (grammatical) forms of a word. Atkinson, Dewar, Evans, Forster, Garrett, Marten, Nichols, Warnow

**MP (Maximum Parsimony).** Procedure for reconstructing the shortest possible (i.e. most parsimonious) tree from the data at hand. The term 'shortest tree' refers to a tree with the minimum number of changes along its branches. The method is applied to character data and is implemented for example in the program **PHYLIP** (see entry). Forster, Holden, Marten, Spencer

**Multilateral Comparison.** Procedure of searching for broadly similar features across several languages simultaneously. This approach was advocated by Joseph Greenberg who also used the synonym **mass comparison**. His approach differs from the pairwise comparative procedure which searches for regularly recurring similarities in a pair of languages, with a view conclusively to prove (or disprove) the pair as being related, before extending the comparison to any other language. Heggarty, Kessler, (Marten)

**Neighbor-Net.** Program for calculating networks from distance data. The program was developed by Bryant and Moulton in 2004 and is also offered as part of the package SplitsTree. Bryant, Heggarty, Holden, Marten, McMahon, Spencer

**Network (1).** A phylogenetic graph which depicts the descent of individual units. The units are typically word lists or DNA molecules. Unlike trees, networks can contain two-dimensional reticulations, three-dimensional cubes etc. which may indicate uncertainty of the true evolutionary pathway, or alternatively which may indicate descent of a unit from more than one ancestor, as is often the case in manuscript traditions. To avoid confusion, it should be noted that Andrew Garrett (Chapter 12 this volume) differs by applying the term 'social network' to a single group of people, which can link with other groups to form higher-order social links; these higher-order social links can then give rise to a network-like descent of language as defined here. Atkinson, Bryant, Forster, (Garrett), Heggarty, Holden, Marten, McMahon, Spencer, Warnow

**Network (2).** Program package for calculating networks from character data. The package contains the median-joining and the reduced median algorithms (see entries), as well as a time estimation method and other tools. The package was co-developed by Arne Röhl and is available free on the internet. Forster, Heggarty, McMahon, Spencer

**NJ (Neighbour-Joining).** A tree reconstruction method for distance data. This popular method was published by Naruya Saitou and Masatoshi Nei in 1987. Holden, Spencer, Warnow

**Node.** A branching point in a tree or network. A node can be full (when the node represents a taxon actually existing in the data table), or empty (when the node represents a reconstructed taxon which has not been sampled, or a reconstructed ancestral taxon that no longer exists, or indeed an artefactual reconstructed taxon that has never existed). Example: In the language network shown in Figure 11.3 of Forster (Chapter 11 this volume), each node, whether full or empty, represents a distinct 56-word list which the reader can compile from the network graph by reference to the data table. Nodes in distance-based methods (such as Neighbour-Joining or UPGMA) do not offer this information. Atkinson, Evans, Forster, Heggarty, Holden, Marten, McMahon, Pagel, Spencer, Warnow

**Noun class system.** Grammatical system that some languages use overtly to categorize nouns. Example: Gender systems and concord systems in Indo-European and Bantu languages are noun class systems. Marten

**Onomastic.** Relating to names. Garrett

**Outgroup.** A distantly related taxon introduced to determine the oldest node in an unrooted phylogeny. Example: An unrooted DNA tree of living humans can be rooted by applying a chimpanzee DNA outgroup. This choice would reasonably assume that living humans are more recently related to each other than to chimpanzees. The chimpanzee itself is of course not the ancestor of modern humans. The rooted tree can then be used to determine whether the speed of evolution has been similar or different in each of the branches, which is a prerequisite for applying a clock. The rooted tree would also reveal which character states are ancestral, and which are derived. Forster, Holden

**Phonemic.** Pertaining to the distinguishing units of sound **(phonemes)** within a specific language. Example: the phonemic composition of *bill* is /b/, /i/, and /l/. The dark /l/ in *bill* would not be distinguished from the light /l/ in *like* because this **phonetic** difference does not convey a difference of meaning in any English word. Evans, Heggarty, Kessler, Warnow

**Phonetic.** Pertaining to actual sounds **(phones)** uttered by a speaker of any language. Example: The dark [ɫ] in *bill* is distinguished phonetically from the light [l] in *like*. Forster, Garrett, Heggarty, Kessler

**Phonological.** Pertaining to the study of sounds in a language. Phonology encompasses the study of phones and phonemes. Atkinson, Dewar, Evans, Forster, Garrett, Heggarty, Marten, Nichols, Pagel, Warnow

**PHYLIP.** Program package for calculating maximum parsimony trees. The package is offered free by Joseph Felsenstein and is, along with the commercial package PAUP, the most commonly used package for tree algorithms. Heggarty, McMahon

**Phylogeny.** A graph depicting the descent of a set of individual units. The units are typically word lists or DNA molecules. The term encompasses both phylogenetic trees and phylogenetic networks. Atkinson, Dewar, Evans, Forster, Garrett, Heggarty, Holden, (Marten), McMahon, Nichols, Pagel, Spencer, Warnow

**Plosive.** Synonym for **stop** (see entry).

**Posterior.** See entry for **Bayesian inference**. Atkinson, Holden, Pagel

**Prior.** See entry for **Bayesian inference**. Atkinson, Pagel

**Probability.** See entry for **likelihood**. Atkinson, Bryant, Evans, Holden, Kessler, Nichols, Pagel, Spencer, Warnow

**Prosodic word.** Word defined as a phonological unit. Counterexample: Latin *-que* (affix, 'and') is not a prosodic word as it cannot stand alone. Garrett

**Quasi-cognates.** Words or morphemes in different languages that fit predetermined semantic and phonological constraints and can be used in measuring distances between languages not shown to be related or lacking regular sound correspondences, much as proven cognates are used within proven families. Example: English *mead* and Chechen (East Caucasian) *moz* 'honey' share generic first and second consonants, and have minimally different glosses. Nichols

**Reduced median (RM) network.** A network produced by network algorithm for binary data. The algorithm was developed by Bandelt and colleagues in 1995 and is available in the program package Network4.109. Unlike some genetic data, language data are typically not binary but multistate data, and thus the **MJ method** (see entry) is often the method of choice for applications in linguistics. Forster, Spencer

**Reflex.** A word descended from a word or root existing at an earlier stage of the language. Example: English *yoke* is descended from and hence a reflex of the Proto-Indo-European **yugom*. Atkinson, Garrett, Heggarty, Marten

**Retention index.** Measure of the proportion of synapomorphy expected from a data table that is retained as synapomorphy on a tree. The retention index is a substitute for the **consistency index** (see entry) because the retention index omits autapomorphies which do not contribute to the reconstruction of a tree from the data. The closer the retention index is to 1 the better the tree is considered to be. Holden

**Reticulation.** A two-dimensional square or parallelogram, or higher-dimensional cube or prism in a phylogenetic network. The synonym 'cycle' is often used. Multistate median-joining networks (unlike binary reduced median networks) can also contain triangular reticulations. A reticulation expresses uncertainty as to the true evolutionary tree. The links in a reticulation represent items (e.g. words) which conflict with each other concerning their evolutionary information. This conflict can be due to parallel evolution, loan events, data errors etc. Atkinson, Forster, Holden, McMahon, (Spencer), (Warnow)

**Segment inventory.** The exhaustive list of **phonemes** (see entry) in a language. Garrett, (Kessler)

**SplitsTree.** Program for calculating networks from distance data. The method was developed by Bandelt and Dress in 1992 and presented as a program by Huson in 1998. Holden, McMahon

**Steiner tree.** A shortest tree linking the given data. The data entries may have user-defined weights. If each data entry is equally weighted, the Steiner tree is equivalent to an MP tree, so MP trees are special cases of Steiner trees.

**Stop.** A sound pronounced with a complete closure of the oral tract. Synonym for **plosive**. Examples: English [p], [d], and [k] as opposed to [f], [θ], and [r]. Garrett, Marten, Warnow

**Syllable structure.** The phonological composition of a syllable. Example: See entry for **CVC**. Garrett

**Taxon.** An individual classification unit such as an organism, text, language, DNA molecule etc. Taxa are defined by characters; taxa and characters together form the data table for any phylogenetic character analysis. Evans, Forster, Holden

**Tip.** The end of a branch in a phylogeny. The synonym **leaf** is often used. A tip is necessarily a taxon which actually exists in the data, rather than being a reconstructed hypothetical node. The term is thus completely analogous to a tip or leaf in a botanical tree. Pagel

**Tree.** A phylogenetic graph which depicts the descent of individual units. The units are typically word lists or DNA molecules. Alternative trees can be superimposed and graphically summarized as a **network** (see entry). ('Tree' is implicit or explicit in all chapters.)

**UPGMA.** Tree building algorithm based on Unweighted Pair Group Method with Arithmetic mean. An early method for distance data. Holden

**Vertex.** Synonym for **node** (see entry).

**Weight.** Importance attached to a particular character by the researcher. Example: In the program package Network4.109, by default all characters are **weighted** 10. In Figure 11.3 of Forster *et al.* (Chapter 11 this volume), if the researcher chooses to assign weight 0 to the character 'small', then Low German and High German would become identical and the reticulation spanned with Dutch would collapse. Conversely, increasing the weight of a character typically also would influence the outcome of the network. Forster, Heggarty, Holden, Kessler, (Marten), (Nichols), Pagel, Warnow